About the Author:

John Perry, Ph.D., is the author of *James A. Herne: The American Ibsen* (Nelson-Hall, 1978). He taught in high schools and colleges for several years and has conducted workshops at the Philadelphia Writers' Conference. Perry's articles have been published in a variety of periodicals including *Dramatics Magazine*, *English Journal*, *Highlights for Children*, and the *Quarterly Journal of Speech*, and he edited *Thirteen Tales of Terror* by Jack London.

Jack London
An
American
Myth

John Perry

Nelson–Hall nh Chicago

Library of Congress Cataloging in Publication Data

Perry, John, 1937-
  Jack London, an American myth.

  Includes bibliographical references and index.
  1. London, Jack, 1876-1916—Biography. 2. Authors,
American—20th century—Biography. I. Title.
PS3523.046z85   818.5209 [B]   81-6458
ISBN 0-88229-378-8 (cloth)   AACR2
ISNB 0-88229-794-5 (paper)

Manufactured in the United States of America

10 9 8 7 6 5 4 3 2 1

To
Paul Green
a wordsman of truth

Contents

Acknowledgments

I wish to express appreciation to the following, who helped make this biography possible:

Clare Abbott, the British Library, London, England.

Constance H. Andrews, Head, Periodical-Microfilm Department, Providence Public Library.

Hazel C. Blackstone, Librarian, Ellsworth City Library, Ellsworth, Maine.

Patricia L. Bodak, Reference Archivist, Manuscripts and Archives; Peter Dzwonkoski, Assistant to the Curator, Collection of American Literature, the Beinecke Rare Book and Manuscript Library, Yale University Library.

Ellen L. Byrnes, Head, Periodical Department, Multnomah County Library, Portland, Oregon.

M. I. Campbell, Head, General Reference Division, the Public Library of Columbus and Franklin County, Columbus, Ohio.

Lynda C. Classen, Research Librarian, Albert M. Bender Collection; Connie Pyle, Reference Librarian, Mills College Library.

Ethel Conrad, Head Librarian, Massillon Public Library, Massillon, Ohio.

Lowell W. Coolidge, Readers' Services Division, Andrews Library, The College of Wooster.

Lois DiGennaro, Reference Department, New Haven Public Library.

Nancy Dubbs, Alameda Free Library, Alameda, California.

Alice A. Dupuis, Interlibrary Loan Librarian, Miami-Dade Public Library.

Thomas M. Fante, California Section, California State Library, Sacramento, California.

Jeannie M. Foersterling, Assistant, Special Collections and University Archives, Utah State University Library.

Thomas R. French, Assistant Reference Librarian, Xavier University Library.

Eleanor M. Gehres, Western History Department, Denver Public Library.

Joyce Guaquinta, Manuscript Librarian, Iowa State Historical Department.

Katherine Grant, Department Head, Art and Music; Judy H. Doumani, Senior Librarian, General Reading Services, City of Los Angeles Public Library.

David Mike Hamilton, Assistant Curator, Literary Manuscripts; Virginia J. Renner, Reader Services Librarian, The Huntington Library, San Marino, California.

James D. Hart, Director, The Bancroft Library; Estelle Rebec, Head, Manuscripts Division; Alda N. Byron, Administrative Assistant, University of California, Berkeley.

Audrey Herman, Reference Librarian, Sonoma County Library, Santa Rosa, California.

Sarah S. Hittig, Interlibrary Loan; Nancy E. Noda, Interlibrary Loan, San Francisco State University Library.

Fran Jackson, University Archivist, University of Hawaii Library.

Robert L. Keel, Assistant Interlibrary Loans Librarian, Southern Illinois University Library.

James M. Knox, General Reference Department; Blodwen Tarter, Manuscripts Assistant, Stanford University Library.

Patricia Maroney, Head, Reference Department, Chattanooga Public Library.

David B. Mason, Assistant Provincial Archivist, Victoria, British Columbia.

Kenneth J. Oberembt, Head, George Arents Research Library for Special Collections, Syracuse University.

Jean Peters, Librarian, R. R. Bowker Company.

Cris Preciodo, Claremont College Library.

Barbara Preece, Library Assistant, Interlibrary Loans Division, Wilson Library, University of Minnesota.

John T. Runk, Newspaper Department, The Free Library of Philadelphia.

David Sauer, Reference Librarian, Mugar Memorial Library, Boston University.

James M. Shebl, Associate Director, The Pacific Center for Western Studies at the University of the Pacific.

Eugene P. Sheehy, Head, Reference Department, Columbia University Library.

Anthony W. Shipps, Librarian for English, Indiana University Library.

M. K. Swingle, Reference Librarian, California Historical Society, San Francisco, California.

Kim R. Turner, Newspaper Reference, Seattle Public Library.

Sayre Van Young, Reference Department, Berkeley Public Library.

Also the following: Boston Public Library, Buffalo and Erie County County Public Library, Chicago Public Library, Cornell University Library, Harvard University Archives, Indiana State University, Indianapolis and Marian County Library, Kansas State Historical Society Library, Kent State University Library, Michigan State University Library, Modern Language Association, Portland State University Library, Rochester Public Library, San Francisco Public Library, San Jose State University, State University of New York at Albany Library, State University of New York at Binghamton Library, University of Chicago Library, University of Illinois Library, University of Kansas Library, University of Michigan Library, and Yeshiva University Library.

Thanks most of all to Mary Kay Ellis, my marvelous copy editor, who patiently labored through endless revisions — her insights and criticisms tempered with wisdom and compassion.

The I. Milo Shepard Estate (formerly the Jack London Estate) denied rights to publish in this biography excerpts from Jack London letters and books still under copyright with the exception of two pamphlets published by Macmillan.

". . . lies are what the world lives on, and
those who can face the challenge of a truth
and build their lives to accord are finally not
many, but the very few."

—Joseph Campbell
Myths to Live By

Chapter 1

A Discarded Wife

"CHANEY—IN THIS CITY, January 12, the wife of W. H. Chaney of a son."[1]

This announcement, buried on the bottom of page four in the January 14, 1876 issue of the *San Francisco Chronicle,* left untold a sensational story behind the baby's birth. The result of a short-lived union between itinerant astrologer William H. Chaney and fervent spiritualist Flora Wellman, the infant would become his age's highest paid author, one of the most controversial figures in history—and an American myth, a heroic figure who mesmerized millions with webs of romantic illusions, millions who led lives of failure, loneliness, and quiet desperation, needing the false hopes of life-lies. He became an extension of their being, someone greater than life, a fantasy enriched and nourished through their personal pain.

His name was John Griffith London.

William H. Chaney, born on January 13, 1821, the sole son among five children, spent his youth on a fifteen-hundred-acre farm near Chesterville, Maine. Although wanting a college education, his father's accidental death separated the family, forcing the nine-year-old Yankee boy to labor for seven masters until he reached sixteen.

My horoscope teaches that Nature did much for me and that I should have been above the average in goodness,'' Chaney wrote in the *Primer of Astrology*, ''but losing my father at nine, without a home, without friends, imposed upon, tyrannized over and cruelly flogged, the good that was in me was dwarfed and the evil so highly developed that when but 16 I enjoyed the reputation of being the worst boy in the county and all predicted that I would die in prison or on the gallows. Disowned by relatives, who looked upon me as a disgrace, I changed from place to place till every door of respectability was closed against me. Then, becoming reckless, I went to sea, secretly resolved to turn pirate, for if mankind would not respect me I would make them fear me. Two years on the ocean completed my primary studies as a wild rover, and I resolved to graduate by entering the Navy, but nine months on a man-of-war seemed to satisfy me, and I deserted in July, 1840, from the receiving ship Columbus, then lying in Boston harbor.[2]

The footloose Chaney soon left Boston, trying to reach New Orleans by flat boat, but he caught chills and fever in Virginia. Sympathetic local farmers, however, led him to settle in Wheeling, where he clerked, stumped, and read law. Several disastrous marriages followed. Then editorial work. He finally returned to Maine and whipped a fellow who had beaten him as a child. Chaney's bitterness towards law grew. He attacked its stale ideas, its back-scratching, its smeared ethics. Such outspoken views made enemies. "School teachers disliked me because I repudiated so much of science and philosophy that they believed true. Lawyers disliked me because I would not run in the old run of 'precedents,' unjust laws, etc., but more especially because if employed to prosecute one of them I did not spare him any more than I would a common thief. Judge Hathaway, at Ellsworth, Maine, once stopt me in an argument to the jury to say: 'It is a filthy bird that fouls its own nest.' "[3]

Such slurs aroused Chaney's social conscience. After becoming editor of the *Ellsworth Herald* in 1853, he advanced such burning issues as Anglo-Saxon superiority and anti-Catholic sentiment, climaxed in his sensational clash with Father John Bapst.

When Father Bapst, a parish priest at Ellsworth, petitioned the Ellsworth School Committee to exempt Catholic school children from reading the King James version of the Bible in classrooms, Chaney attacked him in print, writing red-hot editorials such as "Immorality of Romanism," "The Dangers of Popery," and "Morals of Nuns and Nunneries." He called Bapst an "ape behind the mask," "an Irish Papist," and "a black-hearted hypocrite." A heated debate followed. Many Maine papers supported Father Bapst. When local authorities denied his petition, the cause reached Maine's Supreme Court. Chaney, meanwhile, called the Roman Catholic Church "the scarlet Beast of Rome." A group who opposed the petition met to raise $600, threatening Father Bapst, now transferred to Bangor.

But Father Bapst made a mistake. He returned to Ellsworth in mid-October to celebrate Mass. A drunken mob stripped, then tarred and feathered the cleric, even stealing his money. The martyred Bapst stirred a scandal. The *Bangor Journal* called the incident a "diabolical deed," and the *Eastern Freedom* labeled Chaney "insane" and "unscrupulous."[4] A grand jury investigation followed, but Father Bapst refused to testify, causing the case's dismissal.

Chaney, forced to leave Ellsworth because of this clash, wandered penniless. "In 1857 . . . I lost everything I possessed, all my books went for rent, I could not find employment of any kind (this was after I had been editor and had been practicing law for ten years) and when my last penny was gone, sooner than beg or steal, I walked the streets of Boston for three days without tasting food. On another occasion I hired to work in a match factory at $4 a week and board myself—cheap food, but the salary kept me alive and paid for lodging."[5]

In 1866 Chaney met Dr. Luke Broughton, the English astrologer who had predicted Abraham Lincoln's death, and was converted to astrological charts, vowing: "I shall now devote my life to Astrology, and come what may, never shrink from being its defender."[6] He later wrote: "A false education has taught us that 'the future belongs to God,' and that it is blasphemus for man to even attempt to pry into it. Trained from earliest infancy in this belief, probably nine-tenths of the people of the United States are disposed to doubt when they hear it asserted that the future can be predicted. They occupy a position

similar to the people before the time of Galileo. . . . If man
would predict the future he must do it entirely by the aid of
reason. . . . Astrology is founded purely in the laws of induc-
tion; that is, the pointers have all been learned by observation.'''[7]

Chaney and Broughton opened an Eclectic Medical University at 814 Broadway, New York City, dubbing each other
"Professor." They lectured on astrology, phrenology, and natural theology. James Gordon Bennett, powerful editor of the
New York Herald, called them charlatans, and, according to
Chaney, hired hooligans, who disconnected the water, ripped
down signs, and rented rooms above, where they pounded fur-
niture on the floor during sessions. This kindled a "reign of
terror," causing the ill Mrs. Broughton to utter "cries and
shrieks enough to drive mad those who heard them."[8] And
behind it all stood the *Herald*. "The place was styled the
'Ghoul's Garrett,' and all who came here denominated as in-
fidels and blasphemers," wrote Chaney. "As for ourselves, we
were described as 'the chief ghoul of the den,' 'a played-out
bruiser,' and a 'used up prize fighter,' together with other
expressions equally flattering, and characteristic of a journal
whose proprietor has been cowhided through the streets, on
sundry occasions, on account of the eloquence of his language
applied to gentlemen who never injured him."[9]

Broughton finally appealed to city authorities through Chaney, who landed in the clink, a target of corrupt politicians.
"My lecturing on Astrology in New York aroused such bitter
hostility among the supporters of 'Boss' Tweed, while he was
mayor, that I was arrested on a false charge, accused of teaching
blasphemy by his pious friends who shared in his millions of
boodle, and cast into Ludlow-street Jail where I was supported
for twenty-eight weeks at public expense. Such were a few of
the provocations that aroused me to fight back. . . . Had I been
a timid dude I could not have done much for Astrology."[10]

Released from jail, Chaney married a third time and resumed
lecturing, then headed West, abandoning the woman. While he
was planning a return trip from San Francisco to New York
City, a thief picked his pocket, changing the course of Chaney's
life—leading him to meet Flora Wellman:

I spent the winter in San Jose, lecturing, teaching and practicing astrology, and had an eight-days debate with Elder Miles Grant, the great Second Adventist of Boston. By May 1874, I had saved money enough to return east, but just before starting, received an anonymous letter from my wife . . . stating that she was divorced and could marry again, but if I ever married again she would have me imprisoned.

This aroused my ire and on June 11th, 1874 . . . three weeks later . . . I took another wife. We lived together till June 3rd, 1875 . . . almost a year . . . then separated.[11]

Born in Massillon, Ohio, on August 17, 1843, Flora Wellman was the daughter of wheat tycoon and canal builder Marshall Wellman, a penny-poor individualist whose vision and fortitude enabled him to gain riches. "In 1829, near the close of navigation, a mercantile firm composed of Hiram B. Wellman and Marshall D. Wellman, by the name of H. B. & M. D. Wellman, brought a large stock of goods into Massillon. H. B. Wellman had a year or two before opened a law office in Wooster, and M. D. Wellman, who had been a cooper and settled in Wooster, left there and went into the State of Pennsylvania, and went to building canals under State contracts, and succeeded in money-making," wrote W. H. Perrin in 1881. "These brothers started the firm under the above name. On opening their store in Massillon, they offered 'cash for wheat,' and advertised the public that they would take all the wheat they could get, and would pay cash; and that was the commencement of the prosperity of Massillon. To the firm of H. B. & M. D. Wellman may be accredited the beginning of the great name that Massillon acquired as the 'Wheat City,' and which it proudly held until the railroad era noticed hereafter. For twenty-five years Massillon knew no competition nor allowed any competition to cross her path."[12]

Marshall built a "sprawling 17-room mansion . . . of sun-dried, handmade yellow brick in 1835."[13] The over-indulged Flora grew up in this home. According to Jack London's daughter Joan in *Jack London and His Times,*

Marshall's first wife, Eleanor Garrett Jones, daughter of a Welsh circuit rider known as 'Priest' Jones, had died when Flora was a baby. Father, older sisters, relatives and nursemaids promptly spoiled the motherless child. When her stepmother entered the scene, Flora was four years old, willful, stubborn, hot tempered. Stormy years followed, although they were years in which every luxury, frocks and toys from New York, tutors, piano and elocution lessons, were showered on the little girl. Flora did as she pleased, received what she demanded. Sentiment was ranged on her side; the stepmother was helpless. And when, some years later, Flora fell desperately ill with the long fever which was to stunt her growth and ruin forever her eyesight and beauty, all efforts to curb her will and soften her sharp individuality were abandoned. She ran away from home when she was sixteen, went to stay with first one, then another married sister. And from this time until she was thirty-one and earning her living by giving piano lessons in San Francisco, nothing definite is known about her.[14]

William and Flora Chaney moved to 314 Bush Street in San Francisco, then to 122 First Avenue, after their marriage. (Joan London doubted the legality of all Chaney's marriages.) While he studied and lectured on astrology, Flora kept house, held séances, distributed pamphlets and magazines during meetings. But time eroded their romance. The *San Francisco Chronicle* detailed in a June 4, 1875, article called "A Discarded Wife" that Chaney drove Flora from their home when she refused to abort an unborn babe.

> Day before yesterday Mrs. Chaney, wife of "Professor" W. H. Chaney, the astrologer, attempted suicide by taking laudanum. Failing in the effort she yesterday shot herself with a pistol in the forehead. The ball glanced off, inflicting only a flesh wound, and friends interfered before she could accomplish her suicidal purpose.
>
> The incentive to the terrible act was domestic infelicity. Husband and wife have been known for a year past as the center of a little band of extreme Spiritualists, most of whom professed, if they did not practice, the offensive free-love doctrines of the licentious Woodhull. To do Professor Chaney justice, he has persistently denied the holding of such broad tenets. He has been several times married before this last fiasco of the hearthstone, but it is supposed that all his former wives have been duly laid away to rest, and now repose, like Polonius, in rural churchyards.

The last marriage took place about a year ago. Mrs. Chaney, formerly Miss Flora Wellman, is a native of Ohio. She came to the coast about the time the Professor took the journey overland through the romantic sagebrush, and for awhile supported herself by teaching music. It is hard to see what attracted her toward this man, to whom she was united after a short acquaintance. The union seems to have been the result of a mania like, and yet unlike, that which drew Desdemona toward the sooty Moor.

The married life of the couple is said to have been full of self-denial and devoted affection on the part of the wife and of harsh words and unkind treatment on the part of the husband. He practiced astrology, calculated horoscopes for a consideration, lectured on chemistry and astronomy, blasphemed the Christian religion, published a journal of hybrid doctrine called the *Platomathean,* and pretended to calculate "cheap nativities" on the transit of the planets for $10 each, for all of which he obtained but slender pecuniary recompense. Astrological knowledge is, of course, highly valuable, but the supply in San Francisco seems to be slightly in excess of the demand, and no matter how much Professor Chaney lectured, scattered circulars, watched the movements of the planets and cast nativities, his exchequer continued painfully bare and his larder nearly empty. Sometimes he almost pined again for the confinement of the tombs Prison, within whose massive walls and gloomy shadows his rigorous assertion of personal freedom is once said to have brought him. The wife assisted him in the details of business, darned his hose, drudged at the wash-tub, took care of other people's children for hire, and generously gave him whatever money she earned and could spare beyond her actual expenses. She never told her sorrows, not since her recent great trouble has she communicated them, except to intimate friends. She says that about three weeks ago she discovered, with a natural feeling of maternal pleasure, that she was *enceinte.* She told her husband, and asked to be relieved for two or three months of the care of the children by means of which she had been contributing to their mutual support. He refused to accede to the request, and some angry words followed.

Then he told her she had better destroy her unborn babe. This she indignantly declined to do, and on last Thursday morning he said to her, "Flora, I want you to pack up and leave this house." She replied, "I have no money and nowhere to go." He said, "Neither have I any to give you." A woman in the house offered her $25, but she flung it from her with a burst of anguish, saying "What do I care for this? It will be of no use to me without my husband's love." This show of sincere affection had no effect upon the flinty-hearted calculator of other people's nativities. He told the poor woman that he had sold the furniture (for which she had helped to pay) and it was useless to think of her remaining there any longer.

He then left her, and shortly afterwards she made her first attempt at suicide, following it up by the effort to kill herself with a pistol on the following morning, as already stated. Failing in both endeavors Mrs. Chaney was removed in a half insane condition from Dr. Rutley's on Mission Street to the house of a friend, where she still remains, somewhat pacified and in a mental condition indicating that she will not again attempt self-destruction. The story as given here is the lady's own, as filtered through her near associates.[15]

This article, admitting information through Flora and "near associates," maligns Chaney, calling him everything from a heretic to "flinty hearted calculator of other people's nativities." Yet the investigating detective claimed an unfired pistol and no powder burns on Flora's face. Another witness, a carpenter working nearby at the time, denied hearing shots. Flora's wound from this self-inflicted gunshot? A grazed forehead.

This scandal shredded Chaney's career and private life, far more than the Father Bapst sensation and clashes in New York City. Newspapers spread the lurid story. Chaney's family, except for one sister, disowned him. Although he wrote an explanation, supported by evidence from the detective, local papers refused to print it or make retractions. Chaney suffered disgrace for years.

The truth behind his birth distressed Jack London, undoubtedly triggering his compulsive need to win life's games, to claim a personal superiority, to consider himself a young god. (He later insisted Japanese servants call him Mr. God.) He finally wrote Chaney at twenty-one, searching for facts, but the aged astrologer denied marriage to Flora Wellman, claiming impotency at the time due to exhaustion. Still unsatisfied, London sent a follow-up letter, this time getting details. Chaney claimed Flora wanted a child and asked for permission to let another man impregnate her. Chaney agreed, with one hitch—the fellow must offer support. Flora, however, wanted to nest with Chaney. Pregnancy followed. She pointed the finger at Chaney, who denied paternalism, throwing her out. Flora pleaded forgiveness, then wounded herself in the head with a revolver, leading a mob to threaten Chaney with a noose.[16] Such was the astrologer's account to Jack London.

It appears that London, who translated his fantasies and frustrations into fiction, reacted to this exchange of letters in "A Thousand Deaths," published several years later in 1899. The hero reveals that his father,

> a very learned man and a celebrated antiquarian, gave no thought to his family, being constantly lost in the abstractions of his study. . . . I can but say that he was the most abnormal specimen of cold-blooded cruelty I have ever seen. . . . Having pleaded in vain, I announced and proved that I was his son. It was my last card, and I had placed all my hopes upon it. But he was inexorable; he was not a father but a scientific machine. I wonder yet how it ever came to pass that he married my mother or begat me, for there was not the slightest grain of emotion in his makeup. Reason was all in all to him, nor could he understand such things as love or sympathy in others, except as petty weaknesses which should be overcome.[17]

Time intensified London's birth-anguish. He wrote in "Bâtard," the prototype for *The Call of the Wild*:

"Bâtard did not know his father—hence his name,—but, as John Hamlin knew, his father was a great gray timber wolf. But the mother of Bâtard, as he dimly remembered her, was snarling, bickering, obscene, husky, full-fronted and heavy-chested, with a malign eye, a cat-like grip on life, and a genius for trickery and evil. There was neither faith nor trust in her. Her treachery alone could be relied upon, and her wild-wood amours attested her general depravity. Much of evil and much of strength were there in these, Bâtard's progenitors, and, bone and flesh of their bone and flesh, he had inherited it all."[18] London also charged in "Which Make Men Remember": "Life's a skin-game. I never had half a chance. . . . I was faked in my birth and flim-flammed with my mother's milk. The dice were loaded when she tossed the box, and I was born to prove the loss. But that was no reason she should blame me for it, and look on me as a cold deck; but she did—ay, she did."[19]

The tone of such sharp conflicts voiced in "A Thousand Deaths," "Bâtard," and "Which Make Men Remember" becomes more meaningful after reading several Chaney essays in *The West Shore*. Sharp similarities exist between both men's ideas. Random remarks suggest this, especially their allegiance to science, although several generations separated them. "Science spans the gap between the present and the past;"[20] "And this evolution, so sublimely grand, is still going on;" and "We are catching the first glimpses of heredity."[21] Chaney also talked about his work drifting "back far into the prehistoric," and his references to extreme temperatures, which also typify London's stories about the Yukon and the South Seas, are startling: "In the frigid zone only a few forms of life survive. . . . The heat increasing, man dies and the beasts all perish."[22] Chaney even reduced man to the level of crawling, creeping things. "Man is always blundering, and in his proudest estate but a mere worm when compared with the Infinite."[23] Such views, including their diction, London echoed in countless essays and stories.

London not only echoed Chaney's views, but tried to duplicate his feats, succeeding where the astrologer failed by sometimes letting characters blaze forbidden trails. Both championed Anglo-Saxon supremacy and attacked organized religion. London claimed Chaney's Yankee pre–Revolutionary war roots through Ernest Everhard in *The Iron Heel*, Kit Bellew in *Smoke Bellew*, Darrell Standing in *The Star Rover*, and both Saxon and Billy Roberts in *The Valley of the Moon*. Chaney crossed the American plains to California, something London managed as Jesse in *The Star Rover* and ancestors of Sun Man in *The Acorn-Planter*. His fanaticism with farming, later shown by what he did at his Glen Ellen estate, flared after contacts with Chaney. He earlier preferred city life in Oakland and San Francisco, ridiculing the rural world. Chaney went to sea "resolved to turn pirate," while London claimed he became "Prince of the Oyster Pirates" on San Francisco Bay. When London failed to earn the college degree Chaney wanted, he populated endless stories with academics, most stately professors.

Similar illnesses also strengthen the "nativities" of Chaney and London. "From my earliest recollection until thirty, I had periodical attacks of the sick headache, which would utterly prostrate me," wrote Chaney. "At seventeen my teeth began to decay and I lost several before cutting my 'wisdom teeth.' At that age I also found a gray hair in my head, and by thirty half my hair was gray. Soon after I began to be 'near-sighted.' " Chaney also had rheumatism, admitting that "of late years my kidneys trouble me."[24] These ailments, especially renal colic, long tortured Jack London.

Most uncanny of all, Chaney was born on January 13, 1821; Jack London on January 12, 1876. Did Chaney, who believed parents could choose their children's characteristics through astrology, somehow, pinpoint the birth of Jack London?

Chaney married twice more after leaving Flora Wellman, losing a fifth wife from an affluent family after accusing her brother of stealing government timberland in the North Pacific. (Chaney and London seemed to share similar temperaments, Luke Broughton calling the former "a hasty, hot headed man,"[25] words friends and enemies used to describe London, who held grudges and sought revenge for slights.) Three years of poverty followed in St. Louis. During the 1893 World's Fair he lived in Chicago, marrying for the sixth time, to another astrologer. Chaney, accepting indigence, once said:

"In my horoscope there is not even *one* testimony of wealth, and yet people are continually expressing astonishment that I am so poor. . . . If I should become wealthy, in my own right, that fact would disprove astrology."[26]

Does Jack London's $1,000,000 fortune disprove the Chaney link? Not really. Pleas for money from London, who scattered wealth on empty dreams and schemes, filled letters to George Brett, editor at Macmillan Company. His bank account once drained to less than five dollars. A money-madness, inspired by overspending, served the main motive for his writing habit that produced over four dozen books.

William H. Chaney died after the age of eighty, unknown and probably destitute, as Jack London's star reached its full ascendancy. The editor of his *Astrologer's Vade Mecum* (1902) wrote in the preface: "He is now in his 82nd year and still retains all his mental faculties as clear and vigorous as ever, but physically he is very feeble, his eye-sight has failed, his hearing is not good, and lately he has suffered severely from disease of the kidneys and bladder; students who have studied the Primer will remember that at his birth he had Saturn in evil aspect to Libra the sign which governs the kidneys and the house of life."[27]

After her loud suicidal theatrics, nearly getting Chaney mobbed, Flora retreated to the home of W. N. Slocum, editor of *Common Sense*, at 615 Third Street—Jack London's birthplace. She had met John London, a widowed father of two daughters, then in the Protestant Orphan Asylum, who needed a wife (John London also had an older son who lived elsewhere). They married on September 7, 1875, naming the boy—born in January 1876—John Griffith London. It took a long time for Flora to recover from her ordeal with Chaney. When her milk failed to. nourish the infant, she hired a former black slave, Jenny Prentiss, wife to a white carpenter, to nurse him.

"When I was thirteen years I had typhoid fever," Flora said in a rare interview. "I never grew any after that, and it curved my spine the way it is now. That fever was also the cause of my hair falling out. The doctors said it never would grow thick again, and that as I grew older it would grow even thinner. I had switches and switches made. I used to wear them all the time, but about seven years ago I said, 'I'm going to have my comfort if I have only two strands of hair on my head.' So I gave my switches to the children in the neighborhood to cut up for their dolls."[28]

Burdened with feelings of inferiority, never certain about his birth, London feverishly hid facts from the public. Both Charmian, London's second wife, and Ninetta Eames, his first ranch manager and promoter, fostered the ruse. In her two-volume biography *The Book of Jack London*, Charmian glossed over the courtship between John and Flora in one sentence, perpetuating the idea that John London fathered her husband. *The Dictionary of American Biography*, however, called these memories "vague, confused, and not wholly reliable."[29] Ninetta Eames styled John "a nomadic trapper, scout and frontiersman [who] in 1873 came to San Francisco where Jack, the youngest of ten half brothers and sisters, was born January 12, 1876."[30] Charmian also fed the paternity myth, even tracing London's roots to English royalty, leading H. M. Tichener to say in *Life of Jack London:* "Two English families have taken their name from the city of London; one Jewish, the other Gentile. Jack London, who was born in San Francisco on January 12, 1876, was of the latter. His ancestors both on his father's and mother's side, came to America before the Revolutionary War, his great-great-grandfather being Sir William London, who fought in Washington's army."[31]

Assuming this material truthful, scores of writers, limiting research to warmed-over sources, misinformed millions of Americans, Kunitz and Haycraft saying in *Twentieth Century Authors:* "The secret of London's paternity was so carefully guarded that Carl Van Doren, writing five years after his death in *The American Novel,* stated that he was the son of a frontier scout and trapper (which is probably a fabrication of Jack's). London, however, was fully aware of his origin, which probably conditioned the uneasy bravado with which he faced life, his occasional longing for conventional respectability—as shown by his wooing of Mabel Applegarth—and his desperate efforts to become a landowner and householder on the grand scale."[32]

Rose Wilder Lane's early serialized biography in *Sunset, The Pacific Monthly,* also waxed romantic, sketching a tear-stained portrait filled with shimmering skies, meadowlarks, and lots of lies. She stated that John London met Flora during the spring of 1869 in San Francisco. Her account of Jack London's birth? Snatched from the pages of a slick dime novel.

It was a gray, cold morning. All night the San Francisco winter rain had fallen drearily on the weather-worn, huddled tenements of Tar Flat. At Fourth and Brannan streets the gutters brimmed full, and the light of the flickering street lamp glistened on sluggish pools spreading slowly over old, uneven wooden pavements. Water dripped from the rickety back stairways of the ramshackle houses on Brannan street and splashed on the roof of John London's shabby rented cottage in the alley. Rain filmed the windows.

John London sat in the kitchen, waiting. The bedroom door was open, so that the fire in the cookstove could fight the dampness in both rooms. The tea-kettle steamed. Blankets and towels were draped over chairs, warming in the heat from the oven. He had tramped out through the rain and brought the Irish midwife early in the evening. She was in charge now. There was nothing more he could do, but wait.[33]

From this serialized biography, readers and writers believed London grew up in Tar Town, among the submerged tenth. London pushed this Horatio Alger "rags to riches" myth, claiming he lacked a store-bought shirt until eight and even stole meat from a girl's basket. The last tale infuriated Flora, who denied London starved, adding he probably meant times when he hung loose on streets, sometimes for entire nights. Go hungry? Not in her house, insisted Flora.[34]

The Reverend C. Jonas Tyler, who studied eight London homes, concluded that "Jack London based many of his stories on his own experiences—but they contained a heavy measure of fictional color." Tyler talked with E. M. Applegarth, one of London's later friends, who agreed: "While Jack London was poor, his poverty has been exaggerated."[35] Joan London added: "Out of his awareness from babyhood of the constant struggle, not to get along so much as to get ahead, developed his firm but erroneous conviction that he had grown up in the midst of privation and want. They lived frugally, it is true, but the necessities and many of the comforts of life were never lacking."[36] The San Francisco Chronicle made the most curious remark about London's youth in 1894—years before he became a celebrated author—after one of his road adventures. "His family is one well known in Oakland. He has a wealthy aunt and a collection of cousins who are in the best society. His immediate relatives are well-to-do, industrious folk. They were not rich enough to allow their son to travel, so he decided to see the country on his own hook."[37]

When Lewis Mumford reviewed Charmian's biography in 1922, he commented that "about the career of Jack London there is a vague and yet definitive myth which will probably prove more durable than the canonical accounts of his existence." Mumford added: "Jack London, contrary to the myth, was equipped from the beginning with the usual complement of parents, with a home, with friends, and with a limited but nevertheless certain share of bed and board. . . . Untutored in the academic sense of the word, London's life was far from being mentally impoverished."[38] Kevin Starr agrees in *Americans and the California Dream 1850–1915,* saying that "through the pseudo-historical terms of an imagined impoverished childhood, London gave mythic structure to his inner trauma of repudiation and rejection, a mythic past onto which he later grafted his version of California's history."[39]

Many London readers, connecting California's hazy history with gold dust and Spanish missions—perhaps the result of too much Hollywood hash—believe he grew up in the "wild and woolly West," a primitive frontier outpost, where Indians scalped settlers, rustlers stampeded cattle, and gunslinging outlaws swaggered down dusty streets, spurs jangling, while rugged sheriffs flashed tin stars. Charmian even told *Theatre Magazine* in 1919, three years after London's death, that he took a covered wagon to Glen Ellen[40] at the century's turn! The real frontier? Frank Norris, a native Californian, wrote in 1902:

> So, lament it though we may, the Frontier is gone, an idiosyncrasy that has been with us for thousands of years, the one peculiar picturesqueness of our life is no more. We may keep alive for many years yet the idea of a Wild West, but the hired Cowboys and paid rough riders of Mr. William Cody are more like "the real thing" than can be found today in Arizona, New Mexico or Idaho. Only the imitation cowboys, the college-bred fellows who "go out on a ranch" carry the revolver or wear the concho. The Frontier has become conscious of itself, acts the part for the Eastern visitor; and this self-consciousness is a sign, surer than all others, of the decadence of a type, the passing of an epoch. The Apache Kid and Deadwood Dick have gone to join Hengist and Horsa and the heroes of the Magnusson Saga.[41]

Harry Hartwick concluded about London's acute self-consciousness that "there is something adolescent in his cult of barbarism, a kind of playing at 'cowboys and Indians,' or confession of basic weakness."[42] Negley Farson, another native author, said that for himself "to have hung on in that haunted country, writing second-rate stories about a mythical Golden

West, in the way empty Rex Beach tried to follow the trail blazed by flaming Jack London—this would have been to accept a make-believe life that, sooner or later, would have made me want to shoot myself."[43]

What about Oakland and San Francisco—stripped of stampedes, wagon trains, and desperadoes? San Francisco, the West's Eldorado, housed fifty printers by 1850, and soon set the region's social and economic pulsebeat. By 1876, the year of London's birth, it ranked fifth among America's largest cities. "San Francisco for several decades had been a teeming seaport and more recently the terminus of the transcontinental railroad," writes John D. Bergamini in *The Hundredth Year*. "In size it was twenty times larger than Los Angeles. The great earthquake was yet thirty years away. San Francisco's Palace Hotel was regarded as one of the most elegant in the country. In 1873 appeared the familiar cable cars which transported people between such diverse sections as the mansion-studded Nob Hill and the flagrantly vice-ridden Barbary Coast. The city boasted several theaters, two opera houses, and eating establishments of all nationalities, attesting to its cosmopolitan nature and spirit."[44] Oscar Lewis also remarked in *San Francisco Since 1872* that "throughout the '70s there was none to dispute San Francisco's claim to preeminence in the West. Not only was she incomparably the largest of Pacific Coast cities, but her influence dominated the financial, economic and social life of the entire region. Residents all over the vast interior not only looked up to 'the city'—it needed no other identification—for their contacts with urban conveniences and luxuries, but they regarded it as the Coast's major center of trade. Here was the logical market for whatever the area produced and here, too, was the source of the wide variety of goods and services demanded by the region's expanding economy."[45]

Oakland—Jack London's home town, across the Bay? Locals called it "The Athens of America" and "Eden of the Pacific." Four daily newspapers existed in 1895, and the university boasted two thousand students that year. Three electric streetcar systems rolled between Oakland and Berkeley. One-time residents of this cultural city included Bret Harte, Henry George, Joaquin Miller, Gertrude Stein, and Robert Louis Stevenson.[46] Karl Baedeker wrote in *The United States with an Excursion into Mexico, A Handbook for Travelers, 1893*: "The 'Brooklyn' of San Francisco, is a flourishing city of 48,682 inhab., pleasantly situated on the E. shore of the Bay of San Francisco. It derives its name from the number of live-oaks in its streets and gardens. The value of its manufactures in 1890 was $6,335,000. The steam-railways which traverse Oakland convey passengers free of charge within the city-limits."[47]

London's putdown of Oakland and San Francisco may have stemmed from two phenomenally popular authors of the age— Ouida (Louisa de la Ramée) and Horatio Alger—whose virtuous and penny-poor characters Signa and Ragged Dick became big successes. How much of their fictional fancies London digested into his lifestream remains a mystery, although he learned to believe anything that advanced his career and income, especially America's long-running "rags to riches" romance. Joan said he had a "faculty for absorbing the experiences of others and living them in imagination."[48] A friend, Oliver Madox Hueffer, added that "like Peter Pan, he never grew up, and he lived his own stories with such intensity that he ended by believing them himself."[49]

Joan believed *Signa* greatly influenced London. A brilliant child, Signa is left to his mother's two brothers, after she falls over a bank and dies. Although one treats the child kindly, the other abuses this prodigy who sings like an angel and even plays the violin magnificently while asleep.

For genius is fanaticism; and the little barefoot hungry fellow, running errands in the dust, had genius in him, and was tossed about by it like a small moth by a storm. . . . To himself he was only a foundling, as he was to everyone else; picked up as any blind puppy might have been motherless on the face of the flood. . . . He was always hungry, and never very strong, and certainly simple and poor as a creature could be, and he knew what a beating meant as well as any dog about the farm. He lived with people who thrashed him oftener than they fed him. He was almost always scolded, and bore the burden of others' faults. He had never had a whole shirt or a pair of shoes in all his life. . . . It is hard work to be good when you are very little and very hungry, and have many sticks to beat you and no mother's lips to kiss you.[50] (The youthful hero of London's "One More Unfortunate," an early short story included in the December 18, 1895 issue of *The High School Aegis,* plays the violin so beautifully that Padrodini praises his virtuosity.)

London also devoured Horatio Alger's stories, mentioning his favorite work, *From Canal Boy to President*—a biography Alger finished in two weeks after James A. Garfield's assassination in 1881. A shy, lonely, balding former minister with respiratory problems, Alger filled his street-stories with simple characters, lots of action, and a sense of place—especially for New York City. His stories exerted a profound influence on American youth for several generations, Harvard's Grolier collection including *Ragged Dick* as one of the hundred most important books written before 1900. One of Alger's autographs, written with book titles, summarizes the values preached in his many stories: "*Strive and Succeed,* the world's temptations flee—/Be *Brave and Bold,* and *Strong and Steady* be./ Go *Slow and Sure,* and prosper then you must—/With *Fame and Fortune,* while you *Try and Trust.*"[51]

Ragged Dick (1868), Alger's most famous story, features a vagrant who sleeps in a box of straw. When he rescues a child from drowning, its wealthy father launches Dick on the road to fame and fortune in his countinghouse. As another character says: "You know in this free country poverty in early life is no bar to a man's advancement."[52] In *Mark, the Match Boy* (1869), Alger reminds his faithful readers that "less than three years before Richard Hunter [the earlier Ragged Dick] was an ignorant and ragged bootblack about the streets. . . . By a series of upward steps, partly due to good fortune, but largely to his own determination to improve, and hopeful energy, Dick had now become a bookkeeper in the establishment of Rockwell & Cooper."[53]

Unlike Jack London, who became America's classic example of Horatio Alger's "rags to riches" formula, John and Flora London, an ill-matched pair, struggled to survive, Flora's dominant character eclipsing John's weak but gentle nature. She held séances, some involving London and his two sisters, Ida and Eliza. These experiences surface in several stories, including "Two Gold Bricks" in *The Owl*, September 1897 (perhaps his earliest known tale), "Planchette," collected in *Moon Face & Other Stories* (1906), and *The Star Rover* (1915), whose central figure masters astral projection. In "The Man with the Gash," London's Klondiker "believed in omens and thought-transference, and he deemed these dream-robbers to be the astral projection of real personages who happened at those particular moments, no matter where they were in the flesh, to be harboring designs, in the spirit, upon his wealth."[54] And in the macabre "Who Believes in Ghosts!" London uses words such as "psychic force," "necromancy," "earth bound spirits," and "disembodied entities," common terms in the occult world.

> It is mysterious, imponderable and powerful; it is invisible, yet oftentimes visible; and it can exert itself in innumerable ways. Opening locked doors, putting out lights, dropping bricks, and strange sounds, cries, curses and moans, are but the lower demonstrations of this phenomena. Also, as we have in this life men inclined to good and evil, so have we, in the life to come, spirits, both good and bad. Woe betide you if you are thrown in contact with evil spirits. You may be lifted up bodily and dashed to the floor or against the walls like a football; you may see grewsome sights even beyond the conception of mortal; and so great a terror may be brought upon you, that your minds may loose their balance and leave you gibbering idiots or violently insane. And again, these evil spirits have the power to deprive you of one, two or all your senses, if they so wish. They can burst your eardrums; sear your eyes; destroy your voice; sadly impair your sense of taste and smell, and paralyze the body in any or every nerve. And even as in the days of Christ, they may make their habitation within your bodies, and then—the asylum and padded cell stares you in the face. I have no advice to give you in dealing with this mysterious subject, for I am ignorant; but my parting words are, "keep cool; may you prosper in your undertaking, and beware!"[55]

At times John London probably wished spirits would swallow Flora. He became agent and collector for the Singer Sewing

Machine Company, while Flora accepted a boarder. This enabled her to buy lottery tickets and hire a Chinese servant. (She seems to resemble the whimsical Mrs. Micawber in Dickens' *David Copperfield*.) Things got worse, then better, then worse again, like a seesaw in constant motion. They moved to Oakland, where John leased land, opening a produce store, but his crooked partner bolted with the cash. Four more houses offered shelter. Again John sold vegetables in San Francisco, settling for awhile in Alameda, where young Johnnie attended the West End School. Henry L. Betten, a classmate, later recalled: "The Londons first moved to Alameda in 1880 when John London, stepfather of young Jack, contracted to farm a tract of land lying south of Pacific Avenue and west of Second Street for Matthew Davenport. They first occupied quarters on the farm but later moved to the Charles Weckerle place in the 200 block, north side of Pacific Avenue, which became known as the 'spook house' because of Mrs. London's deep interest in the supernatural. These occult activities doubtless had an ill influence on a youngster who had also inherited disturbed emotional qualities from both natural parents, idiosyncrasies he evidenced in his early schoolboy days."[56] Charmian also mentioned that Johnnie caused trouble in school, attributing it to his imperious air and inability to communicate with intellectual inferiors. Flora recalled temper tantrums, sometimes over trivial issues, resulting in her loss of control over the child.

Thomas J. London, a stepbrother, once commented about the young Jack London:

> Jack was a little baby when I got to California. We always called him 'Little Johnnie.' He grew pretty tall when he was a young boy, but was never very strong and all the time wanted to be reading. He went to school, of course, and when he got old enough father sent him over to a night school in San Francisco. I wasn't at home a lot but when the circus would come in from the road, I always went back to Oakland and lived with them. I remember about Jack, when he was quite a boy, he would work all day, writing something or studying but when it came to other kinds of work, he just naturally wouldn't do it. He didn't seem to be lazy, only he wanted to keep his own way all the time. He was only a boy when I left California and came back to Iowa but I haven't forgotten these things about him.[57]

The Londons next moved to Livermore Valley near San Mateo, the high-strung young Johnnie trailing along, wondering where he'd live next. Here John London raised horses and vegetables on an eighty-acre ranch, once part of a Spanish heritage. The family owned vineyards, fruit and olive trees, Morgan and Blackhawk horses, and modern facilities. Yet after Jack London's half-sister Eliza (born during John London's first marriage) married at sixteen, the Londons abandoned this property, again returning to Oakland—without any explanations regarding the financing of such a farm. In a brochure published many years later by the Macmillan Company, Jack London wrote:

My work on the ranch at one time was to watch the bees, and as I sat under a tree from sunrise till late in the afternoon, waiting for the swarming, I had plenty of time to read and dream. Livermore Valley was very flat, and even the hills around were then to me devoid of interest, and the only incident to break in on my visions was when I gave the alarm of swarming, and the ranch folk rushed out with pots, pans, and buckets of water. I think the opening line of "Signa" was "It was only a little lad, yet he had dreams of becoming a great musician, and having all Europe at his feet." Well, I was only a little lad, too, but why could not I become what "Signa" dreamed of being?

Life on a California ranch was then to me the dullest possible existence, and every day I thought of going out beyond the skyline to see the world. Even then there were whispers, art promptings; my mind inclined to things beautiful, although my environment was unbeautiful. The hills and valleys around were eyesores and aching pits, and I never loved them till I left them.[58]

Even Charmian questioned this remark, asking how a ranch with vineyards, fruit, and olive trees, besides Spanish touches, could be an eyesore and aching pit? Did Johnny prefer the city? Life seemed idyllic enough: "I had plenty of time to read and dream."

After his return to Oakland, John London invested his last savings in an eight-room house on East Seventeenth Street, where Flora planned to run a boarding house for women workers, another shortsighted scheme. Weary from work and a nagging, impractical wife, the elder London drifted from house to house, job to job, once serving as a deputy constable in the tenderloin, taking Johnnie along sometimes, where the boy learned about society's lower depths and its degradation. It's said they fished together, dug clams, and studied the ships.

Johnnie attended the Garfield and Franklin Schools. He sold newspapers, traded junk, helped the ice man, set pins in a bowling alley—and started smoking. "I belonged to a 'street gang' in West Oakland, as rough and tough a crowd as you'll find in any city in the country," he once said. (William H. Chaney also was a young toughie.) "Yet while I always got along with the crowd—I was sociable and held up my end when it came to doing anything—I was never in the center of things; I was always alone, in a corner, as it were."[59]

London did make one friend, Frank Atherton, the popular hobby of collecting picture coupons bringing the boys together. Frank taught Johnnie how to swim. Once they stole fruit from an orchard, narrowly escaping an irate farmer with loaded gun. The Londons invited Frank to supper. Homemade slingshots, filled with lead bullets, soon inspired other ideas: why not shoot ducks in the estuary and marshes, then sell them, making a pretty profit? When a Chinaman bought several mud hens, they started talking about wildcat and grizzly bear steaks. "If we found our enterprise a paying proposition," Atherton wrote, "we both planned to quit school for awhile. For after we had made a small fortune at the wildcat business we could well afford private teachers."[60]

The boys purchased two old pistols and found targets on San Leandro Bay, targets that avoided the spray of bullets. Johnnie fumed. Pistols weren't any better than slingshots. He flung his gun in the water. When Frank wouldn't get it, the hot-tempered youth threw the oars away. Frank's family moved that spring, leading Johnnie to withdraw again into the escapist world of writers like Horatio Alger. "As a child I dreamed awake, with my eyes open to the day, and when I spoke of the strange things I saw I was laughed at, and the other children were afraid and drew away from me," says a character in "Li Wan, the Fair." "It was a sickness, I believe, like the falling-sickness that comes to old men; and in time I grew better and dreamed no more."[61]

Chapter 2

Prince of the Oyster Pirates

AFTER FINISHING grammar school at thirteen, London expected to join the labor force, like most proletarians in those days. Few Americans attended college. Typical Horatio Alger types struggled from the bottom up, including Henry Ford, Andrew Carnegie, and John D. Rockefeller. For awhile, however, London knocked around the San Francisco area, doing odd jobs, sailing the estuary and San Leandro Bay in a small skiff, hanging his hat at home. Such experiences offered a framework for "The Apostate," London's short story about a child who slaves eighteen to twenty hours in a mill, then returns to a filthy shack. Irving Stone treated this tale autobiographically in *Sailor on Horseback*, although Horatio Alger's *Ragged Dick*, begins with similar words: " 'Wake up there, youngster,' said a rough voice,"[1] and continues with the poor lad's troubles. How much of "The Apostate" is Ragged Dick and how much is Jack London?

After several months of factory work, London said he became an oyster pirate on the Oakland waterfront, searching for fast profits. "That he remained at liberty and lived to become something else," noted the *San Francisco Chronicle*, "proves his [him] the exception, for most of them died young in waterfront brawls or at the end of a prison rope, or were shot to death in gunfights with oyster bed watchmen."[2] According to London's account, he bought a tall-masted sloop from an oyster pirate named French Frank for $300, mostly financed by Mammy

23

Jenny, his black wet nurse. But where would she, presumably poorer than London's family, find such enormous funds? And why lend them to an unemployed fifteen-year-old with dreams of playing oyster pirate during a vicious depression? It carries the logic of dime novel thrillers.

The derring-do London with patched-up skiff evokes images of "a miniature Nietzschean 'blond beast' with a touch of Norman Rockwell sentimentality."[3] Even his wharf-rat chums—Whiskey Bob, Joe Goose, Nick the Greek, Young Scratch, and Spider Healy (whose sister, the queen of the oyster pirates, supposedly became London's mistress)—seem like penny-dreadful cartoons. London later confesses in *John Barleycorn* his love for this roguish life, fighting winds and storms, the fish patrol—even French Frank with a shotgun, while steering the *Razzle Dazzle* with his feet! Besides bringing in the biggest hauls in the shortest times. Charmian, London's second wife, however, claimed he just knocked around the bay with hoodlums, drinking and loafing, when out of work.[4]

Perhaps a 1917 article in *St. Nicholas* unknowingly tapped London's source for these romantics:

Jack wandered into the Oakland Public Library. His roving eyes fell on a set of bound volumes of *St. Nicholas*. He opened volume twelve, containing the number for November, 1884. At page thirty-two he stopped. Here was a story which, he felt, fitted into his own life. It was called "The Cruise of the Pirate-Ship *Moonraker*," written by Mr. F. Marshall White. Briefly, it was the story of a boy, *Harry Bronson,* who fell under the evil influence of trashy, juvenile fiction which led him to run away from a good home. Becoming the leader of a gang of "wharf-rats," he cruised about New York harbor on a captured yacht. This he renamed the *Moonraker,* and, as its captain, he styled himself, "The Boy Terror."[5]

Did London later embroider this fiction into his life when trying to shape a heroic American myth? Instead of "The Boy Terror," he became "Prince of the Oyster Pirates" in writings of later years, saying his oyster raids sometimes netted nearly $100 a night. Yet in January 1891 the *Oakland Tribune* reported that "the abandoned oyster beds of the Morgan Oyster Company on Bay Farm Islands present a very busy scene, hundreds of persons going there in search of oysters, and last night there was oyster hunting by moonlight. It is estimated that during the past week more than $5,000 worth of oysters have been carried away. . . . They are fast disappearing, however, and it will not be many days until the beds are exhausted. All that a person needs to go hunting for them is a pair of rubber boots, as there is much mud in the beds. They can be reached by land, but more directly by a boat from the county bridge."[6]

London later wrote a juvenile novel about oyster pirates, *The Cruise of the Dazzler* (1902). Its surface values preach the bourgeois platitudes he hated: "For he felt that he was fighting for principle, as his forefathers had fought for principle," and "I believe in liberty. The finest souls grow in such soil," and "A human life the money of the world cannot buy; nor can it redeem one which is misspent; nor can it make full and complete and beautiful a life which is dwarfed and warped and ugly."[7]

A closer look at *The Cruise of the Dazzler* reveals a polarization between the two opposites in London's personality—the proletarian who wanted to be a prince, and the prince who wanted to be a proletarian. Arthur Calder-Marshall writes that "there are two boys, each displaying one aspect of London's boyhood psyche" in the book. "There is Joe, the tough son of a well-to-do San Franciscan living on the Heights, who hates all he learns at school, except literature, and who wants to run away to sea. And there is 'Frisco Kid, an orphan living aboard the *Dazzler,* working for French Pete, a brutal and drunken pirate. 'Frisco Kid pines for the education and security which Joe despises."[8]

London played both social classes against the middle in this book, letting the prosperous Anglo-Saxon boy call equals, "milk-and-water chaps," kids in white collars and clean clothes, "the kind—afraid of their own shadows, and no more spunk in them than in so many sheep," while 'Frisco Kid, one of the pit people, devours books in a reformatory, where the inmates were "mostly street boys of the worst kind—lying, and sneaking, and cowardly, without one spark of manhood or one idea of square dealing and fair play."[9]

Tired of high jinks on San Francisco Bay, London hit a new adventure path—crossing the Sierra Nevada on railroad rods for a few weeks, then bumming his way home. Back in 'Frisco, he tried to commit suicide in the Bay, according to *John Barleycorn*, but a Greek fisherman rescued him. Flora later commented: "I guess Jack was a pretty good boy when you come to figure it all out, but he fell in with bad company. He used to have terrible fights with the boys of the neighborhood. He got to going down to the waterfront. He became awfully bossy in the house. We couldn't stand him sometimes."[10]

What succeeded the wicked oyster-pirate capers? London said he changed sides, joining the fish patrol with thug Young Scratch, using their boat, the *Reindeer,* to catch thieves, mainly ruthless Chinese shrimp-fishers hated by many Californians. Even Horatio Alger called one Chinese man a "barbarian" and "a rather superior order of monkey"[11] in *The Young Explorer*. London crowed that he fought offenders with "a steel table-fork, but I felt fearless and a man when I climbed over the side of a boat to arrest some marauder."[12] The real San Francisco waterfront?

Relates Herbert Asbury in *The Barbary Coast,*

For half a century after the beginning of the gold rush one of the most dangerous areas in San Francisco was the waterfront, along the eastern and northeastern fringes of the Barbary Coast. Murderers, footpads, burglars, hoodlums, and Rangers prowled the streets in such numbers and carried on their depredations with such boldness that the police walked their beats in pairs and went in even greater force whenever they found it necessary to enter any of the dives with which the district abounded. Every policeman assigned to waterfront duty was specially chosen for strength, bravery, and huskiness. He was equipped with the regulation night-stick and pistol and also carried, in a large outside breast-pocket within easy reach of his hand, a huge knife a foot or more in length. This fearsome weapon was infinitely more effective at close quarters than a club or the cumbersome, unreliable fire-arm of the early days. Nor did the police hesitate to use it. Several battles occurred in which beleaguered policemen chopped off the hands of their assailants or inflicted other wounds equally frightful, and at least one in which an attacking hoodlum was decapitated.[13]

London, nevertheless, fantasized a clash with "Yellow Handkerchief," a wicked Chinese in *Tales of the Fish Patrol* (1905):

A big Chinaman, remarkably evil-looking, with his head swathed in a yellow silk handkerchief and face badly pock-marked, planted a pike-pole on the *Reindeer*'s bow and began to shove the entangled boats apart. Pausing long enough to let the jib halyards, and just as the *Reindeer* cleared and began to drift astern, I leaped aboard the junk with a line and made fast. He of the yellow handkerchief and pock-marked face came toward me threateningly, but I put my hand into my hip pocket, and he hesitated. I was unarmed, but the Chinese have learned to be fastidiously careful of American hip pockets, and it was upon this that I depended to keep him and his savage crew at a distance.

I ordered him to drop the anchor at the junk's bow, to which he replied, "No sabbe." The crew responsed in like fashion, and though I made my meaning plain by signs, they refused to understand. Realizing the inexpediency of discussing the matter, I went forward myself, overran the line, and let the anchor go.

"Now get aboard, four of you," I said in a loud voice, indicating with my fingers that four of them were to go with me and the fifth was to remain by the junk. The Yellow Handkerchief hesitated; but I repeated the order fiercely (much more fiercely than I felt), at the same time sending my hand to my hip. Again the Yellow Handkerchief was overawed, and with surly looks he led three of his men aboard the *Reindeer*. I cast off at once, and, leaving the jib down, steered a course for George's junk. Here it was easier, for there were two of us, and George had a pistol to fall back on if it came to the worst. And here, as with my junk, four Chinese were transferred to the sloop and one left behind to take care of things.[14]

An argument between London and his sidekick follows, leading to a gun grab, while the sadistic Chinese watch, waiting for a chance to strike:

My brain seemed smitten with a dazzling brightness. The whole situation, in all its bearings, was focussed sharply before me—

the shame of losing the prisoners, the worthlessness and cowardice of George, the meeting with Le Grant and the other patrolmen and the lame explanation; and then there was the fight I had fought so hard, victory wrenched from me just as I thought I had it within my grasp. And out of the tail of my eye I could see the Chinese crowding together by the cabin doors and leering triumphantly. It would never do.

I threw my hand up and my head down. The first act elevated the muzzle, and the second removed my head from the path of the bullet which went whistling past. One hand closed on George's wrist, the other on the revolver. Yellow Handkerchief and his gang sprang toward me. It was now or never. Putting all my strength into a sudden effort, I swung George's body forward to meet them. Then I pulled back with equal suddenness, ripping the revolver out of his fingers and jerking him off his feet. He fell against Yellow Handkerchief's knees, who stumbled over him, and the pair wallowed in the bailing hole where the cockpit floor was torn open. The next instant I was covering them with my revolver and the wild shrimp-catchers were cowering and cringing away.[15]

London also tackled other rascals in *Tales of the Fish Patrol,* including six-foot-three Big Alec, The Centipede, The Porpoise, Barchi of the Sporting Life Gang, and Demetrios Contos. One fish patroller predicts, "The youngster takes naturally to the water, and if, when he finishes high school, he takes a course in navigation and goes deep sea, I see no reason why he shouldn't rise to be master of the finest and biggest ship afloat."[16]

Although this account seems amusing, Shannon Garth's biography for juveniles, *Jack London: Magnet for Adventure,* portrays the "Yellow Handkerchief" incident as *fact,* the text even heightened with a drawing showing London facing the heathen, its caption reading: "The decks became alive with yelling, half-naked Chinese."[17] Irving Stone spent two pages in *Sailor on Horseback* detailing these roughshod romantics, without any skepticism, although London admitted to an editor at *The Youth's Companion* that he stretched events for young readers.

Factory slave, oyster pirate, road-kid, and fish patroller. All these experiences London claimed by age sixteen. On January

20, 1893, several days after his seventeenth birthday, he signed the articles of the *Sophie Sutherland,* a three-topmast schooner bound for the seas of Japan.

Although extensive experience in seamanship still clings to London's reputation, Joan London said her father's seven months aboard the *Sophie Sutherland* were "the only time he ever sailed before the mast."[18] Charmian agreed. His earlier adventures passed within the Golden Gate, most in a fourteen-foot skiff. Yet the myth persists that he spent years on the high seas. The cover of Ruth Franchere's *Jack London: The Pursuit of a Dream* shows a sailor with duffle bag, a schooner in the distance; Shannon Garth's title page of *Jack London: Magnet for Adventure* pictures a handsome youth at a ship's wheel, books at his feet; and the *Jack London Newsletter'*s romantic jacket has depicted London below a full-masted schooner.

London remarked in *John Barleycorn* that a harpooner called Peter Holt offered him a job as his boat puller on the *Sophie Sutherland,* a 156-ton gross and 148-ton net sealing schooner built in 1889 at Tacoma, Washington. Although the rank of able-bodied seaman required proof by affidavit and examination that sailors were nineteen, with a minimum of three years on deck, the captain signed London, accepting Holt's word. (Johnny Heinold, barkeeper of the Last Chance Saloon, who knew London, later said he influenced the skipper's decision.[19]) Herbert Asbury wrote in *The Barbary Coast* that crooked captains shanghaied kids and derelicts, beating and drugging them, even murdering hard-nosed seadogs. (Eugene O'Neill, who read London's salt-water stories, dramatized such incidents, based on experience, in his realistic one-act sea dramas.) Several questions remain unanswered: Why would a captain accept London? He had slight knowhow, sensitive hands and feet, couldn't swim well,[20] and was poorly coordinated. Could such a teenager survive schooner life? London thought so in memoirs. He even claimed mastering the schooner's rigging overnight. Nautical specialists expressed these views on London's seamanship:

Frederick P. Schmitt, Curator, The Whaling Museum. "I have been around salt water for the majority of my life, but have never seen anything like Jack London's self-confidence toward the sea, save for those who are foolhardy or naive. . . . His other claims are nothing short of tall 'sea stories' to say the least. There is no way he could learn the ropes in an 80-ton three master in ten minutes or even ten months, because a ship presents constant new challenges."[21]

Waldo C. M. Johnston, Director, Mystic Seaport: "I am still learning about the sea, and good seamanship takes years of experience to acquire. You simply can't 'learn the ropes' in ten minutes, ten hours, or ten days, and in fact the rigging design of a large sailing vessel takes months to learn at sea."[22]

Did Jack London stretch his feats on the *Sophie Sutherland*? Written years later, perhaps he confused fact with fancy—or did he ever go to sea? That remains the biggest mystery.

London later bragged that during his 1907 cruise through the South Seas on the *Snark* with Charmian, he learned to use a compass for the first time in a few afternoons. Waldo C. M. Johnston adds that "the vagaries of a compass to a landlubber are mysteries which require time to understand, and much more time to execute at the wheel or helm and, in fact, some helmsmen never learn really well how to steer instinctively by compass."[23] And William A. Baker, Curator of the Francis Russell Hart Nautical Museum at the Massachusetts Institute of Technology, wonders how London could have first learned to use the compass in 1907, when he sailed on the *Sophie Sutherland* in 1893, taking the wheel during a typhoon. Sailors who took the wheel used a compass. "The comment about the 1907 *Snark* cruise makes no sense unless London meant that it took a half minute to recall an old skill,"[24] comments Baker.

According to Ninetta Eames Payne, the seventeen-year-old London earned respect from his messmates on the *Sophie Sutherland* by beating a chesty sea dog in a fight.

> Our sailor man one day sat on his bunk weaving a mat of rope yarn when he was accosted by a burly Swede taking his turn at "peggy-day" (a fo'castle term, signifying a sailor's day for cleaning off the meals, washing up the dishes, and filling the slush-lamps), a part of which disagreeable tasks the man evidently hoped to bull-doze the green hand into doing for him.
>
> "Here, you landlubber," he bawled with an oath, "fill up the molasses. You eat the most of it!"

Jack, usually the most amiable of the hands, bristled at his roughness; besides, he had vivid memories of his first and only attempt to eat the black viscous stuff booked "molasses" on the fo'castle bill of fare, and so indignantly denied the charge.

"I never taste it. 'Tain't fit for a hog. It's your day to grub, so do it yourself."

Not a messmate within hearing of the altercation but pictured disaster to this beardless, undersized boy.

Jack's defiant glance again dropped to his mat, and he quietly went on twisting the yarn. At this the sailor, both arms heaped with dishes, swore the harder, and threatened bloodcurdling consequences if he were not obeyed, but Jack kept silent, his supple hands nimbly intent on the rope strands, though the tail of his eye took note of his enemy. [Charmian said that London was very clumsy, that he couldn't rig fishing gear or even button buttons.]

Another threat, met by exasperating indifference, and the incensed Swede dropped the coffee pot to give a back handed slap on the boy's curled mouth. The instant after iron hard knuckles struck squarely between the sailor's eyes, followed by the crash of crockery. The Swede, choking with rage, made a lunge at Jack with a sledge-hammer fist, but the latter dodged, and like a flash vaulted to the ruffian's back, his fingers knitting in the fellow's throat-pipes. He bellowed and charged like a mad bull, and with every frenzied jump, Jack's head was a battering ram against the deck beams. Down crashed the slush-lamp and the lookers-on drew up their feet in the bunks to make room for the show; they saw what the Swede did not, that Jack was getting the worse of it. His eyes bulged horribly and his face streamed blood, but he only dug his fingers deeper into that flesh-padded larynx and yelled through his shut teeth: "Will you promise to let me alone? Eh—will you promise?"

The Swede, tortured and purple in the face, gurgled an assent, and when that viselike grip on his throat loosened, reeled and stumbled to his knees like a felled bullock. The sailors, jamming their way through a wild clutter of food and broken dishes, crowded around the jubilant hero of the hour with friendly offers of assistance and a noticeable increase of respect in their tone and manner. Thence on Jack had his "peggy-day" like the rest, his mates risking no further attempt to take advantage of his youth or inexperience.[25]

Sealing schooners like the *Sophie Sutherland* exploited the failure of international law to prohibit the ravaging of rookeries beyond the three-mile limit. This led to the indiscriminate killing of both young and old seals, including pregnant females, until by 1911, most herds in the north seas had been destroyed. Earlier ecologists, like present-day preservers, raged about the seal slaughters. A July 11, 1890, article in the *New York World* called "How to Save the Seals," for example, reported Washington, D.C.'s concern. "It is apparent that to permit the destruction of the seals by the use of firearms, nets or other mischievous means in Bering Sea would result in the speedy extermination of the race," said a spokesman. "There appears to be no difference of opinion on this subject among experts."[26]

London recorded such a seal bloodbath in *The Sea Wolf,* praising the sealers as "a very superior breed to common sailor-folk"[27]—although William A. Baker, Curator of the Francis Russell Hart Nautical Museum at the Massachusetts Institute of Technology, says schooners weren't high-class ships. It's also peculiar that London called sailors "the scum of the metropolis"[28] in "One More Unfortunate," published several years after his stint on the *Sophie Sutherland.*

Unwilling to accept accountability for his actions in the Bering seal slaughter, London blamed the mess on American women who wanted seal coats. Humphrey Van Weyden, the effete author whom Wolf Larsen kidnaps in *The Sea Wolf,* details: "And north we traveled with it, ravaging and destroying, flinging the naked carcasses to the shark and salting down the skins so that they might later adorn the fair shoulders of the women of the cities. It was wanton slaughter, and all for woman's sake. No man ate of the seal meat or the oil. After a good day's killing I have seen our decks covered with hides and bodies, slippery with fat and blood, the scuppers running red; masts, ropes, and rails spattered with the sanguinary color; and the men, like butchers plying their trade, naked and red of arm and hand, hard at work with ripping and flensing knives, removing the skins from the pretty sea creatures they had killed."[29]

Regarding London's experience with the "pretty sea creatures," Richard O'Connor writes that "the memory of that floating slaughterhouse in the Bering Sea, so far as his writings indicate, made no lacerating impression."[30] In his Afterword to a reissue of *The Sea Wolf,* Franklin Walker comments: "The occupation that took [London] adventuring in 1893 might well have served him later, when he became an enthusiast of the ideas of Karl Marx as an outstanding example of the abuses of predatory capitalism and imperialism."[31]

The *Sophie Sutherland* sailed for Japan after the Siberian sea hunt, anchoring for two weeks in Yokohama, where London caroused with comrades. Before the boat embarked, he swam a mile at midnight to the ship, while policemen scoured the harbor for his remains. He also claimed to have taken the wheel of the *Sophie Sutherland* on its return voyage during a typhoon for one hour, fighting several million tons of water to save crew and precious seal furs. William A. Baker says that "it seems incredible that there was not one or two others on deck watch while London was steering, but sealing was not one of the higher class enterprises and anything might have happened on board the schooner. On the other hand, the master might have sensed that whatever the helmsman did would have little real effect on the typhoon and London made a good yarn of the situation."[32] Edward V. Lewis, Director of the Center for Maritime Studies at The Webb Institute of Naval Architecture, adds that "since the ship had reached Japanese waters, the young man must have had practice at the helm."[33]

How curious that one of Horatio Alger's most famous poems, "John Maynard," tells about a sailor boy who takes the helm, preventing a shipwreck, but sacrifices his life in the process. Perhaps the helmsman incident can also be traced more directly to London's "Chris Farrington, Able Seaman" (*The Youth's Companion,* May 1901). Chris, age seventeen as was London on the *Sophie* voyage, becomes the boat's second best steerer, an honor London also claimed in *John Barleycorn.* Chris is also "a slender though strongly built young fellow of seventeen, with Yankee ancestry writ large all over him." The name of the ship he steers? The *Sophie Sutherland.* It even sails from San Francisco harbor. (London often used the names of real people, places, and things in stories, which confused readers, giving his fictions more creditability.) During the terrible typhoon, Chris is left alone on deck with the eighty-year-old captain, a sailing

master who suffers from broken arms and ribs, and an inefficient
Chinese cook. An "ocean of water" hurls Chris one hundred
feet, but the one hundred forty pound boy returns to the wheel,
though bruised and bleeding. "It was no child's play to steer
a vessel under single-reefed jib before a typhoon." He struggles
for hours against the wretched storm, while the old captain
stuffs cake-chocolate into his mouth. After several days, Chris
dozes at the wheel, but still saves the ship. "So small and
insignificant the schooner seemed on the long Pacific roll! Pushing up a maddening mountain, she would poise like a cockleshell on the giddy summit, breathless and rolling, leap outward
and down into the yawning chasm beneath, and bury herself
in the smother of foam at the bottom. Then the recovery, another mountain, another sickening upward rush, another poise,
and the downward crash!"[34] After the devastating typhoon,
Chris even turns around the *Sophie,* rescuing its stranded seal-
hunting crew. (Humphrey Van Weyden, by the way, also sails
the *Ghost* alone after Wolf Larsen dies in *The Sea Wolf.*)

London's first mention of this typhoon—minus the helms-
manship—appeared in a gripping tale called "Story of a Typhoon off the Coast of Japan," which won first prize in a contest
sponsored by the *San Francisco Call.* The following excerpt
shows London's early potential:

> It was on deck that the force of the wind could be fully appre-
> ciated, especially after leaving the stifling fo'castle. It seemed
> to stand up against you like a wall, making it almost impossible
> to move on the heaving docks or to breathe as the fierce gusts
> came dashing by. The schooner was hove to under jib, foresail
> and mainsail. We proceeded to lower the foresail and make it
> fast. The night was dark, greatly impeding our labor. . . . Some-
> times several seas following each other with great rapidity and
> thundering down on our decks filled them full to the bulwarks,
> but soon they were discharged through the lee scuppers.
>
> To reef the mainsail we were forced to run off before the gale
> under the single reefed jib. By the time we had finished the wind
> had forced up such a tremendous sea that it was impossible to
> heave her to. Away we dash on the wings of the storm through
> the muck and flying spray. A wild sheer to starboard, then an-
> other to port, as the enormous seas struck the schooner astern
> and nearly broached her to.

As day broke we took in the jib, leaving not a sail unfurled. Since we had begun scudding she had ceased to take the seas over the bow, but amidships they broke fast and furious. It was a dry storm in the matter of rain, but the force of the wind filled the air with fine spray, which flew as high as the crosstrees and cut the face like a knife, making it impossible to see over a hundred yard ahead. The sea was a dark lead color, as with long, slow majestic roll it was heaped by the wind into liquid mountains of foam. The wild antics of the schooner were sickening as she forged along. She would almost stop as though climbing a mountain, then rapidly rolling to right and left as she gained the summit of a huge sea, she steadied herself and paused for a moment as though affrighted at the yawning precipice before her. Like an avalanche she shot forward and down as the sea astern struck her with the force of a thousand battering rams, burying her bow to the catheads in the milky foam at the bottom that came on deck in all directions—forward, astern, to right and to left, through the hawse pipes and over the rail.[35]

Returning from the Siberian seal hunt on the *Sophie Sutherland,* London's interest in the Oakland waterfront faded; most of his rawboned buddies were either dead, in jail, or dodging the law. A fierce depression, meanwhile, had strangled the country's economic lifelines. Several hundred banks folded. Mines and factories shut. Endless thousands found themselves unemployed, without benefits but with families to feed. Things got worse. The bitter Chicago Railroad Union strike followed in 1894. Rains ruined over $10 million worth of crops in the midwest. Although London found several short-lived jobs, that adventure itch returned, and he again headed for the road.

Chapter 3

The Hobo in Theory and in Practice

ONE OFFSHOOT OF THE crippling 1893 depression was Coxey's army, a forced march from Massillon, Ohio—Flora's hometown—to Washington, D.C., which started on March 25, 1894. Its leader, Jacob Sechler Coxey, "a breeder of fine horses and a comparatively rich man,"[1] wanted Congress to legislate $500 million for a public roads program. Coxey's wife, meanwhile, divorced him, while locals ridiculed the scheme. It appears, however, that Chief Marshall Carl Browne of San Francisco, "a Buffalo-Bill like figure,"[2] masterminded the movement, inspiring Coxey with a doctrine of natural theosophy. In simple language? He claimed to be Christ's reincarnated soul. That's why followers called themselves the "Commonwealth of Christ" and decorated banners with Christ's head, whose features resembled Browne's face. Second in command to Browne stood "an Indian patent medicine vendor" whom he'd met in Chicago and called "the Great Unknown." Under the auspices of Christ, Coxey and his colleagues devised a massive protest in the Capitol "before which, hell, not to mention 'the subservient tools of Wall Street' (Congress), could not stand."[3]

Charles T. Kelly's Industrial Army, a complement of fifteen hundred tramps, unemployed laborers, and knight-errants, also pushed from California to Washington, expecting to link with Coxey somewhere on the trail. *Harper's Weekly* called Kelly

"a small, pale, intellectual-appearing, and rather pensive-look-
ing man. Fortunately, his authority over the rabble, which was
made up by him in a few days, and which was without any
other restraint than that imposed by his word of command, was
excellent. . . . He was merely a creature of circumstances and
of the moment."[4]

London joined Kelly's last recruits as a fling, he and a friend
planning to couple with the exodus at Sacramento. Arriving too
late, they took a train east, London spending some money given
him by his half-sister Eliza and his mother Flora. The *San
Francisco Chronicle* published an article about London's
"trampings" on December 16, 1894, called "His Travel Is
Cheap," saying he "joined the Industrial Army at Lovelock.
This was a clever move, as he had exhausted his money and
understood that the Industrialists were well supplied with food.
This proved to be a mistake. They had scarcely anything to eat,
so the Oakland boy left them and went on to Salt Lake."[5]
William McDevitt, London's platform manager between 1905
and 1909, also remarked: "Jack's penciled diary of a part of
his road experience at this period indicates that he regarded
himself as a member, temporarily, of the 'army,' but George
Speed himself told me more than once that Jack was never *in*
the army nor *of* it, so far as the 'Colonel' himself ever knew.
In either event it is quite obvious that the young wanderer from
home (he was then eighteen) became infected with a socio-
political disease that he kept until his death, twenty-two years
later."[6]

In their article, the *San Francisco Chronicle* tagged London
"The Pastor Kid," tracing his tramp tour from Salt Lake City
through Butte, Yellowstone Park, Baltimore, Philadelphia, New
York, and Boston. The only mention of Washington, D.C.,
involves tourism and a sympathetic letter from Flora, which
disregards Kelly's Industrial Army.[7] Although London detailed
the Kelly experience in both a diary and *The Road* (1907), he
reduced it to several sentences in *John Barleycorn*. The diary,
on the other hand, relates many impressions, such as log houses
in the Rockies, a blinding snow in Laramie, a spark that fired
his overcoat. The sun peeled London's face, and he suffered
from blistered feet.[8]

Although London admitted pilfering from people in an advance unit, instead of collecting food and materials for marchers navigating down the Des Moines and Mississippi rivers, Andrew Sinclair calls his escapades "random and aimless and innocent, as lawless as snowflakes,"[9] in *Jack: A Biography of Jack London* (1977). Robert Barltrop disagrees in *Jack London: The Man, the Writer, the Rebel* (1976), saying that "the picture of a glorious lark, in which initiative and ability were reaping their reward, leaves out that it took place at everyone else's expense. The doctrine of the survival of the fittest, which was to be a dominant theme in Jack's stories, was already affirmed in his outlook. Loyalty, which he extolled to Charmian as the greatest of virtues, was always over-ridden by his conviction that he would be top dog and the weaker others would go to the wall."[10]

What about Coxey's "Commonwealth of Christ"? Most abandoned the march before reaching Washington, D.C., where police arrested Coxey for walking on the Capitol lawns. The *Washington Post* commented on April 30, 1894:

It may not be an heroic, but it is at least a comfortable consummation that the Coxey movement should have dwindled from a great moral crusade to a cheap catch-penny show. Some of them, who seem to think they are entitled to help themselves to other people's property without reference to any of the vulgar formalities observed by ordinary human beings, have been gathered in by the police. Others, who have so far escaped the myrmidons of despotism, are the objects of an earnest and painstaking pursuit. And still others, who have so far done nothing to merit serious consideration, are meeting with a playful if somewhat contemptuous reception, which must make them question the reverence of those who extend it. Altogether, the much-talked-of Commonweal movement appears to have degenerated into a particularly forlorn burlesque. With one lot under arrest for grand larceny, and another in full flight from the constables; with a section here receiving a charivari at the hands of the college boys, and another there being held up for purpose of disinfection by the sanitary authorities; and, finally, with Coxey's own immediate Commonwealers safely caged for exhibition in a suburban resort like so many five-legged calves or wild men of Borneo, it really does begin to seem that the great moral demonstration of 1894 is likely to figure in history as the most ridiculous of humbugs.[11]

London continued to ride the rails after leaving Coxey's Army. His exact route remains a mystery. Was it direct, or did he zigzag across Canada and the States? (In 1893 he also saw the World's Columbian Exposition in Chicago and visited his Aunt Mary Everhard in St. Joseph, Michigan, staying for several weeks.) In "Jack London in Boston" (*Boston Evening Transcript*, May 26, 1900), he recalled drifting into America's cultural cradle during the fall of 1894, a "professional hobo" thrown off some train by an irate "shack" (brakeman).

"Brrr! It's a raw old wind that blows in Boston, about 2 A.M., especially along in September. I shivered and shook, collar pulled up and cap down, vainly trying to sleep, till a policeman tapped me. Now, gentle reader, a word of warning should you ever go on the 'road': Always placate the policeman. He is at once the dispenser and obfuscator of life, liberty and the pursuit of happiness." After swallowing a sob story, this cop, according to London, handed him a silver quarter and apologized for not having any whiskey.

Before moving on to Montreal and Ottawa, London said he met several other road bums. He jawed philosophy with one: "As it was rather early, we sunned ourselves on the benches beside the Bunker Hill Monument, and, discovering an affinity of tastes and studies, discussed till breakfast time the possibilities of a reconciliation of Kant and Spencer. After having satisfied the material man by 'slamming gates' and 'back-door collections,' we returned to the monument. Here we took the sunshine and talked Karl Marx and the German economists, until, in a sort of bashful way, he announced the possession of antiquarian propensities. Thereat I was hauled across the bridge to the North End, where he resurrected all manner of architectural antiquities and fairly bubbled with the histories of the old buildings." London added, "Needless to speak of my delight in all this, for I was fresh from the 'new and naked lands' of the great West, where the elder inhabitants antedated history, and there was nothing old save the soil."[12]

In Niagara Falls, however, London failed to sweet-talk the law. Passing through on a sidedoor Pullman, he flopped in a nearby country field, snoozed soundly, and tramped into town the next morning. A fly-cop pinched him, along with several dozen other bums, which led to a thirty-day vagrancy stretch in the Erie County Penitentiary.

"Incidentally, while tramping some ten thousand miles through the United States and Canada," he later related in *War of the Classes,* "I strayed into Niagara Falls, was nabbed by a fee-hunting constable, denied the right to plead guilty or not guilty, sentenced out of hand to thirty days' imprisonment for having no fixed abode and no visible means of support, handcuffed and chained to a bunch of men similarly circumstanced, carted down country to Buffalo, registered at the Erie County Penitentiary, had my head clipped and my budding mustache shaved, was dressed in convict stripes, compulsorily vaccinated by a medical student who practised on such as we, made to march the lock-step, and put to work under the eyes of guards armed with Winchester rifles—all for adventuring in *blond-beastly* fashion."[13]

In *The Road* London wrote that, while in jail, he was appointed a hall man after two days through a pal's influence, forcing inmates to give kickbacks for better food and conditions, smashing prisoners in the face with a broom handle if they talked during morning wash. Joan, who thought London imagined much of this, wrote: "Prison bit deeply. He described it in *The Road,* as in other books he described his brief experiences with the oyster pirates and fish patrol, and the gold hunters in the Klondike, as if he had spent years there instead of a few weeks."[14]

After London's release, he begged on the streets of Buffalo, then said in *The Road* that he ditched a jail comrade, who had arranged the trusteeship, by ducking out the rear of a saloon and over a fence, then boarded a southbound freight on the Western New York and Pennsylvania Railroad, beating his way across the United States and Canada. He returned to San Francisco as a deckhand on the *Umatilla,* the ship destined to deposit him at the Klondike's doorstep two years later.

In his later experiences on the road, London called himself a tramp elitist, writing in *The Bookman*: "Thousands of men on the road are unfit to be 'profesh;' it is impossible for them to be 'profesh.' The 'profesh' are the aristocracy of their Underworld. They are the lords and masters, the aggressive men, the primordial noble men, the *blond beasts* of Nietzsche, lust-fully roving and conquering through sheer superiority and strength. Unwritten is the law they impose. They are the law, the Law incarnate. And the Underworld looks up to them and obeys.''[15]

Josiah Flynt, to whom London dedicated *The Road,* must have eased down different roads without the Quixotic charac-ters. "It is the man who wilfully and knowingly makes a busi-ness of crime or is experimenting with it from commercial mo-tives that I have found in largest numbers 'on the road',''he said in *Tramping with Tramps* (1899). "He thinks that if all goes well he may become an aristocrat; and having so little to lose and so much to gain, he deliberately takes his chances.''[16]

Flynt met many tramps on the road. His conclusions?

> The tramps; theory of them is that they are possessed of the "railroad fever," and I am inclined to agree with them, but I accept the expression in its broader sense of *Wanderlust.* They want to get out into the world, and at stated periods the desire is so strong and the roar so handy that they simply cannot resist the temptation to explore it. A few weeks usually suffice to cool their ardor, and then they run home quite as summarily as they left, but they stay only until the next runaway mood seizes them. I have been successful in getting really well acquainted with several of these interesting wanderers, and in each case this has been the situation. They do not want to be tough, and many of them could not be if they tried; but they have a passion for seeing things on their own hook, and if the mood for a "trip" comes, it seems to them the most natural thing in the world to indulge it. If they had the means they would ride on Pullman cars and imagine themselves princes, but lacking the where-withal, they take to the road.

Flynt recalls one fellow. "Now it was a wish to go West and play trapper and scout, and then it was the dream of American boyhood,—a life cramped but struggling, and emerging in glo-rious success as candidate for the Presidency. Garfield's bi-ography, I remember, once started him on such a journey, and it took years to get the notion out of his head that simply living and striving as Garfield did was sure to bring the same results. [Horatio Alger's biography on Garfield, *From Canal Boy to*

President, remained one of London's favorite childhood books.] Frequently his wanderings ended several hundred miles from home, but much oftener in some distracting vagabond's hangout in a neighboring city."[17]

Unlike Josiah Flynt, London romanticized his tramp sketches, saying in the *War of the Classes* that the bum "has loafed, seen the country and green things, laughed in joy, lain on his back and listened to the birds, singing overhead, unannoyed by factory whistles and bosses' harsh commands; and, most significant of all, *he has lived.* That is the point! He has not starved to death. Not only has he been care-free and happy, but he has lived!"[18] Hoboes in London's two short stories "Local Color" and "The Hobo and the Fairy" are stuffed with straw. "Local Color" is a pretentious tale about an intellectual drifter, while a bum is reformed by a little girl and her kind mother in "The Hobo and the Fairy." When London sent this to George Sterling, his longtime poet friend, for approval and correction, Sterling replied: "I see you're giving the damned magazines what they want—but what pap that reformed tramp stuff is! If you'd been true to life you'd have had to make him rape her. Then where would the story have sold?"[19]

Critics called *The Road* (1907), London's hitchhiking reminiscences, shallow and dishonest. The *New York Times,* similarly to George Sterling, noted: "The trouble is that Mr. London is not a realist; the form is the form of realism, but the spirit that of sentimentality. The shifty-eyed, lazy, dirty tramp of common experience could never, to a genuine realist, be confused with Nietzsche's blond beast, his overman, as Mr. London confuses him."[20] *Independent* questioned that "in spite of his frankness, [London] does not give the impression of sincerity and strict accuracy. He is too smooth a story-teller to be altogether plausible and he takes such manifest delight in his skill and success as a liar when he was beating his way across the continent that we involuntarily wonder at what date he abandoned the habit. There are photographs to back up the text but when and how were they taken?"[21] A good question. As Josiah Flynt said about "The Children of the Road" in *Tramping with Tramps*: "The law of the survival of the fittest is just as operative in low life as in any other. In such spheres

the worst natures are the fittest, and the partially good must
yield to them unless zealously defended by outside help.''[22] Did
the teenage London take photos? How long would a camera
have survived in such a low-life jungle? A similar situation
resulted in 1903, when Macmillan published *The People of the
Abyss*, London's tract on East-side London. George Brett,
Macmillan Company's editor, rejected London's photos, so he
found someone in England to supply them, yet took credit.[23]
Was *The Road*, published nearly fifteen years after the fact, a
replay of such mischief?

Macmillan Company remaindered *The Road*, while critics
continued to fume over London's rusty romance. *The Dial* published an essay which discussed *The Road* and Edmond Kelly's
The Elimination of the Tramp.

> As to the reliability of [London's] information, he tells us himself
> of half a dozen times when he lied for his own advantage, and
> it will be a credulous reader who does not at least suspect the
> possibility of becoming one case more. . . . One has to search
> diligently through the book to find any quality or trait (not purely
> physical) that is not vicious. Mr. Jack London in his tramp days
> was, of course, a professional beggar and thief, and lived by
> what he could get out of the good-hearted and foolish. But he
> was otherwise a poor type. He tells us (among other such mat-
> ters) how he made friends with a man for what he could get out
> of him and deserted him at the first possible minute. He tells us
> how he joined a set of people and sold them out the first chance
> he got, and then sold out those who helped him sell out the
> others. He does not seem to have been a person who would be
> much improved by a farm-colony, even with forced labor.[24]

When London wrote "How I Became a Socialist" (*The Comrade*, March 1903) he forgot all the road's romance, its hoboes
lying in the sunshine and soaking up life. He seethed: "All my
days I have worked hard with my body, and according to the
number of days I have worked, by just that much am I nearer
the bottom of the Pit. I shall climb out of the Pit, but not by
the muscles of my body shall I climb out. I shall do no more
hard work, and may God strike me dead if I do another day's
hard work with my body more than I absolutely have to do.''[25]
He kept this solemn oath.

London decided that education offered life's shortcut from the social pit, accepting Horatio Alger's belief that "education often enables a man to make money."[26] So he enrolled as a tobacco-chewing freshman at the Oakland High School on Twelfth and Clay, a lot older, a lot more worldly, and a lot rougher than the other kids, who ignored him. Georgia Loring Bamford, one of his classmates in French, recalled in *The Mystery of Jack London*:

> His general appearance was really unbelievably shabby, careless and uncleanly; unlike anything I had ever seen in a school room. The other boys were all neatly dressed and wore short trousers, while his were long and baggy. . . . For a time I thought he had some physical debility, he was so "slouchy." When called upon to recite he never stood straight up beside his seat but raised himself with apparent difficulty to a half upright position, usually keeping both hands on his desk as if to steady himself. His answers came promptly even though they were breathed out rather than spoken. When through reciting, he would sit down quickly and abruptly showing every indication of exhaustion. However, he always developed speed in his departure when the session was over.[27]

Georgia Loring Bamford also shuddered at the remembrance of a Christmas week exercise at school that showed London's radicalism and early defiant attitudes. "One feature was a debate with Jack London as a chief participant. How it was arranged, or engineered, as some of the audience called it afterwards, is more than I know; but before people knew it their ears were being assailed by the most truculent Socialistic diatribe that I have ever heard. He was ready to destroy society and civilization; to break down all resistance with any force and commit the most scientific atrocities."[28] London later advanced extermination and early sterilization of inferiors. (The boy in his early "A Thousand Deaths" undergoes a strange and painful breast operation.) Charmian said he supported vivisection. The Nazis later executed some of the scientific theories that Jack London espoused.

London held part-time jobs while attending high school. He washed windows, beat carpets, polished floors, and became assistant janitor at the high school. He also contributed to the *Aegis,* Oakland's high school paper. This attracted attention, especially articles like "Pessimism, Optimism, and Patriotism," an essay supporting the class struggle. Other pieces ranged from "Bonin Islands" and "The Run Across," accounts of his seafaring days, to "Who Believes in Ghosts!" besides several 'Frisco Kid stories.

A sympathetic socialist at Oakland's Public Library named Frederick Irons Bamford (who later married Georgia Loring Bamford) encouraged London's interest in the socialist party. Here London also met Fred Jacobs, a young librarian who introduced him to Ted Applegarth and Mabel Applegarth, his first love, and to Bess Maddern, subsequently his first wife. Jacobs wore spectacles, subdued clothes, and attended night school, saving enough to enroll at a "cramming" institute for the state university. He sometimes helped London with English assignments, taught him photography, exposed him to a circle of close friends.

For awhile, Ted's sister, Mabel Applegarth, mesmerized London with her lacy femininity, slender shape, and proper speech. Charmian called her the "White Lily." Mabel Applegarth's father, a successful mining engineer, left his charming wife at home to play chaperone while he travelled. "She had reared Mabel carefully as a typical young English girl of good family but, youthful and attractive herself, she would not permit her to forsake her role of ingenue," wrote Joan. "It never occurred to Mabel to question her, and besides, she fitted the role perfectly, with her soft, golden curls, appealing blue eyes and beautiful hands. She was the oldest of the group, but none of them seemed so young and inexperienced. Her habitual langour was no pose; she had never been strong."[29]

London suddenly left Oakland High School, rationalizing the decision, mainly that he lacked time or money. Yet he failed to find a job, later claiming that he wrote, although Charmian dated his first query toward publication in September 1898. According to his scattered remarks, London frolicked during this period. He became Oakland's "boy Socialist," visited the homes of the Madderns and the Applegarths, went on bicycle trips, picnics, sailing excursions on Lake Merritt, joined the Ruskin Club, played chess with Ted Applegarth, and read a lot. Then he entered the University of California.

In *John Barleycorn,* London said he attended a "cramming" academy, absorbing material so fast that the master refunded his tuition, adding he'd give the place a bad name, maybe lose its accreditation. Joseph Noel, friend to London and author of *Footloose in Arcadia,* later scoffed: "We are asked to believe that not only did the headmaster request Jack to leave the school for no other reason than that he was making too rapid progress, but by way of a bribe to get him to go without making trouble, paid him back his tuition fee. Did you ever hear of anything so childish? I happen to know Jack's mental range. It was good, but not that good. I also happen to know somewhat of headmasters of cramming schools. Can you imagine one who would miss the advertisement lying in his institution's possession of a faculty of miracle workers." [30] Joan London explained that Fred Jacobs, not London, had attended the academy as a shortcut to the university; London said, "After leaving the high school, in three months' cramming by myself, I took the three years' work for that time and entered the University of California." [31]

London entered Berkeley that fall as a special student, partly because he thought college would make him an instant brain merchant, partly because of Mabel's influence, besides other friends, partly because this offered new root extensions. On his "Application for Admission as a Special Student," [32] he listed his address as 1327 25th Avenue, Oakland, including John London as guardian and J. B. McChesney and James H. Shepard (half-sister Eliza's husband) as references. His academic credits included two history courses (Europe during the Middle Ages and political history of the nineteenth century), and three English courses (composition, history of English literature, and composition based on nineteenth-century writers of science, including Darwin, Huxley, Spencer, Tyndall). Perhaps here he became a disciple of Spencerian individualism, later praising: "Mr. Spencer's contribution to the world's knowledge is so great that we cannot really appreciate it. We lack perspective.

Only future centuries may measure his work for what it is; and when a thousand generations of fiction writers have been laid away, one upon another, and forgotten, Spencer will be even better known than in this day."[33]

Little information survives about London's brief splash in academe. James Hopper, then editor of *The Occident,* recalled he still dressed "sloppily," wearing the usual shirt and soft collar, while convention dictated high starched collars, carried "about sixteen books under his arms," and had two front teeth missing, which he admitted losing "in a fight somewhere."[34] London left Berkeley with an Honorable Dismissal on February 4, 1897, receiving a 1 and 2—the equivalency of A and B—in the history courses, but three incompletes in English.[35] When London enrolled, James Hopper said he called English "simple," but lacked patience, expecting everything in weeks, not years of intensive study. "Well, when with this in my mind I looked him up some few weeks afterward," said Hopper, "I found him gone! Bag and baggage gone, with the enterprise, of which he had spoken to me so glowingly, unfinished, hardly begun."[36]

Georgia Loring Bamford detailed another incident at the university that may have contributed to London's early withdrawal.

> Jack London used to frequent the gymnasium and always wanted to box, but the students were a bit afraid of him on account of his reputation as a prizefighter. On the day in question he had induced a young freshman to "put on the gloves" for a little sparring. Jack sailed in with his old "windmill" tactics so powerful on the waterfront; and in a very few minutes beat the poor, surprised freshman unmercifully and, in fact, knocked him out.
>
> A junior then stepped up and told Jack that he ought to be ashamed of himself for doing such a thing to a boy less than his own weight. This junior, the son of a wealthy man, was a fine student and a well trained athlete. In fact, in the fall of that year, he was on the football team.
>
> To be "called down" in anything relating to sports, especially by one of the hated "Capitalist" class, infuriated London. He was elated over his inglorious victory and told the junior to "go to —, or you will get some of the same stuff yourself." "Oh,

I don't think so," replied the junior. Jack London, without warning, then struck at him. He had not taken off his gloves and the other had no gloves on, but made a quick duck and escaped a powerful blow. "As you wish," said the junior as he put on the gloves.

Again the "windmill" went to work but now he found things different. The junior "put up a guard like a stone wall" and, until he was ready, made no attempt to land a blow. Fast and furious Jack went at him only to wear himself out while the crowd of students who had now gathered looked on silently. They had never seen a real fight in the gymnasium before—such things were not common and they could not understand it. They knew the junior was a fine boxer but could he withstand the vicious onslaught of his opponent who had been in the Prize Ring?

Then two blows were struck like lightning. One "landed" on Jack's nose and the other "got his jugular," so that he was content to lie on the floor and, as the saying goes, "listen to church bells and the singing of birds." He recovered very quickly but had had enough of fighting, for the time being, at least. He was helped to his feet by some of the students who tried to lead him to the wash room; but he threw down the gloves, grabbed his coat and rushed away unwashed, just as he was.

The next time London saw Georgia Loring Bamford, he "turned aside into another path,"[37] trying to avoid her, later claiming that he had beaten a classmate. How long did London remember this incident? In *Burning Daylight,* published twelve years later, Elam Harnism returns to civilization, where an athletic student from the university beats him at arm wrestling, creating a similar psychological shock.

London admitted another humiliation at Berkeley, one that could have spurred his hatred of soldiers. "Do you know what happened to me over there, in that State university at Berkeley, supported by the taxes of the people? I was called out before a whole regiment of students undergoing, as I was, enforced military drill, and I was publicly humiliated by an officer of the regular army because my uniform was shabby, because I lacked forty dollars to buy a new one. My uniform was a second-hand one. I bought it from a fellow for five dollars; and he had bought it from one before him. It was handed down from one poor student to another, and no doubt it did lack style. But was that any reason why the poor boob who had to wear it because he couldn't get a better one should be humiliated?''[38]

Although London pinned his leaving Berkeley on money and the corrupt academic system, he wanted a college education, something Charmian conceded. Johnny Heinhold, whose bar on the waterfront London visited, recalled, "Jack came in one day and I knew he was thinking about something. I asked him what it was and he said, 'I have decided that education is the only thing to make a man out of men.' I told him he was right, but he must be careful not to make a plaster out of it.''[39] In 1903 London remarked in the *Berkeley Daily Gazette*: "A university is a place where hard facts of the past are encountered, and no great attention is paid to the theories and fancies in store for us in the future, but I have often wished that I could have come back and finished my course. The half year was not very much.''[40]

How did London compensate for this failure? By filling stories with dozens of academics. In *The Kempton-Wace Letters*, Herbert Wace is an economics instructor studying for the doctorate at Berkeley. *The Star Rover* is narrated by a former professor at Berkeley, and the hero of *The Scarlet Plague* is also a former professor of English at Berkeley. Dick Forrest in *The Little Lady of the Big House* has a University of California degree and hires college professors as coaches and agricultural consultants, taking some on a summer cruise in his gasoline yacht, the world's first. The widow of an economics professor even guides Saxon and Billy in *The Valley of the Moon* on the right road to scientific farming. *The Iron Heel*, of course, remains the closest London came to writing a doctoral dissertation, being filled with superfluous footnotes, many pedagogical, some spilling over several pages. Teachers also make a respectable showing in the short stories: John Messner in "A Day's Lodging" teaches English; Avery Van Brunt in "In the Forests of the North" is a geology professor; and Freddie Drummond in "South of the Slot" another Berkeley professor. This obsession became ridiculous in *On the Makaloa Mat*, London letting characters earn degrees from Harvard, Vassar, and Oxford, while in *The House of Pride,* Chun Ah Chun's kin attend Harvard, Oxford, Yale, Mills Seminar in California, Vassar, Wellesley, and Bryn Mawr. And Frona Welse in his first novel, *A Daughter of the Snows,* holds a Vassar B.A.; her milk-toast man Vance Corliss is Yale-educated. Ruth Morse in *Martin Eden* also attends Berkeley.

Yet, on the other hand, London cut education in work, tottering on the academic fence, slapping what he needed most—respectable sobriety. In "Phenomena of Literary Evolution" (*The Bookman,* October 1900) he wrote: "The student refuses to sit under a professor who lectures after the fashion of the kindergarten. It drives him mad to have all things and the most obvious things explained at length. He would as soon sit down and read Defoe in words of one syllable or do sums in arithmetic on his fingers."[41] Then he slurred students and librarians in "Their Alcove" (*The Woman's Home Companion,* September 1900). "He entered the library. At this hour, save for the noiseless attendants and certain weird creatures that infest such places, it was deserted. He passed by the shelves, whose transient occupants came and went unceasingly. In the upper galleries they rarely left their peaceful abode, and were consulted at infrequent periods by musty antiquarians and eager, hungry-looking collectors of worthless facts and figures. In these alcoves pale-faced students were wont to study, and it must be confessed, sometimes to doze over the weary text."[42]

The bitter Berkeley experience pained for years. London, meanwhile, added preachers, politicians, and publishers to his hate list in "What Life Means to Me" (*Cosmopolitan,* March 1906), all symbols of middle class decadence. "Where they were not alive with rottenness, quick with unclean life, they were merely the unburied dead—clean and noble, like well-preserved mummies, but not alive. In this collection I may especially mention the professors I met, the men who live up to that decadent university idea, 'the passionless pursuit of passionless intelligence.' " In the same article London unconsciously exposed other deep resentments, again peeled from proletariat roots. "I looked at the daughter of the cannery owner, in her carriage, and knew that it was my muscle, in part, that helped drag along that carriage on its rubber tires. I looked at the son of the factory owner, going to college, and knew that it was my muscle that helped, in part, to pay for the wine and good fellowship he enjoyed."[43]

College a sore memory, mainly because it failed to offer instant answers, London worked in a steam laundry at the Belmont Academy for $30 a month, after writing awhile—not bad wages during a severe depression. But London loathed labor. He ironed duck trousers and starched shirts for leisure-class boys and professors, more reasons for college grudges. (Charmian said he overstarched the women's linen in revenge.) This incident later appears in *Martin Eden,* its hero also a struggling young author from society's cellar. Writers, however, have misused London's idea of the "social pit." He didn't mean Tar Town, the gutter people, the penniless without hope. He meant working-class Americans. "I was born in the working class," he said in "What Life Means to Me," continuing, "I early discovered enthusiasm, ambition, and ideas; and to satisfy these became the problem of my childhood. My environment was crude and rough and raw. I had no outlook, but an uplook rather. My place in society was at the bottom. Here life offered nothing but sordidness and wretchedness, both of the flesh and the spirit; for here flesh and spirit were alike starved and tormented."[44]

London soon traded laundry steam for the freeze of ice when news of the Klondike gold rush reached Oakland—the road episode that eventually panned a million bucks in words, making Jack London one of history's highest-paid authors.

Chapter 4

Snowshoes, Sleds, and Sourdoughs

ALTHOUGH THE Klondike's white wilderness had lured prospectors for several decades, its historic gold rush didn't erupt until 1897, nearly a year after George Carmack, along with Skookum Jim and Tagish Charlie, made a strike at Rabbit Creek on August 17, 1896. Within weeks, sourdoughs staked the richest claims, leaving scraps for tinhorns. Newspapers warned gold-seekers that winter's freeze-up would prevent their reaching Dawson, that it took money and muscle to strike it rich, that some would die on the trail. But Klondikitis struck hard. And Jack London caught the fever.

When the *Excelsior* docked at San Francisco on July 14, 1897, talk of gold dust melted men's senses. A near stampede to reach the new El Dorado possessed thousands. "Early in July of '97 there sailed through the Golden Gate and up to the docks of San Francisco a treasure-ship bearing a motlier crowd that ever swarmed upon a buccaneer's deck and greater riches than ever lay hidden in the hold of a Spanish galleon," reported one writer. "The human freight was two score men, young and middle-aged, ragged, unkempt and weather-browned; but in their eyes shone the light of triumph, and smiles of anticipated pleasures lighted up their rugged faces. The treasure consisted of more than a million dollars' worth of virgin gold in dust, flakes and nuggets, wrapped in blankets, tied up in canvas bags and the skins of animals, and poured into bottles and cans."[1]

The gold rush offered London another chance to hit life's adventure path, another chance to run free, to become Oakland's symbol of Horatio Alger's pipedream. He quit the laundry, although the bedridden John London neared death, and asked local newspapers for credentials as a correspondent. Most laughed. William Randolph Hearst—later to pay London thousands—had already contracted five seasoned reporters, including Joaquin Miller, "the Poet of the Sierras," so London turned to his half-sister Eliza and his brother-in-law J. H. Shepard.

Past sixty with a bad heart, Shepard became London's partner. He and Eliza collected $1,500 through savings and a home mortgage, ignoring newspaper warnings, expecting to strike paydirt. Charmian said London bought fur-lined caps and coats, boots, shirts—the works—money running like water.[2]

Mable Applegarth, meanwhile, wrote London a loving letter, begging him to forget such schemes, but thoughts of golddust blind man's senses.[3] On a buying jamboree, he planned to return home rich, like thousands of other Americans headed for economic disaster.

Sometime during the voyage, London and Shepard joined with three others—J. M. Sloper, Jim Goodman, and F. C. Thompson, possibly because Shepard had suffered a mild heart attack. Franklin Walker writes:

> Merritt Sloper was forty years old and weighed about a hundred pounds. He had come "direct from adventure in South America" and was not only cheerful and brave but very resourceful, with a knowledge of carpentry and sailing which would come in handy when it came to making a boat and shooting the rapids. Jim Goodman, "Big Jim," knew something about hunting and mining and would obviously be able to outpack most men on the trail. Fred Thompson, a slender, red-whiskered young man, may have had no experience in roughing it, but he was temperamentally fitted to be an organizer and recorder. It was Thompson who kept the diary and it is that diary which is the principal source of information on the itinerary which London followed in going into the Klondike.[4]

London's party arrived at Dyea on August 7, 1897, discovering it lacked both facilities and a landing dock, forcing all the cheechakos (tenderfeet) to forage for themselves. London re-counted this in *A Daughter of the Snows* (1902), his first Alaskan novel:

Everybody was in everybody else's way; nor was there one who failed to proclaim it at the top of his lungs. A thousand gold-seekers were clamoring for the immediate landing of their outfits. Each hatchway gaped wide-open, and from the lower depths the shrieking donkey-engines were hurrying the misassorted outfits skyward. On either side of the steamer, rows of scows received the flying cargo, and on each of these scows a swearing mob of men charged the descending slings and heaved bales and boxes about in frantic search. Men waved shipping receipts and shouted over the steamer-rails to them. Sometimes two and three iden-tified the same article, and war arose. The "two-circle" and the "circle-and-dot" brands caused endless jangling, while every whipsaw discovered a dozen claimants.[5]

Shepard overstepped himself. Within a few days he returned home, like many other misled romantics, leaving London with his money—a big mistake.

Starting his long trek to Dawson, London climbed the eight-mile canyon, then Chilcoot Pass, another three-quarters of a mile beyond. Pack animals seemed useless because of the steep incline, so many hired Indians from the nearby Siwash village to carry goods. London's party bought a boat for ten dollars and went by river, a journey taking four days and several trips. Once reaching the Chilcoot, the portage problem again faced them, although London claimed he out-packed the Indians, lug-ging a hundred and fifty pounds for hours each day. As Franklin Walker says in *Jack London & the Klondike*, "This performance fitted in well with his theory of Anglo-Saxon supremacy."[6]

Ten days passed. London finally reached Sheep Camp, where he met an old-timer called Tarwater, whom he took on in ex-change for work, something Canadian authorities prohibited, mainly because of acute food shortages in the Klondike. "I have paid a dollar's worth of dust for a drink of root beer served in a little cracked teacup, and 'four bits' for a potato, which I had to eat raw," recalled one gold-seeker. "One evening I saw a man pay sixteen hundred dollars for his entertainment at one of the dance halls; and although it all went for champagne and poor whiskey, the man was sober when he paid the bill. Late newspapers have sold as high as three dollars each, and a good dog team for no less than four thousand dollars."[7]

Abandoned horses, many starving, others dead or broken-boned, became one of the land's most savage sights. Oats and hay prices soared. Some horseshoes sold for ten dollars, nails a quarter each. In "Which Make Men Remember" (*God of his Fathers and Other Stories* [1901]) London wrote:

> The horses died like mosquitoes in the first frost, and from Ska-guay to Bennett they rotted in heaps. They died at the Rocks, they were poisoned at the Summit, and they starved at the Lakes; they fell off the trail, what there was of it, or they went through it; in the river they drowned under their loads, or were smashed to pieces against the boulders; they snapped their legs in the crevices and broke their backs falling backwards with their packs; in the sloughs they sank from sight or smothered in the slime, and they were disembowelled in the bogs where the cor-duroy logs turned end up in the mud; men shot them, worked them to death, and when they were gone, went back to the beach and brought more. Some did not bother to shoot them—stripping the saddles off and the shoes and leaving them where they fell. Their hearts turned to stone—those which did not break—and they became beasts, the men on Dead Horse Trail.[8]

London's party reached Lake Linderman on September 8, 1897, then quickly built a boat, fearing the October freeze-up would arrive before they reached Dawson. Some men bought boats like Rasmunsen in "The One Thousand Dozen." Others bought passage. Half-breed Sitka Charley let a woman share his canoe in "The Sun-Dog Trail" (*Harper's Monthly Maga-zine,* December 1905). Everyone, however, shared the same growing fear—freezing to death. London wrote in "The One Thousand Dozen" that "men worked frantically, early and late, at the height of their endurance, caulking, nailing, and pitching in a frenzy of haste for which adequate explanation was not far to seek. Each day the snow-line crept farther down the bleak, rock-shouldered peaks, and gale followed gale, with sleet and slush and snow, and in the eddies and quiet places young ice formed and thickened through the fleeting hours. And each morn, toil-stiffened men turned wan faces across the lake to see if the freeze-up had come. For the freeze-up heralded the death of their hope—the hope that they would be floating down the swift river ere navigation closed on the chain of lakes."⁹

London's party joined with another, all making their boats together, naming them the *Yukon Belle* and *The Belle of the Yukon*. After sailing across Lake Linderman, they portaged to Lake Bennett, stopping for news, learning that food shortages existed in both Dawson and the Klondike diggings. Fighting against time, the two boats sailed down Lake Bennett. London saw two prospectors swept overboard and drowned.

Then came Lake Marsh and the Sixtymile River, which deposited these modern argonauts at the dreadful Box Canyon (or Miles Canyon) and White Horse Rapids, forcing them to decide whether to run the canyon and rapids or portage around them. They decided to run the rapids. London later detailed this experience in "Through the Rapids on the Way to Klondike."

> Lashing the steering oar so that it could not possibly escape, I allotted my comrades their place; for I was captain. Merritt Sloper, direct from adventures in South America and who knew a little of boating, took his position in the bow with a paddle. Thompson and Goodman, landlubbers who had never rowed before this trip, were stationed side by side at the oars. That the run may better be appreciated, it is well to explain that our twenty-seven-foot boat was carrying over five thousand pounds in addition to human freight, and hence did not possess the buoyancy so requisite for such an undertaking.
>
> "Be sure to keep on the ridge," cried the men on the bank as we cast off.
>
> The water, though swift, had a slick, oily appearance until we dashed into the very jaws of the Box, where it instantly took on the aspect of chaos broken loose. Afraid that the rowers might catch a crab or make some other disastrous fumble, I called the oars in.
>
> Then we met it on the fly. I caught a glimpse of the spectators fringing the brink of the cliffs above, and another glimpse of the rock walls dashing by like twin lighting express trains; then my whole energy was concentrated in keeping to the Ridge. This

was serrated with stiff waves, which the boat, dead with weight, could not mount, being forced to jab her nose through at every lunge. . . .

After running "the mile of canyon in two minutes by the watch," London and Sloper then "ran a friend's boat through." Their next major obstacle was White Horse Rapids with its "Mane of the Horse," which could kill boaters.

> When we struck the "Mane," the *Yukon Belle* forgot her heavy load, taking a series of leaps almost clear of the water, alternating with as many burials in the troughs. To this day I cannot see how it happened, but I lost control. A cross current caught our stern and we began to swing broadside. Then we jumped into the whirlpool, though I did not guess it at the time. Sloper snapped a second paddle and received another ducking. . . .
> The bank was alarmingly close, but the boat still had the bit in her teeth. It was all happening so quickly, that I for the first time realized I was trying to buck the whirlpool. Like a flash I was bearing against the opposite side of the sweep. The boat answered, at the same time following the bent of the whirlpool, and headed upstream. But the shave was so close that Sloper leaped to the top of a rock. Then, on seeing we had missed by a couple of inches, he pluckily tumbled aboard, all in a heap, like a man boarding a comet.
> Though tearing like mad through a whirlpool, we breathed freer. Completing the circle, we were thrown into the "Mane," which we shot a second time and safely landed in a friendly eddy below.[10]

Within a week the *Yukon Belle* conquered Lake LeBarge, made famous by Robert Service's poem "The Cremation of Sam McGee," and London's crew waited out fierce winds. When the *Belle of the Yukon* caught up, they tried rowing down the lake, a snow storm forcing them into a cove, where they listened to winter rage. Then they rowed to Thirtymile River below LeBarge, faced with rocks that churned the waters. At Little Salmon (a hundred miles below LeBarge) frightful looking Indians wearing rings in their ears and noses offered to sell them fish, meat, and moccasins. Although they neared the Stewart River, eighty miles above Dawson, the Big Salmon and Little Salmon kept pushing mush-ice into the Yukon River, a bad sign. When they briefly stopped at Fort Selkirk, the Pelly River, which joins with the Yukon, also seemed icy. That meant freeze up.

The *Yukon Belle* and *Belle of the Yukon* split on October 8, 1897, old Tarwater moving on to Dawson, while the rest of London's party stopped at the Stewart. Here Jack London spent the winter of 1897–98.

Except for a short-lived prospecting venture and several jaunts to Dawson, one around six weeks, London remained on Split-Up Island, where he played cards, made biscuits and probably "grew high-stomached with overeating and enforced idleness,"[11] like the characters in "The Men of Forty Mile." Did his future plans include writing about the Klondike? Charmian attributed London's use of the Yukon as raw literary material to one thing: empty pockets when wildcat whims left him broke.[12] London also admitted: "After three months' trial I gave up writing, having decided that I was a failure, and left for the Klondike to prospect for gold. At the end of the year, owing to an outbreak of scurvy, I was compelled to come out, and on a homeward journey of one thousand miles in an open boat, made the only notes of the trip."[13]

Regarding the prospecting venture. Franklin Walker says that London, along with Jim Goodman, a former placer miner, and two other fellows called Charles and Elma, went to Henderson Creek for three days, where they "staked eight claims."[14] London waited eighteen days to file the claim, also failing to work it, and after leaving the Klondike, it reverted back to the Crown. A profitable mining operation involved good weather, the building of a dam and flume, and back-breaking work.

Like most greenhorns London disliked Dawson, later calling it "dreary, desolate Dawson, built in a swamp, flooded in the second story, populated by dogs, mosquitoes, and gold-seekers."[15] He used ramshackle locales in Dawson like the Moosehorn bar, the Opera House and Eldorado gambling house as background for Northland stories, besides dance-hall girls and romantic prostitutes. Freda Moloff, a Greek dancing girl, who called herself "The Turkish Whirlwind Danseuse," became one of London's most celebrated characters. He wrote "The Scorn of Women" about her, adapting it into a play. She was "a woman, flexible of form, slender, yet rhythmic of strength in every movement. . . . Her furs were the most magnificent in all the country from Chilcoot to St. Michael's, and her name was common on the lips of men. . . . It was not for nothing, the saying which has arisen in the country, that Freda played with men as a child with bubbles."[16] Freda is also mentioned in *Burning Daylight* and "The Wife of a King," included in *The Son of the Wolf*.

Edward E. P. Morgan, among the few who remembered London in the Klondike, encountered him in a Dawson bar during fall of 1897, recalling that he "was surely prospecting, but it was at bars that he sought his material. I believe that he had staked a claim, and it is probably that his hatred of capitalism did not extend to acquiring wealth for himself, but I never saw him working one, never met him on the trail, and do not remember ever having seen him except in some Dawson bar."[17]

London's life on Split-Up Island—also known as Upper Island—can be sketched through his stories and articles, although these color actual incidents, which he frankly admitted. In "The Scorn of Women," a typical cabin is described:

> It was very cold without, but it was not over-warm within. The only article which might be designated furniture was the stove, and for this the men were frank in displaying their preference. Upon half of the floor pine boughs had been cast; above this were spread the sleeping-furs, beneath lay the winter's snowfall. The remainder of the floor was moccasin-packed snow, littered with pots and pans and the general *impedimenta* of an Arctic camp. The stove was red and roaring hot, but only a bare three feet away lay a block of ice, as sharp-edged and dry as when first quarried from the creek bottom. The pressure of the outside cold forced the inner heat upward. Just above the stove, where the pipe penetrated the roof, was a tiny circle of dry canvas; next, with the pipe always as centre, a circle of steaming canvas; next a damp and moisture-exuding ring; and finally, the rest of the tent, sidewalls and top, coated with a half-inch of dry, white, crystal-encrusted frost.[18]

Although London seldom wrote humor, a form he considered difficult to master, "Housekeeping in the Klondike" offers amusing sidelights about life in an isolated Klondike cabin.

"Housekeeping in the Klondike—that's bad! And by *men*—worse." This set the piece's tone. Then he tells how to make the three B's—bread, beans, and bacon, concluding that the Klondiker's worst woe was lack of sugar, not the bitter cold, silence, or darkness. The cooking account is both entertaining and informative.

> It is no sinecure, being cook in the Klondike. Often he must do his work in a cabin measuring ten by twelve on the inside, and occupied by three other men besides himself. When it is considered that these men eat, sleep, lounge, smoke, play cards, and entertain visitors there, and also in that small space house the bulk of their possessions, the size of the cook's orbit may be readily computed. In the morning he sits up in bed, reaches out and strikes the fire, then proceeds to dress. After that the centre of his orbit is the front of the stove, the diameter the length of his arms. Even then his comrades are continually encroaching upon his domain, and he is at constant warfare to prevent territorial grabs.[19]

Too many sourdough biscuits and too few vegetables, however, caused many Klondikers, including London, to get scurvy. "In a Far Country," the "blood [of characters] became impoverished, and a loathsome, purplish rash crept over their bodies. Yet they refused to heed the warning. Next, their muscles and joints began to swell, the flesh turning black, while their mouths, gums and lips took on the colour of rich cream."[20] London's teeth fell out, forcing him to later wear false teeth, several pairs of which he broke.

Life with Sloper, Thompson, and Goodman worked for awhile. They sat around the stove, played cribbage and whist, chewed countless words, and cursed the white wilderness. Few gold-seekers had books. Men backpacked food and critical supplies, not heavy, cumbersome books, although Jeremiah Lynch recalled that one fellow brought Edward Gibbon's six volumes of *The Decline and Fall of the Roman Empire.* Written words didn't fill empty stomachs or warm freezing frames. Food and blankets did. Emil Jensen, one of London's acquaintances, said London had copies of Charles Darwin's *Origin of the Species,* John Milton's *Paradise Lost,* and a borrowed copy of Rudyard Kipling's *The Seven Seas.* Perhaps London borrowed from

Dawson's library, located in a bank, or exchanged books with others.

Sometime during that wicked winter of 1897–1898, London's cabin grew too small for four men. They bickered. London packed his gear, joining Doc B. F. Harvey, Judge E. H. Sullivan, and W. B. Hargrave in a nearby cabin. With such intellectuals as comrades, the walls must have trembled with talk about everything from atheism to the socialist state.

London later included some of these Klondikers in his stories: Emil Jensen became the Malemute Kid, and Sloper slipped into both "In a Far Country" and "Like Argus of the Ancient Times." Father Robeau, Louis Savoy, and John Thornton, Buck's master in *The Call of the Wild,* were also based on gold rushers. It's remarkable these people didn't sue London. "To a British writer, dogged by fears of libel, this is fantastic," says Arthur Calder-Marshall. "To give a real person's name in the description of a real incident is perilous enough. To introduce a real person's name into the description of an incident with which he had no connection is asking for trouble."[21]

Tired of beans and bread, flush lamps and Yukon ice, London welcomed the spring thaw, forgetting about Eliza's $1,500 investment. He just wanted out. This really irked Klondiker Wilson Mizner. Mizner's biographer, Alva Johnston, says

> Fifteen years after the death of Jack London, Mizner still got indignant at hearing him praised. London skipped through the Yukon in a season or two and had eighty-eight short stories and novels to show for it; Mizner was there for six years and had nothing but smoking-room anecdotes to show for it. Mizner was a stern debunker of the Arctic literary tradition. Jack London had taught the world that the Yukon had some magic that turned ribbon clerks and ladies' tailors into ferocious primordial monsters. "The truth is," said Mizner, "that most of the fellows up there were the worst sissies on earth. I was in court when two hundred of them were robbed of their claims by a crooked judge and a set of thieving politicians. Did they string up the judge, as the forty-niners would have done? Did they tear the politicians limb from limb? No. They just sat there crying into their beards.

Then they slunk back to their cabins and had to be treated with smelling salts."[22]

London drew his best account of the long-awaited Klondike breakup in *A Daughter of the Snows*, filled with fresh memories of this awesome sight:

> The ice was in motion. Slowly, very slowly, it proceeded down stream. There was no commotion, no ear-splitting thunder, no splendid display of force; simply a silent flood of white, an orderly procession of tight-packed ice—packed so closely that not a drop of water was in evidence. . . . The islands drove their wedged heads into the frozen flood and tossed the cakes high into the air. But cake pressed upon cake and shelved out of the water, out and up, sliding and grinding and climbing, and still more cakes from behind, till hillocks and mountains of ice upreared and crashed among the trees. . . . The whole river seemed to pick itself up and start down the stream. With the increasing motion the ice-wall broke in a hundred places, and from up and down the shore came the rending and crashing of uprooted trees.[23]

London and Doc Harvey made a raft of logs from their Klondike cabin and floated downstream to Dawson, receiving six hundred dollars for the logs. While in Dawson, London stayed with Emil Jensen, who lived in a tent because of high-priced rooms, usually $100 or more a month. It's also possible that London received medication for his scurvy at St. Mary's Hospital, run by Father William Judge, otherwise known as The Saint of Dawson. He is mentioned in both *Burning Daylight* and *Smoke Bellew*.

Along with John Thorson and Charley Taylor, a Kentuckian with Annapolis training, London left the Yukon in late June 1898, heading for St. Michaels at the mouth of the Bering Straits. Two detailed accounts of this trip exist: London's notes and an article called "From Dawson to the Sea," published in the *Buffalo Express* on June 4, 1899. It carried the subtitle: "Two Thousand Miles on the Mighty Highway of the North—The Voyage of an Express Correspondent Down the Yukon River—Scenes and Incidents in the Alaskan Wilderness."[24] (The "express correspondent" tag was an eye grabber.)

London's three-man team shoved off at 4:00 P.M., a peculiar time to launch a two-thousand-mile voyage in an unnamed "home-made, weak-kneed and leaky"[25] skiff, a craft without bunks, forcing them to devise a makeshift living-room-kitchen-bedroom. "All labour was to be performed by gravitation, and all profit reaped by ourselves. And what a profit it was to us who had been accustomed to pack great loads on our backs or drag all day at the sleds for a paltry twenty-five or thirty miles. We now hunted, played cards, smoked, ate and slept, sure of our six miles an hour, of our 144 a day."

Three hundred miles below Dawson, London camped at Circle City, a dreadful place rooted on the fringe of the Yukon Flats. "The 'Flats' are a vast area of low country extending for hundreds of miles in every direction, into which the Yukon plunges and is practically lost. The river, hitherto flowing between mountains, rugged and sternly outlined, with few islands on its breast, now begins its heart-breaking dividing and subdividing. One finds himself in a gigantic puzzle, consisting of thousands of miles of territory, and cut up into countless myriads of islands and channels. Men have been known to lose their way and wander for weeks in this perplexing maze."

One morning they sighted a moose that had wandered into the river, trying to flee hordes of mosquitoes. London grabbed an axe. Taylor seized a rusty shotgun filled with birdshot that either misfired or shot both barrels at once. One blast failed to reach the moose, its noise driving the beast into the forest. A chase followed. While the Kentuckian stumbled in pursuit, London and Thorson waged war against mosquitoes. Taylor lost the moose, returning to the craft, slapping bites that took a day to subside. Inhabitants at nearby Anvik, however, welcomed the party, giving them tomatoes and potatoes, which relieved London's scurvy.

Although London praised the whites, local Indians intrigued him. At the old Hudson's Bay Company post at Fort Yukon, where food was plentiful, he wrote: "All was gaiety, noise and laughter. The bucks were skylarking or flirting with the maidens; the older squaws were gossiping in bunches, while the young ones shrank and giggled in the corners. The children played or squabbled, and the babies rolled in the muck with the tawny wolf-dogs. Fantastic forms, dimly outlined, flitted to and fro, surged together, eddied, parted, in the smoke-laden atmosphere. Only by nosing and poking about could one see anything; for the reeking smoke rose from untold smudges, bringing grief to the mosquito, tears to the soft eyes of the white men and giving to the whole affair a mysterious air of unreality."

The half-breeds, whom London called one of nature's perversions, bothered him. Yet he saw them everywhere among the papooses at settlements like the fishing village of Nuklukyeto:

We landed our heavy craft amid the litter of flimsy bark canoes which lined the banks and found ourselves in the great fishing camp. Picking our steps among the tents and wading through the sprawling babies and fighting dogs, we made our way to a large log structure where a dance was in progress. After much pushing and shoving, we forced an entrance through the swarming children. The long, low room was literally packed with dancers. There was no light, no ventilation, save through the crowded doorway, and, in the semi-darkness, strapping bucks and wild-eyed squaws sweated, howled and revelled in a dance which defies description. With the peculiar elation of the traveller who scales the virgin peak, we prepared to enjoy the novelty of the situation; but, imagine our disappointment on discovering that even here, 1,000 miles beyond the uttermost bounds of civilization, the adventurous white man already had penetrated. In the crowded room, dizzy with heat and the smell of bodies, we at last discerned the fair bronzed skin, the blue eyes, the blond mustache of the ubiquitous Anglo-Saxon. A glance demonstrated how thoroughly at home he was. [London mentioned Anglo-Saxon four times in this article.]

One hundred miles below Nuklukyeto, our midnight watch was beguiled by a wild chant, which rose and fell uncannily as it floated across the water. An hour later we rounded a bend and landed at a fishing village, so engrossed in its religious rites that our arrival was unnoted. Climbing the bank, we came full upon the weird scene. It brought us back to the orgies of the cavemen and more closely in touch with our common ancestor, probably arboreal, which Mr. Darwin has so fittingly described. Several score of bucks were giving tongue to unwritten music, evidently born when the world was very young, and still apulse with the spirit of primeval man. [This early in his career, London talked about the spirit of primordialism, Anglo-Saxon superiority, and the genetic perversion of mongrelism.] Urged on by the chief medicine men, women had abandoned themselves to the religious ecstasy, their raven hair unbound and falling to their hips, while their bodies were swaying and undulating to the swing of the song.[26]

Here London saw a half-caste woman nursing a child, "slender-formed, with her Caucasian features and delicate oval face, she seemed as a pearl cast among swine," and at the mouth of the Koyokuk, he wandered into another camp, where he saw "a most beautiful child—flaxen-haired, blue-eyed and rosy-complexioned, a typical Saxon lass."[27]

The hovel-loving Malemutes London liked even less, using them as raw material for "Nam-Bok the Unveracious," a tale about a tribesman who travels West where he sees marvels such as schooners, steamboats, and iron monsters that walk across the land. When the tribesman returns home to pots of "putrid fish" and "greasy ill-smelling furs,"[28] his people laugh, saying such stories refute their immutable laws of nature.

London's Indian characters remain paradoxes—his finest creations—although he considered them racially inferior to Anglo-Saxons. Fred Lewis Pattee called the half-breed Indian women "his only additions to the gallery of original characters in American fiction. Their doglike fidelity and honesty, their loyalty and self-sacrifice, their primitive resourcefulness in danger and privation, excite unconsciously our admiration and our pity."[29] These fascinating figures include: Ruth, the wife of Mason in "The White Silence," Madeline in "An Odyssey of the North," and Li Wan in "Li Wan the Fair."

The *Buffalo Express* article concluded: "Our last taste of Bering Sea was a fitting close to the trip. Midnight found us wallowing in the sea, a rocky coast to leeward and a dirty sky to windward, with splutters of rain and wind squalls which soon developed into a gale. Removing the sprit and bagging the after leech, we shortened to storm canvas and ran before it, reaching the harbor of St. Michael just twenty-one days from the time we cast off the lines at Dawson." Before docking at St. Michael's, London met Father Robeau, a Jesuit priest who became a character in *The Son of the Wolf* collection, a "jolly fellow," less stern and cold than the Anglo-Saxon, a scholar who smoked a pipe and told tales, "an illustration of the many strange types to be found in the Northland."[30]

The rest of London's return trip echoed earlier road days. He travelled steerage on a ship bound for Seattle, then rode the rails to San Francisco, arriving home in August—busted.

Chapter 5

The Salt of the Earth

JACK LONDON RETURNED to a changed American landscape. As Hawthorne said: "Time flies over us, but leaves its shadow behind." The U.S.S. *Maine* had exploded in Cuba, killing over two hundred crewmen, causing the Spanish American War. Hawaii was annexed to the United States. The battleship *Oregon*'s trip from San Francisco to Key West spurred interest in a Panama Canal. Rough Rider Theodore Roosevelt became a legend at the Battle of San Juan Hill. The war, in general, offered a new sense of power and prosperity after hardship years stemming from the panic of 1893.

After wasting Eliza's $1,500 in the Yukon (coal miners earned $560 a year during this period) London ended where he started— broke and without great expectations, still looking for short cuts to success. John London had died during his absence, leaving Flora with a Civil War pension that paid bills, and this was helped by music lessons, according to Joan London. Flora had also adopted Johnnie Miller, an infant London's sister Ida brought home, its parentage wrapped in mystery. London, meanwhile, sought work on the open market. He advertised in newspapers, mowed lawns, trimmed hedges, washed windows, beat carpets, offered to pose for art students, according to his reminiscences in *John Barleycorn*. He took the civil service examinations for mail carrier. Then he hit the road again, this time for a gold rush in the Sierras, leaving more unanswered questions. Who backed this new venture to nowhere? What happened in the territory? Didn't he feel committed to family after John's death? London did write an article in 1902 for *Collier's* called "The Stampede to Thunder Mountain," comparing this rush in the Sierras to Klondike fever.

> Not since Klondike has there been such a stampede as that now underway to Thunder Mountain. Despite the warning that it is no poor man's country, at least one hundred 'sooners' are going in daily on snow shoes, packing their outfits on their backs or dragging them on toboggan-sleds. Further, all the towns adjacent to the gold fields—such as Boise, Ketchum, Council, Red Rock, Lewiston, Weiser and Salmon—are jammed with an army of cooler-headed gold-seekers, waiting for the opening of the trails. And each train swells these towns to overflowing, with more men hastening eagerly from the north, south, east and west. . . . There are two reasons for the magnitude of this stampede. Thunder Mountain is the only excitement of the year, and money is easy, which is to say that the chronic stampeders and adventurers have nowhere else to go and work off their unrest, and that the good times of the last several years have put the money in their pockets wherewith they may go. That there are all the possibilities for a new Eldorado goes without saying. Idaho has already added $250,000,000 to the world's gold supply, while thousands of square miles of mineral territory remain practically unexplored. As Thunder Mountain is to-day likened to Cripple Creek, who knows but in some future day new bonanzas may be likened to Thunder Mountain? Anyway, 75,000 men are hitting the high places to find out.[1]

One day London read that authors could earn ten dollars for writing a thousand words, an easy way to chase cash, so it seemed. He queried *The Youth's Companion*, then America's leading youth magazine excluding *St. Nicholas*, about serials, whereupon he wrote a twenty-one-thousand-word tale in seven days; another went to a contest sponsored by the *San Francisco Examiner*; the Fifth Ward Republic Club, which offered prizes for essays, poems, and songs, received others. Then London rushed a horror story called "A Thousand Deaths" to the *Black Cat* magazine. Both the *San Francisco Examiner* and *Youth's Companion* rejected his pieces, and although he won several cash prizes from the Republican Club, they failed to pay.

"All my manuscripts came back. They continued to come back. The process seemed like the working of a soulless machine. I dropped the manuscript into the mail box. After the lapse of a certain approximate length of time, the manuscript was brought back to me by the postman. Accompanying it was a stereotyped rejection slip. A part of the machine, some cunning arrangement of cogs and cranks at the other end, (it could not have been a living, breathing man with blood in his veins), had transferred the manuscript to another envelope, taken the stamps from the inside and pasted them outside, and added the rejection slip."[2] London also lamented: "I lived in California, far from the great publishing centers. I did not know what an editor looked like. I did not know a soul who had ever published anything; nor yet again, a soul, with the exception of my own, who had ever tried to write anything, much less tried to publish it. . . . I had no one to give me tips, no one's experience to profit by."[3]

Regarding California, "far from the great publishing centers," San Francisco, for example, housed fifty printers by 1850. A few years later they boasted more newspapers than London and published more books than all other trans-Mississippi towns combined. "Everyone who reached the Golden West, from the days of the explorers, trappers, and miners on down to the era of the fruit canners, freeway builders, showmen, and hippies, wanted to talk about it and write about it," says W. Storrs Lee in *California: A Literary Chronicle*. "At one time or another the state, too, drew most of the literary commentators of the East for a reconnaissance, and they also wrote about it, until California possessed a formidable body of literature."[4] Lee's eighty selections from California authors include work by Gertrude Atherton, Bret Harte, Oscar Lewis, Ambrose Bierce, John Muir, Mary Austin, Joaquin Miller, Frank Norris, Gelett Burgess, Will Irwin, George Sterling and Upton Sinclair—hardly a literary crowd of nobodies. (Later on California added Robinson Jeffers, William Saroyan, Ray Bradbury, and John Steinbeck to this imposing list.)

What about London's lament that he lacked literary friends willing to share tips and experiences? Georgia Loring Bamford recalled that Charley Howell, the Oakland editor of the *San*

Francisco Call, was one of London's closest friends, besides
Sol Sheridan, editor of the *Oakland Times,* George Hatton,
editor of the *Tribune,* and the *Enquirer*'s A. A. Denison, a
member of the Ruskin Club, all forgotten names. Fred Jacobs
and Ted Applegarth, both aspiring writers, encouraged London,
exchanging ideas and techniques, besides Mabel Applegarth,
who taught him the rudiments of composition. Bessie Maddern
and Anna Strunsky, whom London nearly married, also helped.
So did Frederick Irons Bamford, Oakland librarian and former
English professor at Hesperian College, especially along political lines, as did left-wing iconoclast Frank Strawn-Hamilton.
London exchanged letters with Cloudesley Johns and Elwyn
Hoffman, two more writers. Georgia Loring Bamford also mentioned Carroll Carrington, saying that "Jack London never had
a better friend than Carroll, not only in literary assistance but
in a social and also pecuniary way." She concluded that "thinking of the things Jack London said and wrote about himself,
it has been forced on my mind that he has emphasized the bad
influences and minimized or forgotten the good."[5]

By January 1899, following several months of writing, "To
the Man on Trail" appeared in *The Overland Monthly,* setting
the scene for London's Horatio Alger rise to fame and fortune.
"London has been more fortunate than some of his contem-
poraries," commented *Outing* in 1904. "While the immature
imaginings of youthful novelists, as a rule, receive but short-
lived appreciation, London's stories have taken a place in literature."[6] His family agreed. Joan wrote that "the goal he had
set himself had been reached too easily."[7] Charmian said likewise.[8] His press agent, Ninetta Eames, admitted: "Few writers,
in fact, have come into such unprefaced notice as Jack London."[9] Even London remarked that only one person in a million
achieved such easy success.

The Overland Monthly, a Western literary magazine once
edited by Bret Harte, gave London his first break, accepting
"To the Man on Trail," a Yukon short story. This sketch introduced the half-breed Malemute Kid, a central figure in *The
Son of the Wolf* collection. "A health to the man on trail this
night; may his grub hold out; may his dogs keep their legs; may
his matches never miss fire,"[10] he says, expressing London's
early talent for Northland tales.

Two stories about London's association with *The Overland Monthly* survive. According to Irving Stone, the magazine failed to pay London for "To the Man on Trail" and "The White Silence." London stormed its editorial offices, threatening Roscoe Eames and Edward Payne, who settled in small change. (Martin Eden thrashes two editors, throwing one downstairs, for the same reason in *Martin Eden*.) Both Eames and Payne played later roles in London's life. Charmian Kittredge was Eames's niece, and Ninetta, the dominant wife of Eames, later managed the Glen Ellen estate for awhile.

The editor of *The Overland Monthly*, James Howard Bridge, told a different version, failing to mention Payne, one of the magazine's editors, in his autobiography.

One day toward the end of '98, my assistant Green came into my office and said there was a man outside who had a story to sell, and wanted an immediate decision as to its acceptability. I went to the outer office and greeted him. He said his name was Jack London. "You mean 'John,' " I said. "No, just Jack," was the reply. He looked like a tramp, and nothing like a man who could have written an acceptable story for Bret Harte's old magazine. But when he said he had just come down from the Klondike, I said "Give me your story and come back tomorrow." I took the manuscript home with me that night and had the surprise of my life. The story was called "To the Man on the Trail; A Klondike Christmas." It was the first of the Malemute Kid stories, and one of the finest things Jack London ever did. I understood that he had never published before, and that he had come into the office because he needed money—was in fact "dead-broke." Of course there was no hesitation when I saw him next morning.

"We will accept your story, and pay our maximum price— $25—for it. If you will write us a series of six stories, I will pay for them as you bring them in, have Maynard Dixon illustrate them, and feature them in other ways, so that you will be able to get into eastern magazines, and get what your work is worth. For I am free to say that your work is worth more than we can pay for it."

London gratefully accepted my offer, and within the next two or three weeks finished the series and brought them in. "The White Silence," was the next, and was copied by the *New York Evening Post*. Thereafter Jack London never had need to hawk his stuff in any editorial office. He told me that he needed money very badly for "a mother and child." I did not ask what mother or what child, as it did not seem to be any of my business, and he did not tell me. The series included "The Son of the Wolf," "The Wisdom of the Trail," "In a Far Country," and "The Men of Forty Mile."[11]

Another acceptance followed "To the Man on Trail." *The Black Cat* took "A Thousand Deaths," paying forty dollars on acceptance, providing that London cut the work in half. "Grant permission? I told them they could cut it down two-halves if they'd only send the money along, which they did, by return mail."[12]

In January 1899, the same month *The Overland Monthly* published "To the Man on Trail," London passed the post office examinations, which promised forty dollars a month to start, with an early raise to sixty-five dollars. This meant he could marry Mabel. Yet London refused the lifetime post, basing his decision on the acceptance of two short stories, although "he needed money very badly." He also refused other jobs. Georgia Loring Bamford said that the *San Francisco Examiner* extended work in the late 1890s, but "he fell down on the job."[13] In December 1900 *Cosmopolitan* offered an editorial post at a yearly wage, but London told Cloudesley Johns he wanted freedom. Charmian said *McClure's* also proffered a staff post.

London's biggest break? The prestigious *Atlantic Monthly* bought "An Odyssey of the North," sending him a check for $120, which nearly equalled his entire writing income for the previous year. In that story, Alex Gunderson, "a king of Eldorado" who stood seven feet tall, became London's first Anglo-Saxon hero. "His chest, neck, and limbs were those of a giant. To bear his three hundred pounds of bone and muscle, his snowshoes were greater by a generous yard than those of other men. Rough-hewn, with rugged brow and massive jaw and unflinching eyes of palest blue, his face told the tale of one who knew but the law of might."[14]

"The Odyssey of the North," published in January 1900, led to bigger bonanzas. Houghton Mifflin, a Boston blue-blooded publishing house affiliated with the *Atlantic Monthly,* offered to publish London's early Klondike stories after reviewing short-story proofs, calling this collection *The Son of the Wolf.* Because this was London's first book, the public overlooked its emphasis on Anglo-Saxon superiority. "In his very earliest fiction," says Richard Vanderbeets, "Jack London found expression for a brand of racism, which, it seems, went largely undetected by his readers. In reviewing *The Son of the Wolf* shortly after its publication, the *Atlantic Monthly* provided an unintended but ironically accurate insight into the message of the book; obviously taking 'race' in the larger, universal sense, the reviewer concluded: 'The book produces in the reader a deeper faith in the manly virtues of our race.' "[15] Grant C. Knight adds in *The Strenuous Age* that the title "was an appropriate label for this conviction, for the Son of the Wolf was the white man, superior to the Indian and the Eskimo in cunning, cruelty, greed and stamina, and therefore justified in robbing the native of his women and his riches."[16]

A second collection of Yukon stories about the cunning, cruel, and greedy Anglo-Saxon called *The God of His Fathers* followed in 1901, published by McClure, Phillips & Company—eleven stories *The Nation* called "vivid, concise and dramatic,"[17] and *The Athenaeum* "strongly dramatic."[18] Among them were "The God of His Fathers," "Where the Trail Forks," and "The Scorn of Women." In these first two collections, *The Son of the Wolf* and *The God of His Fathers,* London shaped two popular characters—the Malemute Kid and Sitka Charley, both illiterate, half-breed Indians.

The Malemute Kid is "a born raconteur" who was "capable of felling an ox at a blow" yet he "could not bear to beat the poor animals, but humored them as a dog-driver rarely does,—nay, almost wept with them in their misery." In "The Men of Forty Mile" he tells two Klondikers, intent on killing each other, that he'll string up the winner, forcing them to listen because he's "accustomed to an obedience which his fellow men never failed to render." The kid also shoots Mason in "The White Silence." His Northland motto: "Life's a game, and men the gamblers."[19]

Sitka Charley, another exceptional half-breed Indian, "alone knew the white man's wisdom, the honour of the trail, and the law. . . . being an Indian, he had achieved the impossible."[20]

He had "walked in honor, and ever has his word been true. . . . his criteria were primitive; but his word was fiat, and his verdict a hall-mark in every camp under the circle."[21] Charley also sees life as a game, an endless struggle that ends in death, a release from life's tortures. He voices London's early pessimism, a pessimism that gradually eroded his mind and spirit:

> Life is a strange thing. Much have I thought on it, and pondered long, yet daily the strangeness of it grows not less, but more. Why this longing for life? It is a game which no man wins. To live is to toil hard, and to suffer sore, till Old Age creeps heavily upon us and we throw down our hands on the cold ashes of dead fires. It is hard to live. In pain the babe sucks his first breath, in pain the old man gasps his last, and all his days are full of trouble and sorrow; yet he goes down to the open arms of Death, stumbling, falling, with head turned backward, fighting to the last. And Death is kind. It is only Life, and the things of Life that hurt. Yet we love Life, and we hate Death. It is very strange.[22]

London's faith in Anglo-Saxon superiority seems at odds with itself, considering his best-drawn and most convincing characters are half-breed Indians, who live simple lives of honor and respect in the wilds, while his brutal whites, the chosen race, are limned as savage elementals. "London translated Darwinism into the vernacular, presented it in a guise so romantic, boisterous, and extravagant that it proved irresistible," maintains Henry Steele Commager. "He wrote it up in dime novels and purveyed it as literature and philosophy."[23]

A foundless belief in the superiority of Anglo-Saxons, popularized by authors such as Rudyard Kipling, attracted attention at the century's turn. An essay in *McClure's* called "Five Hundred Years of the Anglo-Saxon" concluded: "At the end of five hundred years, the Anglo-Saxon, once weakest of the four races, now leads, while its nearest rival is fast crumbling to pieces. . . . And that race will swell in numbers till, in another hundred years, it will embrace a population larger than the present population of the entire world. These four—Anglo-Saxon, Latin, German, Slav—to-day dominate the earth; but the greatest of these is Anglo-Saxon."[24]

London's essential creed, a reflection of the time, he best expressed in "The Salt of the Earth" (*The Anglo-American Magazine*, August 1902). "Anglo-Saxon? Undeniably he is the most significant figure on the world-stage. . . . It is the mightiest and most prodigious empire the world has yet witnessed. . . . It is the most successful political adventure man has as yet achieved. . . . So it must be granted that the Anglo-Saxon is a race of mastery and achievement." London made it clear that "in the struggle of type with type, it is ethnics which determines, not ethics." This is how he justified the strongest of the strong enslaving mankind. "So evolution deals with force and matter. It has no concern with human right and wrong." Such abstractions, according to London, belonged to sentimentalists, not practitioners of Darwinism. Wolf Larsen expresses this view in *The Sea Wolf*. "So we must confess the truth; our civilization has not yet proved itself aught but a veneer, and a very thin veneer. Underneath we are as savage and elemental and barbarous as primitive man. More than ever to-day is the race to the swift, the battle to the strong. Nor have the meek and lowly yet come to inherit the earth. In the struggle for food and shelter, for place and power, the weak and less efficient are crowded back and trampled under, as they always have been."

He continued in "The Salt of the Earth" that the "Anglo-Saxon is brutal. . . . When Kipling sings his savage songs of sweat and toil and blood-welter, the race as savagely responds." London rationalized: "The history of civilization is a history of wandering—a wandering, sword in hand, of strong breeds, clearing away and hewing down the weak and less fit. In the misty younger world, peoples, nobody knows whence or whither, rise up in blood-red splendor, conquering and slaying, and, like phantoms, conquered and slain pass away. True, those who rise by the sword perish by the sword; but be it remembered, in that day as in this, that those who forswear the sword none the less perish by the sword. It is the history of all life."[25]

The Son of the Wolf, The God of His Fathers, and *Children of the Frost*, London's first three short-story collections, support the genetic superiority of Anglo-Saxons. In "The Son of the Wolf" Scruff MacKenzie has sprung from a woman's loins "with a kingly inheritance—an inheritance which gave to him and his dominance over the land and sea, over the animals and the people of all the zones. Single-handed against fivescore, girt by the Arctic winter, far from his own, he felt the prompting of his heritage, the desire to possess the wild danger-love, the thrill of battle, the power to conquer or to die."[26] Anglo-Saxons are "the dominant, evolved race—the salt of the earth and the masters thereof" in "The Great Interrogation"; they are "fair-faced, blue-eyed, indomitable men, incarnations of the unrest of their race" in "The God of His Fathers," and filled with "lusty freshness" in "Where the Trail Forks."[27] Avery Van Brunt in "In the Forests of the North" was "full-blooded Saxon, and his blood was pounding fiercely through his veins to the traditions of his race."[28]

Most of London's heroes share this kingly inheritance, from Klondike kings to Mexicans and South Sea islanders, perhaps extensions of an idealized self-concept, a feverish attempt to erase bastard birth and proletarian roots. Granville Hicks says that "there is only one character London could depict, and that one character is so much a product of his dreams, so nearly a personal myth, that we cannot find it convincing."[29]

"Have you ever thought that in ten generations of my ancestors 1,022 people happened to concentrate in some fashion on the small piece of protoplasm that was to eventuate in me?" asked London in an interview. "All the potentialities of these 1,022 people were favorable in my direction. I was born normal, healthy in body and mind. Many a life has been ruined by inheriting a tendency to a weak stomach, or liver, or lungs. In my case all were perfectly strong and vigorous. Then, too, you know that in a row of beans, all grown from the same seed, you will find one pod that surpasses all the others, and in that pod one bean that you may call 'the king bean.'"[30]

Richard O'Connor states in *Jack London: A Biography*: "Just where all the 'Saxon' blood was coming from, [London] didn't make clear. Jack himself was at least half Welsh while Bess was of Cornish (also Celtic) extraction."[31] Edwin Watts Chubb recalled, "I do not know his own descent; in person he was more Celtic than Teutonic—small, dark, full of movement, with eyes that could glow like topazes when something excited was toward."[32] And Henry Meade Bland thought that "in personal appearance [he wasn't] especially striking. He has light curly hair, blue eyes, square face, firm-set chin, and rather prominent cheek bones. He is of medium height, and now weighs about one hundred and sixty pounds."[33] This was in 1904.

The writing of Friedrich Nietzsche, German philosopher and author of *Thus Spake Zarathustra,* nourished London's attitudes, especially its emphasis on slave-master morality and the will-to-power ideology, although Nietzscheism related to neither genetic superiority nor Anglo-Saxon dominance. "Only where there is life is there also will; not will to life but—thus I teach— will to power," preached Nietzsche, a shy recluse who mastered Homeric Greek instead of man, venerated Wagner, and once taught classical philology at Basel. "For men are not equal; thus speaks justice. . . . The weaker should serve the stronger." The mainspring of this credo? Probably Darwin's and Spencer's theory of the survival of the fittest. London, like other Americans, mangled Nietzsche, who insisted man must conquer the inner beast in his search for power, not unleash its reckless and destructive powers. "Man is something that must be overcome."[34]

Although exerting a profound influence on modern thought, much of Nietzsche's work remains empty rhetoric. Mrs. Havelock Ellis called it so "obscure and apparently contradictory that it is very difficult to find out what his fundamental aim is."[35] *The Nation* also commented in 1913: "Nietzsche has become quasi-popular for two reasons: first, as a mere writer, as a poet of startling phrases and occasional insight, but with no systematic doctrine; and, secondly, as one of the innumerable forces of change and of rebellion against the existing order of things. It is a fact, we believe, that nowhere will you find more men who regard Nietzsche favorably or tolerantly than among those Socialistically inclined: they feel and welcome the destructive energy of the man, while caring little that his programme of construction is entirely opposed to their own."[36]

London, who became self-appointed spokesman for America's socialistic party, converted Nietzsche's complex system into a "biological Superman, with the result that a character like Wolf Larsen is close to the popular misconception of the Superman, but far indeed from embodying Nietzsche's essentially spiritual idea,"[37] writes Patrick Bridgwater in *Nietzsche in Anglosaxony*. Charles Child Walcutt relates this to London's work:

> *Remove the large sociological framework* and you have the atavistic, red-blooded brute who makes such wonderful material for stirring romance. To call such a creature a superman is a mistake. Rather he is instinctive, physical man set free to roam at large in terrific conflicts outside the restraining influences of society. He is not capable of endless conquest under all conditions. Indeed he is ill-fitted to triumph in the struggle for existence of civilized society. He has little in common with the superman described by Nietzsche. But he is physically strong; the native transition from a creature who is only physical to one who is strong physically is quite understandable, though not therefore reasonable; and in a world where strength counts he will flourish until cunning or accident destroys him.[38]

London's first exposure to Nietzsche? Humphrey Van Weyden says in the second line of *The Sea Wolf* (1904) that his friend "loafed through the winter months and read Nietzsche and Schopenhauer to rest his brain."[39] London earlier mentioned Nietzsche in "Rods and Gunnels" (*The Bookman,* August 1902), calling road bums, "the lords and masters, the aggressive men, the primordial noble men, the *blond beasts* of Nietzsche, lustfully roving and conquering through sheer superiority and strength."[40] Even more to the point, *Metropolitan Magazine* published London's short story "A Hyperborean Brew" in July 1901. The word "hyperborean" appears in the first paragraph of Nietzsche's *The Anti-Christ*. This could mean he first read Nietzsche in 1900.

Nietzsche's impact on London's thought remains questionable, because London freely lifted ideas and material from authors that reinforced his morals and manners, twisting and turning them into dollar signs and pop philosophy. Joan London wrote,

> Darwin, Spencer, Nietzsche, and Marx—these have generally been considered the sources of Jack London's so-called philosophy. Many, seeking to gloss over his chauvinism, have regretted

that he was more impressed by Nietzsche than by Marx; others, weary of his monotonous twanging of the "struggle-for-exist-ence" theme, have wished that he had followed more closely the modifications science made within his own lifetime of the Darwinian concept of evolution.

As a matter of fact these four thinkers did not influence Jack London as greatly as has been supposed. He read very little of any of them, and studied none. Darwin and Spencer were gobbled in one excited reading, although he later returned to Spencer and read him more carefully. His knowledge of Nietzsche was derived largely from listening to Strawn-Hamilton, and when he did turn to Nietzsche's own pages he was so enchanted by the philosopher's vocabulary and slogans that he noted little else.[41]

It's reasonable that Nietzsche heightened London's free-thinking religious views. "God is dead!" announced Nietzsche in *Thus Spake Zarathustra,* still his most famous three words. "Alas, my brothers, this god whom I created was man-made and madness, like all gods!"[42] Nietzsche's most seething in-dictment of religion appears in *The Anti-Christ:* "I *condemn* Christianity, I bring against the Christian Church the most ter-rible charge any prosecutor has ever uttered. To me it is the extremest thinkable form of corruption, it has had the will to the ultimate corruption conceivably possible. The Christian Church has left nothing untouched by its depravity, it has made of every value a disvalue, of every truth a lie, of every kind of integrity a vileness of soul. . . . I call Christianity the *one* great curse, the *one* great intrinsic depravity, the *one* great instinct for revenge for which no expedient is sufficiently poi-sonous, secret, subterranean, *petty*—I call it the *one* immortal blemish of mankind."[43]

London, like Nietzsche, admired Christ, calling him and Abraham Lincoln the two great men of history, but London hated Christianity, including the celebration of Christmas. As early as 1898 he called life "chance" to Mabel Applegarth. The next year he admitted agnosticism to Cloudesley Johns. The narrator of "The Men of Forty Mile" says that Klondikers held "an unswerving faith in the God of Chance,"[44] and in "The God of His Fathers," the missionary Sturges Owen forsakes faith to save his skin, while Hay Stockard dies, loyal to the

God of his fathers. Even Charmian said London held lukewarm ideas about the beyond.[45] He also advanced anti-Christian ideas in "The Human Drift" and "The Eternity of Forms," besides comments in other essays, novels and short stories. In *The People of the Abyss*, London suggested that "the 'soul-snatchers' . . . should study the physiological basis of psychology a little, if they wish to make their efforts more effective. . . . And equally stupendous is the callousness of the people who believe in Christ, acknowledge God, and go to church regularly on Sunday. For the rest of the week they riot about on the rents and profits which come to them from the East End stained with the blood of the children."[46] In *The Little Lady of the Big House* (1916), Paula Forrest laughs at the weaklings who live the Bible, turning their cheeks. Muscles ruled the world. Dick adds that man creates God in his own image. In "When Alice Told Her Soul," in *On the Makaloa Mat*, a character claims sainthood for Judas Iscariot, because the divinity of God made him betray Christ.

And in *The Star Rover*'s Ragnar Lodbrog episode, a Jewess resembling Anna Strunsky converts to Christianity—after denouncing Christ's carousing, mocking his stupid entrance into Jerusalem, denying that he, a man of the mob, could be descended from the kingly David. Ragnar turns against Christ, portrayed as a bum who roams the countryside peddling miracles to dupes. Lodbrog even says Pilate crucified an abstraction, something fabricated by the priests to degrade Jews. London's ultimate statement on religion? When you're dead— you're dead. Just like a crushed insect. Annihilated.[47]

Although Joan said London swallowed Nietzsche, Marx, Darwin, and Spencer in convulsive doses, she credited a "profound"[48] influence to one writer—Benjamin Kidd, author of *Social Evolution* (1895) and *Principles of Western Civilisation* (1902). Close readings of these two books, however, contest Joan's conclusion. The core of Jack London's and Benjamin Kidd's social philosophy run counterclockwise, sharing few similarities.

Kidd attacked primitive social structures in *Social Evolution:*

Now, from the beginning it may be noticed that those societies which existed under stress of circumstances as fighting organisations, presented everywhere certain strongly-marked features. In their early stage the social relations may be summed up briefly. The individual is of little account; the men are the warriors of the chief or the state; the women are the slaves of the men, and the children are the property of the parents. Infanticide is universal; the society is of necessity rudely communistic or socialistic, and the population is kept within due bounds by the simple plan of killing off all undesirable accessions to it. The individual *per se* has few rights "natural" or acquired; he holds his property and even his wife at the mercy of a despotism tempered only by religious forms and customs.[49]

London's social system, as will be seen, incorporated all the elements Kidd despised. London considered women chattel. He advanced power through violence and strong-armed tactics. Infanticide appears in a number of stories. And he believed in the elimination of undesirables. He put forth in his work repeatedly the idea of Anglo-Saxon superiority, an idea which disturbed Kidd.[50] The entire social thesis of Kidd was stitched together with one word—ethics[51]—which London replaced with ethnics and economics.

It seems doubtful that Benjamin Kidd exerted a "profound" influence on Jack London as Joan said. London praised Herbert Spencer's progressivism, yet preached primitivism; he supported socialism, yet became a zealous capitalist; he populated stories with savage brutes, yet befriended aesthetes and bred thoroughbred animals. One might surmise that London skimmed Kidd, but according to evidence in his early work, he *read and used* Kidd. Kidd mentioned the shrinkage of the planet. London wrote an article called "The Shrinkage of the Planet" for *The Chautauquan* in 1900. Kidd used the word "phenomena" in most chapters of *Social Evolution* and *Principles of Western Civilisation*. London contributed "Phenomena of Literary Evolution" to *The Bookman* in 1900. Kidd also discussed the laws of development. *The International Socialist Review* published London's "Wanted: A New Law of Development" in 1902. London collected the ideas, the plots, the catchwords of other

authors; then, like alchemists of old, turned them into gold—
the gold of the written word.

Other writers besides Kidd and Nietzsche influenced London,
among them the overlooked Bret Harte. "Everywhere the Bret
Harte paradoxes; the seeming villain proves to be a saint, the
holy man of God turns out to be a blackleg and a murderer.
Everywhere the rush of the narrative is compelling and the
seeing fidelity to the minute facts of the background convincing,"[52] wrote Fred Lewis Pattee. "Bunk is the fashionable
novel; and Bull applies to the Jack London School," said James
Gibbons Huneker, "ramping, roaring, robust rough-riders and
heroes from the wild and woolly West; bastards of the Bret
Harte fiction."[53] And Arthur Voss concludes that although
"reviewers praised [*The Son of the Wolf*] and likened London
to Kipling, . . . in most of the stories the characters, situations,
sentiment, and style are more reminiscent of Bret Harte."[54]

About Kipling. This Nobel Laureate, the first Englishman so
honored, also captivated American readers during the late nineties, including Jack London, who often referred to him in his
stories. He quotes snatches from "Galley Slave" in *The People
of the Abyss*. Dane Kempton and Herbert Wace discuss Kipling
in *The Kempton-Wace Letters*. Dede Mason of *Burning Daylight* carries Kipling's work in her purse. Even Wolf Larsen
likes him. King Hendricks and Irving Shepard list nearly two
dozen Kipling remarks in *Letters from Jack London*.[55] The
Overland Monthly first published London's work in 1899, the
year Kipling's career peaked; as the Englishman's fame re-
ceded, London's advanced, some critics calling him "The Kipling of the Klondike" following the incredible success of *The
Call of the Wild*.

"The race wants its reading matter to be not only concen-
trative, compact, but crisp, incisive, terse," wrote London.
"It tolerates Mr. James, but it prefers Mr. Kipling."[56] Perhaps
so, but London ignored his own advice about crisp and compact
language, cluttering early work with heavy-handed words and
phrases. In a filler called "What are We to Say?" (*Journal of
Education*, July 1899), he forced such phrases as "arithmetical
proposition," "a chance is at once manifest," and "converting
the proposition"[57] in four paragraphs. Verbiage characterizes

some short stories. In "A Thousand Deaths" (*The Black Cat,* May 1899) the reader plows through such pseudoscientific clatter as "tangential," "predilection for scientific pursuits," "technical nomenclature," "speculative hypotheses," "aerotherapeutical apparatus," "quiescent," "manifestation," and "apotheosis."[58] Writers noticed this tendency. "His philosophical ideas came out of books rather than out of life," said Stephen Graham. "Hence at times his appallingly bookish phraseology. . . . This personal literary weakness he imputed also to the heroes of his stories, and the maniacal captain of the sealer, Wolf Larsen, who trampled men to death yet read Herbert Spencer, quoted Kipling and Milton, and did not fall asleep over Browning. Even *Burning Daylight,* the wild man of Alaska, was left chanting *Tomlinson.* This is inartistic and nauseating. One feels that much of London's writing ought to be judged as journalism rather than as literature. He used the fictional form for self-expression, because it gave him most scope."[59]

London admired Joseph Conrad, saying the legendary literateur managed more in two words than his entire career, adding that only Conrad's skill could equal *Martin Eden,* hardly a comment showing humility. Charmian recalled that during the 1907–1909 *Snark* voyage, London read several Conrad stories to the crew, among them *Youth.* He wrote Conrad after reading *Victory.*

London's sensationalism, however, appalled the titanic Conrad. Learning that Sweden considered him "literarily a sort of Jack London," he remarked: "I don't mean to depreciate in the least the talent of the late Jack London, who wrote to me in a most friendly way many years ago at the very beginning, I think, of his literary career, and with whom I used to exchange messages through friends afterwards; but the fact remains that temperamentally, mentally, and as a prose writer, I am a different person."[60] David Thorburn firms Conrad's attitude towards London: "Once, examining a Norwegian translation of one of his books, Conrad complained about its luridly illustrated cover and said with annoyance, 'These people seem to think I am a sort of Jack London.' Though he had intelligent foreign critics during his lifetime, Curle reports that 'it was galling to

(Conrad) . . . to think that many people who read him in trans-
lations regarded him as a blood-and-thunder writer of adventure
stories, while accepting with solemn approval some quite inferior writers.' ''[61]

Although London may have been influenced by the works of
Bret Harte, Rudyard Kipling, Joseph Conrad, and Friedrich
Nietzsche, the changing mainstream of America's social climate
made his success possible. London entered the writing game
during the country's "Golden Age" of short stories, an age
when syndicates handled submissions, textbooks and college
courses taught its techniques, and correspondence schools
fleeced would-be writers. Magazines first serialized novels,
swelling the income and exposure of pen men: London received
$400 for "To Build a Fire," $500 for "The Chinago," and $750
for "Brown Wolf." Hearst's *Cosmopolitan* paid him $1,000 a
shot, besides another $12,000 a year for one serialized novel,
their 1912 contract upping the latter to $24,000. A mere handful
of magazines offer such rates in today's shrunken short-story
market, and few publishers hazard collections, most losing
money.

   Photoengraving techniques replaced engraving and woodcuts,
revolutionizing American publishing. Lithographic posters also
delighted the millions, from Mucha's artistic creations for Sarah
Bernhardt, to tasteless sidewalk billboard monstrosities. Pa-
perbacks, then called dime novels, kept escapists in wonder-
land. (During his lifetime the books of Horatio Alger sold around
800,000 copies. After his death in 1899, when paperback publishers entered the picture, they soared to over a hundred million, some historians doubling and tripling this figure.) Other
influences included more cash flow because of more jobs during
prosperous times, wider magazine advertising, and the expansion of railroads, ensuring fast delivery of magazines from coast
to coast. The increased use of flash powder and dry plates
permitted longer indoor photographic settings, also raising magazine circulations. The end result? Greater emphasis on visuals
instead of copy. "The revolution in the art of engraving, not

to say its destruction, is threatening a change in the conduct of magazines," predicted *The Independent*. "What will be the effect on the high-priced illustrated magazines, like *Harper's, The Century* and *Scribner's*, it may not be easy to foresee; but it seems probable that they will not find it wise to reduce their price to a like figure. . . . The reason is that they will wish to maintain that higher, purer literary standard which succeeds in securing the best but not the most numerous readers."[62] This was wise advice. Nearly all the faddish magazines appealing to "numerous readers" have vanished, while *Harper's* and the *Atlantic* still survive.

One other element also spread magazine sales. The rise of illustrators. These artists dressed stories with classy, eye-catching drawings, some gaining greater fame than writers. Charles Dana Gibson's "The Gibson Man" still remains a kind of romantic logo of the entire period. Crowds followed J. C. Leyendecker, originator of the "Arrow Collar Man" and "New Year's Baby" everywhere, even watching him at railroad stations. Frederic Remington, Howard Pyle, and James Montgomery Flagg—like Maxwell Parrish and Norman Rockwell of later eras—also became national celebrities. (These artists, it must be remembered, worked much faster than earlier wood engravers. Magazines also photographed their work, another time-saving factor, instead of worrying about the cutting techniques of wood and steel engravers.)

It was S. S. McClure, founder of *McClure's Magazine,* a ten-cent periodical, who siphoned sales from the higher priced literary magazines. "Golden Ages, of course, do not just happen along by chance," writes Peter Lyon, McClure's biographer. "In this case a complex of factors—technical, economic, cultural, and purely fortuitous—combined to yield a crop of magazines cheap in price, national in circulation and unprecedented in their influence on the social scene. On each score, *McClure's Magazine* led the way."[63] McClure published glossy work by Anthony Hope, Arthur Conan Doyle, Robert Louis Stevenson, and Rudyard Kipling, along with muckraking essays by such notables as Ida Tarbell and Lincoln Steffens. He also published London's "Grit of Women," "The Man with the Gash," "The Law of Life," "The God of His Fathers," "Love of Life,"

"The Unexpected," "The House of Mapuhi," and "The Unparalleled Invasion." McClure's only reference to London in
his memoirs, however, involves a manuscript reader whom he
said "seized upon the early stories of O'Henry, Jack London,
Rex Beach, Myra Kelley, and the 'Emmy Lou' stories when
their writers were unknowns." He also remarked, "I could give
a new writer such an instrument of publicity as had probably
never been built up before."[64]

From the start London explored mass magazines such as
Ainslee's Magazine, *The Smart Set*, and *Frank Leslie's Illustrated Popular Monthly*, besides juveniles such as *St. Nicholas*
and *The Youth's Companion*. Between 1897, when "Two Gold
Bricks" appeared in *The Owl*, and 1904, the year *Century Magazine* serialized *The Sea Wolf*, London contributed nearly seventy stories to periodicals.[65] Yet only two: "An Odyssey of
the North" and "Li-Wan the Fair" appeared in the *Atlantic
Monthly*, none in *Harper's*, *Century Magazine* or *Scribner's*.
(It must have irked London. Humphrey Van Weyden remarks
in *The Sea Wolf*'s first chapter about his current critical article
on Poe in the *Atlantic*.)

America's trailblazers in the territory of realistic literature
had fought their bitter fight before London stormed the literary
scene with frosted tales from the Klondike. Hamlin Garland's
Main-Travelled Roads stung readers in 1891; Stephen Crane's
Maggie: A Girl of the Streets followed in 1893; Frank Norris
added *McTeague* in 1899; Theodore Dreiser's then-sensational
Sister Carrie briefly appeared in 1900.

Harlan Hatcher, typical of most literary critics, concluded in
Creating the American Novel that "in spite of his immense
popularity in America and abroad, Jack London's work is of
minor importance in the development of our modern fiction."[66]
The kinds of pieces London wrote flooded new mass magazines.
As James I. McClintock says in *White Logic*, an incisive analysis of London's short stories:

> Anyone who turns to the magazines to acquire "a knowledge
> of literature as it [was] produced" in 1898 and 1899 cannot avoid
> having adventure stories forced upon his attention. A glance at
> the magazine contents at this time attests to the overwhelming

trend in public taste and literary expression for aggressive, adventurous materials; they dominate page after page of the leading big circulation magazines. . . . *The Overland Monthly,* London's first consistent market, specialized in stories and articles featuring outdoor life in the West, and more than any other magazine printed articles capitalizing upon the Klondike gold mania. [In October 1897 *The Overland Monthly* noted twenty-eight Alaskan articles they had published before London reached the Yukon wilds.][67] All major publications participated in the worship of active strength and virile adventure. The materials of London's life automatically blended with the materials he studied in the magazines, and eventually he would find markets for his stories in all these magazines.[68]

This strenuous age that worshipped ferocious strength, the superiority of Anglo-Saxons, the thrill of exotic settings, reached its peak with Theodore Roosevelt, presidential pacesetter of his time, the man who made "bully" a household word and inspired a national Teddy-bear craze. Although Roosevelt sought big sticks when arbitration failed, he hated violence for the sake of violence, a long-ignored fact. "It is never well to take drastic action if the result can be achieved with equal efficiency in less drastic fashion." He also hated anarchists. "I treated anarchists and bomb-throwing and dynamiting gentry precisely as I treated other criminals. Murder is murder. It is not rendered one bit better by the allegation that it is committed on behalf of a cause."[69] Roosevelt's diplomacy during the Russo-Japanese War earned him the 1906 Nobel Prize.

American literature, for awhile at least, leaned towards Roosevelt's big-stick side. Best sellers by the score filled bookstalls, many styled after such Roosevelt sagas as *Big Game Hunting in the Rockies and the Great Plains, The Wilderness Hunter, Hunting the Grizzly and Other Sketches,* and *Life Histories of African Game Animals.* Most reduced outdoorsmanship to slick dime novels. London, the pulpists' prince, pocketed the most from this trend, stamping out red-blooded supermen, stacks of pseudoscientific tracts, folktales about the heroic present in distant lands. His landscapes, carefully colored for dramatic effect, evoked romantic images: road bum, sailor on the *Sophie*

Sutherland, Alaskan adventurer, rugged individualist, poor boy
from Tar Town.
"He was writing for money and for little else, and he studied
his market like a broker," assessed *The Cambridge History of
American Literature* in 1918. "Earlier literature was aristocratic—it was written for the refined few; the latest literature
is democratic—it is written for the mass, and the mass is un-
critical and unrefined. Its demands are gross: sensation, movement, physical thrill. London gave the mass what it demanded,
every sensation which the brutal underworld he knew had af-
forded him, and he sold his work well."[70] Van Wyck Brooks
added: "But consider [London's] style, the treatment, that bra-
zen style, that noisy style; never for an instant does the per-
former shift his foot from the loudpedal."[71] London knew his
audience. Theodore Dreiser's powerful and penetrating *Sister
Carrie* earned $68.40 because he played down the pedals.

Jack London exploited the Klondike's white wilderness, its
cult of the cold, frightful sense of the unseen, and remoteness
from civilization in handfuls of sensational short stories, leading
readers to believe he recorded experiences. *"The Son of the
Wolf, A Daughter of the Snows,* and *The God of His Fathers*
represent London's early attempt to create myth out of his own
Arctic adventures,"[72] remarks James R. Giles, while A. Grove
Day writes that "although Jack never panned an ounce of gold,
he was building a myth so powerful it was to be accepted even
by men who had toiled in the dreary northland."[73] California
author Thomas Williamson recalled: "Jack London apparently
knew that he was describing a non-existent Alaska. He was
very bitter about the country when I knew him in Oakland. I
was a kid, a hero-worshipper; and I asked him a lot of questions
about his life up there. Mention of Alaska made London scowl
and curse. It was a hell of a place; it had ruined his health. He
went up there to get rich and all he brought back was the scurvy.
'I'm making up for it though,' he said. 'I'm giving the public
what it likes to think Alaska is, and I'm getting gold for it.
Writing is my strike.' "[74]

London's early short stories reflect this bitterness towards the Yukon. During the death throes of Mason in "The White Silence," he mumbles, "This country was not made for white men," and characters in "To the Man on Trail" and "The Grit of Women" call the Yukon a "God-forsaken hole"[75] and a "God-forsaken land." Wertz in "Where the Trail Forks" echoes them: "Our concern is to get the dust and then get out of this God-forsaken land. 'T n't fit for naught else but beasts." Another Klondiker in "Jan, the Unrepentant" curses, "Gawd never intended this here country for livin' purposes, an' that's a cold frozen fact,"[76] while Hutchinson calls it a "falling off place for the damned"[77] in "The Faith of Men." Success, however, seemed to mellow London's hindsight. "It was in the Klondike that I found myself," he said in a Macmillan Company promotional pamphlet years later. "There nobody talks. Everybody thinks. You get your true perspective. I got mine."[78]

Most Northland tenderfeet agreed with London's earlier views. "I would not be tied up in this lorn, large, desolate largeness another winter for all the Klondike gold you could point to me with a dozen North Poles in a thousand years,"[79] declared Joaquin Miller. Hamlin Garland wrote in *The Trail of the Goldseekers* that prospectors "appeared to drift on and in toward that human maelstrom going irresolutely to their ruin. They did not seem to me strong men—on the contrary, they seemed weak men—or men strong with one insane purpose."[80]

London sketched a Klondike of such insane, irrational powers, a terror terrain of frozen ice and snow where man, a speck on the horizon, struggles against natural forces that clutch his most elemental emotion—*fear*. "Deep down in the roots of the race is fear," he wrote in "The Terrible and Tragic in Fiction." "It came first into the world, and it was the dominant emotion in the primitive world. To-day, for that matter, it remains the most firmly seated of the emotions."[81] Nietzsche advanced the same idea in *Thus Spake Zarathustra*: "For fear is the original and basic feeling of man; from fear everything is explicable, original sin and original virtue. From fear my own virtue too has grown, and it is called: science. For the fear of wild animals, that was bred in men longest of all—including the animal he harbors inside himself and fears: Zarathustra calls it 'the inner beast.' "[82]

London's "brooding land; the ghastly silence, which made the echo of each heart-beat a sacrilege"[83] led *The Bookman* to predict that "very few readers who take up [his work] will lay it down without feeling more keenly than ever before all the ghastly horror and loneliness of life in the frigid zone."[84] *The Critic* called the Klondike "a horrible land and its stern savagery is unspeakable. You have only to watch the faces of men who have come back from the Klondike to see what havoc it makes of ordinary human nature."[85]

The paradox of London's Yukon stories, with all their blood-letting and pulsating action, is that they're studies in stasis—nature's attempt to stop action by freezing man's blood. The white silence loathes movement. "Nature has many tricks wherewith she convinces man of his finity—the ceaseless flow of the tides, the fury of the storm, the shock of the earthquake, the long roll of heaven's artillery—but the most stupendous, the most stupefying of all is, the passive phase of the White Silence. All movement ceases, the sky clears, the heavens are as brass; the slightest whisper seems sacrilege, and man becomes timid, affrighted at the sound of his own voice. Sole speck of life journeying across the ghostly wastes of a dead world, he trembles at his audacity, realises that his is a maggot's life, nothing more."[86]

London later transferred this idea of stasis, of man's impotence, to his hell-ship the *Ghost* in *The Sea Wolf.* "Without moving and being part of the yeast there would be no hopelessness," Wolf Larsen philosophizes to Humphrey Van Weyden. "But,—and there it is,—we want to live and move, though we have no reason to, because it happens that it is the nature of life to live and move, to want to live and move. If it were not for this, life would be dead." Larsen calls this lust to live "piggishness," later adding that "another way of expressing the joy of life is that it is alive, the triumph of movement over matter, of the quick over the dead, the pride of the yeast because it is yeast and crawls." Larsen, like the white wilderness's eternal silence, reflects London's growing death-wish, yet primal need to be. "To crawl is piggish; but to not crawl, to be as the clod and rock, is loathsome to contemplate," says Larsen. "It is loathsome to the life that is in me, the very essence of which is movement, the power of movement, and the consciousness of the power of movement. Life itself is unsatisfaction, but to look ahead to death is greater unsatisfaction."[87] Larsen beats nature's silence, existing without movement before death, his body still, but brain alive, functioning in its capacity to think and reason. His inner spirit remains unimpaired.

Such irreconcilable feelings—a thirst for life and a thirst for death, to be or not to be, to move or become nothingness—deeply scored Jack London's work, personal associations, and tormented being, as he tried to exist in a hated world.

Chapter 6

Race Epic Without a Race

AFTER HIS RETURN from the Klondike, London saw less and less of Mabel Applegarth, although they once talked of marriage. She thought the post-office job would make him sink roots, but London wanted freedom. Yet several years later he warned aspiring authors: "Don't quit your job in order to write unless there is none dependent upon you."[1] Perhaps visions of Mabel's mother and Flora battling, one demanding breakfast in bed, the other feigning heart attacks, helped the decision.

Mabel also failed to feed London's fantasies. She criticized the slipshod style of his work, its flat characterizations and elemental philosophy. He talked cash. When did style fill empty stomachs? "So it were well that we, moved towards literature by belly need, should judiciously decide what part of us is the best to put on paper. Frankly, which pays the best—fiction, poetry, essays, history, philosophy, or science? The circulating library is an artery where one may feel the pulse of the market. That which is most read is most in demand, and was there ever a circulating library which did not put forth more fiction than all other forms of printed thought combined?"[2] He also declared in "Again the Literary Aspirant" (*The Critic*, September 1902) that "the deepest values of life are to-day expressed in terms of cash. That which is most significant of an age must be the speech of that age. That which is most significant to-day is the making of money."[3] As Joan London later remarked: "It was not a living he wanted to make, but money, and writing, for which he was aware he had a certain talent, was a convenient, readily exploited means to that end."[4]

Two other women soon replaced Mabel in London's life—the lovely socialist-student Anna Strunsky and Bessie Maddern, his first wife. Bessie had been involved with Fred Jacobs, London's chum at the Oakland Library, but Jacobs enlisted in the army and died of fever aboard a ship en route to the Spanish-American War. London and Bessie, having dated a short time, suddenly announced wedding plans at the time Houghton Mifflin published *The Son of the Wolf,* surprising everyone, probably themselves the most. London told Bessie—a gray-eyed motherly type with engaging smile and pompadour styled hair—that he did not love her. His reason for marriage? To perpetuate seven Saxon sons. Bessie, instead, produced two daughters, Joan and Bess. "He blundered into his first marriage . . . in order to escape from another woman [Mabel] with whom he was in love but who, as he realized, would have kept his artistic conscience uneasily awake,"[5] suspected *The Freeman* in its 1922 review of Charmian's biography. Louis Kronenberger said that London "had—or thought he had—a great love, but married a woman he did not love at all, and left her for a woman [Charmian] who snared him with mush that would have sickened the soul of Marie Corelli,"[6] then a popular authoress.

Jack London and Bessie Maddern took vows on April 7, 1900, in the Maddern's home. Flora, London's mother, failed to show. After honeymooning in the nearby hills for several days, the newlyweds returned to Oakland, living at 1130 East Fifteenth Street, along with Flora and Johnny Miller. When trouble flared between Flora and Bessie, London removed his mother, along with Johnny, to a nearby cottage on Sixteenth Street.

Domestic duties irritated London, from gas bills to groceries and the garbage, yet Bessie made a fine wife, the kind his works praised. She washed dishes, corrected manuscripts, and continued tutoring on the side, while he wrote short stories, newspaper articles for the *San Francisco Examiner* and struggled through a stillborn first novel, *A Daughter of the Snows,* which sold only several thousand copies.

S. S. McClure, who then paid London around $125 a month, refused to serialize *A Daughter of the Snows,* his book-publishing subsidiary following suit, so they peddled the novel to

J. P. Lippincott. McClure kept most of the $750 advance to cover funds earlier given London. Stuffed with material for a stackful of novels, *A Daughter of the Snows* violated London's own literary advice: "The race wants its reading matter to be not only concentrative, compact, but crisp, incisive, terse. . . . The race does not want novels and stories teeming with superfluities. The unpruned shall be cast aside unread. What it wants is the meat of the matter, and it wants it now."[7]

The public ignored this "unpruned" work. "He lacks the craftmanship of the novelist," said *The Athenaeum*. "He does not show the sustained power of thought which is essential to the production of a first-rate novel. Page after page, particularly in the early part of the present book, consists simply of condensed, detached short stories."[8] This problem plagued London's entire career. Although early work showed obvious writing skills, his journalese, lacking creative artistry, resulted in "a shambles of idealizations that personal neuroses often confused and defeated."[9] *The Athenaeum* caught this failure to weave novels with complex characters in *A Daughter of the Snows*, his first effort. He "brushstroked," sketching people and places, even in later fictions like *Smoke Bellew* and *The Star Rover*. *The Call of the Wild* is seven short stories stitched together by Buck.

Critics ridiculed Frona Welse, the central character of *A Daughter of the Snows*. *Book Buyer* concluded London wasn't "living up to" his earlier promise, calling Frona "unbelievable," predicting that "if she had never left Alaska she would have been a heroine of parts, but now we shake our heads over her and feel convinced that ultimately she abandoned canoeing and sledge driving and organized a woman's club in Dawson."[10] Frona Welse became the first of London's mate-women, who could both drive dog sleds across the Arctic wastes and putter with poetry. Although Frona is Paris-educated, reads Browning, stages Ibsen's *A Doll's House* in Dawson, and loves "the things which rose straight from the heart," her biceps bulge: "Oh, I can swing clubs, and box, and fence," she cries, successively striking the typical postures,"and swim, and make high dives, chin a bar twenty times, and—and walk on my hands. There!"[11] London called her "fair and flaxen haired, typically Saxon," using her as a sounding board for his racism:

We are a race of doers and fighters, of globe-encirclers and zone-conquerers. We toil and struggle, and stand by the toil and struggle no matter how hopeless it may be. While we are persistent and resistent, we are so made that we fit ourselves to the most diverse conditions. Will the Indian, the Negro, or the Mongol ever conquer the Teuton? Surely not! The Indian has persistence without variability; if he does not modify he dies, if he does try to modify he dies anyway. The Negro has adaptability, but he is service and must be led. As for the Chinese, they are permanent. All that the other races are not, the Anglo-Saxon, or Teuton if you please is. All that the other races have not, the Teuton has. What race is to rise up and overwhelm us?[12]

Nearly a decade later, London resurrected Frona Welse, shifting her remains from the Klondike to the Melanesian Islands in *Adventure,* a tropical thriller written aboard the *Snark.* Her new name is Joan Lakeland, and she is another literary transvestite who wears heavy braids, a cowboy Stetson hat, and slings a .38 Colt revolver; she also hunts alligators, swims in shark-infested waters, and blackbirds in the Solomons. Yet Joan's very feminine, a girl who plays the piano, sews, and even cooks.

Frona's father, Jacob Welse, emerges as London's first millionaire. (Later characters Burning Daylight, David Grief in *Son of the Sun,* and Thomas Regan in *Hearts of Three* also roleplay J. P. Morgan.) Welse is "a captain of industry and a splendid monopolist [who] dominated the most independent aggregate of men ever drawn together from the ends of the earth," an "economic missionary" who "bore the country on his shoulders." Darwinism drives this Klondike king's will to power: "Competition was the secret of creation. Battle was the law and the way of progress. The world was made for the strong, and only the strong inherited it, and through it all there ran an eternal equity. . . . The stubborn earth yielded only to force. Brain was greater than body. The man with the brain could best conquer things primitive."[13]

London defended *A Daughter of the Snows* in "Stranger than Fiction," claiming he fashioned Frona from a real-life girl seen in the Sierra Nevadas, taking literary liberties with her persona. "The reviewers swiftly proved to me how signally I had failed. I quote at random: 'One cannot believe in her, but one likes her and forgives her culture'; 'a projection of the writer's ideal woman upon paper'; 'a monster'; 'a thing contrary to nature'; 'remains at the end of the story utterly incredible and even inconceivable.' " London concluded from these reviews that "it is incontrovertible that one cannot do on the printed page what one does in life."[14] Yet he later complained that critics misunderstood both *Martin Eden* and *The Sea Wolf*, ignoring his own premise.

When spring rains flooded the London's home on Fifteenth Street, they moved into a rococo Italian villa called La Capriccioso, whose bohemian designer, Felix Peano, was a sculptor-member of the Ruskin Club. "I climbed the hill in Oakland according to directions and was soon lost in a maze of back streets; but I knew the freak house instantly when I found it," recalled Ray Stannard Baker. "I am certain that there was not another like it in America. It had been built by an imaginative Italian musician, of highly colored stucco with the bottoms of blue and yellow glass carboys set in around the front entrance. Over the door a bar of the music of 'Home Sweet Home' had been worked into the stucco, with flourishes. It seems that the inventive Italian had neglected to make room inside the house for a stairway to the second floor; but this had caused him no anxiety; he built a kind of ramp rising up the wall outside of the house which seemed to serve perfectly well."[15]

The goose hung high, although London couldn't afford such posh style, any more than he could later spend a fortune on the Glen Ellen estate. He smoked Russian cigarets, wore silk shirts and long ties, sailed on San Francisco Bay, and threw his usual Wednesday night parties that attracted Jim Whitaker, Frank Strawn-Hamilton, Xavier Martinez, James Hopper, Austin Lewis, Anna Strunsky—and lots of leeches. It didn't take Bessie long to tire of "The Crowd," the way Charmian later tired of them at Glen Ellen.

The Londons soon left La Capriccioso, moving to the suburban Piedmont hills, a move encouraged by London's poet friend George Sterling, and one Bessie resented because grocery and butcher shops were a mile away. After Joan, their first child, arrived on January 15, 1901, Bessie worried about doctors. Suppose the infant got sick during the night? But London liked the view. What else really counted?

Credit bends so far—then snaps. This happened to London in 1902, one incident making newsprint. A grocer named Benninger threatened to sue over a $35 bill. London wrote Benninger. "After a sarcastic introduction," reported the *San Francisco Bulletin,* "London writes that he will make an endeavor to teach the couple common courtesy, to be gentlemanly and ladylike in their methods. He also, in the paragraph, asks them to send him his bill and not to fail to credit him with"[16] thirty cents spent on bread. In the second paragraph, London warned the grocer not to blackmail him or cause trouble. Then he'd never get paid. Benninger read this letter several times to the Grocers' Association, but members failed to take action, probably because of the amount involved.

As might be expected, home life between London and Bessie soon soured, mainly because of his egocentric and footloose nature. In "The Proper Girlie" (*The Smart Set,* October–November 1900), London, whose female characters feel and express his views, says about Maud, a young married girl: "Perhaps it was the unconscious radiation of his present mental attitude, or the sum of his attitudes through many days, that made Maud lonely on her side of the table. At least, she felt depressed and isolated, as if in some way the bonds that once so tightly bound them were undergoing an extraordinary expansion. She had expected that the fervid kisses that so sweetly punctuated their engagement period would change to the staid homage of tried affection, but not that they would become only a meaningless duty, the mere mechanical performance of a function. His whole demeanor had come to lack that subtle seriousness and enthusiasm the absence of which a woman is so quick to detect."[17]

When the American Press Association asked London to cover the aftermath of the Boer War, he accepted, although Bessie was again pregnant. On the way, he planned to meet George P. Brett, editor at Macmillan Company in New York, who offered letters of introduction to British connections but, enjoying the "big city," he forgot to meet Brett. A letter of apology followed.[18] (London also forgot to tell Bessie about the *Children of the Frost* manuscript. When she received it in early August from Macmillan for revisions, uncertain what to do, she asked Brett if it should be returned to Macmillan.)

After reaching London, England, the first lap of his long trip, London got a surprise. The American Press Association had cancelled his assignment, leaving him stranded on foreign soil. So he decided to undertake and finish in six weeks a sociological study of London's East End slums that the Macmillan Company commissioned him to do. He named this tract *The People of the Abyss*. Andrew Sinclair calls this work "planned and artificial," adding that he "deliberately hunt[ed] for the worst areas of poverty in the East End."[19]

Arriving in London Town, he secured guides for the most depressing and dangerous dens of the abyss, traveled with half-crowns and florins sewed in his pockets, and found housing in a detective's home. "While living, eating, and sleeping with the people of the East End, it was my intention to have a port of refuge, not too far distant, into which I could run now and again to assure myself that good clothes and cleanliness still existed. Also in such port I could receive my mail, work up my notes, and sally forth occasionally in changed garb to civilization." This half-hearted immersion into the East End, with its "noisome and rotten tide of humanity,"[20] London undertook in rags, detaching himself with a camera lens, attempting to support his own prejudices.

This led *The Bookman* to comment:

If Mr. London imagines that he really did this, then his idea of how "the other half" lives is vastly amusing. He confesses that he was never without sufficient money for an emergency, and that he kept within reach of a comfortable room to which he could always retire to rest, bathe, receive his mail, and, most important of all, write up his notes. Mr. London can scarcely believe that the typical East Ender goes about with sovereigns sewed up in his clothes; and that he has a comfortable haven of refuge open to receive him when the tooth of poverty gnaws too keenly. I prefer to believe that his remark about living the life of the slum inhabitant was a mere by-product of his too exuberant imagination, not intended to be taken literally.

The magazine concluded: "It is the pretence of Mr. London's book to a character which it does not possess that is exasperating, and that induces a doubt whether nine-tenths of all the slumming books are not sheer rot."[21]

Even before reaching his destination, London launched research by calling East Enders beasts in a letter to Anna Strunsky. Instead of sympathizing with the submerged tenth in *The
People of the Abyss*, London indicted them as "some vile spawn
from underground . . . sodden and forlorn creatures, uncouth,
degraded and wretched below the beasts of the field," predicting
that "not of their sort are revolutions bred. And when they are
dead and dust, which will be shortly, other fools will talk bloody
revolution as they gather offal from the spittle-drenched sidewalk along Mile End Road to Poplar Workhouse." He also
charged: "These men of the spike, the peg, and the street, are
encumbrances. They are of no good or use to any one, nor to
themselves. They clutter the earth with their presence, and are
better out of the way."[22] This was hardly the scientific objec-
tivity that characterizes slum studies, seeking solutions to better
the lives of the poor and downtrodden. *The Dial*, unable to
believe that London actually wanted to exterminate the submerged tenth, questioned: "He does not, perhaps, sufficiently
distinguish between the inferiority due to birth and that due to
environment. It is a comforting doctrine to some, that the poor
are so because of their natural inferiority. It need not be doubted
that the two things often go together; but it has been well shown
that the children of the poor, removed to better surroundings,
will exhibit undreamed of abilities."[23]

One of the things, in general, that irked Jack London about
English culture was its response to the coronation procession,
something he compared to "Yankee circuses and Alhambra
ballets,"[24] failing to recognize the people's pride in king and
royal family. And even this was a toned-down version of the
book's original condemnation, which Brett pressured him to
alter.

London's contempt for the English "gutterwolves"[25] also
surfaced in *The Kempton-Wace Letters*, published the same
year, 1903. Herbert Wace (London) advances scientific breeding
of human beings like fine horses, calling the husband in London
slums "a very natural beast who expresses himself in a very
natural manner. . . . The half brute of the London slums had
not food enough when a child, and malnutrition is deadly. Later,
he stole and lied in order to eat, and he was bullied and kicked

for it out of human shape. The trick was passed on to him. The unfortunate of the London slums will push us all from heaven's gate, because we do not do battle with the conditions that make him. It is not such as he that should lead you to scorn love, for he is a mistake and a crime." Anna Strunsky (Dane Kempton) responded to London's eugenics: "Your race epic omits the race."[26]

The People of the Abyss leaves an unsettled taste, considering contents of London's earlier work and his personal prejudices. Were these case studies fact—or fiction? Heroes are burning socialists who read the books London read. He calls American sailors tramps royal. The book even includes a corrupt judge, who sends a boy to jail for thirty days; this is highly reminiscent of London's experience in Niagara Falls. And a drunken sailor voices London's apparent resentment toward wife and domestic routine:

> "Wimmen!" he thumped his pot upon the bar and orated eloquently. "Wimmen is a thing my edication 'as learnt me t' let alone. It don't pay, matey; it don't pay. Wot's a man like me want o' wimmen, eh? jest you tell me. There was my mar, she was enough, a-bangin' the kids about an' makin' the ole man mis'rable when 'e come 'ome, w'ich was seldom, I grant. An' fer w'y? Becos o' mar! She didn't make 'is 'ome 'appy, that was w'y. Then, there's the other wimmen, 'ow do they treat a pore stoker with a few shillin's in 'is trowseys? A good drunk is wot 'e's got in 'is pockits, a good long drunk, an' the wimmen skin 'im out of 'is money so quick 'e ain't 'ad 'ardly a glass. I know. I've 'ad my fling an' I know wot's wot."[27]

It's uncertain—aside from the hope of quick cash—why London wrote *The People of the Abyss*. He padded the work with quotes, tables, statistics, nearly five pages from the police blotter, and began each chapter with a famous quote. Many photos consume space, *The Nation* saying, "Mr. London's statistics must have been obtained by the same process as some of his photographs."[28] *The Bookman* later said that "the thing was being done constantly by sociologists, by economists, by people who made a business of writing or speaking on just such subjects."[29] A consultant at Columbia University, for similar reasons, advised Brett to reject *The People of the Abyss*.

American reformists had been criticizing social ills for decades, yet Jack London called the field of sociological studies virginal to Brett.[30] Was he lying—or uninformed? "We have fallen into a serious misconception," wrote Edward B. Cassady, "in assuming that the muckraking era followed a long period of public and literary complacency toward social evils. The connotations of the term 'Gilded Age' have been taken so literally as to constitute a real barrier to an intelligent understanding of American civilization between the Civil War and the end of the nineteenth century. . . . One has only to thumb through the bound volumes of such periodicals as the *Atlantic, North American Review, Nation,* and *Harper's* to discover how active our writers were in exposing the evils of their day. The longer works, fiction and nonfiction, tell the same story."[31]

Rebecca Harding Davis, the mother of Richard Harding Davis, wrote a scalding indictment of worker abuse in "Life in the Iron-Mills," published by the *Atlantic Monthly* in April 1861. "A Reality of soul-starvation, of living death, that meets you every day under the besotted faces on the streets," she sketched the terrible scene, calling mills "a city of fires, that burned hot and fiercely in the night. Fire in every horrible form; pits of flame waving in the wind; liquid metal-flames writhing in tortuous streams through the sand; wide caldrons filled with boiling fire, over which bent ghastly wretches stirring the strange brewing; and through all, crowds of half-clad men, looking like revengeful ghosts in the red light, hurried, throwing masses of glittering fire. It was like a street in Hell."[32]

Charles Bellamy, brother of Edward Bellamy, wrote *The Breton Mills* in 1879, letting his mill owner admit: "I climb to heights on another's body. Everybody knows life is only a fight—the weakest goes to the wall."[33] The same year Henry George's *Progress and Poverty* reached Americans. His family nearly starved before its publication. Benjamin Orange Flower, maverick publisher of *The Arena,* also accused in *Civilization's Inferno* (1893): "Within cannon-shot of Beacon Hill [Boston], are hundreds of families slowly starving and stifling; families who are bravely battling for life's barest necessities, while year by year the conditions are becoming more hopeless, the struggle for bread fiercer, the outlook more dismal."[34] Richard Watson

Gilder, editor of the *Century*, served on committees with Jacob A. Riis, generously giving his time to reform projects. Riis, "knight of the slums" and friend of Theodore Roosevelt, contributed many works on American slums. He called them "dens of death" in *The Battle with the Slum* (1902), hell-holes where children were "damned rather than born," their tenement homes "infant slaughter houses." Riis painted a frightful picture of such existence:

> Imagine, if you can, a section of the city territory completely dominated by one man, without whose permission neither legitimate nor illegitimate business can be conducted; where illegitimate business is encouraged and legitimate business discouraged; where the respectable residents have to fasten their doors and windows summer nights and sit in their rooms with asphyxiating air and one hundred degrees temperature, rather than try to catch the faint whiff of breeze in their natural breathing places—the stoops of their homes; where naked women dance by night in the streets, and unsexed men prowl like vultures through the darkness on "business" not only permitted, but encouraged by the police; where the education of infants begins with the knowledge of prostitution. . . . Where small boys are taught to solicit for the women of disorderly houses; where there is an organized society of young men whose sole business in life is to corrupt young girls and turn them over to bawdy houses; where men walking with their wives along the street are openly insulted; where children that have adult diseases are the chief patrons of the hospitals and dispensaries; where it is the rule, rather than the exception, that murder, rape, robbery, and theft go unpunished—in short, where the premium of the most awful forms of vice is the profit of the politicians.[35]

Many writers tussled with social ills like these, despite London's statement to the contrary. (Louise Ware, by the way, lists nearly seventy articles on social reform in *Jacob A. Riis,* all before 1904.[36])

Such wretched conditions also existed on San Francisco's Barbary Coast. Thugs knifed innocents. Sailors were shanghaied on ships. The red-light district flourished. "As late as 1895 a slave-dealer named Charley Hung, together with an old Chinese woman called Dah Pa Tsin, kept a hundred girls, all under

fourteen, in pens in the rear of a building in Church Alley,"
reported Herbert Asbury in *The Barbary Coast.* "When the
sale began, the girls were brought in one by one to the block.
They were stripped, punched, prodded and in some cases ex-
amined by Chinese physicians who had, more likely than not,
been bribed to warrant them sound in wind and limb."[37] Yet
London grappled with London's East End, while his own back-
yard reeked with social stench.

Why did Macmillan Company accept *The People of the
Abyss?* They specialized in sociological studies. Their publications included: Benjamin Kidd's *Social Evolution* (1895), Joseph Lee's *Constructive and Preventive Philanthropy* (1902),
The Tenement House Problem (1903), edited by R. W. DeForest
and L. Veiller, and the definitive seventeen-volume *Life and
Labour of the People of London* (1902–1903) by Charles Booth,
a social scientist who spent seventeen years collecting data,
while running a private business.[38] London probably relied heavily on Booth's books as resource materials. (Even Benjamin
Kidd praised them.) Paralleling *The People of the Abyss* with
Jacob A. Riss's *The Battle with the Slum* (released a year earlier
by Macmillan Company) shows striking similarities. They look
like twins: same size, same typeface, same layouts, including
photographic format. Was *The People of the Abyss* planned as
a spin-off? London, still an obscure author, didn't gain fame
until *The Call of the Wild*—also published by Macmillan Company in 1903.

The People of the Abyss eventually sold over twenty thousand
copies, most likely due to the success of *The Call of the Wild,*
boosting London's reputation as the "high priest of the Socialist
party."[39] Philip S. Foner says in *Jack London: American Rebel,*
a socialistic study, that "*The People of the Abyss* brought Jack
London to the attention of the entire socialist movement in the
United States. Previous to its appearance he was only well
known on the Coast. Then *Wilshire's* printed *The People of the
Abyss* serially, beginning with the March 1903 issue and running
it through January 1904. Thus several months before Macmillan
released the book, socialists all over the country were reading
London's burning indictment against capitalism, and overnight
his name became a household word among Party members."[40]

Many of these party members were also devouring *The Call of the Wild*.

After completing *The People of the Abyss,* London briefly toured Europe, while Bessie struggled through a second pregnancy. Bess arrived on October 20, 1902. Shortly afterwards, London returned home, eager for new adventures.

Chapter 7

War on the Classes

LONDON'S CONNECTION with Anna Strunsky, who was invited to his home during their collaboration on *The Kempton-Wace Letters,* became a key issue in his scandalous separation from Bessie. The divorce petition, among other grievances, claimed he had gonorrhea. A former student at Stanford University, Anna had debated, tramped in protest parades, had even been suspended for entertaining a fellow in her room, then highly irregular. After fleeing Czarist Russia, the Strunskys settled in San Francisco, clinging to Old World traditions of camaraderie among friends and family, although welcoming guests such as anarchist Emma Goldman. (Anna's sister Rose, delight of Sinclair Lewis, wrote a book on Lincoln and translated into English Leo Tolstoy's *Journals* and Maxim Gorky's *My Confessions.*)

London first met Anna at the Turk Street Temple in December 1899 during a socialist labor party meeting. Her dark eyes, curly brown hair and radicalism intrigued him. A friendship blossomed. In letters to her London lamented about deep despairs, his loss of sentiment, and willful nature. Although still married to Bessie, he asked for Anna's hand in May 1902, suggesting they live in New Zealand or Australia.[1] Tempted to test fate, Anna still declined, probably unready for domestic duties like Bessie, the mother of one infant and pregnant with a second, besides questioning London's erratic emotional state. When Bessie finally divorced London, she called Anna "the other girl," unaware that Charmian Kittredge, her own confidante,

109

not only relayed their discussions to London, but played his latest whirl.

London encouraged Anna's writing, analyzing her work, teaching her techniques, even letting her edit his short stories. They also collaborated on *The Kempton-Wace Letters,* a novel structured as letters between Dane Kempton (Anna) and Herbert Wace (London) on love, Anna defending romance, London scientism, one of the ages popular pastimes.

The Macmillan Company anonymously published *The Kempton-Wace Letters* in 1903, after London assured Brett it wouldn't clash with *The Call of the Wild,* a book that Macmillan wanted to push. (The authors' names appeared on the title page of the second edition.) This work, essentially an attempt on London's part to justify his empty marriage to Bessie Maddern, defended a union based on sexual comradeship instead of romance. "In all marriages love—passionate, romantic love—must disappear, to be replaced by conjugal affection or by nothing." A clear reference to Bessie evolved in his fiction as the idea of "Mother Woman," whom he called the "highest and holiest in the hierarchy of life," as opposed to the "wanton"[2] Mate Woman, later personified, one would assume, by Charmian Kittredge. London used Herbert Wace as a mouthpiece for the following ideas:

> Love is a disorder of mind and body, and is produced by passion under the stimulus of imagination.
>
> We see it every day, for love is the most perfectly selfish thing in the universe.
>
> During the time romantic love runs its course in an individual, that individual is in a diseased, abnormal, irrational condition.
>
> Now this is the law: Love as a means for the perpetuation and development of the human type, is very crude and open to improvement. What the intellect of man has done with the beast, the intellect of man may do with man.[3]

Anna (Dane Kempton) disputes London's views in *The Kempton-Wace Letters,* telling Herbert Wace: "You picture a scientific Utopia where there are no lovers and no back-harkings to the primitive passion, and you appoint yourself pioneer to the promised land of the children of biology." She also says that man doesn't choose a wife like a saddle horse, nor are marriages planned like horses. "It is not whether people can live together, but whether they should live together."[4] London defined mating in scientific terms—without emotional ties or self commitment—the way he viewed most things through test-tube sights. "No activity was strictly human for London, not even administering a charity or producing a work of art," says Malcolm Cowley. "They were all applications of biology."[5]

Although *The Kempton-Wace Letters* could have been re-duced to several essays, the book remains a valuable index to London's thoughts, Symes and Clement concluding that it holds "the essence of that wish-fulfillment dream that was finally to carry London through the pages of Hearst's *Cosmopolitan* to the mastery of a rancho and blooded stock in the Valley of the Moon."[6] The work's resolution? Herbert Wace's fiancée leaves him, unwilling to become part of a diseased disorder of the emotions, unwilling to become part of the universe's most self-ish end.

The Kempton-Wace Letters baffles reason after reading *A Daughter of the Snows,* written during the same period. "First, and most necessary of all, there was that physiological affinity between them that made the touch of his hand a pleasure to her," London says about Vance Corliss and Frona Welse. "Though souls may rush together, if body cannot endure body, happiness is reared on sand and the structure will be ever un-stable and tottery."[7] Trying to pinpoint a consistent philosophy in London's work fails, mainly because he considered all rel-ative in an absurdistic universe, a rationalization for shifting attitudes without moral accountability, a more common view in today's society. As Eugene Debs said: "His was a romantic mind, an adventuresome spirit, and that combination cannot be expected to sink into the grooves of logic and practicality."[8]

Anna Strunsky contributed a romantic memoir to *The Masses* on London after his death in 1916, one filled with evasive re-marks and contradictions. After admitting "he mortgaged his brain in order to meet the market demand," and that "he threat-ened to study Marie Corelli [a popular author] in order to dis-cover those qualities which made her success inevitable and to make them a part of himself," she adds that "his was not a vulgar quest for riches." Then she states that he "justified war," "believed in the inferiority of certain races," and supported "the biological inferiority of woman to man." After calling London a "revolutionist,"[9] she later said that he lived by the rules: "Law, Order and Restraint."[10] Such double-talk improved with time. Years later she romanced: "His standard of life was so high. He for one would have the happiness of power, of genius, of love and the vast comforts and ease of wealth. Napoleon and Nietzsche had a part in him, but his Nietzschean philosophy became transmitted into Socialism and it was by the force of his Napoleonic temperament that he conceived the idea of an incredible success, and had the will to achieve it."[11]

Anna's personal view? A few years after his death, she wrote,

> Our friendship can be described as a struggle. Constantly, I strained to reach that in him which I felt he was "born to be." I looked for the Social Democrat, the Revolutionist, the moral and romantic idealist; I sought the Poet. Exploring his personality was like exploring mountains, and the valleys which stretched between troubled my heart. They did not seem to belong to the grandiose character he was, or could, by an effort of the will, become. He was a Socialist, but he wanted to beat the Capitalist at his own game. To succeed in doing this, he thought, was in itself a service to the Cause; to "show them" that Socialists were not derelicts and failures had certain propaganda value. So he succeeded—became a kind of Napoleon of the pen. This dream of his, even when projected and before it became a reality, was repellent to me. The greatest natures, I thought, the surest Social Democrats, would be incapable of harboring it. To pile up wealth, or personal success—surely anybody who was a beneficiary of the Old Order must belong to it to some extent in spirit and in fact!
>
> So it was that our ancient quarrel, and many, many others, took their rise in the same source—a doubt, not as to himself— I never doubted the beauty and the warmth and the purity of his own nature—but as to the ideas and the principles which he invited to guide his life. They were not worthy of him, I thought; they belittled him and eventually they might eat away his strength and grandeur.[12]

Anna married William English Walling, affluent American socialist, and powerful stockholder in *Wilshire's Magazine.*

Along with Jane Addams and others, he founded the National Woman's Trade Union League in 1903, and helped organize the National Association for the Advancement of Colored People in 1909.

When racial strife erupted in Springfield, Illinois, against blacks, Walling and Anna rushed to the scene. After blaming "the masses of the people," Walling predicted: "The day these methods become general in the North every hope of political democracy will be dead, other weaker races and classes will be persecuted in the North as in the South, public education will undergo an eclipse, and American civilization will await either a rapid degeneration or another profounder and more revolutionary civil war, which shall obliterate not only the remains of slavery but all the other obstacles to a free democratic evolution that have grown up in its wake."[13]

Jack London, a different kind of social reformer from William English Walling, once told Charmian that if he ever became a sociologist, he'd study submerged peoples impersonally, out of curiosity, intellectually—based on his superior self-concept.[14]

London's hell-fire socialism flared years before he met Anna Strunsky, Georgia Loring Bamford tracing its roots to 1893. By 1896, however, London had gained local recognition. The *San Francisco Chronicle* reported on February 16:

> Jack London, who is known as the boy socialist of Oakland, is holding forth nightly to the crowds that throng City Hall Park. There are other speakers in plenty, but London always gets the biggest crowd and the most respectful attention.
>
> London is young, scarcely 20, but he has seen many sides of the world and has traveled extensively. He was born in San Francisco in the Centennial year, and went through the California grammar schools before he started out in the world. . . . He is a High School boy, and supports himself as a janitor in the institution. At present he is fitting himself for a course at the University of California, where he will make a specialty of social questions.
>
> The young man is a pleasant speaker, more earnest than eloquent, and while he is a broad socialist in every way, he is not

an anarchist. He says on the subject when asked for his definition of socialism, "It is an all-embracing term—communists, nationalists, collectionists, idealists, utopians, altrurians, are all socialists, but it cannot be said that socialism is any of these—it is all."

Any man, in the opinion of London, is a socialist who strives for a better form of government than the one he is living under.[15]

London's muddied definition of socialism, dumping everyone from idealists to collectionists in the philosophic pot, didn't clear with time. When *Charities* reviewed *War of the Classes* in 1905, they concluded that "except that socialism stands for discontent with the present industrial order, the reader gains no clear idea of what the movement really is."[16] London also ignored a tenet of many socialists—that the future hope of American progress lay in industrialism, a social system he called worse than war.[17]

More notoriety followed in 1897. Although the mayor enforced a ruling that the park around Chabot Observatory on Eleventh Street be a free forum for soapboxers, local socialists wanted more freedoms and more attention. They needed a test case—something London provided for the cause. At 7:30 P.M. on February 10, 1897, he spoke on the corner of Tenth Street and Broadway, attracting a crowd before ordered to stop by an officer. London refused and was arrested. A group of socialists, intent on political reform, trailed him to police headquarters, where they "made a little socialist speech to Chief Lloyd at the station, and the ordinance depriving them of the dearest right assured by the Constitution was roundly denounced." After paying $5 bail, he spoke on the city hall steps.

We will see whether a city ordinance of Oakland is greater than the Constitution of the United States. I claim that this ordinance which prevents speaking upon the street corners is in direct violation of that section of the Constitution which guarantees free speech to all, and upon that ground I shall fight it. I applied to Mayor Davie for a permit to speak upon socialistic doctrines, but he refused it to me, saying that no other political leader had asked for or been granted a similar privilege. I then determined to test the law that stops free speech, and went out on the street and spoke, expecting to be arrested. I am a candidate for School Director at Large upon the ticket that will be placed in the field by the Socialist Labor party, and while I do not expect to be elected, I hope to be able to do something for my party in spreading its doctrines, and I am going to begin by defeating this city law if I can.[18]

The following morning London appeared in police court, but his hearing was postponed, the judge eventually releasing him after a severe lecture. The *San Francisco Chronicle,* who called London "the idol of the Socialists,"[19] mentioned his nomination for school trustee by the socialist labor party. London later ran for mayor of Oakland several times.

London wrote for socialist magazines when it involved profits or publicity. "Let us have an eye to the ills of the world and its needs; and if we find messages, let us deliver them. Ah, pardon me, purely for materialistic reasons," he said in "First Aid to Rising Authors." "We will weave them about with our fictions, and make them beautiful, and sell them for goodly sums."[20] *The American Magazine* paid him $200 for "A Question of the Maximum," and *Collier's* $500 for "Revolution," higher figures than most current magazine rates. When the *Appeal to Reason* asked to publish *The Iron Heel* serially, London held out, waiting for bigger bites, also refusing a request from *Wilshire's Magazine* to do a socialistic essay, while pounding out other copy to finance the *Snark's* voyage around the world. He also made several hundred dollars a day during his 1905–1906 cross-country lecture tour for the Intercollegiate Socialist Society. One of London's few quarrels with George Sterling stemmed from his refusal to invest in a socialist paper that Sterling and Harry Lafler, former editor of the *Argonaut,* planned to publish, although at the time he was making investments in Glen Ellen holdings. London also crossed socialists in several other ways: he published material in magazines that used scabs; he exploited laborers on his ranch, hiring itinerant Italians for $1.75 a day, forcing them to pay for room and board, refusing wages when it rained; he also refused Brett's suggestion that *The Iron Heel* be published in a fifty-cent edition, saying the better classes would spend $1.50.

"The conversion of Jack London to the philosophy of Marx had more to do with rising in the world than with world revolution," says Kenneth S. Lynn. "London's socialism clearly reflects the success aspirations of an ex-newsboy; stated more abstractly, it reveals the impingement of the outlook of Horatio Alger on that of Karl Marx. . . . His socialism was dominated by the success mythology."[21] Critics have also noted that London's five books about the Klondike (*The Son of the Wolf, The God of His Fathers, Children of the Frost, A Daughter of the Snows* and *The Call of the Wild*) evade socialistic issues. London realized this because Vance says to Flora in *A Daughter of the Snows*: "Then you would preach two doctrines? . . . One for the elect and one for the herd? You would be a democrat in theory and an aristocrat in practice? In fact, the whole stand you are making is nothing more or less than Jesuitical."[22]

Joan London commented on London's grasp of Marxist socialism.

> He had relied on second and third sources and listened uncritically while this one and that, forgetting his meager equipment, had expounded their understanding of Marxian theories. Further, like most laymen of his time, he really knew very little about modern science. . . . As for Marx, only the first volume of *Das Kapital* was then available in English; socialists who could not read German were to wait until 1906 for Ernest Untermann's first complete English edition of "the entire Marxian theories of capitalist production." There is no evidence, however, to indicate that Jack studied even the one volume. His exacting schedule had always been based on the rapid acquisition of knowledge. If a subject could not be so acquired, and if he could find no short cut, it was put aside until that future date when, his ambitions realized, there would be time for everything. So Marx, save for *The Communist Manifesto,* went by the board, although, in all fairness, it must be stated that letting Marx go by the board was not an uncommon practice among American Socialists in those days.[23]

London's remarks in "The Scab" also show confusion about American labor. He stated that "a scab is one who gives more value for the same price than another. . . . It is not nice to be a scab. Not only is it not in good social taste and comradeship, but, from the standpoint of food and shelter, it is bad business policy. Nobody desires to scab, to give most for least."[24] London missed the point. "Scabs didn't work for less," said Philip S. Foner. "They worked for more. Didn't London know this?"

Foner added that "professional strike-breakers were being paid more for a month's work than the men on strike received during the entire year. Nor does [London] point out that the refusal of the craft unions to organize Negro and women workers often lead them to scab against their will."[25]

London praised socialists in the most glowing terms, calling them noble and heroic, the essence of humanism, nearly transcendently unselfish in their actions. This is seen in "What Life Means to Me" (*Cosmopolitan Magazine*, March 1906):

> Here I found keen flashing intellects and brilliant wits. . . . Here I found, also warm faith in the human, glowing idealism, sweetness of unselfishness, renunciation and martyrdom—all the splendid, stinging things of the spirit. Here life was clean, noble, and alive. Here life rehabilitated itself, became wonderful and glorious; and I was glad to be alive. I was in touch with great souls who exalted flesh and spirit over dollars and cents; and to whom the thin wall of the starved slum-child meant more than all the pomp and circumstance of commercial expansion and world-empire. All about me were nobleness of purpose and heroism of effort, and my days and nights were sunshine and starshine, all fire and dew, with before my eyes, ever burning and blazing, the Holy Grail, Christ's own Grail, the warm, human, long suffering and maltreated, but to be rescued and saved at the last.[26]

Reporters, who looked at London's extravagant life-style, his independent spirit, his strongest-of-the-strong creed, naturally questioned such revolutionary romance. This angered him. Sophie Treadwill broached the issue in one interview. "No, a capitalist is one who lives off capital, who makes money earn money," snapped London. "I don't. I live off wages, the wages that I coin out of my own brain."[27] Hobart Bosworth, later film producer of *The Sea Wolf,* also made the mistake of questioning London's socialism. "He flared up and asked what was he, if not a Socialist. I tried to laugh it off and grinned and sparred a good bit but he demanded to know what he was if not a Socialist. I saw disaster ahead, but I had to say it, and so I took my courage in both hands, and said 'Jack, you're just a grand author searching for material.' I thought he would have struck me, but little by little the blaze went out of his eyes, his muscles loosened up, and finally, and to my eternal gratitude and relief, and with his rare, quizzical smile, he said with a nod of his head, 'I guess maybe, you're right at that.' And you can depend upon it I never referred to the topic again."[28]

Although London often romanticized socialists in his works, he didn't romanticize their overthrow of capitalism in fiction. He called for a bloodbath, a purgation, an old-fashioned revolution. *The Iron Heel* (1908), his name for the oligarchy, became his most ambitious assault on American capitalism. Philip Foner called it "the most revolutionary novel in American literature."[29]

Set between 1912 and 1932, this futuristic tract involves an underground socialist revolt under the leadership of an intellectual, power-starved elitist called Ernest Everhard, who believes terrorist tactics answer victory's call, not the ballot box, even though he becomes a Congressman. (His last name denotes muscular manhood, parallel to the spelling of *male* backward for the name of Elam Harnish in *Burning Daylight*.) The book contains a savage workers' revolt in Chicago, stemming from an earthquake (this is presumably based on London's experiences in the San Francisco earthquake, but little looting occurred in that catastrophe) in which horrors and terrible barbarisms happen. Like many of London's heroes, however, Everhard fails and is executed.

Critics—both socialist and capitalist—attacked *The Iron Heel.* "This is not a pleasant book to read," charged *The Outlook.* "As a work of fiction it has little to commend it; and as a Socialist tract it is distinctly unconvincing. In fact, there are passages in it which should open the eyes of many Socialists who have at present no clear perception of whither the cause they have so ardently espoused is leading them."[30] *The Nation* added: "Theoretically Mr. London's role as a socialist is that of apostle of peace, but his nature—his imagination, at least— is, one recalls, a trifle bloodthirsty. A future such as Socialism hopes for, of steady progress, of peaceful conquest by propagandism and the ballot, would afford small material for his talent. The gore through which, in the course of these pages, we are invited to wallow, is far more to his taste; three hundred years of it is not a day too much for him."[31] *The Independent* also groaned about the gore.

> An open-minded inquirer into Socialism who should read *The Iron Heel* and *New Worlds for Old* would be equally bewildered. Jack London is a boy buccaneer. He gloats over bombs, Gatling guns and war automobiles; over secret glens, Argus-eyed spies and traitors foiled, over heroes of spotless virtue and tyrants with horns and hoofs. To him capitalists are monsters red in tooth and claw. Society he shakes over the pit and with—oh! such gusto. So fond is he of fury, so obsessed with a mania for blood and battle, that he reduces his own argument to absurdity. He sides with the Marxians who hold that society is splitting inevitably into just two classes; that capitalist and proletarian will face each other presently in a final Armageddon, and that immediately thereafter a co-operative commonwealth will, hey presto, occupy the stage. But *The Iron Heel* pictures the failure of this prediction. Instead of the oppressed workmen winning, their revolts thru several centuries are drowned in blood. However, the drowning gives a good chance for painting a gory picture, an opportunity welcome to the boy buccaneer. We surmise that sane socialists pray to be saved from such rampant, uproarious friends. Semi-barbarians, to whom this sort of stuff appeals, may possibly tear down our civilization; they will never lay a single brick of a nobler civilization.[32]

Even the radical *Arena,* usually sympathetic towards London, questioned *The Iron Heel*'s socialistic value: "We believe it is the kind of prophecy that will tend to defeat the objects which the author undoubtedly desired to further. . . . All talk of forcible revolution is not only foolish, but it is bound to injure the people's cause; and to picture the plutocracy as invincible, and the desperate attempts of the people as successive and tragic failures, is little calculated to in any degree help on the cause of social justice."[33] The *International Socialist Review* agreed: "The picture he gives is well calculated, it seems to me, to repel many whose addition to our forces is sorely needed; it gives a new impetus to the old and generally discarded cataclysmic theory; it tends to weaken the political socialist movement by discrediting the ballot and to encourage the chimerical and reactionary notion of physical force, so alluring to a certain type of mind.''[34]

One sore-thumb attitude stands out in *The Iron Heel*: Jack London's bitter resentment toward America's plain people, the working class, beneficiaries of the Marx-Engels socialistic theory, who would seize the factories, making them public property. (Benjamin Kidd details this in his chapter on "Modern Socialism" in *Social Evolution*.) London called both English and American workers stupes, scratching their destruction as a small loss to the socialistic movement. Noted socialist Floyd Dell declared that "if Percy Byssche [sic] Shelley had lived in our era, he would have been another Jack London; and if Jack London had lived in our era, he would have been another Jack Reed, he would have been in the Communist party.''[35]

London's malice towards the proletariat, essentially an attempt to retaliate against his own roots, surfaced long before *The Iron Heel*. A few examples between 1902 and 1908 follow.

"The Dignity of Dollars" (*The Overland Monthly*, July 1900): "But the common clay-born man, possessing only talents, may do only what has been done before him. At the best, if he work hard, and cherish himself exceedingly, he may duplicate any or all previous performances of his kind; he may even do some of them better; but there he stops, the composite hand of his whole ancestry bearing heavily upon him. . . . The clay-born are a pitiful, pitiless majority.''[36]

"Again the Literary Aspirant" (*The Critic*, December 1902): "Whenever the mass is admitted into living, whenever the common men for the first time grip hold of life, there must follow a falling away from all that is fine of tone and usage, a diminishing, a descending to a something which is average, which is humanely average.''[37]

A Daughter of the Snows (1902): "The mass is nothing; the individual everything; and it is the individual, always, that rules the mass and gives the law.''[38]

London also called the masses miserable in "Revolution" (*The Contemporary Review*, January 1908),[39] published the same year as *The Iron Heel*.

As the Reverend Edward Biron Payne, who gave the oration at London's funeral recalled:

It may be that in the early days the young soap-box orator, who used to harangue the crowds at the Oakland street corners, was wont to voice the well-known ideals of socialism, especially its doctrine of the universal brotherhood of man. But under the influence of the materialistic evolutionary theories he later declared socialism not to be for all men impartially, but for an elect group of men, represented first of all by the Anglo-Saxon breed. For this order of men, he held, socialism would constitute a new way of industrial and administrative public life, which would give them a determining advantage in the great struggle for the possession and exploitation of the world. Sociologists and economists who object to socialism as a system which would fill the world with derelicts, incompetents and defectives, should take note of Jack London's conception of it. He apparently relegates these lower grades of humanity to destruction. The earth and its resources are not, he believes, for all sorts and conditions of men universally and impartially.[40]

London admitted this in *War of the Classes,* saying that "the capitalist must learn, first and for always, that socialism is based, not upon the equality, but upon the inequality of men." His solution to "lower grades of humanity" in "The Scab": that tramp "waste must be eliminated. Chloroform or electrocution would be a simple, merciful solution to this problem of elimination; but the ruling ethic, while permitting the human waste, will not permit a humane elimination of that waste."[41] London denied interest in the brotherhood of man in 1899 to Cloudesley Johns. Such attitudes hardly seem socialistic or humanistic, yet the mythomania surrounding London's image acclaim him champion of the underdog, the downtrodden, the waste existing on society's cellar floor.

While writhing over the working class and borderline derelicts, London also called for the elimination of American government, an anarchist view. According to Emma Goldman—whom he met several times, once inviting her to Glen Ellen—anarchism meant "the philosophy of a new social order based on liberty unrestrained by man-made laws. The theory that all governments rest on coercion and force, that they are therefore harmful and unnecessary."[42] The result of such a system is uncontrolled chaos and social disintegration, but London bought the idea. As early as 1895 he wrote in the *Oakland High School*

Aegis: "Our anarchists, socialists and labor leaders, with the great masses which they represent, are the components of that great tidal wave of humanity, which a few of our talented observers have already taken notice of and classified as the 'Coming Terror.' "[43] He also called himself a revolutionary during a 1905 speech in Boston. "I consider the Russian Nihilist assassins my comrades. . . . There are to-day over seven million people in the world enrolled with the sworn purpose of overthrowing society. When it is possible we work through the ballot boxes. In Russia we meet murder with assassination. I speak or think of these assassins as my comrades and would canonize them."[44]

Most theoretical anarchists like London and Emma Goldman exerted a corrosive influence on losers and malcontents. Take Emma Goldman. In early May 1901 she spoke at Cleveland, Ohio: "Under the galling yoke of government, ecclesiasticism, and a bond of custom and prejudice, it is impossible for the individual to work out his own career as he could wish. Anarchism aims at a new and complete freedom. It strives to bring about the freedom which is not only the freedom from within but a freedom from without, which will prevent any man from having a desire to interfere in any way with the liberty of his neighbor. . . . We merely desire complete individual liberty, and this can never be obtained as long as there is an existing government."

One mesmerized member of Emma Goldman's audience was Leon Czolgosz, a failure who assassinated President William McKinley on September 6, 1901, at the Pan-American Exposition in Buffalo, New York. Czolgosz later admitted: "I never had much luck at anything and this preyed upon me. It made me morose and envious, but what started the craze to kill was a lecture I heard some little time ago by Emma Goldman. She was in Cleveland and I and other Anarchists went to hear her. She set me on fire. Her doctrine that all rulers should be exterminated was what set me to thinking so that my ear nearly split with the pain. Miss Goldman's words went right through me and when I left the lecture I had made up my mind that I would have to do something heroic for the cause I loved." The same cause Jack London preached. What startled Czolgosz most after the murder? That Americans didn't make him a national hero. "I thought I would be killed and was surprised the way they treated me."[45] Emma Goldman's reaction when arrested for possible complicity in the assassination was to deny her identity. (Goldman's lover, by the way, was Alexander Berkman, who tried to assassinate Pittsburgh mogul Henry Clay Frick in the industrialist's office.)

London's handful of socialist short stories failed to advance the cause. "The Dream of Debs" involves a national strike that immobilizes the country, turning everyone into savages who ravage and kill for food—a favorite London theme. Terror also stalks through the pages of "The Strength of the Strong," a peculiar title for a socialist tract. In this narrative set in primordial times, Old Long Beard tells a parable about brutes who slayed those desiring a collective tribe. *The Bookman* called this "rather tedious, blatantly unreal, and to the reader who does not happen to share Mr. London's economic convictions, quite unimportant."[46] Both "Goliah" and "The Minions of Midas" propose seditious means of revolt. In "Goliah" an anarchist gains control of the world through a destructive substance, while in "The Minions of Midas" a secret organization demands millions from a magnate, killing innocent victims who ignore them.

"South of the Slot" is valuable because of Freddie Drummond, another London split personality, a sociology professor at the University of California by day, a class-conscious agitator by night. (Wolf Larsen in *The Sea Wolf*, Frona Welse in *A Daughter of the Snows*, and the two tenderfeet in "In a Far Country" are other London schizoids.) Freddie eventually abandons academe, although he's a prestigious author of sociological works, to become a labor leader who chooses the common girl over the bourgeois beauty. Most American socialists found more in *The Communist Manifesto* than a cry for machine guns and wholesale slaughter. Intellectuals advanced such municipal reforms as public baths, concerts, and refrainment from alcohol, tobacco, and promiscuity. The socialists'

reaction to "Revolution," London's firebrand essay first published in *The Contemporary Review*,[47] then included in *Revolution and Other Essays*, can only be conjectured. This became
his basic speech that startled thousands on the cross-country
tour.

Although American socialists tired of London's polemics, the
Russian proletarians read everything from *White Fang* to *Martin
Eden*, calling him "Yacklunnen." (Several countries, however,
ignored London's work. He whined to Brett in 1909 that British
publishers were scarce. The Germans also disliked his work,
and few royalties came from Australia and New Zealand.) Leo-
nid Andreyev and Maxim Gorky were among the first Russians
to promote London abroad, Andreyev calling him "the repre-
sentative of the Anglo-Saxon race, the race of doers. . . . the
enemy of impotence and decrepitude, of fruitless lamentation
and pity." Kuprin called him another Kipling, and Volsky
wrote: "dark, devious passion is the business of old Europe;
the American is enamored of force. Primitive love, primitive
hate, stubborn will, the storming of life, inability to generalize,
and a distrust of generalization—such is Jack London, for such
is America."[48]

All of Russia's intellectuals, however, didn't applaud London.
K. Chukovsky defined him as 'a Yankee, a salesman in a derby,
playing Zarathustra or Byron, and dealing in oceans, tempests,
Lucifers, prairies. Working for the firm of 'Struggle and Elemental Powers' he forces upon us all kinds of shop-worn stuff
which has been lying about on the European market since the
days of Chateaubriand."[49] During the twenties and thirties,
Russian critics became more suspect of London's inflated reputation, although the masses continued to buy his books. As
early as 1923, L. Rozenthal wrote that *The Iron Heel* did "not
belong among the author's best works." The more severe Din-
amov added in 1933: "*The Iron Heel* is a continuous cry of
despair, it is a retreat before the might of capitalism. . . . London, like Upton Sinclair now, tried to combine revolution with
evolution . . . and it is clear that he could not understand the
nature of revolution." Startsev further remarked in 1938: "Indeed, all of Jack London is in this contradictory combination
of hybrid elements: heroics, the pathos of struggle with nature

and human bravery which are close to us, and bourgeois individualistic motives which are alien to us." The 1932 *Literary Encyclopedia* said: "The socialism of London is merely a 'promised land' for which those who would save themselves from the misfortunes of capitalism yearn, while still dedicating themselves to the individualism of the petty bourgeois milieu."[50]

The Russians bought London's Klondike stories mainly because they voiced a sense of comradeship, but even this lacked full endorsement, the most famous instance being Lenin's response to several his daughter read shortly before his death.

Two days before his death I read to him in the evening a tale of Jack London, *Love of Life*—it is still lying on the table in his room. It was a very fine story. In a wilderness of ice, where no human being had set foot, a sick man, dying of hunger, is making for the harbour of a big river. His strength is giving out, he cannot walk but keeps slipping, and beside him there slides a wolf—also dying of hunger. There is a fight between them: the man wins. Half dead, half demented, he reaches his goal. That tale greatly pleased Ilyich. Next day he asked me to read him more Jack London. But London's strong pieces of work are mixed with extraordinary weak ones. The next tale happened to be of quite another type—saturated with bourgeois morals. Some captain promises the owner of a ship laden with corn to dispose of it at a good price: he sacrifices his life merely in order to keep his word. Ilyich smiled and dismissed it with a wave of his hand.

That was the last time I read to him.[51]

Chapter 8

The Dominant Primordial Beast

As EARLY AS 1901 London told Cloudesley Johns that he tired of writing Klondike stories, but because of public appeal, he continued creating endless cakes of ice, howling wolves, and frostbitten half-breeds, most tales poured into the same mold with predictable plots and terrifying ends. *McClure's* published "Love of Life" in 1906, nearly a decade after the gold rush. He wrote "To Build a Fire" during the *Snark*'s 1907–1908 South Seas cruise, and "The Return of Marcus O'Brien" appeared in 1908. One of his last stories, "Argus of the Ancient Times," retains the same tone and treatment as the first *Overland Monthly* pieces. Today London's fame still hangs on a handful of Klondike short stories and *The Call of the Wild*, the work that catapulted him to fame and American mythdom.

First serialized by *The Saturday Evening Post* between June 20 and July 18, 1903, then published by Macmillan, *The Call of the Wild* fulfilled Jack London's longtime ambition. "A name is a very excellent thing for a writer to possess; and the achievement of a name is an ambition which dominates every normal unknown who ever entered the field. The word 'normal' is used understandingly. Whether a materialist or an idealist, no normal writer is insensible to the benefits which accrue from such a possession. To the one it will give greater scope and opportunity for the gathering in of shekels; to the other, a larger hearing and a more authoritative rostrum."[1]

The Saturday Evening Post paid London three cents a word for the American serial rights to *The Call of the Wild,* amounting to around $700. Although Brett of Macmillan wanted exclusive rights, he contracted without them, persuading London to accept an outright $2,000, a figure both found fair. (Neither Brett nor the *Post* liked the title, Brett telling London it reminded him of Roberts's *Kindred of the North*) Macmillan then "pushed" the novelette, spending thousands on deluxe bindings, beautiful illustrations, and promotion—editorial treatment authors dream about. After its release, London praised the layouts, even telling Brett he hoped Macmillan would find it profitable. *The Call of the Wild* represented one of the biggest breaks in the history of publishing, and because of "chance," that elusive element in Horatio Alger's fortune formula, paid off. London's first five books before *The Call of the Wild,* all published by different houses, received lukewarm receptions. Carl Van Doren thought that London "never rose above his first marked success, *The Call of the Wild,*"[2] which is probably true, considering the disastrous *A Daughter of the Snows,* a 1902 prelude to several dozen potboilers. It was as hard to sell novels in 1903 as it is today. Few became bombshells. Henry Holt once said that in forty years only two novels that he published made reputable profits! He compared best-sellers to playing the lottery.

The Athenaeum, in its 1903 review of *Children of the Frost,* suggested: "If the author would be well advised (there is a cocksure note about his work, a fluent complacence, which makes one doubt the likelihood) he would write nothing more for at least a year or two, and in the meantime set himself to read a good deal of the genuine masters of prose. . . . The stories, some of which are in themselves good, are full of strange and graceless locutions, crude affectations, and astonishing misuse of 'dictionary words.' "[3]

Critics made similar remarks about *Moon Face* (1906), *The Independent* calling London "a great disappointment."[4] *The Nation* also criticized: "These stories present Jack London at his shallowest, but by no means at his worst. Everything in them, even their brutality is subordinated to a trivial ingenuity of plot. With the exception of the longest of them, 'Planchette,' they are not dull; but they do not reassure us that this writer is what he was hailed to be when first he flashed upon our ken; a second Kipling. We would suggest as a sub-title, 'Diversions of a Literary Bounder.' "[5]

In 1907 *The Athenaeum* remarked in its review of *White Fang*: "We note, however, that Mr. London does not write so well now as when his first book appeared. . . . His tale is packed full of absurdly precious idioms, literary clichés, and pompous little mannerisms."[6]

Things got worse, not better, and most important magazines failed to review his books during the last years. In 1913 *Current Opinion* made a cutting comment on *The Night-Born*: "Jack London has recently informed a listening world that he could do much more work if only he did not sleep so much. We are sometimes tempted to wish that Mr. London would not sleep a little longer but not work quite so hard when he is awake; in other words that he would stop and think a little more. Then he might really become a great American storyteller (for he has the gift), and not merely a popular romancer."[7]

The $2,700 London received for *The Call of the Wild* provided enough cash in 1903 to live well for several years, a figure higher than many present novels return. (Mario Puzo made $6,500 from two novels before *The Godfather*.) According to *John Barleycorn*, London had stormed *The Overland Monthly* offices a few years earlier, threatening to whip its editors for $5! London, by the way, told George Brett that he earned around $150 a month from magazine contributions, giving him a solid middle-class income at the time.[8] One thing he wasn't: broke and starving. The brilliant Stephen Crane received $90 for the serialization of *The Red Badge of Courage* from the *Philadelphia Press,* lamenting in the fall of 1893, "I'd trade my entire future for twenty three dollars in cash."[9] S. S. McClure, whose magazine helped revolutionize American publishing, recalled, "I remember at one time I agreed to select and file newspaper clippings for the librarian for $3.50 a week."[10] And Richard Harding Davis got $7 a week for writing nearly twenty assignments a day at the *Philadelphia Press*—after publishing a book. Malcolm Cowley recalls that in the 1920s "freelance work was paid for at the rate of about a penny a word for reviews. *The New Republic* and *The Dial* paid *two* cents; that was high, and besides, you were always glad to be printed in *The New Republic* or *The Dial.*"[11]

Critics gave *The Call of the Wild* good reviews, several of which follow.

The Atlantic Monthly: "*The Call of the Wild* is a story altogether untouched by bookishness. A bookish writer might, beginning with the title, have called it An Instance of Atavism, or A Reversion to Type. A bookish reader might conceivably read it as a sort of allegory with a broad human application; but its face value as a single-minded study of animal nature really seems to be sufficiently considerable."[12]

The Bookman: "As for *The Call of the Wild,* It may be summed up simply by saying that it is far and away the best book that Mr. Jack London has ever written."[13]

The Critic: "Buck will live long among the dogs of literature, if, indeed, he does not 'lead the team.' "[14]

Current Literature: "This is by far the best piece of work which has come from the pen of this gifted author. . . . The book rises above mere story telling, and possesses elements of the best in literature—scope, vitality, and fulness."[15]

The Athenaeum: "It is the best thing the public has had so far from the pen of a young author who, though he made his first bow but yesterday, has already shown a fresh and vigorous bent in story, combined with a certain amount of originality and dramatic power."[16]

The Dial: "Mr. Jack London has certainly done a clever and appealing piece of work in *The Call of the Wild,* which must rank high among animal stories and, *pace* Mr. Burroughs, is made sufficiently convincing to dull skepticism while it is being read. Doubts arise afterwards, and they are probably legitimate, but while the spell of the story is upon us, we are willing to allow that a dog may have the complex inner life which is here depicted."[17]

Why did *The Call of the Wild* become a phenomenal bestseller? To answer this is to answer the success of Mother Goose or Kahlil Gibran. Chance played a key role in London's jackpot novelette. Macmillan's massive push also planted seeds in the public's mind. Its subject matter—dogs—helped a lot. "In the many years of my incumbency as a magazine editor, it was a general, and occasionally embarrassing, fact that any even half-way good dog story usually attracted wider attention among the readers," recalled George Jean Nathan, "and certainly a lot more enthusiastic letters to the editor—than almost anything else, however highly creditable to the art of belles-lettres, in the particular issue."[18] In *The Call of the Wild: 1900–1916*, a study of American culture between 1900 and 1916, Roderick Nash offers another reason for Buck's bonanza:

> In the case of *The Call of the Wild* the significance is comparatively clear. The book is an allegory; it deals with dogs but pertains to men. In describing Buck's progress from tameness to wildness, the author passed judgment on his contemporaries. They too, he implied, suffered from overcivilization, and in the early 1900s the idea struck a sympathetic chord. For many the growth and change of the United States over the previous hundred years seemed to have brought not the millennium once expected but rather a state of confusion, corruption, and debilitating abundance. For such people, Buck's simple, vigorous, unrestrained life in the North was very appealing. As the twentieth century dawned, the nation found itself drawn toward virility, toward novelty, toward nature. Significantly, London's *White Fang* (1906) in which a wolf became a family dog, never enjoyed the popularity of *The Call of the Wild*.[19]

An earlier short story called "Diable, A Dog" (*Cosmopolitan*, June 1902) became London's prototype for *The Call of the Wild*. James I. McClintock calls this diabolical tale "a place of horrors that is grotesque because the 'abnormal' has become the universal norm. Evil has become the active force in man and the cosmos."[20] (Diable means devil.)

London pits two demons against each other in "Diable, A Dog": Black Leclère, a Klondiker whose "upper lip had a wolfish way of lifting and showing the white, cruel teeth," and his monstrous devil-dog Diable, known everywhere as "Hell's Spawn." For five years "the very breath each drew was a challenge and a menace to the other. Their hate bound them together as love could never bind." The sadistic Black Leclère beats and whips Diable, even breaking his ribs, yet he refuses to sell the beast, protecting him from both humans and wild animals. Both hunger for revenge, finally clashing:

It was a primordial setting and a primordial scene, such as might have been in the savage youth of the world. An open space in a dark forest, a ring of grinning wolf-dogs, and in the centre two beasts, locked in combat, snapping and snarling, raging madly about, panting, sobbing, cursing, straining, wild with passion, in a fury of murder, ripping and tearing and clawing in elemental brutishness.

Black Leclère, later found guilty of murder by Klondikers, discovers himself on a cracker box, ready for the noose. When vigilantes locate the real killer, they leave Black Leclère tottering on the flimsy crate. The fiendish Diable "faced about and paused. He showed his white teeth in a grin, which Leclère answered; and then hurled his body through the air, in full charge, straight for the box."[21]

The Call of the Wild, expanded from "Diable, A Dog," opens on a restful note, Buck living "at a big house in the sun-kissed Santa Clara Valley. Judge Miller's place it was called," a far cry from the savage wilderness of Diable and Black Leclère. (The real-life Buck belonged to Louis Bond, someone London knew at Dawson during the gold rush, and Louis's father, Judge Bond, owned the Santa Clara Valley ranch.) Reading into the story, one soon realizes that Buck symbolizes Jack London's Anglo-Saxon theories and harsh racist views. Buck lives "the life of a sated aristocrat" on the ranch, having "a fine pride in himself, was ever a trifle egotistical, as country gentlemen sometimes become because of their insular situation." He's "king over all creeping, crawling, flying things of Judge Miller's place, humans included," something especially true regarding "Toots, the Japanese pug, or Ysabel, the Mexican hairless,—strange creatures that rarely put nose out of doors or set foot to ground."[22]

Instead of evolving according to the progressivism of Herbert Spencer and Benjamin Kidd, Buck regresses, both morally and socially, London hinting this in the novelette's prefatory poem: "Old longings nomadic leap,/Chafing at custom's chain;/Again from its brumal sleep/Wakens the ferine strain." When conditions awaken primitive instincts, civilization's surface veneer vanishes, leaving an atavistic brute who survives through raw physical strength. This happens to Buck through Manuel, a gardener's helper on the Miller ranch, who kidnaps the "high-strung and finely sensitive" dog, selling him to money-grubbers as a Klondike sled dog. The trusting Buck, thrown into the primitive, soon learns a big lesson: "that club was a revelation. . . . A man with a club was a lawgiver, a master to be obeyed, though not necessarily conciliated."[23] Pain teaches this lesson. Thereafter Buck avoids the club through cunning and dominance of weaker creatures, leaving them to suffer his savage abuses and exploitations.

Two French-Canadians, Perrault and Francois, eventually buy Buck, taking him to the Yukon. As he does Charley and the Malemute Kid, London sketches these half-breeds sympathetically, particularly Francois, who makes moccasins for Buck's sensitive feet, saves him several times from the treacherous dogs, and weeps when they part. Buck learns fast in this white wilderness. "They were savages, all of them, who knew no law but the law of club and fang." When the gentle Curly, "a good-natured Newfoundland," is devoured alive, "screaming with agony, beneath the bristling mass of bodies," the second law is implanted on Buck's sharp mind: "So that was the way. No fairplay. Once down, that was the end of you. Well, he would see to it that he never went down."[24] The dog Spitz, who laughs at Curly's horrible end, becomes the archenemy of Buck, each waiting for a chance to kill the other.

Once Buck realizes what operates on Yukon ice, he becomes a thief, stealing to live in this "dog eat dog" world on the edge of civilization, where one needs strength, imagination, and the ability to adapt to changing environmental conditions, something Curly lacked. Violent death becomes the ultimate fate of inferiors. As the narrator says in "The Wisdom of the Trail," "I, I, I, want to exist!—the dominant note of the whole living universe."[25] So Buck becomes a bully, an agitator who undermines "the solidarity of the team.... it was a greater delight slyly to precipitate a fight amongst his mates and tangle the traces." When he finally kills Spitz, he realizes that "mercy was a thing reserved for gentler climes. . . . Buck stood and looked on, the successful champion, the dominant primordial beast who had made his kill and found it good."[26]

As Buck's muscles toughen through the toil of traces, his sense of morality weakens, while instincts strengthen. Past harkings of the forests primeval begin to possess his will. "The

domesticated generations fell from him. In vague ways he remembered back to the youth of the breed, to the time the wild
dogs ranged in packs through the primeval forest and killed
their meat as they ran it down. It was no task for him to learn
to fight with cut and slash and the quick wolf snap. In this
manner had fought forgotten ancestors."[27]

Diable also muses about past howling ages of the world's
youth when weaklings cringed in fear. "The philosophy of *The
Call of the Wild* consists in a glorification of sheer strength and
cunning," writes Walter Fuller Taylor. "London's hero is—
insofar as human traits can be attributed to a dog—a savage
individualist, exulting with the strength of the strong in the
struggle for existence, fighting his way to mastery with the
ruthlessness of the dominant primordial brute."[28] Philo C. Buck,
who wrote a scathing essay in the *Methodist Review* on London,
called him "The American Barbarian," saying: "He is an atavism. But it is this very return to the primitive in the present,
like the romantic stories of the strenuous day of the past, that
arouses the enthusiasm of hero-worshiping youth. It is this that
explains the huge popularity of such stories as *The Sea Wolf,
The Call of the Wild, Burning Daylight,* and even *Martin Eden.*
Their 'elemental strength,' as a critic phrases it, their war
against the conventions of society, their love of combat, their
delight in pure physical existence—in a word, their essential
barbarity is cause sufficient for their magnetic hold upon our
imaginations."[29]

While Buck dreams about hairy cavemen and senses nature's
primal call of the wild, he passes through the hands of several
more masters, including a Scotch half-breed, then three tinhorns—Hal, Charles, and Mercedes, all symbolic of decadent
civilization. These losers first feed the dogs too much, then too
little, and Mercedes—another of London's weak-minded women—
adds to the dogs' exhaustion by riding on the sleigh. When her
husband and brother remove her, "she let her legs go limp like
a spoiled child, and sat down on the trail. . . . And through it
all Buck staggered along at the head of the team as in a nightmare." They finally reach the mouth of White River, where
John Thornton cuts Buck's traces, forcing them to continue
without him. When a section of ice collapses, they're killed,

vanishing into the Yukon's yawning jaws, their terrible death
ignored by John Thornton, who merely looks at Buck, saying:
"You poor devil."[30] And Buck licks his hand.

John Thornton becomes Buck's ideal master, London calling
this chapter "For the Love of Man." Written from Buck's point
of view, however, the true nature of Thornton, another London
"hairy" loser, becomes blurred. (In one paragraph he repeats
the word "hairy" five times, stressing the man's primitivism,
saying he "seemed as much at home among the trees as on the
ground." Like Hans and Pete, his two partners, Thornton lives
close to nature, a clear thinker unafraid, yet accident-prone like
London, who even told Brett about his many mishaps on the
Glen Ellen ranch. Thornton loafs away the months. (Hans and
Pete left him behind the previous December after a foot-freezing
accident.) Buck saves him twice, once from Black Burton in
a barroom knockdown, the second time from rapids, both courageous canine acts of devotion. But Thornton shows thought-
less concern for Buck, once asking him to jump off a cliff, a
command the dog begins to obey. Reduced to their last two
hundred dollars, Thornton and his partners hope to win sixteen
hundred dollars, boasting Buck could do the impossible: start
a thousand pounds on a frozen sled. Buck achieves this tor-
turous feat, of course, as Thornton follows the sled, "cursing
Buck, and he cursed him long and fervently, and softly and
lovingly."[31] (London based the sled race on an actual happening,
detailed in "Husky—The Wolf Dog of the North" [*Harper's
Weekly*, June 30, 1900].)[32]

Greedy for gold and using the $1,600, the three men start east
"after a fabled lost mine," spending nearly two years tracing
it, then luckily find "a shallow placer in a broad valley where
the gold showed like yellow butter across the bottom of the
washing pan." While Buck runs free through the forests, "a
killer, a thing that preyed, living on the things that lived, un-
aided, alone by virtue of his own strength and prowess, sur-
viving triumphantly in a hostile environment where only the
strong survived," Yeehat Indians surprise the three men, who
failed to post a guard, and slaughter them. Returning to camp,
satiated with nature's throbbing call that takes him into the wild
for longer and longer periods, Buck scatters the Indians, killing

several, which possesses him with an exhilarating sense of ecstasy: "He had killed man, the noblest game of all, and he had
killed in the face of the law of club and fang. He sniffed the
bodies curiously. They had died so easily. It was harder to kill
a husky dog than them. They were no match at all, were it not
for their arrows and spears and clubs."[33]

His ties severed with civilization, Buck becomes a legendary
Ghost Dog, an Evil Spirit, creating a superior strain of animal
by mating with a wolf. (This, of course, contradicts London's
theory that crossbreeds perpetuate inferior stock.) London ends
The Call of the Wild with his most famous lines: "But he is not
always alone. When the long winter nights come on and the
wolves follow their meat into the lower valleys, he may be seen
running at the head of the pack through the pale moonlight or
glimmering borealis, leaping gigantic above his fellows, his great
throat a-bellow as he sings a song of the younger world, which
is the song of the pack."[34]

London's absorption with nature's "dominant primordial
beasts," his work roving between the worlds of romance and
raw primitivism, borders on the ridiculous, the kind of thing H.
L. Mencken called "muck for the multitudes." This even mars
The Call of the Wild, in which Buck dreams about a caveman
sitting around an ancient fire, sometimes scurrying up trees for
protection from wild beasts. "The hair of this man was long
and matted, and his head slanted back under it from the eyes.
He uttered strange sounds, and seemed very much afraid of the
darkness, into which he peered continually, clutching in his
hand, which hung midway between knee and foot, a stick with
a heavy stone made fast to the end. He was all but naked, a
ragged and fire-scorched skin hanging part way down his back,
but on his body there was much hair."[35] (London later wrote
a pulpish novelette called *Before Adam,* which elaborates on
the nature of primitive man. He told Brett kids would like it.)

After London's remarks in "Revolution" that cavemen loafed,
generally ate well, and breathed fresh air, their children enjoying
the good life, critics raved, the *Berkeley Advance* roasting his
idea that "the man who crawled in and out of a hole in the hill
was better fed than millions of people today."[36] The *San Francisco Chronicle* jeered:

Jack London declares that the cave dweller was much better off than the laboring man of today. He thinks that the mental and material welfare of the latter would be improved by reverting to the anarchism which prevailed in the days of the cave dwellers, and insists that there are today seven million people in the world enrolled with the sworn purpose of overthrowing society. If there are so many avowed enemies of society as London declares, they ought to be able to form a big enough colony in some part of the world to furnish a practical demonstration of the beauties of their ism. The chances are if such a colony should ever be formed it would not be in existence long before society would have to step in to prevent its members cutting each other's throats.[37]

Why London's interest in cavedom? It certainly didn't embrace the period's "return to nature" talk, an American pipe dream since the time of Thoreau. Perhaps *The Bookman* explained: "It is the animal side of human nature that Mr. London always delights in exalting, in all the relations of life."[38] In such a woeful world, man's fighting instinct dominates, so does human depravity. Ethics become absurd, man's assurance of broken bones and starving stomachs. Primitivism also negates the spine of Herbert Spencer's credo that humanity evolves, not devolves. Regression, of course, spells out decay, another central London theme, from Alaska's white wilderness to the decayed tropical vegetation of South Sea islands—a peculiar slant during America's strenuous age of Rooseveltian virility and optimism.

The period's literary preoccupation with European naturalism, which often reduced men to wild, elemental beasts, provided a popular framework for London's primitivism, which Frederick J. Hoffman calls "an interesting sideshow in the naturalistic carnival."[39] London compared one of the mob's hands in *The Iron Heel* to claws and hoofs. A Goat-Man and Fish-Man play roles in *The Son of the Sun*. Humphrey Van Weyden and Maud Brewster revive "like bugs and crawling things"[40] on their deserted island. The narrator of "Li Wan, the Fair" comments: "And over all, like a monstrous race of ants, was flung an army of men—mud-covered, dirty, dishevelled men, who crawled in and out of the holes of their digging, crept like

big bugs along the flumes."[41] In "The End of the Story," a
rabbit bone is grafted to a man's arm, creating the perfect limb.
And in *The People of the Abyss,* London compares the submerged tenth to wolves and other animals of prey, calling one
boy "a young cub seeking his food in the jungle of empire,
preying upon the weak and being preyed upon by the strong."[42]

Such remarks support London's view, one stated in such
articles as "The Somnambulists"[43] that beneath the skin, man
and beast share common inheritances. Remove civilized man
to a remote region? He's soon reduced to an elemental force,
devoid of values, stalking food to survive. "Morals are not the
important thing, nor enlightenment—nor civilization," said
Mark Twain. "A man can do absolutely well without them, but
he can't do without *something to eat.* The supremest thing is
the needs of the body, not of the mind & spirit."[44] London
illustrates this in "Bâtard, a Dog." It also happens to the peaceful Buck in *The Call of the Wild.* Man even resembles the
beasts, assuming their physical features, their instinctual behavior. "What with the Fear of the North, the mental strain,
and the ravages of the disease," wrote London in "In a Far
Country," "they lost all semblance of humanity, taking on the
appearance of wild beasts, hunted and desperate."[45] Both Buck
and White Fang are men dressed in furs. When they brutally
maim and devour opponents, London means humans, releasing
complex hostilities in his makeup against the world, hostilities
again traced to his birth and feelings of inferiority. Even Macmillan Company admitted this in *Jack London: His Life and
Literary Works*: "In his two most important books, *The Call
of the Wild,* and *White Fang,* he has reduced thought and
emotion to their lowest terms. He has dared to treat animals
like human beings—not symbolically, be it noted, but realisti-
cally and naturally—because he recognizes no essential difference between the so-called lower animals and man."[46]

Other American authors heard naturalism's call, including
Theodore Dreiser and Frank Norris, without the pathological
overtones. Dreiser details in *Sister Carrie*:

> Our civilization is still in a middle stage, scarcely beast, in that
> it is no longer wholly guided by instinct; scarcely human, in that

it is not yet wholly guided by reason. On the tiger no responsibility rests. We see him aligned by nature with the forces of life—he is born into their keeping and without thought he is protected. We see man far removed from the lairs of the jungle, his innate instincts dulled by too near an approach to free will, his free will not sufficiently developed to replace his instincts and afford him perfect guidance. He is becoming too wise to hearken always to instincts and desires; he is still too weak to always prevail against them. As a beast, the forces of life aligned him with them; as a man, he has not yet wholly learned to align himself with the forces. In this intermediate stage he wavers— neither drawn in harmony with nature by his instincts nor yet wisely putting himself into harmony by his own free will.[47]

In *McTeague* Frank Norris compares McTeague's jaw to "that of the carnivora," adding that "every other Sunday he became an irresponsible animal, a beast, a brute, crazy with alcohol. Zerkow, the Polish Jew in *McTeague,* "had the thin, eager, cat-like lips of the covetous; eyes that had grown keen as those of a lynx from long searching amidst muck and debris; and clawlike prehensile fingers."[48] Ernest Marchant, Norris's biographer, says: "Frank Norris is by every right the founder of the red-blooded school in America. . . . Norris' immediate successor was Jack London, who owed much to him."[49]

Psychological depth, however, separated the work of Jack London from Frank Norris, whose McTeague, for example, remains a highly textured literary figure, a human being with inner feelings and motives, a crude character, yet one who involves readers in his personal life-conflict. London, on the other hand, sets scenes in primitive societies, where animals and atavists like Wolf Larsen survive through brute force, instead of reason, which involves moral decisions and accountability for one's acts. Savage romances. As Theodore Dreiser remarked: "I have read several short stories which proved what he could do. But he did not feel that he wanted want and public indifference. Hence his many excellent romances."[50] And Sherwood Anderson echoed that London "became merely a romancer and, I think, has not had any very definite influence on the march of literature. Such men, while their work is very fine in some respects, are outside the great tradition. They are, I presume, romancers rather than artists."[51]

London told Brett in 1904 that he planned a companion piece to *The Call of the Wild*, a story in which he would reverse the atavistic process, letting a wolf-dog raised in the white wilderness become domesticated on a California ranch. Although magazines like *Harper's* offered ten cents a word for serialization, they also wanted book publication rights; these belonged to Macmillan, who offered London 15 percent royalties on the first 5,000 copies and 20 percent thereafter, a rarity today. London called this book *White Fang*. It sold over 400,000 copies.

As in *The Call of the Wild*, London hewed a convulsive "dog eat dog" world of raw violence—literal and figurative—in which the strongest of the strong survive, leaving the weak, old, and infirm to be eaten alive. A hawk digs its sharp talons into the soft flesh of a ptarmigan, while the frenzied bird screams in agony; the weasel, a drinker of blood, sucks life from the throat of smaller creatures; the once powerful moose falls to the she-wolf, like some men. (This she-wolf, who refuses to let One-eye touch the cubs in her nest, afraid he'll devour them, contains parallels to Bessie who, according to London, wouldn't let him touch Joan or Bess after his trips to San Francisco whorehouses with George Sterling.) Man, who lights the fire and carries clubs, stands highest in nature's chain. He is god, the lawgiver in this Nietzschean slave-master system, someone dictating the destiny of nature's creatures who live by instinct, rather than superior intelligence. Both Buck and White Fang learn to exist in this primitive place of ice and snow on the edge of civilization through submission to their master's will, but craftily erode order among the other dogs through "tough" tactics, then shift the blame on them. Unlike Buck, however, White Fang is a loner, a fearful killer despised by men and beasts.

"Mr. London has fortunately obeyed the call of the wild and returned to the field of his early triumphs," wrote *The Independent*. "This is quite a relief after the mediocre short stories he has been giving us of late. He apparently understands the psychology of brutes, animal and human, better than ordinary tamed and civilized men and women."[52] "This is the kind of thing Jack London does best," added *The Nation*. "In this atmosphere he wears neither his street swagger nor his distressing company manners. As a biographer of wild animals he has hardly an equal."[53] *The Bookman* admired the illustrations by Charles Livingston Bull, commenting that the book was "full of blood and death, rough, rugged strength, horror and beastliness, passing glimpses of kindliness and love."[54] *The Dial* compared *White Fang* to *The Call of the Wild*, concluding that "there is as much that goes against the reader's sympathy in one book as in the other; but because the story of White Fang ends happily, much of the cruelty in it will be forgiven and forgotten."[55] Which is what happened. *The Forum* even detected socialistic overtones: "It would be an exaggeration to call this novel a Socialistic tract in disguise, but it is certainly not the least clever stroke of its author's that he has succeeded in interweaving into a dog-and-wolf story so subtle a reminder of the pressure of feral conditions in the midst of civilized human society."[56]

For all its furious action and bloodlust, *White Fang* becomes a sedate dog romance. The moment a character, whether man or beast, becomes imprisoned by civilization in a London book, its credibility slips. Once White Fang reaches ordered California climates, he grows lazy like Burning Daylight, whose paunch bulges. White Fang becomes the father of playful pups, although he foils a convict who tries to rob Judge Scott's home, killing the man. This frightful conclusion again reinforces London's vision of a chaotic universe: an inmate from San Quentin, the victim of White Fang's force, has been falsely imprisoned by Judge Scott, the true social criminal.

Like thousands of other Americans, President Theodore Roosevelt read *White Fang* and bristled at each page, because the public believed London truthfully depicted animal behavior in the Klondike. "You will be pleased to know that I finally proved unable to contain myself, and gave an interview of statement, to a very good fellow, in which I sailed into Long and Jack London and one or two others of the more preposterous writers of 'unnatural' history,'' Roosevelt wrote a friend. "It will be coming out soon, but I do not know in which magazine." He concluded, "I know that as President I ought not to do this; but I was having an awful time toward the end of the session and felt I simply had to permit myself some diversion."[57] The article called "Roosevelt and the Nature Fakirs" appeared in *Everybody's Magazine.*

Take the chapter from Jack London's "White Fang" that tells the story of a fight between the great northern wolf, White Fang, and a bulldog. Reading this, I can't believe that Mr. London knows much about the wolves, and I am certain that he knows nothing about their fighting, or as a realist he would not tell this tale. Here is a great wolf of the northern breed; its strength is such that with one stroke it can hamstring a horse or gut a steer, and yet it is represented as ripping, and slashing . . . again and again and again a bulldog, not much more than a third its size, and the bulldog, which should be in ribbons, keeps on fighting without having suffered any appreciable injury. This thing is the very sublimity of absurdity. In such a fight the chance for the dog would be only one in a thousand, its victory being possibly only through getting a throat grip the instant that the fight started. This kind of realism is a closet product.

In the same book London describes a great dog-wolf torn to pieces by a lucivee, a northern lynx. This is about as sensible as to describe a tom cat tearing in pieces a thirty-pound fighting bull terrier. Nobody who really knew anything about either a lynx or a wolf would write such nonsense. Now, I don't want to be misunderstood. If the stories of these writers were written in the spirit that inspired Mowgli and we were told tales like those of the animals at the Council Rock, of their deliberations and their something more than human conclusions, we should know that we were getting the very essence of fable and we should be content to read, enjoy, and accept them as fables. We don't in the least mind impossibilities in avowed fairy tales; and Bagheera and Baloo and Kaa are simply delightful variants of Prince Charming and Jack the Slayer of Giants. But when such fables are written by a make-believe realist, the matter assumes an entirely different complexion. Men who have visited the haunts of the wild beasts, who have seen them, and have learned at least something of their ways, resent such gross falsifying of nature's record.[58]

All this rankled London, who retaliated in *Collier's*.[59] He attacked Roosevelt's ideas about animals, admitting his exaggeration of dog heroics in earlier stories, but denied the president's "Fakir" award. London also attacked Roosevelt's remark that a lynx killed a wolf-dog in *White Fang*, denying the inclusion of the incident. Roosevelt, in a letter to Mark Sullivan, had fumed about the lynx's victory over White Fang, adding that someone recently returned from an Alaskan winter in the region London mentioned, found that female lynxes weighed around twenty pounds. Yet London allowed a fighting wolf, weighing six or seven times as much, to be defeated in battle. Roosevelt suggested, "Mr. London should take the trouble to read what he himself has written before he again makes a denial of this type."[60] London, taking his advice, reread *White Fang*—discovering it included the incident. Calling his own textual perceptions lousy, he admitted to *Collier's* editor that three fights occurred in the novelette with lynxes, not one, rationalizing the clash Roosevelt mentioned took one line.

London also misinformed readers about animal behavior in *The Call of the Wild*. Buck, returning to the spoils of a kill, finds a dozen wolverines, among nature's most vicious creatures. "He scattered them like chaff; and those that fled left two behind who would quarrel no more."[61] (London used *wolves* and *wolverines* interchangeably in his stories, not realizing that vicious wolverines would have slaughtered White Fang.) Buck also beats an entire wolf pack. In the 1918 posthumous *Michael, Brother of Jerry*, Michael, a fox terrier puppy, breaks the back of a gigantic Persian cat, its tail the size of a muscle man's arm, then takes on two full-grown fox terriers, crushing the foot of one and nearly severing the other's jugular vein. He even leaves the ship's captain bleeding on deck. As Theodore Roosevelt reasoned: "The modern 'nature faker' is of course an object of derision to every scientist worthy of the name, to every real lover of the wilderness, to every faunal naturalist, to every true hunter or nature lover. But it is evident that he completely deceives many good people who are wholly

ignorant of wild life. Sometimes he draws on his own imagination for his fictions; sometimes he gets them second-hand
from irresponsible guides or trappers or Indians."[62]

The wolf remains Jack London's most outrageous deception,
an animal he associated with cunning, fierce strength, and legendary inheritance traced to Romulus and Remus. "In spite of
our sober biological outlook," writes Barry Lopez, "we can't
seem to escape our fear of . . . [the wolf] hunter, any more than
we can deny a fondness for the . . . [animal] because he seems
to represent valued things that are slipping away from us—
courage, wildness, self-sufficiency. Our fascination with the
wolf may be rooted in a perception of him as the symbol of an
internal war, the conflict between rational and instinctual behavior. This is the wolf of Aesopian fable."[63] Lopez adds in
Of Wolves and Men that "London's novels show a preoccupation with 'the brute nature' in men, which he symbolized in
the wolf. . . . But it is, ultimately, a neurotic fixation with mach-
ismo that has as little to do with wolves as the drinking, whoring,
and fighting side of man's brute nature."[64]

In London stories, wolves track adventurers across Klondike
trails, sniffing blood stains on the virgin snow, devouring them
alive. In "The Story of Jess Uck," Neil Bonner brings a brute
into his post, "but the beast, mere domesticated wolf that it
was, rebelled, and sought out dark corners and snarled and bit
him in the leg, and was finally beaten and driven forth."[65] Old
Kooskoosh, of course, is eaten alive by wolves in "The Law
of Life." "He saw the flashing forms of gray, the gleaming
eyes, the lolling tongues, and slavered fangs. . . . A cold muzzle
thrust against his cheek. . . . He waved his brand wildly, and
sniffs turned to snarls; but the panting brutes refused to scatter.
Now one wormed his chest forward, dragging his haunches
after, now a second, now a third; but never a one drew back."[66]
In "Love of Life," a sick man and sick wolf try to outwit each
other, the man finally strangling the anemic beast, sucking blood
from its throat. London spent an entire chapter in *White Fang*
on wolves: After eating Henry's partner, the pack chase Henry
across the white wilderness, snarling and salivating, leaping at
limbs and throat in camp. A fire frightens them until help miraculously arrives at dawn.

Millions of Americans swallowed London's cruel fantasies as truth, not realizing human beings terrify wolves. "In North America, no scientifically acceptable evidence is available to support the claim that healthy wild wolves are dangerous to man," writes L. David Mech in *The Wolf*. "Even stronger evidence that healthy North American wolves are harmless to humans can be found in the many well-documented accounts of various researchers who have worked in wolf country. . . . In my own experiences with wolves I have never come close to danger."[67]

Farley Mowat tells this story in *Never Cry Wolf*: "Quite by accident I had pitched my tent within ten yards of one of the major paths used by the wolves when they were going to, or coming from, their hunting grounds to the westward; and only a few hours after I had taken up residence one of the wolves came back from a trip and discovered me and my tent. . . . It was true that I wanted to be inconspicuous, but I felt uncomfortable at being so totally ignored. Nevertheless, during the two weeks which followed, one or more wolves used the track past my tent almost every night—and never, except on one memorable occasion, did they evince the slightest interest in me."[68]

Naturalist-cinematographer Bill Mason, who filmed "Cry of the Wild" for the Canadian Wildlife Services, writes me: "My captive wolves were terrified of me, despite all my efforts to befriend them. Only pups taken from the mother before two weeks old could be tamed and raised to accept the presence of humans without fear. If there is one single thing that I learned from all my experiences with wolves, it's that I would stake unequivocally that wolves are terrified of people. In fact I staked my life on it by travelling unarmed among them and alone. The only dangers I faced were from the extreme cold."[69]

Perhaps Roger A. Caras (author of *The Custer Wolf*, ABC-TV news correspondent and former vice-president of The Humane Society of the United States) makes the most penetrating remark about London and wolves, writing me that London was "an incurable romantic whose truth was instantly made and served up as needed. . . . He was not an authority on wolves, dogs, people, places or truth. He wrote and they bought it so

he wrote some more."[70] Caras comments about London's Yukon stories: "He certainly was also devoted to the macho image.
I have been around sled dogs (I cared for a championship team)
and I have been in the Arctic and in Eskimo villages. It is rather
more peaceful than super jock Jack London portrays."[71]

An obsession with wolves haunted London's life, another
expression of his pathological involvement with symbols of fear
and violence. As Sidney Alexander says, "The trouble with
Jack London was that he wasn't sure whether he was a man
or a wolf."[72] London used the name in the title of two books:
The Sea Wolf and *The Son of the Wolf,* dedicating *The God
of His Fathers* "to the daughters of the wolf who have bred
and suckled a race of men." He also wrote a short story called
"Brown Wolf," a pet husky's name. *White Fang* is called "The
Fighting Wolf." Burning Daylight sleeps beneath wolfskins.
Other characters wear wolfskin caps. Thomas Regan in *Hearts
of Three* is called "The Wolf of Wall Street." London had a
wolf's head on his engraved stationery and bookmarks, signed
his letters "Wolf," and named his sprawling ranch at Glen Ellen
"Wolf House." George Sterling called him "Wolf,"—something he asked Charmian to do more often. "In all his writings
Jack London is changing dogs into wolves and wolves into
dogs," remarked Stephen Graham. "In the course of it all London himself became a civilized dog, reconciled to kennel and
master. But he constantly bays at men and the moon to assure
them that he is wolf at heart."[73]

Chapter 9

The Cult of Red Blood

THEODORE ROOSEVELT'S "nature faking" charges aroused other writers such as naturalist Arthur Stringer, who ridiculed London's amphibious fish in "Love of Life." "Either there are indeed amphibious fish in the Valley of the Coppermine, or the laws of gravitation fail to operate in their usual manner in this strange country of the North." He also faulted the open water holes that didn't freeze in temperatures of fifty degrees below zero, trainers who commanded "Marche!" to huskies instead of "Mush On!" and the birchbark sled that transported four hundred pounds of freight in *White Fang*, which Stringer said would have had the strength of tar paper. "Yet if he knew this country as he claims to do, he would never make the fatal mistake of substituting birch-bark for birch-wood."[1]

Stringer concluded: "The sin that lies darkest at Mr. London's door, let me hasten to add, is not one of mere local color and detail, such as I have mentioned. It is, rather that general and persistent tendency to 'foreigneer' things, to translate everything northern into the lurid. The map of the North must be all red or nothing. Everything above the forty-ninth parallel must be written down as blood and raw beef."[2]

The pages of Jack London's stories drip blood-red. His seas are blood, his sunsets are blood, his clouds are blood, his sands are blood, his poppies are blood. The old chieftain in "The Death of Ligoun" says, "Yet do I speak of the law of blood for blood, and rank for rank."[3] Lone Chief in "The Sickness of Lone Chief'' also chants, ''I knew that I had killed, and the taste of the blood made me fierce.''⁴ Scruff MacKenzie in ''The Son of the Wolf'' at first ''felt compassion for his enemy; but this fled before the primal instinct of life, which in turn gave way to the lust of slaughter.''⁵ And superdog Buck ''got a frothing adversary by the throat, and was sprayed with blood when his teeth sank through the jugular. The warm taste of it in his mouth goaded him to greater fierceness.'' Buck becomes maddened with ''the blood lust, the joy to kill,'' which achieves the ultimate experience according to London: ''There is an ecstasy that marks the summit of life, and beyond which life cannot rise. And such is the paradox of living, this ecstasy comes when one is most alive, and it comes as a complete forgetfulness that one is alive.''⁶

London liked the title, ''Father of Red-Blooded American Literature,'' saying he enjoyed writing bloody stories, once remarking that ''The House of Pride'' failed because it didn't end with death. He also wrote in ''The Terrible and Tragic in Fiction'' that ''the great short stories in the world's literary treasure-house seem all to depend upon the tragic and terrible for their strength and greatness. . . . Talk with the average man or woman of the reading public and it will be found that they have read all, or nearly all, of the terrible and horrible tales which have been written. Also, they will shiver, express a dislike for such tales, and then proceed to discuss them with a keenness and understanding as remarkable as it is surprising.''⁷ As George Orwell said about ''The Francis Spaight'': ''The starving crew of a waterlogged ship have decided to resort to cannibalism, and have just nerved themselves to begin when another ship heaves in sight. It is characteristic of Jack London that the second ship should appear after and not before the cabin boy's throat has been cut.'' Orwell added: ''The answer is surely that London could foresee Fascism because he had a Fascist streak in himself: or at any rate a marked strain of brutality and an almost unconquerable preference for the strong man as against the weak man.''⁸

This ''streak of physical cruelty''⁹ surfaces in many London short stories such as ''Mauki.'' Set on the rotting, steaming island of Malaita, this horrid tale tells about a native servant,

Mauki, tortured for years by an evil trader named Max Bunster, who punches him in the mouth, burns him with cigars, rips cartilage from his nose—and runs a shark's skin over his body, which removes the skin, causing agonizing pain. Mauki finally gets revenge, skinning the sadistic Bunster with this glove, turning the brute German into a raving maniac. In "Lost Face" a Cossack is tortured, presumably including castration, until he becomes a howling beast. "Mr. London, in particular, seems willing to spare us nothing," wrote *The Nation*. "In his latest collection of tales, we find several of the familiar horrors retailed with the customary detail—men who die by inches of cold and hunger, and so on. But in the title story, the writer makes a really distinguished addition to his series of brutal exhibits; describing in detail the (one might think) unspeakable torturing to death of a huge Cossack by a band of Nulato Indians. We recognize Mr. London's talent; but he seems to us the victim of a disease of the fancy from which, and from the effects of which, it is impossible not to shrink."[10]

Yet such sinister tales as "Mauki" and "Lost Face" pale compared to London's treatment of children, who play negligible roles in his stories: a girl in "The Dream of Debs" gloats when someone's face is smashed, egging on the wholesale bloodletting. In "The God of His Fathers," a child's "puny body circled through the air, dashing to death against the logs,"[11] and in "The Master of Mystery" an Indian boy "with shrieks and laughter, was flinging stones with the rest of the tribe's 'blood-cry,' "[12] helping them murder a code violator. The cruel Red Eye in *Before Adam* crushes a child's head against a wall. David Grief in *A Son of the Sun* carries a black child from a hut, minus its head, and in "When Alice Told Her Soul," a mother tramples her own child, crushing in its brains.

Even London's lovers dabble in sadomasochistic foreplay. As Wace says in *The Kempton-Wace Letters*, "I have shown that the natural expression of the love instinct is bestial and brutal and violent."[13] Billy pinches Saxon until she squeals with pain in *The Valley of the Moon*, pressing his finger into her arms, making her dizzy with chin taps. Joe, who bearhugs Genevieve in *The Game*, hungers "to make the embrace crushing till she should cry out with the hurt."[14] Ape men in *Before*

Adam make mincemeat of their mates who whine for more.
And Floyd Vanderlip bruises Freda Moloff in *The Scorn of
Women,* twisting her arms until she yelps.
Most of London's fragile females, however, like a man's man.
"The masculinity of his heroes is always emphasized by reference to their high sexual attraction,"[15] remarked C. Hartley
Grattan in *The Bookman.* It is Martin Eden's rippling muscu-
lature that quickens Ruth's pulse, even leading her to offer
services as his mistress. "She is surely and steadily drawn to
his phallic power," says Jonathan Harold Spinner. "Freud
would have been delighted."[16] Lute in "Planchette" tells Chris
that she relishes the bruises and finger imprints on arms, the
joyful pain that made her holler, even wishing bruises would
remain discolored. Joan Lakeland in *Adventures* also derives
a subliminal thrill from watching the whipping of black slaves,
seeing their muscles quiver as the whip draws blood. The same
subsurface phenomenon is true regarding Buck. In his quasi-
critical *Jack London,* Earle Labor admits that "London hid sex
under a heavy cloak of fur"[17] in *The Call of the Wild.*
    Critics have questioned this bizarre element in London's
psychic makeup for generations, trying to relate such literary
statement to an inner death wish and psychoneurotic tendencies.
T. K. Whipple calls London's obsessiveness with physical
prowess and primordial sexuality "the regressive myth of the
primitive, barbaric hero."[18] "A quietly maturing male human
will gradually grow into manhood and take the social responsibility of manhood in organised human society, by becoming
a gear wheel in the social machine and not make a loud scraping
noise in doing so," psychoanalyzed Wilfred Lay. "He will not
suddenly and spectacularly shout, full lunged, that he is a
man. . . . On the contrary, Jack London is impressed with the
fact that at the age of fourteen he is a man and tells it emphatically, when, at the age of thirty-seven he published *John
Barleycorn.*"[19]
    Such shouting also bothered Joan London. "So frequently
in his writing recurs his chant of pride in brute strength in
general and his own in particular, that one can scarcely fail to
realize that this achievement must have been difficult and dearly

bought."[20] Asked about macho men, James Jones replied: "Macho? I think anybody who has to wear his masculinity on his sleeve like a target, is someone who is pretty insecure about his masculinity. One of the great parts of man in the full sense of the word is an ability to be gentle with people. Macho generally is not."[21]

London's red-blooded barbaric heroes, cardboard caricatures of man's darker side, have offended many literary critics:

John McCole remarked that London "dipped the beam of our scales of fictional values by piling on more red meat than any other early American novelist."[22]

Van Wyck Brooks added that "The Red-Blood . . . is oddly enough the most neurotic of men. Whatever his physical equipment may be, he is always the victim of an exaggerated sense of inferiority that drives him to assert himself; he wants to 'beat' society, and this desire inhibits his own growth. So it appears to have been with Jack London."[23]

Carl Van Doren said: "What was elemental in Frank Norris became abysmal in Jack London. He carried the cult of red blood in literature to an extreme at which it began to sink to the ridiculous, as in his lineal descendants of the moving-pictures."[24]

And Alfred Kazin remarks that his "thick slabs of bleeding meat were essentially only a confession of despair."[25]

The principal symbolic expression of London's despair, his self-hatred and sense of nothingness, is death and the demonic, James I. McClintock saying that "death is the center of almost all of London's important stories."[26]

Anna Strunsky revealed that London "kept a loaded revolver in his desk ready to use it against himself at any time,"[27] and he made Eliza promise not to commit him in case of insanity. Suicide creeps into several stories: both Paula Forrest in *The Little Lady of the Big House* and Martin Eden self-destruct. So does David Rasmunsen in "The One Thousand Dozen." "Semper Idem" involves a doctor who advises suicide as life's cure. "One More Unfortunate" involves suicide. Humphrey Van Weyden entertains the idea, and Alousius Pankburn tries it in *A Son of the Sun.* So does London in *John Barleycorn.*

Death stalks through London's terror tales, whether in the
Klondike, on the South Seas or devil ships, his characters vic-
timized by the whims of a convulsed, incoherent universe devoid of reason and sanity. This includes Ernest Everhard in
The Iron Heel, John Thornton in *The Call of the Wild*, and
Wolf Larsen in *The Sea Wolf*. Wolves devour Old Koskoosh
in "The Law of Life." Mason dies in "The White Silence."
The traveler in "To Build a Fire" perishes. Hay Stockard is
brutally murdered in "The God of His Fathers." Percy Cuthfert
and Carter Weatherbee kill each other over sugar in "In a Far
Country."

Whether weak or strong, London's characters die, some
wretchedly, denying the essential premise of the power of brute
force in his work. Maxwell Geismar calls his entire career
"demonical in essence," his characters "victims of obsessions,
delusions and grotesque missions of self-destruction," and himself "a species of devil-worshiper invoking forces of darkness
which rule a cosmos of death."[28] In "In a Far Country" London
says about Cuthfert: "There was no sun. This was the Universe,
dead and cold and dark, and he its only citizen. . . . He was
a Caliban, a monstrous phantom, fettered to him for untold
ages, the penalty of some forgotten crime." Then about Weatherbee: "He lived with Death among the dead, emasculated by
the sense of his own insignificance, crushed by the passive
mastery of the slumbering ages. The magnitude of all things
appalled him. Everything partook of the superlative save
himself."[29]

Endless allusions to demons and devils appear in Jack London's stories. Diable is a devil dog. Buck is two devils. White
Fang is also a devil. Dan Cullen in "Make Westing" worships
the devil. Both the *Ghost* and *Elsinore* are devil ships; *The Dial*
wrote in its review of *The Mutiny of the Elsinore* that "Mr.
London's real object is to revel in sailing a ship round the Horn
with a crew of devils,"[30] and that the *Ghost* is "a floating hell."[31]
After reading Milton's *Paradise Lost*, Wolf Larsen praises Lucifer: "He led a lost cause, and he was not afraid of God's
thunderbolts. . . . Hurled into hell, he was unbeaten. A third
of God's angels he had led with him, and straightway he incited

man to rebel against God and gained for himself and hell the major portion of all the generations of man.''[32]

London sent Brett a synopsis of *The Sea Wolf* in September 1903. *Century Magazine* had already offered $4,000 for serialization rights, but questioned the novel's factual details. L. Frank Tooker, an editor, called it farcical. ''It was not intended to be farcical; that was the irritating thing. It took the reader's lack of intelligence for granted. One may be unintelligent, but one dislikes to have the fact paraded as a historical truth no one questions. 'The Sea Wolf' had come to us on the heels of London's great success, 'The Call of the Wild,' and in their satisfaction at having obtained the work of the popular author of the hour the editors were somewhat disposed to hold it sacrosanct.''

Although Tooker opposed publishing *The Sea Wolf,* the business boys at *Century* voted yes. As a youth Tooker had studied the draft books of a master sailmaker, leading him to question the *Ghost*'s dimensions; local shipmasters and sailmakers confirmed his suspicions. London admitted the errors, and encouraged revisions. Tooker said of London,

> A man of strong peculiarities, he was also an egoist, and his little world was bounded by his own individual thoughts and beliefs. Thus he did not envisage the actual world; he envisaged himself moving through a creation of his own habitudes of mind. A dominant creature, he dominated his own thoughts, colored them. One always finds him in his books. Indeed, in 'The Sea-Wolf' he divides himself, as it were, into two. In his mental apprehension of himself as intensely masculine, a radical, a protestant, a believer in evolution, and a lover of accepted literature, he created *Wolf Larsen* in the likeness of his own image; *Van Weyden* is the embodiment of his own imagined power to triumph over environment through evolution. Personally, I think that in his eager haste to catch the advantage of his golden tide of popularity he had rushed his work, paying little heed to details.[33]

Joan London agreed. ''*Hurry!* Faster, faster! This [was] the dominant characteristic of Jack London's activity until the end of his life."[34] He even let Charmian and George Sterling make final revisions on *The Sea Wolf,* while he tramped through Manchuria, reporting the Russo-Japanese War.

Century editor Robert Underwood Johnson, who also edited *Battles and Leaders of the Civil War,* admired L. Frank Tooker, saying in 1923 that he "kept the proof reading of the magazine up to its high standards of style, and who is now, editorially, the one link between the old *Century* and the new." Johnson also commented on taste, sensibility, and sympathy in literature: "No writer represents life exactly as it is and no one wishes to contemplate merely the facts of life. That is the difference between pathology and art, which is a compromise with facts to obtain an effect of truth through beauty and illusion. The person who sneers at taste should betake himself to a slaughter house or a lazaretto."[35]

London, who turned Larsen's *Ghost* into a human slaughterhouse, dripping with blood and violence, sneered at taste the way he sneered at ethics. One thing dominated his mind—how to make money. "Nowhere in his works does he show that he understands the artist mind," wrote Porter Garnett, a founder of the *Lark* magazine, in 1907: "He has drawn characters such as Humphrey Van Weyden and Maud Brewster in *The Sea Wolf* who have artistic sensibilities; but these sensibilities are interpreted only as they appear when brought into violent contact with the brute force of humanity as expressed in the character of Wolf Larsen."[36] *The Literary World* concluded after London's death that "to the last, culture and highbrow were synonymous to him, states of mind to be suspected, scorned, and combated."[37] London, for example, hated both Henry James and William Dean Howells. He once ridiculed James' *The Wings of the Dove,* asking some Carmelites, "Do any of you know what all this junk is about?"[38]

It was the same with music, painting, and sculpture. Although Charmian claimed London loved classical music, both Joseph Noel and Georgia Loring Bamford disagreed. Noel said that Charmian played Edvard Grieg, while London chose "a Sicilian folk song, done in rollicking style by a singer who accompanied himself on the accordion . . . played twice. Other songs, all second-rate followed."[39] Georgia Loring Bamford concurred.

"He liked a little music of the home variety, but scorned a concert of classical music by a famous pianist, and Grand Opera, although he subscribed to the latter." London's artistic insensibilities to painting and sculpture also surprised her. "It is almost impossible to believe that Jack London had no interest in painting and almost none in sculpture. This fact was well known to many of his friends. George Sterling once said to me, 'Why, Jack can't even see a picture. The best paintings mean nothing to him.'"[40]

London's stationery reflected the same tastelessness. As late as 1908, after making half a million dollars, he still corresponded on scrap paper with George Brett, using a rubber-stamp heading, usually applied crookedly. (He also had a rubber-stamp name, using it once in a Brett letter, which led Charmian to apologize.) London's early typewritten letters to Brett, by the way, were full of strikeovers and words added in pen.

Macmillan launched *The Sea Wolf* in 1904, selling 40,000 copies before publication, then half a million more. Wide-eyed Americans, famished for fantasy, relieving sexual and sadistic impulses, clutched their seats as Larsen jumped nine feet, lifted sailors off the decks with iron fists, and shamed Humphrey Van Weyden, the bourgeois literateur. Ludwig Lewisohn used this novel to explain London's popularity among the masses for awhile:

The average, ignorant reader, shorn by civilization of the full expression of his primitive instincts, both sexual and aggressive, identifies himself with sadistic joy with the pseudo-Nietzschean captain and through this identification satisfies his lust for ferocity and raw force. Nor is that all. The satanic captain's cruelty is directed against a boy belonging to the most sheltered section of capitalistic society. Thus there enters the further motive of satisfied envy, parading sincerely as a desire for leveling justice and there enters, in the case of many readers, a satisfaction (through the relations of the cruel captain and the delicate lad) of unconscious homo-erotic wishes. No wonder that Jack London is popular and continues so. "The Sea-Wolf" also contains,

however, an unconscious confession: the formidable captain collapses in the end, paralyzed and impotent. Something had slowly
hollowed out that gigantic frame and that will of steel. Brutality,
in brief, is the mask of inner weakness and aggressive cruelty
a confession of ultimate impotence.[41]

Many of these thirsty readers failed to realize that *The Sea
Wolf* indicted them as human beings. They missed its central
theme that "might is right, and that is all there is to it. Weakness
is wrong. Which is a very poor way of saying that it is good
for oneself to be strong, and evil for oneself to be weak."[42]
London's might doesn't include moral strength—just muscle.
In this deranged world of jungle beasts disguised as humans,
raw force tramples intellect, leaving in its wake broken bones
and crushed skulls. The Reverend Edward Payne wrote: "Morals have no sanction, he maintained, except as an evolutionary
development; and this appears only with man. The animals,
surely, know nothing of it. It is a strictly human invention. . . .
Accordingly, man may change or modify it to meet his pragmatic
needs."[43] In London's language that meant "might spells right."
The Sea Wolf, like *White Fang* and *The Call of the Wild,*
unleashed another dominant primordial beast, this time a psy-
chotic sealing-schooner captain caught between two irreconcilable opposites in his nature.

Most reviewers criticized *The Sea Wolf*'s contrived plot, flat
characterizations, and hideous exhibition of violence. Besides
mentioning the book's "padding of the most tedious kind," *The
Nation* remarked that "never has sickening brutality been more
gloatingly described than in this story,"[44] a remark echoed by
The Outlook: "One sickens at the excess of brutality."[45] *The
Bookman* agreed: "The book is a record of brutality, pictured
with such pitiless vividness that more than once even a hardened
reader flinches from it a little, and falls to turning over the pages
at a quickened pace, from the same instinct that makes one
hurry past the scene of an accident."[46]

Several sources contributed to *The Sea Wolf.* Many writers
of the time, London included, relied heavily on newspaper articles for ideas. Humphrey Van Weyden's salt water dunking
after falling off a ferry derived from a collision between the *San*

Rafael and *Sausalito* on November 30, 1901. Two other novels, Rudyard Kipling's *Captains Courageous* and Frank Norris's *Moran of the Lady Letty,* helped set the scene. The *Athenaeum* commented that London owed "a good deal to the writer of 'McAndrew's Hymn' in most of his work."[47] The Bering Sea sequences at the seal rookery should be credited to David Starr Jordan, mentioned several times by Van Weyden and Maud Brewster, who wrote a report on pelagic seal fishing. Part of Wolf Larsen's makeup belonged to Captain Alexander McLean, a sea poacher known as the "Sea Wolf."[48]

Mostly written after his separation from Bessie, *The Sea Wolf* mirrors London's deepening bitterness towards life. Wolf Larsen, the incarnation of cosmic evil, someone with an amoral drive unconquerable by man who symbolizes Nietzsche's over-man, became his spokesman. "I believe that life is a mess. . . . It is like yeast, a ferment, a thing that moves and may move for a minute, an hour, a year, or a hundred years but that in the end will cease to move. The big eat the little that they may continue to move, the strong eat the weak that they may retain their strength. The lucky eat the most and move the longest, that is all."[49]

Larsen, "a magnificent atavism, a man so purely primitive that he was of the type that came into the world before the development of the moral nature. . . . The piercing glitter that arose at times in his eyes was the same glitter I had observed in the eyes of caged leopards and other preying creatures of the wild. [Frank Pease wrote that London's "eyes changed with the changing color of his soul, and often seemed filled with the anguish of sins impossible to commit."[50]] It was a strength we are wont to associate with things primitive, with wild animals and the creatures we imagine our tree-dwelling prototypes to have been—a strength savage, ferocious, alive in itself, the essence of life in that it is the potency of motion, the elemental stuff."[51]

Perhaps indicating his essential despair (and in one way to advance his theories about Darwin's "survival of the fittest" and Nietzsche's "will to power"), London made the *Ghost* "a miniature floating world," a hell ship of abysmal brutes "whose bunks looked like the sleeping dens of animals in a menagerie," a hell-hole where "life had become cheap and tawdry, a beastly and inarticulate thing, a soulless stirring of the ooze and slime." Van Weyden says: "It seems to me impossible sometimes that they ever had mothers. It would appear that they are a half-brute, half-human species, a race apart, wherein there is no such thing as sex; that they are hatched out by the sun like turtle eggs, or receive life in some similar and sordid fashion; and that all their days they fester in brutality and viciousness and in the end die as unlovely as they have lived." He concludes: "How God must have hated them that they should be tortured so!"[52]

Larsen, a godlike figure to these brutes, had raped women, killed a sailor with his bare fist, and shot four others during a previous trip. He terrorizes the *Ghost*'s crew, savagely beating and punishing them without relief. When Johnson rebels, Larsen and his mate "struck him with their fists, kicked him with their heavy shoes, knocked him down, and dragged him to his feet to knock him down again. His eyes were blinded so that he could not see, and the blood running from ears and nose and mouth turned the cabin into a shambles. And when he could no longer rise they still continued to beat and kick him where he lay."[53]

The plot curds after Larsen rescues Humphrey Van Weyden, "The Dean of American Letters, The Second," from the waters, and reduces him to a menial cabin boy, flinging him down society's cellar stairs. (Van Weyden may be London's literary expression of William Dean Howells.) Larsen then teaches this squeamish, aristocratic sissy, "a miserable weakling," a scholar-recluse detached from reality, about life's piggishness. Hump soon realizes you can't live on belles-lettres at sea. So he strengthens stringy muscles, especially after the cook Mugridge—whose words speak for London—browbeats him day and night, accusing: " 'Ump. You was born a gentleman. You never knew wot it was to go 'ungry, to cry yerself asleep with yer little belly gnawin' an' gnawin' like a rat inside yer. It carn't come right. If I was President of the United Stytes tomorrer, 'ow would it fill my belly for one time w'en I was a kiddy and it went empty?" One day Mugridge talks too much and Larsen indulges in some man-play, throwing him overboard tied to a rope, a pastime interrupted when a starved shark devours his foot. "Then he came in like a fresh-caught fish on a line. . . . But a fountain of blood was gushing forth. The right foot was missing, amputated neatly at the ankle."[54]

Although Larsen despises weaklings like Van Weyden, he values the author's insights and rich literary background, leading to philosophical discussions that shake the rational Hump. Larsen accepts a universe with inverted ethics—bad is good and good is bad. "Don't you see? How can two particles of the yeast wrong each other by striving to devour each other? It is their inborn heritage to strive to devour, and to strive not to be devoured. When they depart from this they sin." Life is cheap. Nature is generous. All that counts is force, the ability to survive by devouring other living creatures. "You have talked of the instinct of immortality," Larsen tells Hump. "I talk of the instinct of life, which is to live, and which, when death looms near and large, masters the instinct, so called, of immortality. . . . To live! To live! To live! you are crying; and you are crying to live here and now, now hereafter."[55] London lets Larsen quote Ecclesiastes for support.

> All things come alike to all; there is one event to the righteous and to the wicked; to the good and to the clean, and to the unclean; to him that sacrificeth, and to him that sacrificeth not; as is the good, so is the sinner; and he that sweareth, as he that feareth an oath.
>
> This is an evil among all things that are done under the sun, that there is one event unto all; yea, also the heart of the sons of men is full of evil, and madness is in their heart while they live, and after that they go to the dead.
>
> For to him that is joined to all the living there is hope; for a living dog is better than a dead lion.
>
> For the living know that they shall die; but the dead know not anything, neither have they any more a reward; for the memory of them is forgotten.[56]

Lavon B. Carroll offers this explanation of London's Ecclesiastical creed:

> He translated the new philosophy and ideology into far older terms, into the pre-Christian or Old Testament conflict of "good"

and "evil" that had come down to us as Puritanism. Instead of
the old "Devil," man is now confronted with the "Brute Force"
which leered out of the pessimistic view of evolution. Man has
to overcome this in order to become a better man, to justify his
humanity, or to find his salvation. But London recognized (here
is possibly the real influence of Nietzsche's transcendental Man-
ichaeism) that the primitive force which threatened man was also
the chief source of his life and strength. Man could only become
estranged from it at the peril of his life, but he must control and
utilize it.[57]

Larsen later reappears in "Make Westing," included in *When
God Laughs* (1911), this time as Captain Dan Cullen, who also
rules a terror ship, another brute consecrated to the forces of
evil. Cullen dedicates himself to the devil, to the deepest dun-
geons of darkness, killing a passenger who threatens to inform
authorities when he doesn't save a sailor.

Neither Wolf Larsen nor Dan Cullen, with their dark designs,
are true Nietzschean disciples. As *The Nation* noted, "The hero
of [London's] 'Sea Wolf' is a methodical superman; not so
much one of Nietzsche's unconscious blond beasts as a man
who had read Nietzsche and acts up to formula."[58] Robert H.
Woodward also concludes: "He is a superman in the same sense
that Milton's Satan is a superman: strong, selfish, vengeful,
referring all values to his own security. But he is not the Nietzschean superman. True, he has energy, intellect, and pride—
the requisites; but he lacks the discipline of self which is the
harmonizing element, the catalyst in Nietzsche's formula. Without this requisite discipline he is but a highly-developed brute,
an embodiment of the gross materialism which results from
naturalism."[59]

Maud Brewster, a hybrid Anna Strunsky and Charmian Kittredge, is also rescued from the sea by Larsen, saving the effete
Van Weyden from moral—and perhaps physical—destruction.
(She enters the novel when London became involved with Charmian.) Maud, also a distinguished American literateur, falls for
Hump, who considers her "a being from another world. . . .
Indeed, she was a slender, delicate woman as women go, but
to me she was so ethereally slender and delicate that I was
quite prepared for her arm to crumble in my grasp. She was

like a bit of Dresden china." The two authors, after Larsen nearly rapes Maud, abandon the *Ghost,* rowing to a deserted island, where they survive under extreme primitive conditions, sharing a platonic relationship. "Truly she was my woman, my mate-woman, fighting with me and for me as the mate of a caveman would have fought, all the primitive in her aroused, forgetful of her culture, hard under the softening civilization of the only life she had ever known."[60]

Although Ambrose Bierce called *The Sea Wolf* "a rattling good story," he wrote George Sterling: "It is a most disagreeable book, as a whole. London has a pretty bad style and no sense of proportion. The story is a perfect welter of disagreeable incidents. Two or three (of the kind) would have sufficed to *show* the character of the man Larsen; and his own self-revealings by word of mouth would have 'done the rest.' Many of these incidents, too, are impossible—such as that of a man mounting a ladder with a dozen other men—more or less—hanging to his leg, and the hero's work of rerigging a wreck and getting it off a beach where it had stuck for weeks, and so forth. The 'love' element, with its absurd suppressions and impossible proprieties, is awful. I confess to an overwhelming contempt for both the sexless lovers."[61] Hump and Maud, incidentally, survive on a seal rookery filled with the bellowing of 200,000 beasts, most of them mating. The lovers also use the skins of virginal bachelor seals to cover their roof.

This romantic paradise on Endeavor Island ends when the *Ghost,* abandoned by all except Larsen, miraculously beaches nearby. Larsen's feared brother, Death, a physical giant who dwarfs Wolf in size and evil, also captains a schooner. After Maud and Humphrey abandoned the *Ghost,* he kidnapped its crew, leaving Wolf on board, alone and dying. The purpose of this cartoon character? None except to unravel plot lines and shift Wolf Larsen to the island, where he tries to wreck Van Weyden's remarkable repairs on the *Ghost.* This he fails to achieve. After Larsen dies, his inner spirit triumphant till the end, calling life "B-O-S-H," the novel degenerates into pure literary bosh, Humphrey and Maud Brewster sailing into the sunset on the *Ghost,* The Dean of American Letters, The Second doing "a thirty-six hour trick at the wheel," then going

below, leaving the seal schooner to self-navigate, while the seas
pound and winds roar. The Van Weydens, presumably, live
happily ever after, correcting each other's proofs. As a rescue
cutter nears, the novel ends with these sentiments: " 'My
woman, my one small woman,' I said, my free hand petting her
shoulder in the way all lovers know though never learn in
school. 'My man,' she said, looking at me for an instant with
tremulous lids which fluttered down and veiled her eyes as she
snuggled her head against my breast with a happy little sigh.
I looked toward the cutter. It was very close. A boat was being
lowered. 'One kiss, dear love,' I whispered. 'One kiss more
before they come.' 'And rescue us from ourselves,' she completed, with a most adorable smile, whimsical as I had never
seen it, for it was whimsical with love.''[62]

London's 1914 melodramatic sea boots thriller, *The Mutiny
of the Elsinore,* published ten years after *The Sea Wolf,* also
indicts society. Its hero, John Pathurst, dissects the life-lie,
saying that man finds escape in fancies such as art, alcohol,
God, love, and socialism. He confesses a loss of faith in mankind, a revulsion for women's primitive nature, a disenchantment with art. George Sterling wrote London: "I don't (and
maybe you don't) particularly admire your smug Pathurst, and
as a brunette, naturally find his 'perishing blond' tirades pretty
tiresome. He's heartless, too, but so are all the others on the
'Elsinore.' I suppose you're merely using him as a foil to the
great characters of the captain and first mate, who are sections,
as it were, of Wolf Larsen.''[63] He added in a follow-up letter:
"I don't call it one of your 'flivvers.' . . . I think the weak spot
in the 'mutiny' is the unlovableness of the 'hero.' Mr. Pike is
your real hero, however.''[64]

The Outlook called *The Mutiny of the Elsinore* "an exciting,
excessively brutal tale of a sea voyage in a sailing sloop, in
which happens nearly every conceivable sensational thing made
possible by a crew of cripples, incompetents, scoundrels and
maniacs.''[65] Captain West, an aristocratic Viking lord who reads
little, showing even less interest in politics and philosophical

issues, becomes an empty echo of the past Nordic glories London once championed. His daughter, Miss West, another cardboard Maud Brewster, sails into the sunset with Pathurst, blushing as they tease each other's lips. As for realism on other levels, Arthur Hobson Quinn quipped in *American Fiction*: "London's heroes, like Van Weyden or Pathurst, the cabin messenger in *The Mutiny of the Elsinore* (1914), who quells the mutiny after the captain and mates are dead, either learn navigation with a rapidity that is startling or else sail a boat cheerfully without it."[66] As *The New Republic* observed: "The Elsinore with its murderous crew, tossing helpless in the Southern seas, gave a chance for something that an artist could have managed superbly. But Mr. London only feebly touches it. He has put his primitive men upon the sea without putting the sea around them."[67]

Chapter 10

Childie Upstages the Yellow Peril

ALTHOUGH *The Call of the Wild* made London famous, his life continued to unravel at the seams. Following the separation from Bessie, he located on Telegraph Hill, sick with depression, struggling through *The Sea Wolf*. The same old restlessness again seized him, a longing for the adventure path, this time finding release in the Russo-Japanese War over Manchuria. *Collier's, Harper's,* and the *New York World* offered contracts, but London chose profiteer William Randolph Hearst, *San Francisco Examiner* owner, sailing to the East on the Pacific Mail liner *Siberia.* Edmond D. Coblentz, a waterfront crony, later recalled that he "poured [London] on board."[1]

Accident-prone and sensitive to diseases, London caught the grippe en route to Japan, then smashed a left ankle. (He told George Brett that many accidents happened on the Glen Ellen ranch.) The tendons healed slowly, and he hopped about on crutches, searching for letters from Charmian Kittredge, a recent flame—but none arrived.

London reached Tokyo on January 24, 1904, finding correspondents loafing in the Imperial Bar, waiting for clearances, while Japanese diplomats played politics, offering harmless interviews at the war office. "The air of the Imperial Hotel was a bright blue from early morn to golden sunset," said correspondent Willard Straight. "Famous journalists, veterans of countless campaigns were held up, bound hand and foot by the dapper little Orientals whose attitude throughout had been greatly wondered at and most profanely admired. . . . The situation was unique in the annals of journalism. A government holding the rabid pressmen at a distance, censoring their simplest stories, yet patting them on the back, dining them, wining them, giving them picnics and luncheons and theatrical performances and trying in every way not to soften their bonds and to make their stay a pleasant one, but siren-like, to deaden their sense of duty and their desire to get into the field."[2]

London, ignoring Japanese directives, took a train to Kobe on January 27. After reaching Moji from Nagasaki, he bought a ticket on the ship *Kanazawa Maru,* bound for Incho, waiting several days. According to his dispatch, a Japanese "flycop" arrested him for snapping photos of children and coolies carrying coal and cotton, all forbidden by the Fortress Area Act. While being taken to the Kokura Ward Court, he pleaded innocent to Russian-spy charges. One Japanese paper reported: "In spite of his earnest pleas that as he was a gentleman who drew a salary of one thousand three hundred yen a month he was not one who would wilfully offend the law, we hear that the Moji Water Police disposed of the case according to the letter of the law."[3] The court fined London five yen and confiscated his camera, which aroused sympathy from both American correspondents and Japanese pressmen in Moji and Shimonseki, who lodged a petition for the camera's return. Lloyd Griscom, United States minister to Japan, revealed how London retrieved his camera:

> One day I had a frantic appeal from Jack London. He was in jail; I must have him released immediately. Investigation showed that he, with his camera, had strayed by mistake into one of the fortified areas along the Inland Sea; and on my assurance that he intended no harm, the Japanese released him. However, he returned to Tokyo, sputtering with wrath because his valuable camera had been confiscated; he could not replace it; it was essential to his livelihood; a war correspondent without his camera was like a plumber without his tools.
>
> On my next visit to Baron Komura, after I had gone through my other business, I brought up the matter of the London camera. He was in a rather irritated mood, and said that he did not see how he could grant this request, but to make certain he would summon the legal counsel of the Foreign Office. I knew

very well that when a Foreign Minister rang the bell for his legal adviser, it meant he needed support, and I would not get what I wanted.

The counsel arrived, an extremely clever lawyer, who, according to the quaint Japanese custom, had sat on the bench for many years to gain experience before being allowed to practise and have clients. As soon as the case was put to him he answered, "What you ask, Your Excellency, is absolutely forbidden. The statute declares that the weapon with which a crime has been committed becomes the property of the court."

"There you are," Baron Komura said to me.

"Does that apply to every crime?" I asked the lawyer.

"Yes, to every crime of every description."

I turned to the Foreign Minister. "If I can name a crime to which this does not apply, will you release the camera?"

Regarding me doubtfully for a few seconds, Baron Komura replied, "Yes, I will."

"Well, what about rape?"

Baron Komura's oriental stolidity dissolved in a shout of laughter. "That's a good one. Wait until Count Katsura hears it."

Later the Foreign Minister called me on the telephone. "Mr. Griscom, your story broke up the Cabinet meeting. Mr. London gets his camera back."[4]

Eiju Tsujii, who researched Japanese newspaper accounts of London's arrest, concluded: "We hear that London had a prejudice against the 'yellow' races even before coming to Japan, and this prejudice was also strong in the U.S. in those days, especially in California, London's home state. Though it can't be denied that his hatred of the yellow races was aggravated by his arrest or examination during his stay in Japan or Korea, the fact that the pressmen sympathized with him and his response to it seem to me that they will bring up another new problem about his outlook on Japanese when we combine this fact over Jack London's scorn and loathing of the Japanese."[5]

London's clash with the Japanese authorities didn't stop him, although it could have sparked an international incident. He knew action would erupt in the north and headed there third-class on a ship leaving Shimonoseki, camera slung over a shoulder, cigarette hanging from his mouth. More trouble followed. Left stranded at Pusan, he boarded a steamer, but was thrown ashore with other passengers at Mokpu. Then he journeyed up Korea's west coast in a sampan with three Koreans, unable to understand their lingo, eating rice and fish, warming himself with a charcoal fire.

Meeting correspondents Frederick Arthur McKenzie and Robert Dunn, London recruited thirteen men and eighteen ponies, most left behind within several days. (An interpreter named Mr. Yamada and a young groom called Manyoungi, who attended him for several years, swelled London's entourage.) With snow falling, roads slippery with ice, winds howling, they started for Pingyang. "We had to go through districts where a foreigner was as rare as a Sioux Indian in Fleet Street,"[6] recalled McKenzie. But they continued, carrying food and other supplies, sometimes encountering hostility from the Koreans.

In one small, walled town, the head man refused them entrance for the night, leading McKenzie to pull a gun, which got fast results. The next morning, all the horses' blankets except one—on an ornery beast that kicked—had vanished, leaving the horses half frozen. The Koreans blamed roving robbers. This enraged McKenzie, who arrested the head man, threatening jail in Pingyang, another strong-armed bluff that worked: "The villagers crowded around, shouting, gesticulating, protesting. My two companions came up and produced their revolvers. Five minutes passed, and the scene was now pandemonium. The head man was warned to hurry up. Then he found himself in a corner of the yard with my .38 Colt covering him, and my friends' revolvers covering the mob. It now dawned on the people that we really meant business. A sharp word was spoken, and suddenly a miserable stable boy knocked aside some snow, pulled away some matting, and revealed the blankets snugly tucked in underneath."[7]

McKenzie realized the Japanese weren't fools. Their insight, initiative, and stubborn persistence showed throughout Korea. Officers knew the language. They held detailed maps of every town, understood local customs, and assigned physicians to scout, marking unsanitary pools and studying health conditions. The Japanese, like American and British correspondents, considered the Koreans a filthy, backward nation.

Each day Pingyang grew closer, and each day food grew scarcer. Dunn caught pneumonia. London suffered from an inferior Japanese saddle, aggravated by his inability to ride. (He also bought a nag that proved blind on the road.) McKenzie slipped on ice and fractured a wrist. Talk focused on food— European clubs, southern dressed chicken, canvasback in San Francisco. Finally reaching Pingyang, informants told them Tokyo correspondents had filed protests against their advance unit. Officials detained McKenzie in Chinnampho. Dunn and London's push ended in Sunan. Authorities returned all three correspondents to Seoul, placing them under top security. Robert Dunn, correspondent for the *New York Globe,* later told the following anecdote.

The two best-paid correspondents in Seoul were Jack London and Richard Harding Davis. London was a hefty version of my Alaska partner, Jack Swann, with lighter, curlier hair. The barrel chest in his gray flannel shirt seemed to move him when he walked. We relived Alaska—"the true white man's country"— and agreed on Japs, or rather his dislike outdid mine. Though a professed socialist, he really believed in the Kaiser's "yellow peril."

After a good deal of vodka, we were off hunting tigers in Korean caves. I took him home and he turned up for lunch next day, shyly worried because he hadn't been asked. His deep blue eyes never more than smiled; but he said, in the manner of his stories, "If we never meet again, Bob, my memory will be your laughing at me and my laughing at you, and your knowing I'm laughing, and my knowing you know I am."

He stayed for dinner too. Afterwards, when he signed the drink chit for the crowd at Martin's bar, he said of a slick stranger with prison pallor, "I've been in jail myself."

"Who hasn't been?" I boasted. "Where were you pinched?"

"Niagara Falls, New York, the first time. I was fifteen. Got thirty days as a vagrant. The injustice helped make me a socialist."

Every man worth his salt has some bug inscrutable to others, and London took his socialism seriously. He went on to explain a dialectic that few of us then understood, and ended with a grin, "I'm a socialist because it's got to come some day. And anyway I like a fight. What are all you bourgeois drinking now?"[8]

Another day Dunn and London wandered beyond the Seoul walls, looking for news, becoming involved with the Japanese Twelfth Division. Reported Dunn,

The cavalry was a relief but one supply train was pathetic. Horses were alien to the *samurai* (hay was scarce in Japan), and these were mere leggy ponies. One officer was held in his seat by a private, and none dismounted at the steep ascents. The transports and the landing had lamed many pack-animals, now treated with callousness that would rile any horse-lover.

"Their pack saddles don't fit, either," Jack observed. "Look at that for cruel ignorance—God damn him."

A loaded pony hobbled on three legs. The off hind one, broken, had been strapped up against his belly. We slipped from our mounts, cursing the soldier who dragged him by a halter. By some miracle he spoke English.

"All right," he told us. "If leg don't touch ground, very soon mend." And the little yellow brother laughed. We wanted to hit him but we didn't—it would have started an "international incident."[9]

Sixteen correspondents finally got clearance to move north. Richard Henry Little recalled that he and London bought a saloon at Chemuplo, then closed the doors, running it themselves for several hours, "taking turns as bartender, and finally giving the saloon away to a poor blind man."[10] Although correspondents attended the Battle of the Yalu, military restrictions prevented field involvement. The Japanese later provided screened accounts.

After the Battle of the Yalu, McKenzie watched the wounded in a field hospital, an experience that renewed his sense of brotherhood: "Here was a Russian officer, his silver-laced coat ripped off, and thrown lightly by the doctors over him, his face graved with pain, every half-conscious thought merged in the one determination not to show signs of his agony before his nation's foes. A Japanese, whose uniform proclaimed him high in the General Staff, came up and spoke gently and pitifully to him in his own tongue. The surgeon touched the shattered limb, and the man was wrung with sharp pain, from him despite his volition. 'Not that.' And then the man was master of himself again, and there was silence."[11]

William Maxwell recorded another intense glimpse of the Russians and Japanese.

The battle was over, and in the courtyard of a Manchurian house sat victor and vanquished. It was a strange and moving picture, such as Verestchagin might have painted. In the dark quadrangle flickered the embers of a wood fire, and around it were seated a prince and a soldier and his captives. The flame threw into relief the face of the solder—a strong, clear-cut face—European rather than Oriental, over which a smile came readily. Between the firm-set lips glowed the red end of a cigar, without which General Kuroki is seldom seen. He sat at his ease, with a cap pushed well over his forehead, and slippered feet crossed. The prince at his side was in full uniform, correct in every detail from spurs to sabre-tache, and his dark, immobile features wore an expression of intense solemnity. In the front of these two on the other side of the fire were seated three Russian officers—tall blond men of Teutonic type, with fierce mustache, and the air of soldiers who know how to face death. They smoked and drank, and talked like comrades who had fought side by side and were telling to friendly ears the story of the passage of the Yalu.[12]

London's reports showed little insight into the pain and suffering of these modern warriors, the brotherhood of man, the pride and mastery of oneself. He clearly supported the aggressive Russians, refusing to admit that Japan had intervened to avoid the Kremlin's takeover of Korea and Manchuria, thus threatening their future freedom. "There was not a man who had not long dreamed of that grim easternmost symbol of Russian aggression," wrote John Fox, Jr., later author of *The Little Shepherd of Kingdom Come,* in *Following the Sun-Flag.* He called Japanese "the cleanest people in the world," and their soldiers "the best in the world."[13] London romanced in "The Yellow Peril" (*San Francisco Examiner,* September 25, 1904) that "back of our own great race adventure, back of our robberies by sea and land, our lusts and violences and all the evil things we have done, there is a certain integrity, a sternness of conscience, a melancholy responsibility of life, a sympathy and comradeship and warm human feel, which is ours, indubitably ours, and which we cannot teach to the Oriental as we would teach logarithms or the trajectory of projectiles."[14]

The race issue, of course, played a key role in London's attack on the industrious Japanese, Frederick Palmer saying that he compared them to "South American peccary pigs in their herd charges."[15] In "The Yellow Peril" London concluded that there was "a weakness inherent in the brown man which will bring his adventure to naught. From the West he has borrowed all our material achievement and passed our ethical achievement by. Our engines of production and destruction he had made his. What was once solely ours he now duplicates, rivaling our merchants in the commerce of the East, thrashing the Russian on sea and land. A marvelous imitator truly, but imitating us only in things material. Things spiritual cannot be imitated. They must be felt and lived, woven into the very fabric of life, and here the Japanese fails."[16]

Other American correspondents found spirituality in the mysterious Japanese. Louis L. Seaman, recalling a soldier returning from the front, wrote: "One would never have imagined that standing in this stolid crowd were those whose hearts were over-welling with joy to greet their loved ones. Occasionally a mother or a sister would recognize a son or brother. The greeting would be almost formal, and with an air of deference on the part of the women. The real welcome, of course, was reserved for the home, where scenes of which the world knows nothing and which are sacred took place later."[17] Frederick Palmer also recorded Japanese farewells: "There is no weeping at the farewell. I saw a reservist parting with his family at the railroad station to-night. He came in with his little boy, olive-skinned, round-faced, smiling—a live Japanese doll of three years—thrown over his shoulder. The women folk formed the inner circle, the men the outer. In the centre of such a group, the soldier in his Occidental uniform seemed to belong to a world apart. There was no weeping; for years they had expected him to go, and now he was going. He smiled, and they smiled at the parting—a variation of that Japanese smile which says: 'We are sad and try to show that we are not by being merry.' "[18]

Palmer told an amusing story about London's startling the curious Koreans at lunch: "Jack's front false teeth were attached to a plate. When the staring sheep faces pressed too close, Jack stuck out his tooth plate on the edge of his tongue, and the Koreans fell back in disorder for four or five yards. Cautiously and curiously they would draw near again; and again Jack would repulse them. Our lunch was finished and still they were unable to stand their ground in face of the strange phenomenon."[19]

London nearly ended his Korean experience with a court-martial for slugging a groom, claiming the man stole fodder from his horses. An arrest followed, his third in four months, this time very serious. (Charmian said London got arrested wherever they went—Cuba, Japan, Korea—for something. Even Hawaii worried her.) Frederick Palmer's efforts failed to free London, so the influential Richard Harding Davis cabled President Theodore Roosevelt, who protested through the United States ministry to Tokyo. Its war office then pressured General Fuju to release London, although Fuju's chief of staff demanded London leave the country.

Without the help of Davis, America's most celebrated war correspondent and personifier of the chic "Gibson Man," London could have become a firing-squad casualty. (Davis later rescued London a second time during the 1914 Mexican revolution. See chapter 16.) Remembered today for "Gallagher," his short story about a daring cub reporter of the nineties, Davis's literary fame once challenged Kipling's, his Van Bibber shorts being immensely popular. *Soldiers of Fortune,* an adventure novel, sold over 500,000 copies. Three other pieces— "The Consul," "The Deserter," and "The Bar Sinister"—illustrate Davis's precise, tailored style. "A perfect day for Mr. Davis," one caustic critic remarked, "would consist of a morning's danger, taken as a matter of course. In the afternoon a little chivalry, equally a matter of course to a well-bred man, then a dash from hardship to some great city, a bath, a perfect dinner nobly planned. Shrapnel, chivalry *sauce mousseline,* and so to work next morning on an article which presupposed in others virtues his code compelled him almost to ignore in himself. Richard Coeur-de-Lion would not have disliked such a day, once he was used to shrapnel."[20]

Still fuming about the barbarian Japanese after returning home, London spoke to Oakland's chapter of the socialist party, shocking some members with his indifference towards international brotherhood. Edmundo Peluso recalled:

With evident pleasure, he described the wiliness of these "human burnt candles," as he called the officers of the Japanese General Staff, and used stronger expressions with regard to them. But his gorge rose not only at the Japanese General Staff; he cursed the entire yellow race in the most outrageous terms. Some of the comrades present were somewhat embarrassed.

The struggle against race prejudice, especially against hatred of the "yellow" races, was part of the daily work of the Socialist branches of the Pacific Coast and it was hard to conceive of Jack London, one of the foremost members of the branch, evincing race chauvinism.

Convinced that there was some misunderstanding, one of the comrades began talking to him about classes that exist in Japan as everywhere else. Another called his attention to the slogan decorating the wall over the portrait of Marx: "Workers of all countries, unite!" But this did not touch him in the least and only served to increase his passion. Pounding his fist on the table, Jack met their arguments with,

"What the devil! I am first of all a white man and only then a Socialist!"

His comrades might have been forgiven if they wondered just what kind of Socialist Jack was turning into, with his imported valet, his individualism that blazed up at every challenge, his drive for money and fame, and his intense convictions about white supremacy. In those days, however, even Marxist Socialism was fairly tolerant with deviationists, hoping that the misguided comrade could be brought back into the line. In its later evolution into Communism and an insistence on party discipline, Jack would have lasted as a member about as long as his career as a correspondent with the Japanese First Army.[21]

Like Edmundo Peluso, correspondent Frederick Palmer also found London a strange brand of socialist. "With the exception of Jack Reed, the knight errant of the Reds, Jack London was the most inherently individualistic, and un-Socialist of all the Socialists I have ever met, and really, I thought, a philosophical anarchist. Although cheery and kindly, and liking conversation with him at the center of it, he preferred to walk alone in aristocratic aloofness, and always in the direction he chose no matter where anybody else was going. He had his own separate mess and tent; general and private of his army of one, he rode in front of his two pack-donkeys, which jingled with bells, the leader bearing an American flag.''[22]

The ''yellow peril'' threat, however, became the last of London's worries after his return from the East. When the *S. S. Korea* docked at San Francisco, a process server welcomed him with Bessie's divorce suit, one filed for extreme cruelty in the Alameda County Superior Court, attaching all his belongings—bank accounts, book royalties, even the *Spray* and *Examiner* income, blaming Anna Strunsky for the split. The *San Francisco Chronicle,* recalling the time when Anna stayed at London's home during their writing of *The Kempton-Wace Letters,* reported that ''divorce proceedings were threatened about two years ago, when, it is said, Mrs. London accidentally found Miss Strunsky sitting in her husband's lap.''[23]

The confused London, neglecting an earlier proposal to Anna, defended her to reporters: ''That is pure, sheer rot,'' he said. ''I cannot imagine how such a report has originated. It seems hardly probable that my wife has started it, for she knows that it is absolutely untrue. Outside of the time that we were thrown together as collaborators on the 'Kempton-Wace Letters,' I have seen very little of Miss Strunsky, as she and I have been away from San Francisco a great deal. We have not even corresponded, except on matters relating to our book.''[24]

It probably startled London that Bessie blamed Anna instead of Charmian Kittredge, the niece of Ninetta Eames, whom he first met in 1900. After he posed in furs one day for an *Overland Monthly* feature article, Charmian joined the group at Young's Restaurant, unmoved by the young author of short stories. More notable men attracted this thirty-ish secretary with the lively step who played piano, mastered horsemanship, and managed a European trip and Swedish maid—on $30 a month. Ninetta, who wanted her ''Childie'' to live happily ever after with a wealthy purse, may have decided London offered chances for both Charmian and *The Overland Monthly,* a literary magazine on its last legs.

Charmian became one of "The Crowd," who resented her presence—especially Carrie, George Sterling's wife.²⁵ Pretending to play Bessie's confidante, Charmian relayed their talks to London through letters. London said he first told Bessie the truth six months after their separation. Bessie, however, never forgave Charmian, painting her as a modern-day Medea to Bess and Joan.

Charmian's chance to net London arrived when Bessie and the babies went to Wake Robin Lodge for the summer, while he stayed at the Piedmont Bungalow, working on *The Sea Wolf*. When a buggy carrying him, George Sterling, and others crashed into a ravine, injuring London's leg, Charmian made bedpost appearances during his recovery, besides writing mawkish letters from her San Francisco apartment.

London resented Bessie's refusal to grant him total sexual freedom, a concession Charmian later made. "She's devoted to purity," he told George Sterling. "When I tell her morality is only evidence of low blood pressure, she hates me. She'd sell me and the children out for her damned purity. It's terrible. Every time I come back after being away from home for a night she won't let me in the same room with her if she can help it. I can see the horror in her eyes when I go near the children. She wants to make me a house animal that won't go anywhere without her approval. And worse than anything else, she's converting that bungalow into a prison. I don't want to live in a prison."²⁶

Keen in "In the Forests of the North" mirrors London's view: "The man who stays in the lodge by the fire grows not cunning and strong. He is not made happy in the eating of my kill, nor is living to him a delight. He does not live."²⁷ London also mentions "hot-house breeds—pretty, helpless, well-rounded, stall-fatted little things, blissfully innocent and criminally ignorant" in *A Daughter of the Snows*. "They are not natural or strong; nor can they mother the natural and strong."²⁸

Charmian, on the other hand, offered London a sense of freedom. She also paraded nice hips, wore frilly dresses and disliked prudes; she smoked, read censored books, and worked—long before the current women's movement. She was Frona Welse, London's idealized "mate-woman," someone wearing a feminine facade who boxed, fenced, and qualified as a comrade. Bessie didn't stand a chance. Yet while involved with Bessie London produced his most enduring stories: *The Son of the Wolf, The God of His Fathers, Children of the Frost,* and *The Call of the Wild.* After marrying Charmian, his work deteriorated, interrupted by occasional good short stories; most of it was hackwork that paid bills and supported their extravagant lifestyle.

That fall, before going to Manchuria, London and Cloudesley Johns vacationed along the Sacramento River, writing in the morning, fishing and bagging ducks in the afternoon. Then Joan caught typhoid fever. London rushed home, ready to renew domestic ties, providing she recovered. When her strength returned, promises evaporated as he headed for San Francisco bay. But like Wolf Larsen, "the old primal melancholy was strong upon him . . . the penalty which the materialist ever pays for his materialism."[29]

After the process server left San Francisco's docks, London scanned the scene: Where was Charmian? What happened to his "mate-woman"? She had retreated to Newton, Iowa, with an aunt. London wondered if she really cared. Her letters to him abroad talked about oriental jewels, Japanese kimonos, and piano rentals—much less about love. She had asked for *The Sea Wolf* manuscript, wanted to sue Bessie for opening her mail, and urged London to hold a hard line in the divorce.

Anna's response to Bessie's allegations appeared in the *San Francisco Chronicle* on June 30,1904, under the title: "Absurd and Vulgar, Says Miss Strunsky." An illustration showed Anna and Bessie, naked Cupid weeping on the side.

> "The affair strikes me as being vulgar above all other things," said Anna.
>
> Miss Strunsky is a slight, frail, spirit-looking woman with brilliant brown eyes. When seen yesterday she looked worn and wearied. The interview took place in Miss Strunsky's reception room, a bizarrely furnished apartment, with framed pictures of Maurice Maeterlinck, and others . . . hung about the walls. A

number of the young Californian novelist's photographs in his customary sweaters and Byronic collar effects adorned tables and mantels.

"Yes, I knew Mr. London for several years before he was married," said Miss Strunsky. "And our literary tastes were such as to establish a bond of mutual interest between us, and make us very good friends indeed. We were both members of the Ruskin Club.

"About three years ago, Mr. London proposed to me that we write a book together, and this was the beginning of the 'Kempton-Wace Letters,' which, as you may know, is a series of episodes on love, passing between a very old man and a very young one, whose points of view are diametrically opposed. I was the former—Mr. London the latter.

"During June, 1901, the book was practically completed, and I received a letter from Mr. London, asking me to come to his home in Piedmont in order that we might revise the manuscript together. He stated in the letter that both his mother and wife added their requests that I might come. Besides this, Mr. London's wife had been to my house to dinner several times, and I knew her slightly.

"I went to Piedmont as requested. During the first few days of my stay Mrs. London was very cordial and manifested great interest in our work, but, after a stay of five days, I became convinced that, for some reason, Mrs. London had begun to dislike me. She said nothing of any importance to make me feel out of place, but, judging from several little occurrences, I decided it was best for me to leave the London home. I carried out my resolve and left Piedmont, much against Mr. London's will, and, apparently, Mrs. London's also. Both husband and wife accompanied me to the train, and the farewell between Mrs. London and myself was that of two acquaintances between whom existed a mutual liking.

"Absurd is hardly a word strong enough to be used with regard to the silly stories about the love-making that went on before Mrs. London's eyes. Mr. London and I were very good friends, and we treated one another as such—no more. Besides, Jack London is hardly the man to make love to another woman in his own house, invited there on another errand altogether. His behavior was most circumspect toward me, and always has been.

"The ridiculous part of the whole thing is in the fact that my visit to the London's house occurred exactly two and a half years ago. At that time there was not a breath of rumor to the effect that their married life was not happy. My observations at the time served to convince me that he was blindly in love with his wife—and whatever other affection he had to give was lavished on his two children.

"Since 1901, I have seen Mr. London but three or four times. Immediately after my visit to his home, I went to New York, from there to London, and I have spent the greater part of my time since then in Italy, returning from Naples only four months ago because of the illness of my mother. This scandalous affair has reduced her almost to the stage of nervous prostration.

"I am more sorry for Mr. London than for myself that Mrs. London has seen fit to do what she has done. He is the kind of man to feel deeply about such a thing."[30]

Flora supported Anna. Bessie, living at 853 West Nineteenth Street, Oakland, with the two girls, refused public comment. A month passed. On August 6 she dismissed the cruelty charges, filing a new suit that charged London with desertion. They reached a property settlement outside court.[31] London agreed to build a new house for Bessie in Piedmont, instructing Macmillan to send her seventy-five dollars a month support. The house, which cost around four thousand dollars, depleted both his pay for the serialization of *The Sea Wolf* and the Hearst income, but these stiff terms meant freedom. Life was too short for haggles over money; besides, he couldn't afford more mudslinging now that *The Call of the Wild* had made his name.

Joan later explained the divorce's prelude and Bessie's changing the suit from cruelty to desertion.

Yielding finally to my father's pressure, my mother consulted an attorney, who was also a friend to whom she could open her heart and speak freely. Anna said that it was the attorney who proposed the plan to which my mother agreed: to draw up the divorce papers, name Anna Strunsky, and file the papers in what Anna described as a "sealed" file in the courthouse. (Such a file, I imagine, has long since ceased to exist.) The next step in the plan was to tell my father, on his return from the Russo-Japanese War assignment, that he could have his divorce, but at the cost of Anna being named in the complaint. This, both my mother and the attorney firmly believed, would end the matter; they knew that my father would not permit Anna to be hurt under any circumstances.

Then, as Anna recalled, a few days before Jack returned, a "curious" newspaperman somehow managed to gain access to the sealed file and promptly broke the news of the London divorce. The result, Anna said, was that my father told my mother, in so many words: You have done your worst. Now get a divorce on the obvious grounds—desertion. Which she did.[32]

Bessie finally withdrew the claim against Anna Strunsky, then living in New York, probably thinking second thoughts about her collaboration on *The Kempton-Wace Letters*. London told Anna that everyone who knew him got hurt, that life had soured, that success had failed to bring happiness. As Wolf Larsen laments: "Life? Bah! It has no value. Of cheap things it is the cheapest. Everywhere it goes begging. Nature spills it out with a lavish hand. Where there is room for one life, she sows a thousand lives, and it's life eats life till the strongest and most piggish life is left."[33]

What happened to Charmian Kittredge? Jack London married her in Chicago on November 19, 1905, a marriage that, somehow, survived bedlam until his 1916 death, after which she told Upton Sinclair's wife: "I now sleep soundly for the first time in many years."[34]

Chapter 11

The Wolf, the Greek—and Plagiarism

AFTER HIS BREAK from Bessie, London found some comfort in companionship with George Sterling, poet, longtime comrade, and fellow author. London called Sterling "Greek." (Others dubbed the poet "Dante.") Sterling called London "Wolf," beginning letters with such salutations as "Oh my Wolf!" "Dearest Wolf," "My Darling Wolf," "You Blessed Wolf," and "Beloved Wolf." He flattered London, the way he flattered Ambrose Bierce, ending messages with names like "The Super Slob," "The Vile Greek," and "The Parched Greek."[1] Both men, possessed by psychic pain and unstable values, helped the other endure existence.

Sterling was born in Sag Harbor, New York, on December 1, 1869, making him seven years older than London. When his learned father, senior warden of the Sag Harbor Episcopal Church, converted to Roman Catholicism, Sterling entered St. Charles College seminary. In 1890, however, he moved to California, monastic studies incomplete, and secured clerical work with a rich uncle. Marriage followed to his secretary, Caroline Rand, in 1896, a marriage destined for disaster.[2]

The bitter Ambrose Bierce, California's most feared critic, now remembered for *The Devil's Dictionary* and the short story "An Occurrence at Owl Creek Bridge," became Sterling's mentor, tirelessly improving his verse, reshaping its style, strengthening its meter and diction. Some poems Bierce printed in his

"Prattle" column for Hearst's *The Examiner*. After three fruitless years of contacts, he finally persuaded *Cosmopolitan* to
publish Sterling's "The Wine of Wizardry," then praised Sterling in a review as "a very great poet—incomparably the greatest that we have on this side of the Atlantic. And of this particular poem I hold that not in a lifetime has our literature had
any new thing of equal length containing so much poetry and
so little else."[3]

Other American writers besides Bierce admired George Sterling. Upton Sinclair called him "the dearest friend I ever had
among men."[4] Joaquin Miller described "A Wine of Wizardry"
as "titanic [and] magnificent."[5] Robinson Jeffers wrote him:
"Other poets have sublimity, but yours is of a different nature,
more literal to the word, more abstract perhaps, I've no analysis
but I recognize yours. The Pathfinders is a magnificent poem,
the same lift of enormous wings, and yet I feel that your more
metrical manner is too beautiful to be abandoned." Jeffers called
"The Cynic" a "beautiful and desolating" poem, "Lilith" a
"terrible and beautiful poem," and lauded, "There is nobody
in the world but you could write a sonnet like 'The Meteor.' "[6]
Sterling's other friends included Theodore Dreiser, Edgar Lee
Masters, and H. L. Mencken, who told F. Scott Fitzgerald that
Sterling should do his *Blix* preface.[7] Gertrude Atherton remi-
nisced: "[Sterling] was the ideal poet in appearance, tall, gracefully built, with a mop of dark hair that fell over his forehead
(but properly cut), large gray eyes 'that had an eternally burning
softness,' a beautifully curved mouth, which was generally smiling, but upon which I detected at times a fleeting expression
of scorn. But he observed none of the sartorial vagaries of the
traditional poet. In fact he wore black broadcloth, well cut, well
fitted, well pressed. He was always gay and friendly in company
and wholly without affectations or mannerisms, a delightful
talker, and as popular with men as with women."[8]

Sterling's greatest flaw was listening too much to others instead of trusting intuition. (He even let H. L. Mencken persuade
him not to accept membership in the prestigious Institute of
Arts and Letters.) Bierce he venerated, publishing several
poems under the pseudonym John Bierce, dedicating *The Testimony of the Suns and Other Poems* to him, eulogizing: "I
trouble at the splendid weight./To my unworth 'tis given to

know/How dread the charge I undergo/Who claims the holy muse as mate."[9] Bierce's biographer M. E. Grenadier says:

> Bierce was sturdily independent; Sterling, narcissistic, egocentric, clinging. Reading over their correspondence, one gets the impression of a parasitic vine wrapping itself about a stalwart oak; until the last year of their correspondence, Sterling, overriding Bierce's objections, addressed him as "Magister" or "Master." Bierce was unmercenary to a degree, yet he understood the necessity for earning a living, and he was a good businessman. Sterling, in spite of the bohemianism he flaunted, appears crass in his attitude toward money, rather like a child who feels that he is entitled to an allowance all his life simply because he exists. Bierce, incorruptible in his personal relationships, preserved a decent reticence about them; Sterling at times came perilously close to insincerity, and his confidences about his wife and his mistress Bierce regarded as appallingly candid.[10]

One thing rattled Bierce more than Sterling's intimate confidences: his association with Jack London. Carrie and Sterling's mother agreed. All considered London a menace. "Carrie, in co-operation with her mother-in-law, sought to find a substitute for London," writes Michael Paul Orth in *A Biography of George Sterling*. "They even accepted [artist] Xavier Martinez as a far better influence than London, although Marty, with his Bohemian habits and wild hair, was not the sort of companion they might have chosen for Sterling. . . . After Sterling's first book, *Testimony of the Suns,* was published, London urged Sterling to be freer in his conduct; as an artist he had earned the right to ignore conventional standards. Sterling took this advice. His mother prayed for his soul. Carrie temporarily moved out of his bedroom. Nothing worked."[11] Bierce, for years, tried to sway Sterling in letters such as the following:

December 3, 1905. "Yes, I was sorry to whack London, for whom, in his character as author, I have a high admiration, and in that of publicist and reformer a deep contempt. Even if he had been a personal friend, I should have whacked him, and doubtless much harder. I'm not one of those who give their friends carte blanche to sin. If my friend dishonors himself he dishonors me; if he makes a fool of himself he makes a fool of me—which another cannot do."

August 14, 1908. "Must the new heavens and the new earth of prophecy and science come in *your* little instant of life in order that you may not go howling and damning with Jack London up and down the earth that we happen to have?"[12]

Bierce and London met at the 1910 Summer Jinks of the Bohemian Club, a meeting that probably shook Sterling, who tried to hide his involvement with London from Bierce.

[Bierce] was a guest at the club (though sleeping at the home of his brother two miles away), and after a few hours in camp inquired as to the whereabouts of London, whom he knew to be attending the Jinks," recalled Sterling. "Oh, you mustn't meet him," I replied. "You'll be at each other's throats in five minutes." "Nonsense!" exclaimed Bierce, drawing his blond, shaggy brows together. "Bring him on. I'll treat him like a Dutch uncle." So I disentangled London from the poker-game to which he gave his forenoons, and presented him. The two men conversed in their friendliest manner, though signs of an armed peace were not lacking to my anxious eye. However, they were never to cross swords in argument, and the midnight of the grove-play saw us accompanying Bierce to his brother's home, to reach which we had to cross the river in a row-boat and then walk over a mile along the railroad track. We managed the river despite the ocean of our potations, and London and I were ambling rather unsteadily along the ties when he suddenly said: "Why, where in hell's Ambrose?"

Sure enough, Bierce had vanished. We retraced the rough way along the track, calling loudly, and were soon rewarded by the sound of his voice from the bottom of the twenty-foot embankment at our right. He had stumbled, lost his arm-clasp on London's shoulder, and slid head-first down the steep bank, to a fern bed where he seemed content to lie. We descended, and helped him to his feet. He was not even scratched, and we proceeded to our destination, where he and London sat up the rest of the night, consuming a bottle each of Three Star Martel. God knows of what they talked! I was to awaken at seven with the worst headache of my life. Truly they were made of the stuff of heroes!

London seemed vastly to interest Bierce, even before their meeting, despite the former's radicalism, and [Bierce] often referred to him, in his letters to me, as well as in his conversation. They were never to meet again. London was even more fascinated by Bierce, and more than once expressed to me a willingness to engage in argument with him on the merits of Socialism, but with the pen, not orally.[13]

Mainly because of London, the Bierce-Sterling axis split, both later slurring the other in print and letters, Sterling saying Bierce "gave too much of his energy to the breaking of butterflies on a wheel."[14] In 1912, repulsed by the London-Sterling clan, Bierce refused an invitation to Carmel, writing a friend, "I never hear from Sterling and his entourage of social impossibilities; there is not enough charitableness in this vale of tears to make them and me personally congenial, or even compatible."[15]

Joan London thought Sterling "mystified Jack for a long time."[16] He tried to immortalize the poet as suicidal Russ Brissenden in *Martin Eden*. Herbert Wace in *The Kempton-Wace Letters* lives with a poet. Dane Kempton is a poet. Sterling's verse paid pennies, forcing him to subsidize most of its publication, while holding temporary jobs, his uncle often helping. When *McClure's* welcomed work, he wrote London, "I'm not anxious to be one of the 'magazine poets.' " *Collier's* paid him only thirty dollars for his "Swimming" poem. "The damned pinders!" he wrote London. "And a red-blooded poem like that! The tight-wads!" He once told London, "I think I'll give up my wretched rhyming and write coon-songs and advertisements. And probably I'll fail at those."[17] Sterling's faith in verse eluded money-minded London. "Poetry is empty these days, empty and worthless and dead," says Herbert Wace. "All the old-world epic and lyric-singing will not put this very miserable earth of ours to rights. So long as the singers of the things of yesterday, glorifying the things of yesterday and lamenting their departure, so long will poetry be a vain thing and without avail."[18] (London, ironically, did likewise in stories, glorifying the things of yesterday, the elemental days when Vikings sacked the earth.)

A number of writers, ignoring the cultural climate and complexity of both writers' minds, have slipped a homosexual tag around London's relationship with Sterling. This would have made friends laugh—and perhaps Carrie to weep. Sterling, who loved the ladies, even rented a retreat on Montgomery Street in San Francisco for amorous pastimes. His many short-lived affairs eventually led to divorce, resulting in Carrie's suicide. (Sterling also, reputedly, committed suicide in 1926.) "Every few weeks I receive a note from some woman offering to sell me a series of his love letters," H. L. Mencken wrote Alfred A. Knopf after Sterling's death. "He wrote them by the thousands, and sent them apparently to hundreds of women. Very often he sent the same poem to as many as a dozen women. One of those who got a long series was Upton Sinclair's present wife. Sinclair is such an ass that he did not know Sterling's habits with women, and so he solemnly printed the letters in a book after Sterling's death. They made his wife look a bit ridiculous."[19]

Michael Paul Orth adds: "[Sterling's] sexual indiscretions of the Coppan and Carmel years grew after Carrie's death into a series of affairs with many women. It is not certain that this kind of sexual activity had any part in the gradual breakdown of Sterling's health, indeed, it may well have served as a reassurance that his youth was not altogether past. There was, however, one probable unpleasant result. Sterling was very interested in the devices of several health quacks who advertised the cure of venereal diseases, and at least one man who knew him [Rudolph Blaettler] remembers rumors that Sterling suffered from one or more venereal infections in the early Twenties."[20]

Sterling's weirdest kink was parading naked before friends, both men and women, exhibitionistic acts he attributed to a dislike of clothes. "He used to have himself photographed in the nude, from all angles, posing at times as a god, again as some brute animal, and at other times in obscene postures," says Bierce biographer Walter Neale. "He used to circulate the photographs among his acquaintances, particularly among the ladies, and Bierce, again to point Sterling's grossness, showed to me a large collection. In every such collection that I have seen—I have seen only those that Bierce showed to me—there were at least several pictures in which Sterling's external genitals were conspicuously displayed."[21] W. A. Swanburg also reveals in *Dreiser* that Sterling, once riding with Dreiser and

Helen Parges Richardson, "asked Helen to stop the car. He got out, disrobed and plunged into the lake. 'And it was a lovely sight to see him, too,' Helen admitted, 'as his slender body gracefully moved through the misty, foggy atmosphere. . . .' He came back with a dripping bouquet of water lilies for Helen as a policeman arrived and seized him. Sterling identified himself and the bluecoat let him go. The story made the morning *Examiner* and *Chronicle,* with pictures of Sterling and Dreiser, but Helen was not named."[22]

Famed photographer Arnold Genthe, who attended Sterling's abalone and mussel parties on Sunday afternoons at Carmel, recalled one situation involving London and Mary Austin, dressed as an Indian princess:

> George Sterling, who was proud of his classic contours, had climbed to the top of the cliff in his bathing trunks. Somewhere or other he had procured a trident and he was standing silhouetted against the sky while Jimmie Hopper was taking his picture. This was too frivolous for Mary who was gazing at the setting sun. Standing on the beach with outspread arms, she began something which sounded like an incantation, but which turned out to be a quotation from Browning.
>
> "Tis a Cyclopean blacksmith," chanted Mary, "striking frenzied sparks from the anvil of the horizon." London was standing with fork in hand, having just disposed of an abalone steak. Taking a look around which included both Mary and the horizon, he exclaimed, "Hell! I say this sunset has guts!"[23]

A need for friendship, not sexuality, seems to have linked the bizarre lives of Jack London and George Sterling, touching some inner spark, sensuous instead of sensual. Neither appreciated women, although both needed them for egocentric reasons—Sterling as potent sexual boosters, London to disarm deep-rooted insecurities. Miriam Allen deFord reasoned: "George Sterling could neither make any woman happy, nor himself be happy with any woman. As Mary Austin says, 'he made a kind of life-philosophy of his dependence upon women. . . . He was never able to enter into the psychic life of any woman!' Sara Bard Field notes that 'the feminine side of his nature was not nourished by the love relation. It fed, rather, on friendship with

men.' ''[24] Adela Rogers St. Johns, London's godchild, also remarked that he "never saw women as *people*. Women weren't
really important to him, nor was sex. I never saw Jack particularly attentive to or engrossed by a woman. He was more
interested in the men in any gathering."[25]

Where does London's preoccupation with manly men and
blond-haired boys fit? Years before Theodore Roosevelt ram-
paged through White House corridors, Americans glorified full-
chested males the way they glorified feminine females. Line
illustrations of men's naked derrieres appeared in family magazines like *Harper's Weekly*. Both men and women flocked to
see Eugene Sandow, who lifted horses and pianos over his head,
while flexing his muscled frame. Wrestlers and well-built actors
also depicted Greek statues in plastic poses on tour. Theodore
Dreiser noted in *Sister Carrie*: "Good clothes, of course, were
the first essential, the things without which [dandies were] nothing. A strong physical nature, actuated by a keen desire for the
feminine, was the next."[26] It took years before the masses accepted "Gentleman Jim" Corbett after he whipped John L.
Sullivan in 1892. Why? He wore gloves, top hat, and twirled
studded canes—all signs of weakness to the proletariat. Recalling one fight when ringmen laughed, calling him a dude,
Corbett said: "There it was! I looked too nice to be a fighter—
though why a fighter can't be careful about his appearance is
something I don't understand. If I had come in wearing a blue
flannel shirt, two days' growth of beard and a lot of scars on
my face, he'd have said I was a real gladiator. But I've always
been fond of my toothbrush and clean living, and I like to shave
every morning."[27]

Women of the times stumbled beneath the wheels of America's double standard. Men could sow oats by the bucket—but
from females society exacted virtue, domestic duty, and lots
of apple pie. Critics fumed when James A. Herne's now historic
Margaret Fleming, the radical drama about a woman who left
her adulterous husband, played Boston in 1891. They called
Margaret "a monster of morality," and the play "bold beyond
the wont of the English-speaking stage." One reviewer sneered:
"When is this Ibsenism nonsense to stop, and how many more
otherwise respectable people are to be infected by it?"[28] London

typified America's attitude towards equal rights. In his first known story "Two Gold Bricks (*The Owl*, September 1897), a character mentions "equal suffrage and all that rot."[29]

London's early stories mirror the age's male-female clichés. In "The King of Mazy May" (*The Youth's Companion*, November 1899), he wrote that "Walter Masters is not a very large boy, but there is manliness in his make-up." Walter also likes to "talk big."[30] On the other hand, he describes twelve-year-old Mabel Armitage of "A Lesson in Heraldry" (*The National Magazine*, March 1900) as being "too delicate, too good, too angelic, for this world. She was an apotheosis of all that was best, a radiant, celestial creature, one who would have surprised no one had she followed in the footsteps of Elijah and taken her rightful seat among the elect."[31]

Sexuality in London's stories reflects a mind cluttered with neuroses. Freudians have cast suspicious glances in the direction of several of his female characters—androgynous creatures capable of wrestling mightily with one hand and playing the piano with the other. Kevin Starr maintains in *Americans and the California Dream* that "London's latent homosexuality was an important element in the creation of these 'mannish heroines.' "[32] Not necessarily. The tickings of a woman's mind, as mentioned, escaped London's sights, the way they escape many narcissistic men devoted to macho myths. London also failed to infuse a sense of sexuality in his women characters. (Joan Lakeland of *Adventure* prefers camaraderie with men to kissing games.) As late as 1904 Humphrey Van Weyden muses in *The Sea Wolf*: "The love of man and woman, I had always held, was a sublimated something related to spirit, a spiritual bond that linked and drew their souls together, the bonds of the flesh had little part in my cosmos of love. But I was learning the sweet lesson for myself that the soul transmuted itself, expressed itself, through the flesh."[33]

Several writers besides Kevin Starr, nevertheless, allege London's latent homosexuality. Robert Barltrop says in *Jack London: The Man, the Writer, the Rebel* that it's "impossible not to notice the homosexual overtones"[34] with George Sterling. Joan London also concluded: "Whether his writing reveals this or not is no longer of much consequence, but the quality of the affection which existed between George and Jack gives a certain validity to the conclusions of the literary analysts. In that relatively simple era before even the man on the street became Freud conscious, both George and Jack naively declared their love for each other. Both would have furiously resented and denied the inference that would be readily drawn today from such a declaration, but it seems probable that the emotional interplay which continued between them for a number of years revealed this latent homosexuality of which neither was aware."[35]

Robert Forrey has attempted a serious psychoanalytic study of London's work. He finds homosexual tendencies, for example, in *The Sea Wolf*, tendencies that seem rational in a Freudian interpretation of data:

> The accusation that Van Weyden is effeminate is not unfounded. From a psychosexual point of view, his strong attraction to the virile Larsen suggests that he may be a homosexual. Van Weyden dwells on his lean muscularity, his strong shoulders and his extraordinary eyes. . . . Waiting on Larsen in his cabin, making up his bed and doing the other domestic chores women were expected to do for their husbands, Van Weyden finds himself admiring the captain in a way a woman might have. "When I finished the bed," Van Weyden says on one occasion, "I caught myself looking at him in a fascinated sort of way. He was certainly a handsome man—beautiful in the masculine sense." Then follows an erotically tinged description of Larsen's "beautiful face. Smooth-shaven, every line was distinct, and it was cut as clear and sharp as a cameo; while sea and sun had tanned the naturally fair skin to a dark bronze which bespoke struggle and battle and added both to his savagery and his beauty. The lips were full, yet possessed of the firmness, almost harshness, which is characteristic of thin lips. The set of his mouth, his chin, his jaw, was likewise firm or harsh, with all the fierceness and indomitableness of the male—the nose also. It was the nose of a being born to conquer and command."
>
> Van Weyden's apparently homosexual feelings reach their intensest pitch when in his capacity as the ship's nurse he dresses the wounds Larsen had received while fighting off an attack by the crew. We should note that in this scene, perhaps because he has consciously put a great deal of distance between himself and the effeminate Van Weyden, London comes as close as he ever does in his novels to openly attributing homosexual longings

to one of his heroes. In the scene London is more consciously identified with Larsen, but unconsciously Van Weyden may express London's own passive need to be loved by a domineering male. . . . [I feel London wanted to be loved by a domineering female.] "I had never before seen him stripped, and the sight of his body quite took my breath away. It has never been my weakness to exalt the flesh—far from it; but there is enough of the artist in me to appreciate its wonder.

"I must say that I was fascinated by the perfect lines of Wolf Larsen's figure, and by what I may term the terrible beauty of it. I had noted the men in the forecastle. Powerfully muscled though some of them were, there had been something wrong with all of them. . . .

"But Wolf Larsen was the man-type, the masculine, and almost a god in his perfectness. As he moved about or raised his arms the great muscles leapt and moved under the satiny skin. I have forgotten to say that the bronze ended with his face. His body, thanks to his Scandinavian stock, was fair as the fairest woman's. I remember his putting his hand up to feel the wound on his head, and my watching the biceps move like a living thing under its white sheath. It was the biceps that had nearly crushed out my life once, that I had seen strike so many killing blows. I could not take my eyes from him."[36]

London's fixation on manly muscles, now tinged with Freudian overtones, should be viewed in terms of early inferiorities as a small, withdrawn child, one feeding on fantasies. Perhaps homosexual urges slumbered within his mind. They do in most people. It must be remembered, however, that he sired two daughters from Bessie, besides two babies Charmian lost.

Besides providing years of companionship, George Sterling also played a feature role in London's writing career, revising more than a quarter million words, including work on *John Barleycorn, The Mutiny of the Elsinore, The Valley of the Moon,* and *The Sea Wolf,* which he and Charmian reshaped while London covered the Russo-Japanese War in Manchuria. (Charmian's writing skills, revealed in *Our Hawaii,* have been slighted. She typed London's manuscripts.) Sterling filled letters with aesthetic and structural comments. He wrote London on December 14, 1911, "I'll be delighted to go over all your proofs, and promise not to be too much of a purist."[37] But Sterling symbolized the poetic purist. Ambrose Bierce made a good mentor. Both Mary Austin and Arnold Genthe corroborated the Sterling touch. Mary Austin said, "At that time one found him reading manuscripts and proofs for London with a meticulous interest that never flagged; his diction was irreproachable, and his feeling for the fall of a sentence and the turn of a figure peculiarly sensitive."[38] Arnold Genthe described their method: "London did considerable writing at Carmel, for he liked to be near Sterling who was his best critic. They would write all day in adjoining rooms and in the evening would go over each other's work. Jack London in those days rarely gave a manuscript its final typing until he had submitted the drafts to Sterling, who had an eagle eye for careless writing or the misuse of words."[39]

Upton Sinclair complicated issues. "I learned that Jack left his manuscripts with George when he went off to sea; and that at such times he gave George full authority to edit and market them. Even more; George was authorized to do 'ghost writing' when and if he needed money; he had Jack's permission to write stories, sign the famous London name to them, and then sell them at the high prices Jack's by-line could command."[40] (Sterling also helped Sinclair sharpen his style at Carmel.)

"The First Poet," a one-act verse play by Sterling, illustrates Sinclair's point. Sterling wrote London on November 18, 1910:

> Since you like the First Poet and would not be ashamed to have written it, it's easier for me to talk business. The whole proposition is: What's the use in throwing away good money? You can probably get a fair sum for the First Poet. I would not be paid half as much and in spite of what you say, I'm of the same opinion still that editors will turn the thing down coming from an unknown person. You see, it's a bit of a whack at them. But they'll be glad to take *anything* with *your* name attached to it. And as for such fame as may be acquired by its publication, you know I care about as much for fame as an albatross for a manhattan. So please take the thing, add something to it, and send it out. If you ever put it in a book, you may state in a footnote that it was written in collaboration with me.[41]

"The First Poet" appeared in *Century* under London's by-line, then included in *The Turtles of Tasman* (1916) without any footnote to Sterling. London did pay Sterling, who worked on *The Assassination Bureau*, $100 for the plot of "The Hussy" and "The Red One." How many Sterling stories were published under London's name? A February 1, 1913, letter implies others: "Forgive, thou Wolf! my misunderstanding of your literary contracts. You must have told me when the repenthe of Picon was in my blood, for my notion was that you could use all stories I could send in, if not entirely bad. Now I'll have to turn them out under my own name—a nice bear-pig-skunk to get down into!"[42]

London also bought plots from desperate young author Sinclair Lewis, later recipient of the Nobel Prize for Literature. According to Franklin Walker: "Lewis submitted at least fifty-five plots to London, that London bought twenty-seven of them, and that he paid Lewis a total of $137.50. Of these it is fairly certain that London used five, three for published short stories, one for a novelette, and one for a novel, which he was never to complete."[43]

When London returned from the *Snark* cruise in 1909, his frayed reputation forced Macmillan to require outlines before book contracting. (This may also have been true with *Cosmopolitan.*) To maintain his lavish baronial estate, he rushed twenty-one books between 1909 and 1916, most potboilers filled with lifeless characters, plus scores of essays and short stories. Although he remained America's highest-paid author, earning around $75,000 a year, his endless need for money forced him to write three or four books a year, (Brett criticized this practice) re-sell stories, ignore contracts, and try to reprint short stories in anthologies. His most incredible re-sale is "The Dignity of Dollars," which *The Overland Monthly* bought twice, first in 1900, then again in 1907, the second slightly altered.[44] Henry Gallup Payne once signed London for twelve short stories, offering a staggering $1,000 each. He later winced when London sent early rejected work, not "even bothering to shake the dust from their pages."[45]

Sinclair Lewis first met London at Yale during the 1905–1906 lecture tour, then again later in California, writing him on September 28, 1910, concerning plots: "I hope to gawd that you will probably finally give me the chance to get back at the free lancing—nothing but writing—which I haven't done for over a year; can the job and really get at decent work. I've saved up some mun, but not enough yet for a sinking fund. Next spring I shall receive between two and three hundred for a novelette; so that if I get started now I shall be able to hike along nicely, with the novelette money as a safeguard if I don't sell much at first. . . . Gawd I'll be glad to get back at writing; for here what I've done—tho it has been a fair quantity—has been only at the cost of sleep—which is too cheap and instructive an amusement, is sleep, to be wasted."[46]

Lewis wrote London after one sale, "Thanks for the fifteen— it is now a part of a winter overcoat, very much needed in these pleasing N.Y. winds."[47] This was November 1911. The previous summer London had invited Lewis to submit plots, an invitation the struggling novelist grabbed, sending seventeen. Six weeks passed. Then Lewis wrote London: "How do you find my plots go, in general? Good investment? I sure hope they are. I've had so much fun reading the stories you have made from them—for instance the capital 'Abysmal Brute.' Do they prove a good business investment? Some time I'll have to get real tactful and try to find a way to get you to make me a *wedding present* of some modest per cent of your profits on 'em. Please tell your pleasant lady, Mme. Charmian, to tell me how to get you to ante up in this cheerful fashion to this youthful and timid partner (or is it local manager?) of yours."[48] Ten days later Lewis received a cool reply from London, saying he was writing the *Smoke Bellew* stories and *Sun Tales,* which limited time for outside ideas. He also accused Lewis of submitting O. Henry-type plots, and that because first-rate magazines had refused *The Abysmal Brute,* based on Lewis's idea (bought for $7.50), he received only $1,200 for it.

At one time Lewis even offered London a collection called *The World Police,* inspired by Sherlock Holmes. "The series should not be touched till you really feel acquainted with the big central figure, the man who *is* the series: everything about him from his ideas on matrimony up to his brand of tobacco. He need not—should not, and with you writing, would not—be

in the least like Sherlock Holmes; but Holmes offers suggestions.''[49] Lewis held high hopes for this series, asking $40, five
times his usual rates, but London refused it.

However London used writers like George Sterling and Sinclair Lewis, charges of plagiarism hounded his entire career.
As early as 1907, *Current Literature* remarked: ''Of late he has
even been charged with being in such a hurry to produce 'copy'
that he was forced to dip his pen into other people's ink.''[50]
When did this ink dipping start? L. A. M. Bosworth showed
in *The Independent* that London copied sections from Edgerton
R. Young's *My Dogs in the Northland* almost verbatim for *The
Call of the Wild*. Several of Bosworth's paralleling passages
follow. (Young's original words appear on the left, London's
recycled ones on the right.)

''He was a magnificent St. Bernard dog, and his name was Jack.'' He was ''accompanied by a very beautiful Newfoundland dog, whose name was Cuffy.'' ''Of the short, curly-haired variety.'' ''I did not have the slightest trouble in breaking him into his work in the harness.''

The father of Buck was ''a huge St. Bernard.'' ''Curly, a good-natured Newfoundland,'' was ''led away'' with him. In the harness ''Buck learned easily.''

The missionary had a dog, who, he says, was ''not what might be called handsome,'' and one of whose eyes had been destroyed. ''He ever resented being silently approached on his blind side.'' ''He was never an affectionate or playful dog. A petting he considered an insult. Kind words he treated with scorn. . . . He was never seen to play with the other dogs.''

Jack London introduces a dog ''with a battle-scarred face and a single eye,'' who ''asked nothing, gave nothing, expected nothing.'' ''He was called Sol-leks. . . . The Angry One.'' ''He had one peculiarity . . . he did not like to be approached on his blind side.''

Speaking of the cries of the Eskimo dogs at night, Dr. Young says: "These strange, weird howlings would begin about nine o'clock. . . . At first it sounded very eerie-like, and not unmusical . . . like a succession of O-O-O-O-'s long-drawn out, rising and falling on the clear frosty air." But as others took up "the doleful notes," it became "the most ear-splitting din that ever mortals heard. . . . At about midnight these horrid choruses were repeated, and then again at about three o'clock in the morning."

Jack London: "Every night, regularly, at nine, at twelve, at three, they lifted a nocturnal song, a weird and eerie chant . . . pitched in minor key with long-drawn wailings and half-sobs."

"Rover, like all of my civilized dogs, had not the hard, firm, compact feet of the Huskies." So for him and others dog shoes were made. The dogs were not long in finding "out the comfort there was in them," and "Rover soon became an adept in asking for his shoes. . . . It was interesting to see how he would wait until we were ready to harness up the dogs, then he would deliberately throw himself on his back, and putting up his feet, eloquently, even if mutely, thus plead for his warm shoes."

"Buck's feet were not so compact and hard as the feet of the Huskies. His feet had softened during the many generations since his first wild ancestor was tamed." "The dog-driver . . . sacrificed the tops of his own moccasins to make four moccasins for Buck. This was a great relief, and Buck caused even the weazened face of Perrault to twist itself into a grin one morning when François forgot the moccasins, and Buck lay on his back, his four feet waving appealingly in the air."[51]

London answered Bosworth in *The Independent*. He admitted indebtedness to *My Dogs in the Northland*, but denied plagiarist charges, rationalizing that all fictionists used factual material. He was skirting the main issue—at what point does fair use become piracy?

The Independent also mentioned Stanley Waterloo's charges of plagiarism against London for *Before Adam,* a hack novelette about primitive man. "I am not personally acquainted with Mr. London, but I am convinced that he is a clever writer when he uses other people's brains. He has accomplished in six weeks what it took me fifteen years of deep study and investigation to produce," wrote Waterloo." 'The Story of Ab' was my pet and I worked on it for fifteen long years. Jack London not only starts out with the same proposition I based my work on, but he employs in some instances practically the same language."[52]

London countered that Waterloo generalized from one *Before Adam* installment in *Everybody's Magazine.* He added that both of them owed background ideas to H. G. Wells, Andrew Lang, and Rudyard Kipling. *The Bookman* reported that "Mr. London's frontispiece was copied bodily from Mr. Waterloo's rough chart of the lands inhabited by his cave men." The magazine noted that "many of the names in *Before Adam* were either imitated or deliberately taken from *The Story of Ab,* as, for instance, that of Sabre-tooth, the dreaded cave-tiger; and that, to go no further than the opening chapters, the incidents of the two stories form . . . [a] close parallel."[53]

George Sterling's letters enlighten matters. "Waterloo and Wells have both done better with that subject. Then, your opening chapters are so far from being convincing (I have to use that word on you!) that I think you'd better have left out all explanations, and approached the theme as Wells or Waterloo did." He also wrote: "Garnett says he's found ten scientific errors in the first chapter of the story, but I think that's absurd." After mentioning Well's *A Story of the Stone Age,* Sterling remarked, "I'm wondering what Wells will think of Everybody's impudent (or ignorant) assumption of your pioneership in the fiction of the primitive." Another remark shows that as late as 1907 London's plagiarism escaped Sterling. "I can't see how you can jus†ly be charged with plagiarism of Waterloo's stuff, unless you paralleled some specific occurrence."[54]

Ambrose Bierce also wrote Sterling about *Before Adam.* "I rather like your defence of Jack London—not that I think it valid, but because I like loyalty to a friend whom one does not believe to be bad. (The 'thick-and-thin' loyalty never commends itself to me; it is too dog-like.) I fail, however, to catch the note of penitence in London's narratives of his underlife, [Bierce meant *The Road*] and my charge of literary stealing was not based on his primeval man book, 'Before Adam.' ''[55] London and Sterling seldom bickered. Bierce's plagiarism charges, however, caused friction when London wrote a satire that maligned Bierce as the father of an illegitimate actress. This incensed Sterling. He demanded the manuscript and destroyed it.

Another plagiarist charge at the time faced London. The *New York World* accused him of lifting "Love of Life" from August Bridle's and J. K. MacDonald's *Lost in the Land of the Midnight Sun*. This led *The Bookman* to chide, "Mr. Jack London has incurred the apparently inevitable charge of plagiarism and the deadly parallel, and appears to be somewhat exasperated."[56] The *New York Telegraph* added: "Examples of unconscious celebration, to use a mild and unirritating phrase, have not been common in the past, but it is seldom that a man of caliber, even if his character is a little bit frayed at the edges, is caught with the goods twice in a single year. . . . London cannot plead poverty. His income from his royalties and other sources is large. He is in demand and could command a good price in the market if he would confine himself to descriptive writing of actual occurrences."[57] London denied all charges.

When Frank Norris's "The Passing of Cock-Eye Blacklock" appeared in the July 1902 *Century* and London's "Moon-Face" in that month's *San Francisco Argonaut*, controversy had also flared. Both writers, it seems, borrowed from earlier sources. London admired Norris's work, including *The Octopus, Moran of the Lady Letty*, and especially *Vandover and the Brute*, in which the central character dropped on all fours, "kept rattling his teeth together, and every now and then he would say, way down in his throat so it sounded like growls, 'Wolf—wolf—wolf.' ''[58] Franklin Walker notes: "It is interesting that six years after Norris brought adventure to the hero in *Moran of the Lady Letty* by having him shanghaied from the San Francisco waterfront, London opened *The Sea Wolf* by having Humphrey Van Weyden forcefully taken to sea by Wolf Larsen, who had pulled him out of the San Francisco waters after a ferry collision in the fog."[59] (*The Sea Wolf*'s first chapter also resembles Kipling's first chapter in *Captains Courageous.*)

London later locked horns with Frank Harris, now noted for *My Life and Loves,* then editor of England's *Vanity Fair,* over the Bishop of London sequence in *The Iron Heel.* London admitted plagiarism to Harris, tracing his source to *The Socialist Voice,* a piece presumed factual. He added that Harris received valuable promotion from their clash. Harris, however, originally called the piece "imaginative,"[60] adding that "when [London] altered a word he has worsened the phrase."[61] Harris fumed for months in *Vanity Fair,* American newspapers reprinting his remarks. He finally charged in its October 27, 1909, issue:

> Mr. Jack London began this controversy by showing himself to be not only light-fingered, but heavy handed as well. Being forced to admit that he had taken an article of mine and had incorporated it bodily and almost word for word in his book, "The Iron Heel," he excused himself by asserting that my pretended report of the Bishop of London's speech was so realistic that he had been deceived by it. . . . That Mr. Jack London was deceived hardly affects the ethics or the esthetics of the situation. [This is an amusing remark, because London substituted ethnics and economics for ethics and esthetics in his life scheme.] Is he justified in taking a speech of the Bishop of London and putting it word for word into the mouth of an American bishop, invented *ad hoc*? Are we to take it that Mr. Jack London's novels are *réchauffé* of newspaper reports? Is that what his readers expect and pay for?[62]

Frank Harris later voiced his views on London to Upton Sinclair: "Jack London it seems to me might have thought but didn't; he was evidently too greedy for money and enjoyment to give himself time to do his best work. . . . The more I read of your praise of Jack London the more I wonder. . . ."[63]

London told Cloudesley Johns in 1899—a year before Macmillan Company published his first collection—that originality eluded him, that he preferred to interpret facts. Soon afterwards Johns found ideas in the essays and short stories that he sent London for criticisms contained in his friend's work. He accused London of modeling "In a Far Country" on his short story "North-Drake Co." London replied that he conceived the idea long before reading Johns's manuscript. When Johns worked on his "Philosophy of the Road," London asked for sections; his tramp articles later appeared in *Wilshire's Magazine,* then were collected in *The Road.*

When Franklin Walker reviewed *The Fiction of Jack London: A Chronological Bibliography* by Dale L. Walker and James Sisson III, he concluded that "one is disturbed by evidence of London's constant search for a market in even the most obscure of journals, by his willingness to sell stories twice under different titles, and by his practice of borrowing and buying plots from established writers like Joseph Conrad and willing friends like Sinclair Lewis and George Sterling. Striking also is his willingness to capitalize on other genres than the fiction for which he was best suited, genres such as the essay, the poem, and the drama."[64]

Forty years before the Walker-Sisson bibliography, Richard Francis made an exhaustive two-year analysis of London's work. "It is time Jack London is pulled off his pedestal and shown as he really was," he wrote in the November 28, 1932, issue of the *Oakland Tribune.* "I found that working on the bibliography I had discovered hitherto unknown or unadmitted facts on Jack London's life." Francis concluded: "He was burnt out as a writer, and knew it. He was deeply in debt. So he turned to stories previously published in national magazines, gave them new names and resold them to obscure journals which were unlikely to meet the eyes of the first purchasers. Thus I found material originally printed in *Cosmopolitan* reappearing in *Uncle Remus' Magazine* in Georgia. 'Martin Eden,' the articles on the 'Snark' expedition, and a dog story variously known as 'Diable' and 'Bâtard' are among the writings thus republished in one place or another."[65]

London's early advice to would-be writers: "The three great things are: GOOD HEALTH; WORK; and a PHILOSOPHY OF LIFE. I may add, nay, must add, a fourth—SINCERITY. Without this, the other three are without avail; with it you may cleave to greatness and sit among the giants."[66]

Chapter 12

Socialist on the Speaker's Trail

BY OCTOBER 1905, eleven of London's books, numerous articles, and over seventy-five short stories had been published, yet his bank account tallied less than $210. "I run out a couple of books a year, but I'm always in debt," he told a reporter in 1905. "Look at that hand! See where the light comes through the fingers? That hand leaks."[1] When the Slayton Lyceum Lecture Bureau in Chicago, therefore, suggested a cross-country tour, London hit the speaker's trail, anxious for extra cash.

The Bureau soon regretted this invitation. P. S. Williams wrote in 1906,

> While on the road, he was guilty of frequent delightfully unbusinesslike performances, such as paying fare at full rates because he had thoughtlessly locked his mileage book in his trunk; nor could he be persuaded but that such as these were not legitimate items for his expense account. On one occasion the whole sixth floor of the . . . Chicago bureau . . . was thrilled with holy terror to encounter an item in London's account: "To one stomach ache—50 cents," which presumably was a bill for medical services. The crowning feature of these little incidents was London's remittance of something over two hundred dollars in currency to the bureau by mail. The night it was sent the remittance was caught in a fire, and was destroyed. Mr. London refused to make it good.
>
> "Why should I?" he asked. "I registered it. I sent $400 to my own bank in California at the same time."

201

"I suppose you would expect them to make that good had it
been destroyed?" commented Secretary Wagner, of the bureau.
"Sure" London assented.
"It's not customary to send such remittances in that manner,"
said Mr. Wagner. "No business man would do it."
"You shouldn't expect me to be a business man," replied
London.
"We'll sue you," declared his manager.
"Go ahead," retorted London, to whom all publicity is grist
for his mill.[2]

The Bureau did sue—and won, forcing London to pay them
$203. What about the registered letter? "The mail car that car-
ried the letter was burned. The government paid London $25
for the letter,"[3] reported the *San Francisco Examiner*.

The Intercollegiate Socialist Society, founded in 1905, sponsored London's lecture tour, although the Slayton Lyceum
Lecture Bureau arranged schedules. An inspiration of Upton
Sinclair, the I.S.S. solicited support from men like millionaire
socialist William English Walling, New York nabob J. Phelps
Stokes, lawyer Clarence S. Darrow, B. O. Flower, editor of
The Arena, and Jack London, its first president. The society
proposed to promote "an intelligent interest among college men
and women, graduate and under-graduate, through the forma-
tion of study groups in the colleges and universities, and the
encouraging of all legitimate endeavors to awaken an interest
in Socialism among the educated men and women of the country,"[4] not to incite revolution through channels outside the constitution's framework.
    With several basic speeches up his sleeve, London shuffled
ideas to suit each audience and situation. For ladies' clubs and
organizations, the Bureau billed him as "daring traveler, an
original Klondiker, an experienced seaman, a prominent Socialist, the American Kipling." He usually entertained these
groups with colorful Klondike tales, his early life as a San
Francisco newsboy, the Russo-Japanese War, and whaling on
the high seas, sometimes reading from his stories. At Bowdoin

College, he spoke about his "experiences as Tramp, Klondiker and Correspondent, with reading."[5] One audience member recalled, "London who, directly after making a dull speech on socialism at Bowdoin College, sat by our fireside and thrilled us half the night with his adventures in Alaska."[6]

To radicals, however, London appeared as "Prominent Socialist" and "Novelist and Socialist friend of the Under Dog." These speeches? Spiked with sharp-edged cant against the capitalistic system, later published in *The Contemporary Review* as "Revolution."[7] Sometimes both socialists and the general public attended appearances. The *Los Angeles Examiner*, which covered his January 1905 "Scab" speech in Simpson Hall, reported that "the Socialists had no monopoly of seats" and that many came out of "curiosity to see the writer for the laborer's field—the romanticist confronting the actual."[8] This happened everywhere. Capitalists, as well as socialists, wanted a glimpse of Jack London, the celebrated author of *The Call of the Wild*, many naive about his revolutionary socialism.

A socialist reporter with *Common Sense* interviewed London before the speech, saying that while "the musicians were doing the opening stunts [he] made connections with the comrade and, between puffs of his cigarette, drew from him some rapid fire comments and observations." When asked the source of his socialism, London referred the reporter to a back issue of *The Comrade*, which, the reporter said, "*Common Sense* might do a great many worse things than republish if I didn't mind the suggestion." A statement from London regarding socialistic writers followed, one knocking both the intellectuals—and himself.

You must not attach too much importance to these artists and literary people in the Socialist movement. Many of them—most of them in fact—are Socialists, but they are not the Socialist movement and never will be. The Socialist movement is made up of people to whom grocery and rent bills are as ghosts that haunt forever. These artists and literary people are parasites. They can afford a fad. No, they are not all sentimentalists. Many of them can give a scientific reason for the faith that is in them and many of them would suffer for the cause if need be. But they are not pressed by the terrible realities that the exploited wealth producers are. I have become a parasite. But I was not always one.[9]

London then showed the reporter his hands, recalling when he sold papers on San Francisco streets and labored for a buck.

On January 20, 1905, he addressed "a large number of students"[10] at the university in Berkeley. President Benjamin Ide Wheeler chaired the occasion. Instead of lecturing on literature, as scheduled, London substituted "The Revolutionary Spirit of the American Proletariat." He opened with the following.

> Yesterday I received a letter from Arizona addressed 'Dear Comrade' and closing with the words 'Yours for the Revolution.' There are 500,000 men in the United States today who are writing thus. In Germany there are 3,000,000; in France nearly 2,000,000. In all there are 15,000,000 working for the same cause in the countries of the world that are civilized. They have before them no figment of the imagination, no Utopia. Their revolution is already with them. It is here now. The movement is unparalleled. It is all other revolutions rolled into one. The American and French revolutions were local, isolated ones compared with this one. It is an organized, international revolution of such tremendous scope that it will prove irresistible. Never in history have men from all countries united in one great movement.[11]

When London finished his "anarchistic declamation," he stepped from the platform, relieving a tense audience. Professor Charles Mills Gayley, one of London's former teachers at Berkeley, commended his literary success, but London continued: " 'Dr. Gayley permit me to make the criticism, that English is not being taught in the right way. You are giving the students for their textbooks such antiquated authors as Macaulay, Emerson, and others of the same school. What you need in your course is a few of the more modern types of literature, for instance—'

"Dr. Gayley interrupted London's remarks, and with a dry smile said: 'Perhaps you are not aware, Mr. London, that we are using your "The Call of the Wild" as a text-book in the University.' London stared for a minute at his former instructor and without a word walked away."[12]

For some strange reason, London enjoyed antagonizing middle-class audiences, especially college and club groups. Once after the publication of *John Barleycorn,* among other things an antisaloon tract, he ordered beer before some teetotalers.[13] During a 1902 speech for the Pacific Coast Women's Press Association he pretended to lose his Kipling notes, presenting instead the tramp essay, which incensed these tea-time socialites. "The lecturer was plied with questions concerning what the several members of the association ought to do with the tramp who sat upon their 'back stoops'—always sitting, never flitting, like the raven on the bust of Pallas above the chamber door. There was a tone of resentment in all these inquiries, and it was apparent that the egotism of the inquiries had been roused to antagonism—that each woman differed from Mr. London upon the specific instance while agreeing with him in the general idea that the tramp is 'the by-product of an economic necessity.' "[14]

London's famous grin, known as "the smile that won't come off,"[15] fooled lots of ladies and small-talk audiences, while his sharp tongue lashed conventional ideas. This tactic didn't work at Harvard. Around two thousand jammed the Harvard Union's great room on December 24, 1905, and punctuated London's remarks with laughter. They roared after his comment, "I was in Colorado with Mother Jones . . . along with our noble leaders of the economic revolution." They also laughed again when he declared about the famous strike agitator, "Fellows, Mother Jones is one of the noblest women in the world. If I were to be born a thousand times I would ask no better birthright than to be born of Mother Jones."[16]

Harvard's papers dismissed London's speech with a few paragraphs, *The Harvard Crimson* calling his address "an arraignment of the capitalist class for its mismanagement of society," adding that "this criminal mismanagement is bringing on the uprising of the working class, the Revolution."[17] *The Harvard Advocate* reasoned that people should be informed about the facts before accepting London's invitation to "line up!"[18] for socialism.

London had earlier applauded the Russian anarchists at a businessmen's meeting in Stockton, California, shortly after Bloody Sunday in St. Petersburg, calling the United States "the greatest 'scab' on earth."[19] *The Miners Magazine* said that this caused near chaos.

"You are drones that cluster around the capitalist honey-vats. You are ignoramuses. Your fatuous self-sufficiency blinds you to the revolution that is surely, surely, coming, and which will as surely wipe you and your silk-lined, puffed up leisure off the face of the map. You are parasites on the back of labor."

A few other well-chosen and graphic remarks followed. There was a terrific uproar. The "drones" and the "parasites" and the "ignoramuses" cried aloud in their wrath. They arose on their 25 cent seats (for the benefit of the socialist cause) and hurled epithets at the lecturer:

"Do you know what will be the result of your revolution?" one millionaire sugar king shouted.

"It is not MY revolution," London broke in. "It is YOURS. Yes, yours and your kind's. You are the cause of it!"

"Anarchy! Civil War! Death and crime! These will be the results of that revolution you are prophesying. National up-heaval"—the millionaire began again—

"I know it," said London. "But what are you going to do about it? How are you going to stop it?"[20]

While in Boston, London spoke at Tremont Temple, shocking his audience with the declaration, "I consider the Russian Nihilist assassins my comrades,"[21] the same declaration made at Harvard. "I shall canonize them."[22] Another oration at Faneuil Hall led the *Boston Post* to remark that "seldom has the old Cradle of Liberty held such a concourse of people, who both championed and denounced the ideas of the now famed author and lecturer."[23] *The Arena* agreed, saying that although the meeting was "on the order of an informal talk," so many attended that "a large proportion of them [were] compelled to stand."[24] Franklin H. Wentworth presided, and "Mother" Jones, labor leader whom London praised at Harvard, urged everyone to show "the revolutionary spirit of your comrades in Russia."[25]

London spoke for nearly two hours, telling his audience, among other things: "The capitalist denies the existence of the misery alleged by the Socialist, but the capitalist class isolates itself from the class it has robbed; it is part of the policy of the capitalists not to see or know how much misery that workmen suffer. But there is a better day coming, and it is something that I should shake up this capitalistic class, blind and greedy as it is, that never before was there so worldwide an organization of labor as there is today, that never before were workingmen in different countries so organized into an international revolutionary movement as we know them to be today."[26]

London's sensational November 19, 1905, marriage to Charmian Kittredge—announced the day after his divorce from Bessie became official—drew considerable attention. The reason for such haste? Michael Paul Orth, who interviewed the wife of Xavier Martinez, says:

> Mrs. Martinez remembers that Carrie [George Sterling's wife] was furious when she heard that London had married Charmian; Carrie did not care for London, but while in Piedmont she found common ground with his first wife, Bess Maddern. Bess was a lower middle-class school teacher, and, according to Mrs. Martinez, a prude. Carrie had her own marital problems at this time, and so she sympathized with Mrs. London. In addition to this, London had, in 1904 and 1905, been showing serious interest in one of Blanche Partington's sisters, who was an opera singer in New York. London had asked the Partington sister to decide between him and her career. He stopped to see her on his 1905 lecture tour through the East. Charmian heard that he was going to New York, and she met him at the station there. That was all for London. He married Charmian a few weeks later.[27]

Fireworks exploded when newspapers reported that because of a new Illinois law that required a one-year interval before remarriage, London was unable to tie the knot. Cancellations poured into the Lyceum Lecture Bureau, especially from America's Bible belt. One prominent Iowan accused the Women's Club of Des Moines of flattering someone who "so lightly treated the marriage relation. . . . To lionize one who is guilty of moral laxity, is to condone the offence."[28] But London retaliated: "I will get married in every State of the union just as fast as I can get from one to another, if it is necessary. The State law of California provides that a divorced person may not marry within a year and to encompass this end the courts grant a divorce and one year later a decree and the decree was granted last Saturday. As to whether this divorce is amenable to the laws of Illinois is something I don't know, but it seems that the Illinois law did not go into effect until last July and it cannot affect my case.''[29] The *San Francisco Call* disagreed, saying it applied to Californians, that London received his final decree on November 18, 1905.

After speaking in Boston at Faneuil Hall, London, Charmian and their Korean servant boarded the fruit steamer *Admiral Farragut* and sailed for Jamaica, Cuba, and Florida, planning a few weeks' vacation. Friends waved good-by at ten o'clock on Long Wharf.[30]

Scheduled by the Intercollegiate Socialist Society to speak in New York's Grand Central Palace on January 19, 1906, at 8:00 P.M., London managed a 9:00 P.M. appearance, having just returned from his Jamaican trip. The *New York Times* reported that ''candy was hawked through the audience and a great number of little red flags at 10 cents each were rapidly bought up. These the fakers cried out to be genuine blood-red Jack London souvenirs of a great and momentous occasion.'' Many women, who outnumbered men by two to one, also wore red dresses and hats accented with red ribbons. Upton Sinclair recalled few collegiates, many present being from the Lower East Side, Jewish boys and girls wearing red badges, serving as ushers. While J. G. Phelps Stokes, society vice-president, introduced London, ''the cries of the peddlers who sold copies of Mr. London's latest socialist book''[31] competed for the audience's attention.

Stokes made one thing clear: he didn't endorse London's message. ''When asked to preside at this meeting I was told that the subject of Mr. London's address would be 'The Message of Socialism.' There is so very much in this message that I was very glad to accept the invitation. Owing to some misunderstanding on the part of those who sent out the call for the meeting a much narrower subject has been announced, and one in regard to which great differences of opinion exist among those who believe in Socialism,'' he qualified. ''The accumulation of power in the hands of a few unscrupulous individuals and the increasing rashness displayed in speculative ventures by men having control of vast wealth endangers the public welfare. Nevertheless, it by no means follows that the catastrophe which these things threaten will necessarily come upon us. Mr. London will present to you this evening the other point of view."[32]

Speaking on "The Coming Crisis" for an hour and fifteen minutes, London expressed hope that his comments wouldn't cause "seas of blood," although he assumed all would be convinced by his facts, by the "science and philosophy" of his logic. (He always advised, "confine yourself to the fact, man, the irrefragable fact," a rule he rarely applied in practice.)[33] Pinning strike failures on scabs and injunctions, London predicted new recruits to the socialist army would say: "To hell with the Constitution," a remark leading one old patriotic soldier to ask whether this was London's observation or a quotation. London answered it belonged to a Colorado soldier, causing the old man to leave, while "Mother" Jones leaned from a box shouting: "Yes, and it was a General."[34]

One *New York Times* interviewer recalled that most of London's audience came to hear a celebrated author, unaware of his fierce socialism that claimed brotherhood with the Russian revolutionists, championing the "magnificent fight against the villainy of capitalism" and the "hidden hand of malice in the kid glove of capitalism." During the interview a cigarette dangled from London's lips, and a Japanese valet "waited upon him noiselessly."[35] Manyoungi, the devoted valet brought back from Korea, made critics fume during this engagement. " 'He even sat in his chair and let that heathen Jap bring him a drink,' indignantly declared one hard-headed capitalist who had become rich by shining his own shoes and shaving himself for some three score years."

" 'That's all right; he is conserving his strength to exploit socialism,' "[36] ingeniously explained a defender.

The day after his Grand Central Palace speech, London met Upton Sinclair, another socialist disciple, in a restaurant, along with Charmian and the editor of *Wilshire's Magazine* and his wife. A teetotaler, Sinclair later wrote: "His eyelids were inflamed, and there were in his face and speech all the signs of alcoholism I had learned to recognize. He ordered drinks throughout the meal and during the hours of talk which followed.''³⁷ Sinclair also said that London told him "tales of incredible debauches; tales of opium and hashish, and I know not what other strange ingredients; tales of whiskey bouts lasting for weeks.''³⁸ Although some have accused Sinclair of exaggeration, London admitted using opium and hashish with Sterling; he also kept a copy of Victor Robinson's *An Essay on Hasheesh: Including Observations and Experiments* (1912) in his library, according to Andrew Sinclair. (Sterling even alludes to poppy-blooms in ''A Wine of Wizardry and Other Poems.'')

Thus ended a friendship, although London and Upton Sinclair exchanged letters for years, even reviewing each other's books. Every now and then, London extended an invitation to Glen Ellen, one Sinclair refused because George Sterling said "Jack's drinking has become tragic.''³⁹ (H. L. Mencken agreed: "I daresay Jack London's finish was due to his chronic alcoholism in youth. He was a fearful drinker for years and ran to hard liquor.'')⁴⁰ Following London's death, Upton Sinclair recalled in *The Masses* that they met again six or seven years after the Palace speech. London's "voice was almost entirely gone from the effects of sore throat. He was trying the drink treatment; my last picture of him in the flesh was very much of the flesh, alas!—with a flask of gin before him, and the stumps of many cigarettes in his dinner-plate, and his eyes red and unwholesome-looking.''⁴¹

London did, however, review Sinclair's *The Jungle* in *Wilshire's Magazine*, comparing its import to *Uncle Tom's Cabin*.⁴² "The book is to come into the world as a straight proletarian proposition with a low royalty for me & a price about ¢50 in quantities,'' Sinclair wrote him, pleading for a five-hundred word review. "You will understand what this book means to me & what a grave decision it has been to trust it to the underground movement. . . . We have *got* to make this go. Among other things I shall die if it doesn't so if you ever want to see me!—''⁴³

While in New York during January 1906, London addressed a wealthy group, later using the experience in "The Philomaths,'' a chapter in *The Iron Heel*. Joshua Wanhope, who attended this meeting, recalled that London's allegations shook the audience.

"You have been entrusted with the world; you have muddled and mismanaged it. You are incompetent, despite all your boastings. A million years ago the caveman, without tools, with small brain, and with nothing but the strength of his body, managed to feed his wife and children, so that through him the race survived. You, on the other hand, armed with all the modern means of production, multiplying the productive capacity of the caveman a million times—you are incompetents and muddlers, you are unable to secure to millions even the paltry amount of bread that would sustain their physical life. You have mismanaged the world, and it shall be taken from you."

"The 'silk-stockinged audience,' " Wanhope recalled, "murmured their perturbation, anger and impatience, but the unrelenting London went on":

"Who will take it from you? We will! And who are we? We are seven million socialist revolutionists and we are everywhere growing. And we want all you have! Look at us! We are strong! Consider our hands! They are strong hands, and even now they are reaching forth for all you have, and they will take it, take it by the power of their strong hands; take it from your feeble grasp. Long or short though the time be, that time is coming. The army is on the march, and nothing can stop it, that you can stop it is ludicrous. It wants nothing less than all you have, and it will take it; you are incompetent and will have to surrender to the strong. We are the strong, and in that day we shall give you an exhibition of power such as your feeble brains never dreamed the world contained."

"There was a loud murmur of protest and dissent," Wanhope continued, "and one or two respectable-looking persons choked up, and seemed as if they were about to have apoplexy. London walked down from the rostrum through a sea of blasted, purple faces distorted with rage, but no attempt was made to detain him. . . . It was not until he was well out of earshot that some of the stunned audience plucked up enough courage to remark that 'he ought to be in jail.' "[44]

Sometimes London's radicalism backfired. When the Oakland High School debating society invited him to speak in April 1905, the principal and superintendent barred him from the public schools.⁴⁵ As to whether it's gossip or not, Herb Caen, columnist for the *San Francisco Chronicle,* explained in 1939 that "popular Jimmy Pond, then principal of Oakland High, invited the great Jack London to come over and address the student body. This was around '04, and Jack was in rare form; his fame was growing and his tongue was sharp and vitriolic. 'Don't take your studies too seriously,' London advised the students maliciously, 'Jimmy here—he's a good guy, but after all he's only doing what he's being paid to do. And remember that half the stuff in your books is phony.' Principal Pond took it as long as he dared; then he arose and said: 'O.K., let's go boys.' Whereupon the Oakland High football team arose as a man, marched onto the stage, grabbed the bewildered London and threw him smack through the auditorium window!'"⁴⁶

London's Yale appearance received wider public notice than did his later visits to Yale and the University of California. Dr. Alexander Irvine, minister of the Pilgrim Church in New Haven and secretary of the local Socialist party, persuaded the Yale Debating Association to sponsor London—an invitation which met with considerable controversy among the faculty. William Lyon Phelps, then a young professor, said: "Yale is a university, and not a monastery; besides, Jack London is one of the most distinguished men in America." Red posters showing London in a red sweater, meanwhile, colored the campus, posters with the word REVOLUTION on them. This caused more academic flutters, one Socialist student writing Irvine, "Yale Union and many of the faculty are sweating under the collar for fear London *might* say something Socialistic."⁴⁷

London finally spoke before twenty-eight hundred. All paid ten cents for admission. (Irving had promised to make up losses in case very few attended.) London used "The Coming Crisis," a variation of his usual "Revolution" speech, leading the *New Haven Register* to comment that "one of the most conspicuous in the country, standing upon the platform of Woolsey Hall and boldly advocating the doctrines of revolution was a sight for gods and men."⁴⁸ The *Yale Alumni Weekly* noted that "the majority of those in the hall were from the city, and included many Germans, Russians, Italians, and Jews, evidently warm sympathizers with the cause of socialism."⁴⁹ London told about his early working-class roots in the "cellar of society," Gorky's phrase, where he "sweated [his] bloody sweats," finally determining to become a "seller of brains." Then he attacked the "rottenness" of America's business world, the decadence of its university system, and the socialist's militant stand against capitalism.

Although Philip Foner says that "when he finished, London received a tremendous ovation from the students and was carried off the platform on the shoulders of a group of Yale men,"[50] contemporary accounts differ. Mark Schorer, more than half a century later, remarks in *Sinclair Lewis* that "the Yale students in that audience, in the recollection of George Soule, behaved very badly, laughed and booed and stamped and brayed. . . . After the lecture London was taken to a student dormitory, where he answered questions for hours."[51] The *Yale Alumni Weekly* at the time said that "from the expressions heard after the lecture it was a disappointment to most of the audience."[52] Alexander Irvine reported: "A woman—a lady—went out swearing. A few students tried hard to sneer, but succeeded rather indifferently. . . . Jack London gripped by the intellect and held them. . . . There was some applause at the beginning and some at the close, but at neither end was it intense or prolonged."[53]

London did write an article called "Things Alive" for the *Yale Monthly Magazine,* again knocking the academic world.

Modern American college life has in it a good many of the characteristics of old monasticism. The students shut themselves up, for a great part of the time, in their college walls, and find their mental pablum principally in books and preachments. It astonished me considerably, and shocked me a little at first, when a hall full of Harvard men almost laughed me off my feet upon my telling them of some particularly harrowing experiences I have had with *les misérables* of our society. I think their amusement was caused by my relation of the incident of a couple of laborers eating filthy apple-cores, picked up from the gutters of a big city. If the same men had realized, had really appreciated, the meaning of such a diet, I don't think they would have laughed; at least, not so openly and whole-heartedly. They might have shrugged their shoulders, and said *laissez faire*; and a few of them might have snickered fastidiously,—but I don't think their laugh would have been one of such delighted amusement. They were good fellows, clean fellows, noble fellows; but they simply couldn't appreciate what I was talking about. They had no real aliveness to the actuality of such conditions as I was trying to describe.[54]

Many American socialists considered London a liability to the cause, resenting his revolutionary remarks, especially those at New Haven. They also opposed London's closing his letters with "Yours for the Revolution," and others hit his "Revolution" lecture, the *Social-Democratic Herald* recommending he "should stop foaming at the mouth."[55] David A. Shannon writes in *The Socialist Party of America*:

> The truly distinguished intellectuals in the ISS [Intercollegiate Socialist Society] gave the Socialist Party a luster, a certain aura of respectability, which was advantageous to it, but unfortunately some of the Socialist intellectuals were eccentric to the point that anti-Socialists could smear the party as a collection of crackpots. Jack London is a case in point. He undertook a lecture tour under ISS auspices in the winter of 1905–06 that aroused a great deal of editorial comment. London, who signed his letters 'Yours for the Revolution,' took with him on this tour a Korean valet, who dressed him for his lecture appearances in as unproletarian a costume as it was possible to devise. London addressed his audiences dressed in a white flannel shirt with a rolling collar that suggested a little boy's sailor outfit, a white silk tie, a black cheviot suit, and patent-leather pumps. London also frequently became involved in charges of plagiarism which appeared to be valid. On one occasion the New York *World* published in adjoining columns excerpts from a London article and the one copied from. Activities such as these certainly did not advance the party's interests.[56]

In February 1906, a *New York Times* editorial commented about London's openness in speeches: "We must commend Mr. Jack London for the perfect frankness with which he tells his audience what Socialism is, and what it aims to accomplish. He does not dissemble. He is not mealy-mouthed. He does not cloak Socialism in timid disguises. He does not profess to regard it as a mere return to the principle of the golden rule, or as a reform altogether beneficial that will harm nobody and make all the world happier. Mr. Jack London's Socialism is bloody war—the war of one class in society against other classes. He says so. It is a destructive Socialism. He glories in it."[57]

Emotionally charged words like "mealy-mouthed," "bloody war," and "destructive socialism" led Upton Sinclair to write the editor: "You say that 'very few Socialists have Jack London's courage,' and imply that the rest of us shrink from stating our purpose fairly. If I may be pardoned the remark, your comments upon Socialism are of a kind to suggest that you are not familiar with Socialist writings and lectures. I heard Jack London's address; I have heard and read many Socialist addresses, and so far as I know there is no such difference to be noted between them."[58]

Three days after the *Times* editorial, the Derby Neck, Connecticut, library passed a resolution to remove London's books from their shelves: "As Jack London publicly announces he is an Anarchist, devoting the Constitution to hell and Government to destruction, we have ordered all his works withdrawn from circulation; and we urge not only other libraries to do likewise, but all lovers of their country to cease buying his books or taking magazines publishing his stories."[59] Several other libraries, including the Pittsburgh Public Library, also banned London's work. The *New York Times*, which had criticized London's "crazy talk," then criticized Derby Neck for its "exceedingly foolish announcement," predicting that "the bad, even when imposed by Derby Neck, is good advertisement for some good books, and no doubt their sale will be largely increased in that part of Connecticut."[60]

One question remains about London's platform tour. Did he speak well? Not according to friends. Will Irwin, a correspondent, said he had "a voice which sounded thin and slight."[61] Joan London supported this: "Jack was a poor soapboxer. He gave it up long before he overcame his dismay at the thinness of his voice in the out of doors and the resultant absence of passion in his tones and gestures, as well as the shyness which almost strangled him."[62] William McDevitt, his platform manager between 1905 and 1909, recalled that he "never acquired, as Upton Sinclair, for instance, has achieved, the ability to hold his own in comparison with the orators of the party." McDevitt told about an incident that illustrates London's awareness of his rhetorical weakness:

As an inting [interesting] echo of London's soapbox adventures, I recall that in 1906 or '07 when the Socialist party of Oakland was in the midst of a prolonged fight with the police of that city over the right to speak on the famous corner of Broadway, and when there had been numerous arrests of socialist soapboxers, including Tuck, the blind leader of the movement in California, and James Osborne, "the blind orator," and several others, including myself as the organizer in charge of the "war," Jack wrote me from his ranch, offering, if it seemed helpful, to come to Oakland and get "pinched," in order to liven up the conflict; but, he insisted, it must be understood that he was NOT to be left on the box, if the police declined to arrest him instanter; in other words, he was not to be asked to make a speech. By that time, after his years of literary fame, he had lost the power to speak extemporaneously and effectively in public, even if he ever had such a facility. Years of intensively concentrated writing had atrophied his ability to "think on his feet" in public and, much more truly, his immensely cultivated power of personal criticism made him completely averse to being publicly associated with his UNDEVELOPED capacity for effective impromptu.[63]

London admitted that he seldom spoke at socialist meetings, reserving his muscle for propaganda purposes. When asked to serve as California's vice-president of the prohibition plan in 1913, he agreed, again refusing to speak, rationalizing that he lacked practice. Charmian thought he despised public speaking.

London's tour for the Intercollegiate Socialist Society ended on February 3, 1906 in St. Paul, Minnesota. Some writers state that London's travels were cut short by illness, but local newspapers reported that London and Charmian, driven by their chauffeur, sped down Robert Street until a police sergeant took the carriage's license number. The *Minneapolis Tribune* said "the chauffeur was arrested in the evening but London and his wife are now speeding toward the Pacific coast."[64]

Back in California, the Londons rented a cabin at Wake Robin Lodge, then started planning, among many things, a seven-year voyage around the world.

Chapter 13

Snarking on the South Seas

A BOOK CALLED *Sailing Alone Around the World,* by Joshua Slocum, appeared in 1900, intriguing both sea rovers and land-lubbers alike, including Jack London. Slocum, a shipmaster for nearly twenty years, "born in the breezes," set sail from Boston Harbor on April 24, 1895, and went around the world, dropping anchor at Newport on June 27, 1898, three years later. "As for myself, the wonderful sea charmed me from the first. At the age of eight I had already been afloat along with other boys on the bay, with chances greatly in favour of being drowned. When a lad I filled the important post of cook on a fishing-schooner; but I was not long in the galley, for the crew mutinied at the appearance of my first duff, and 'chucked me out' before I had a chance to shine as a culinary artist. The next step towards the goal of happiness found me before the mast in a full-rigged ship bound on a foreign voyage. Thus I came 'over the bows,' and not in through the cabin windows, to the command of a ship.''[1]

Seduced by Slocum's pluck, London named a boat, the *Spray,* after Slocum's boat, telling Brett in March 1903 that his plans included an eventual trip through the South Seas on a boat to be built by himself. This incubated four years. During that time, he charted a loose plan that included the Hawaiian Islands, Australia, India, and Russia—seven years on the world's waters. Charmian endorsed the idea. Old salts, social-ists, and reporters, however, called it "London's Folly." More intent on naming the craft, London ignored such slurs, baptizing it the *Snark,* a bizarre creature from Lewis Carroll's poem, "The Hunting of the Snark: An Agony in Eight Fits." George Sterling pleaded: "For God's sake don't call your boat the 'Snark.' 'Gull' was a fine name."[2] But London insisted.

Why did Sterling beg London not to name his boat the *Snark?* Because visions of Carroll's tale sent shudders up his spine. R. S. London—no relation to Jack London—says in the introduction of a recent reprint of "The Hunting of the Snark" that it may have symbolized "the supreme moment of anguish when you realize that perhaps you don't exist anymore; that there is nothing between you and a total void. Anti-religion. Carroll is credited with having a subconscious motive for writing the Snark. Other theories include the Snark as a political satire containing a hidden moral and as an allegory on the pursuit of happiness, which is the one Carroll himself liked best. That the Snark represents material wealth or even an unsound business venture and business in general."[3]

Several of these interpretations, ironically, relate to London's macabre life-view—its pain, its anguish, its frightful void. Even the subtitle "An Agony in Eight Fits" makes one shake. This fictional sailing venture, captained by a fool who, as one character recalls, "bought *us* the best—A perfect and absolute blank!"[4] also parallels London's ill-conceived and absurdistic voyage, one that strains credulity.

London also designed the *Snark,* instead of hiring professionals from San Francisco or spending $5,000 on a new craft. To finance this scheme, he mortgaged both the Glen Ellen property and Flora's house, secured advances from Brett, and sought magazine assignments through multiple queries. He wrote *Cosmopolitan,* saying that both *Outing* and *McClure's* wanted his work, then sent similar letters to *Collier's, Outing,* and *McClure's.* The editor of *Cosmopolitan* contracted for a maximum ten articles on the voyage at ten cents a word, with a $2,000 advance. He also furnished film, camera, and paid processing costs. *The Woman's Home Companion* settled for domestic articles about the South Seas, while *Collier's* agreed on timely pieces. *Cosmopolitan,* meanwhile, led readers to believe they were financing the trip and had exclusive rights to his wanderings. *The Woman's Home Companion* did likewise. *McClure's,* on the other hand, refused London's offer. They questioned similarities between his "Love of Life" and August Bridle's and J. K. MacDonald's "Lost in the Land of the Midnight Sun." *McClure's* also rejected "When God Laughs" and *Before Adam.*

Snags with magazine contracts continued. Accusations and counter accusations between London and editors filled letters. Things got tighter. The *Times Magazine,* which promised $1,000 for "The Wit of Porportuk" published in their first issue, folded, without issuing a check. So London counted on *White Fang,* his play *The Scorn of Women,* and *Moon-Face and Other Stories* for revenues. He finally broke the *Cosmopolitan* contract, owing them around $1,600, persuading the editors to publish *The Road* series, which brought between $6,000 and $7,000. (*Cosmopolitan* later signed a ten-year contract with London for one novel a year. They paid him $2,000 a month.) Even *Harper's Weekly* eventually contracted for articles on the South Sea trip.

London estimated the *Snark*'s cost at $7,000, but this swelled to $30,000 and then some, forcing him to push *The Iron Heel,* a caustic indictment of capitalism. (Joshua Slocum, by the way, spent $553.62 on the *Spray,* building it himself in thirteen months.) After *The Iron Heel*'s release, *Bookman* published a photo of the Londons aboard the *Snark,* commenting that "the photograph that we present herewith does not indicate that he is spending his days in brooding over the coming cataclysm. On the contrary, he looks remarkably well fed, happy and contented—for a socialist. But there are socialists and socialists."[5]

London made weak choices of crew for the *Snark.* Magazine ads brought hundreds of replies from doctors, dentists, draftsmen, engineers, electricians, reporters, ranchers, retired sea captains, students, socialists, and stenographers. A famed chef, earning $200 a week, wanted to cook, a millionaire's son offered $500, a college professor $1,000 to do anything. Yet besides

himself and Charmian, London's choices included Roscoe
Eames, Charmian's gray-bearded uncle, as co-navigator and
building supervisor, whose sailing experience had been confined
to San Francisco Bay. "If you take Uncle Roscoe with you,"
warned George Sterling, "it will be a surer sign than others that
he writes your books. I'd think you'd be scared to do it."[6] Bert
Stoltz, a Stanford student who became a Rhodes Scholar, became the *Snark*'s engineer, although engine mechanics eluded
him. And London's $25-a-month cook, a later famous cine-
matographer of Africa, couldn't cook. His name was Martin
Johnson.

Young Martin was working in his father's jewelry store in
Independence, Kansas, when he applied for the cruise, and had
already traveled from Chicago to London and Brussels, returning with twenty-five cents of an original $5.50 investment. He
never learned why London chose him. When Martin received
the telegram asking if he could cook, he got a fast job at a
friend's lunch room, then replied to London, "Sure, just try
me."[7] He studied cookbooks, wrote recipes in notebooks, and
learned how to make gravies and biscuits. His friend's wife
helped. So did Martin's mother. He even made Thanksgiving
dinner that year. In *I Married Adventure* Osa Johnson later
wrote: "With his old canvas suitcase pressed into service and
the latest type camera (a parting gift from his father) as his only
luggage, Martin boarded the San Francisco-bound Santa Fe. As
he settled himself once more on the plush cushions he heaved
a sigh of relief. But as he listened, the click of the wheels
seemed to say: 'Can-you-cook . . . can-you-cook . . . can-you-
cook?' He opened his suitcase and fished out his notebook. A
glance through its grease-stained pages dispelled all misgivings
and he answered the wheels, saying: 'Sure! Try me!' "[8]

Preparation for the voyage was fraught with trouble. Uncle
Roscoe Eames, paid $60 a month to supervise the *Snark*'s con-
struction, let workers loaf, failed to examine materials, and
ignored slipshod work. London, who remained at Glen Ellen
writing to meet bills, bought expensive Oregon pine for planking, Indian oak for the ribs, copper instead of conventional nails
and screws, even installing electricity, a modern bathroom, and
a seventy horse-power engine on the boat. "We spent money

like water," recalled Martin, who lived with the Londons for three months before sailing. "Before the buying was finished, there were few luxuries or facilities we did not have aboard the Snark."[9]

Workmen planned to lay the *Snark*'s five-ton keel on April 18, 1906. That morning at 5:00 A.M., tremors awakened the Londons at Wake Robin Lodge. Riding to the ranch, they found its barn in ruins, smoke clouds rising over San Francisco. George Sterling wrote: "We had a hell of an earthquake in Carmel (and assumably everywhere else in America). You should have seen Carrie getting from her bed to the front veranda in 1 1/2 seconds! . . . The dog was so scared that his heart hasn't stopped thumping yet and all the hens yelled 'bloody murder.' "[10]

According to Walter Lord, the Londons had this experience in the fallen city:

> Just before the crest of the hill, Jack and Charmian London rested on the steps of a more modest house. About 5:15 the owner appeared, turned his key in the lock, and on sudden impulse asked them in. He said his name was Perine, explaining, "Yesterday morning I was worth $600,000. This morning this house is all I have left. It will go in fifteen minutes."
>
> His tone was cheerful—almost matter-of-fact—as he showed them around: "This is my wife's collection of china. This rug upon which we stand is a present. It cost fifteen hundred dollars. Try that piano. Listen to its tone. There are few like it. There are no horses. The flames will be here in fifteen minutes."
>
> His feelings broke through only once. That was when Charmian did try the piano. Quickly he raised his hand in a gesture that begged her to stop.[11]

Although first swearing he wouldn't touch the disaster, London grabbed an offer of twenty-five cents a word from *Collier's*, who published his account on May 5, 1906, as "The Story of an Eye-Witness, by Jack London, Collier's Special Correspondent." His lead follows.

> The earthquake shook down in San Francisco hundreds of thousands of dollars' worth of walls and chimneys. But the conflagration that followed burned up hundreds of millions of dollars' worth of property. There is no estimating within hundreds of

millions the actual damage wrought. Not in history has a modern
imperial city been so completely destroyed. San Francisco is
gone. Nothing remains of it but memories and a fringe of dwelling-houses on its outskirts. Its industrial section is wiped out.
The factories and warehouses, the great stores and newspaper
buildings, the hotels and the palaces of the nabobs, are all gone.
Remains only the fringe of dwelling-houses on the outskirts of
what was once San Francisco.[12]

This lead reveals much about London—his ideas, his style,
his contradictions. It also reveals the leverage a best seller or
two—in London's case *The Call of the Wild* and *The Sea Wolf*—
gives an author. The lead sentence, "San Francisco is gone,"
lies buried, losing its powerful impact. London's first concern
is with financial losses instead of human life. He spends three
sentences on this subordinate detail. Any editor, of course,
would have revised the work of an apprentice author, one without a reputation, but London stood on his author's prerogative,
attested by Brett in several letters. So *Collier's* sacrificed style
for a popular by-line. London, who had painted San Francisco
as an uncivilized "Wild West" town, the dust of stagecoach
wheels rising from dirt streets, now calls it a "modern imperial
city," closer to its 1906 cultural and economic standing. (The
colossal cost of rebuilding this city helped cause the 1907 depression.) He then mentions nabobs, affluent capitalists, another
cut, and concludes his lead statement with a redundant sentence
about dwelling-houses. London's paragraph pales compared to
the top-flight reportage of someone like Richard Harding Davis.
But by-lines are by-lines.

Goods and labor costs soared in the San Francisco area after
the disaster, forcing London to acquire materials for the *Snark*
from New York City. A strike closed shipbuilding factories.
And Roscoe Eames's blunders started showing. The *Snark*'s
oak beams were pine, its planking warped and knotted. Parts
wore out faster than they could be replaced. The gears and
castings that transferred power from the engine to windlass were
flawed and cracked. The bed-plate was also bad, and the sev-
enty-horsepower engine ripped from its shattered foundation,

wrecking connections and fastenings, then collapsed. Instead of sailing on October 1, 1906, London pushed the date to April 21, 1907. Sailors laughed. Editors grumbled about deadlines. Annoyance after annoyance. Two lumber-scows squeezed the *Snark* one night, giving her a lopsided bulge. The anchor slipped during a night storm, although Martin managed to start the engine after hours of struggle, narrowly avoiding a smashup. London finally determined to sail on April 21. He planned to finish the *Snark* in Honolulu, their first stop, but before embarking, a United States marshal met them at the wharf with a $247.79[13] claim from Sellars & Co., grocers, attaching the sloop. When London tried to pay, the marshal vanished, so did the grocer's lawyer and United States judge, all away for the weekend, which meant another two-day wait for launching.

At 12:20 P.M. on April 23, however, the *Snark* sailed from the Franklin Street wharf. Dozens of friends, including George Sterling and James Hopper, whose sweater hung from the masthead, waved good-bys. "The author appeared to take his departure in a matter-of-fact fashion," said the *San Francisco Chronicle*. "He stated that he apprehended no more delays and that his next port would be Honolulu. He gave his orders in a quiet way, and in short sleeves, with collar of negligee shirt thrown carelessly open, he looked the part of a seafaring man."[14]

But more accidents plagued the *Snark*. Its dynamo failed. The bow wouldn't heave-to, and the sea anchor collapsed. Then the rigging's ironwork broke. The ship's planking leaked, forcing the use of pumps. The watertight compartments weren't watertight, causing slushing into the galley and stateroom. Charmian once slipped and tumbled onto the dinner table. Even the gasoline tanks leaked, making everyone sick and worried about striking matches, and the bathroom facilities failed within twenty-four hours. "The boat was leaking like a sieve," recalled Martin. "Yes, the *Snark,* the famous *Snark,* that had cost thirty thousand dollars, that had been built by expert shipbuilders, and that was declared to be the tightest craft afloat, leaked!"[15]

In *They Took to the Sea,* a study of small-boat voyagers, including London and Joshua Slocum, David Klein and Mary Louise Johnson say:

London, who knew nothing about yacht design, decided to build the *Snark* according to his own specifications. He was assisted by his wife, who knew less, and by their friend and prospective navigator, whose little knowledge did as much damage as the Londons' lack of it. . . . The building took nearly two years. The specifications were changed every time someone had a new whim, but they were never changed correctly and so the building was a continuous process of alteration and shifting to make all the requirements fit into the 54-foot hull. The *Snark* cost—this was before the First World War—$30,000 and London paid every cent of it by writing articles at so much a word, some of them making fun of his own unhappy experiences.[16]

Macmillan collected these articles, along with photos, in *The Cruise of the Snark*. In their book, Klein and Johnson said of *The Cruise of the Snark*: "Delightful or idiotic, depending upon the reader's temperament and technical background. London made every mistake possible, but he was too clearly aware that his plight made good copy. A mixture of condescension, corn, and travelogue." They called Joshua Slocum's *Sailing Alone Around the World* a "masterpiece of literature, navigation, seamanship, and understatement."[17]

Before the *Snark* was far out to sea, food shortages complicated matters. "Martin hadn't the remotest idea of how to provision a ship," wrote Osa, although he brought enough spices "to supply several large restaurants for years."[18] The oranges froze, and kerosene ruined the carrots. They tossed mushy vegetables overboard. Coal had been delivered in rotten sacks, and the kindling wood wouldn't fire. Constipation plagued Roscoe Eames. Other crew members grew seasick.

London later called their twenty-seven days at sea uneventful to Honolulu reporters, although Martin dubbed them "hell on the high seas."[19] A storm would have wrecked the tiny *Snark* that dragged its anchor, couldn't heave-to, and carried a defective lifeboat. London, waiting until after launching to study sextants, claimed that he mastered the technique in several afternoons. Joshua Slocum, however, remarked in *Sailing Alone Around the World*: "I hope I am making it clear that I do not lay claim to cleverness or to slavish calculations in my reckonings. I think I have already stated that I kept my longitude, at least, mostly by intuition. A rotator log always towed astern, but so much has to be allowed for currents and for drift, which the log never shows, that it is only an approximation, after all, to be corrected by one's own judgment from data of a thousand voyages; and even then the master of the ship, if he be wise, cries out for the lead and the lookout."[20]

It seems that co-navigators Eames and London battled their way across the seas. Edwin Emerson later wrote:

I was in California with Jack London when he built his unfortunate ketch, the Snark, and when he set out on her to cruise the Pacific. I was at her launching and was consulted by Jack London concerning her equipment. The first question he asked me was how to equip her with machine-guns and other arms and munitions.

"What for?" I asked.

"Why to fire on anyone who should attempt to steal anything off the Snark," he replied.

Yet Jack London pretends to hold with Louis Blanc that all ownership of property is a crime.

Mr. London himself has told how the cruise of the Snark became a nightmare because he could not agree with his navigator, and so came to blows with him on the high seas.

Why?

Because the navigator, having his own ideas of navigation and of his sea duties, would not obey the master's orders concerning technical points of navigation. So the master—Mr. London— flew at his throat.[21]

Fish seemed to avoid the *Snark*. "It's queer we see no fish," wrote Martin, "for by all the books we have on fish, this is where they should be found. Jack throws out his trolling line every day, but catches nothing."[22] They did sight whales, which attracted many flying-fish, but aside from a seven-foot shark, they saw nothing else until bonitas and porpoises began to surface when they reached Hawaiian waters. London, of course, wrote each day, sometimes reading sea stories or manuscripts to the crew at night.

Every day, Jack wrote two hours," said Martin. "Just two hours, no more, no less. He would get up in the morning and take his trick at the wheel, have breakfast, and then shut himself in his

stateroom for just two hours and write. He always laughed at
what he called the tomfoolery of waiting for inspiration to come.
He doesn't believe there is any such thing as inspiration—he
himself can write just as well at one time as at another. It is
plain work, he says, and the only way he can do it is to go ahead
and do it. Incidentally, I may mention that Jack London never
rewrites a story. He writes it just once, and never goes over it
to change it. He writes with a fountain pen, and nobody can
read his writing but Mrs. London. He turns his manuscript over
to her, and she types it and gets it ready for the publishers.[23]

London had first seen Hawaii in the early 1890s, when he
sailed on the *Sophie Sutherland* bound for Japan. He visited
Waikiki for one day in January 1904 en route to the Orient as
a Russo-Japanese War correspondent, and stopped in Honolulu
on his return six months later. This time, however, members
of the Hawaiian Yacht Club met the Londons, escorting the
Snark into Pearl Harbor, where astonished reporters thought
they had been lost at sea because of erroneous newspaper reports. Interviews followed. "Everybody is rated on the ship's
articles in accordance with the requirements of the United States
navigation laws," London answered a reporter's question. "But
in practice we knew none of the distinctions between foremast
hands and others. We were not only the ship's company, but
we were company for each other. The trip was an ideal one,
in all but speed, and as I see that a merchantman has just arrived
at Honolulu twenty-five days from San Francisco, I do not see
that it should be thought wonderful that we took twenty-seven.
We were in no hurry. We were not like the merchantman eager
to get to our destination, counting every hour as so much
money, every sail full of wind as so many dollars."[24]

During the *Snark*'s repairs, however, London did worry about
so many dollars. Earlier he had counted on *The Iron Heel* for
revenues to keep him afloat, but magazines wouldn't touch its
revolutionary theme. The *Snark* cost $1,000 a month. California
expenses also continued. What to do but keep writing. So he
sat down in his kimono and completed "To Build a Fire," still
his most famous short story of the freezing Klondike.

London wrote two versions of "To Build a Fire." The first
appeared in the May 1902 issue of *The Youth's Companion,* a

Boston-based juvenile magazine with half a million circulation. He received fifty dollars. In this earlier story, tenderfoot Tom Vincent survives, mainly because of superior human intelligence, resourcefulness, and a love of life. The tale concludes with this tacked-on moral: "In a month's time he was able to be about on his feet, although the toes were destined always after that to be very sensitive to frost. But the scars on his hands he knows he will carry to the grave. And—'Never travel alone!' he now lays down the precept of the North."[25]

London expanded the second "To Build a Fire," evoking moods of impotence and loneliness through images of cold, deriving the story line from Jeremiah Lynch's *Three Years in the Klondike*. The hero is a frosty unnamed fellow. He's usually called a tenderfoot, someone without brute intuition or imagination who ignores the old sourdough's advice at Sulphur Creek—always travel with a companion on the trail. But this Northlander really possesses sharp insights. He studies the land's topography, its snow formations and creek changes, even forcing his dog—not a devoted canine—to scout ahead for danger spots. He falls through the ice in an area free from treacherous signs, another instance of London's gnawing pessimism and belief in an erratic universe. Both facts and logic betray the traveler in this wasteland beyond time on the world's edge, where things haven't changed for millenniums. He eventually freezes to death when snow, shaken from a tree limb, deadens his life-giving fire. *Century Magazine* published this grim tale in August 1908. "It was a weird scene; an anachronism," London had written in "The Son of the Wolf." "To the south, the nineteenth century was reeling off the few years of its last decade; here flourished man primeval, a shade removed from the pre-historic cavedweller, a forgotten fragment of the Elder world."[26]

Hawaii seemed a paradise. While crew remained aboard the *Snark,* London and Charmian dined at the Royal Hawaiian Hotel, visited the Honolulu Aquarium, and climbed the Diamond Head crater. It made London's eyes puff, lips swell, tender skin blister and joints ache, putting him to bed for awhile. Charmian details this in *Our Hawaii*.

During their two-month Hawaiian vacation, the Londons rubbed shoulders with numerous important capitalists. They dined with Charles L. Rhodes, editor of *The Star,* toured the Ewa Plantation with its manager, mixed with judges and congressmen, met Joseph P. Cooke, financial wizard, and befriended the Portuguese consul, Senor A. de Souza Canovarro. Hawaiian royalty entertained them. London fished by torchlight with Prince David Kawananakoa, met the former Queen Lydia Liliuokalani, visited the Haleakala Ranch on the Island of Maui, and tramped through the remote "ditch country" of Haleakala, where tangled vegetation grew lush.

Lorrin A. Thurston, publisher of Honolulu's *Pacific Commercial Advertiser,* invited the Londons to his cottage on Tantalus for several weeks, giving him a chance to study London's writing ways. He recalled that

> after breakfast at Tantalus, [London] would get a small wire basket, in which he had numerous small writing pads covered with scribbled notes. These he would arrange in a circle before him on the dining room table, and compile them and write them up in longhand. The rest of us would be laughing and talking in the room, but London was absolutely oblivious of everybody and everything except his notes and writing. He studiously and laboriously concentrated on his work until eleven or twelve o'clock, when he suddenly would throw down his pencil, and say with a sigh: "Well, my job's done for today!" After he had written a thousand words, nothing could induce him to write another word until the morrow.[27]

Thurston took the Londons to the Haleakala Ranch on Maui, on the steamer *Claudine*. After reaching Kahului, Thurston suggested they continue by carriage, an idea London liked. A mishap on the way, however, nearly killed them. "As we met [a plantation wagon] the two horses of our rig gave a snort of terror, and plunged into a dry ditch at the side of the road, capsizing the vehicle, rolling Mrs. London and Mrs. Thurston, who were in the back seat, into a conglomerate mess, and throwing Jack upon his head into the dirt. The two horses jerked loose from the traces; and I, clinging to the reins, was dragged headfirst over the dashboard, landing upon my stomach with the two horses facing me, their ears projecting in wonder. We slowly gathered together the scattered remains, rescued the two ladies, and discovered that nobody had been killed."[28] They finally reached the Haleakala Ranch, rode through the "Ditch Country" where annual average precipitation exceeded four hundred inches, and saw the massive crater of Makawao.

But Thurston made a mistake during London's visit, asking him to speak on "Revolution" to an audience of Hawaiian industrialists. "Jack London created quite a sensation here in an address on 'Revolution' before the Research Club, in which he declared that under present economic conditions, the laboring classes had a harder time than they did in the stone age," relayed the *San Francisco Chronicle*. "He said that, barring a few degenerates, who always appeared on such occasions, the man who threw a brickbat at a strikebreaker was actuated by as good motives and was doing as noble a thing as the colonists who, from behind fences and stone walls, shot at the British redcoats at Lexington."[29]

More bad feelings erupted in Hawaii after London and Charmian visited Molokai, the leper island, for five days. In his article "The Lepers of Molokai," London found these unfortunates happy, productive, and intelligent people, concluding after five days that leprosy wasn't dangerous. Their energetic colony of a thousand had built assembly halls, a race track, bandstand, and other facilities. Some even ran stores. Comparing the island with British and American ghettos, London said he'd prefer to live on Molokai. Yet he wrote three sensationalistic short stories about lepers that enraged Hawaiians: "Koolau the Leper," "Good-by Jack," and "The Sheriff of Kona," calling them monsters, misfits and hideous creatures.

Martin commented on the lepers in *Through the South Seas with Jack London,* admitting that he "was never on" Molokai, and that "everything here set forth was gotten direct from [London] or from others who had intimate knowledge whereof they spoke." Then he supports London that "the horrors with which Molokai is associated in the average mind, *simply do not exist*. The sensationalists have done their work well." But several pages later, he refers to "the horribleness of the disease—

for horrible it is, beyond the power of the most unprincipled inkster to exaggerate—and its absolutely incurable character, one cannot wonder much at the sentiment existing among all peoples in countries where any of its forms are known. . . . Leprosy is usually slow, vile, hideous. One dies by inches. Terrible in contemplation, what must it be when fastened insidiously upon one's flesh." But he glibly added that "the days are peaceful and the nights are happy" on Molokai, and that the lepers "while they live, they live in paradise. No wonder Jack London knew, without debate, which place he would choose."[30] Charmian also mentioned the hideous appearance of lepers.[31]

London's three stories caused an editorialist to call him a sneak and bounder in the *Honolulu Advertiser*.[32] London, of course, retaliated in a letter to the editor, complaining about Hawaii's provincialism, claiming its natives robbed him. Lorrin A. Thurston resented such remarks, and an exchange of letters followed, London criticizing him for lack of support. Thurston responded,

> Your expressed opinion of me does not worry me, for the reason that I know that it is not founded on fact, and further that I do not believe that you believe it yourself. I think that I rather "got under your skin," in my reply to you, and that with somewhat of a smart to your conscience, you have assumed the "offensive defensive," rather than admit that your treatment of Hawaii has been ungenerous. . . . You came to Hawaii and absorbed local color enough to give realism to your tales. You then began a series of gruesome stories in which leprosy was the theme and Hawaii the setting. None of them were true. They were pure fiction; but like the historical novel, worked in so much fact with the fiction, that they give the impression to the uninitiated that. they are more fact than fiction, the net result of which is to create an untrue impression, injurious to Hawaii, that this is an unsafe and undesirable place to live in.
>
> If I really thought that you were so mentally deficient as to be unable to distinguish between a "funny story" and a series of publications harping upon the fact that some of your "loved" neighbors are afflicted with a loathsome disease, I should no more think of appealing to you to stop it, than I would try to stop a sewer from discharging its contents. . . .

Really, you've laid yourself open to the above, because in endeavoring to score a point on me to cover up your own offense, you have ignored the main issue, which is that it is ungenerous to exploit the troubles and afflictions of your friends, unless for the purpose of helping them, especially when you know that it hurts.[33]

When London planned another Honolulu trip in 1915, George Sterling wrote him: "I'd think you'd be afraid to tackle the latter place, after the way you've revealed the presence of leprosy there!"[34]

Returning to the *Snark* from Hawaiian sight-seeing, London found its decks rotting and everything else disordered. Eames hadn't scraped the masts, oiled the teakwood railings, or replaced the rigging. He also lacked a log. London fired both Eames and Bert Stoltz. Hidashisa Tochigi left to join the ministry. The *Snark* needed new recruits.

Yoschimatsu Nakata, the new cabin boy, was to stay with the Londons for years. He later became a dentist. T. Wada, who signed on at Hilo as the new cook, deserted once to live with natives. He called London a "piker, quitter [and] grouch,"[35] complaining his moods changed with the weather. Hermann, a young Dutchman, became the *Snark*'s sailor.

Andy Rosehill succeeded Roscoe Eames, but he swore and resented Martin and tried to get him fired. Rosehill also ran the *Snark* into a freight steamer. London replaced him with Captain J. L. Warren, a convicted murderer whom he persuaded the governor of Oregon to pardon.

The repaired *Snark*, with the help of another five-hundred-dollar advance from Brett, left Hawaiian waters on August 15. When engine troubles resumed, London told Martin "he would not go back to Honolulu if the boat were sinking."[36] Yet the *Snark* kept sailing. A mariner's miracle.

"All the sea sharps are 'saying things' about Jack London and his ketch craft the *Snark*, because the vessel was more or less unmanageable on its recent voyage from San Francisco to Honolulu," wrote *Sunset Magazine*. "The report is that the scuppers fouled the binnacle and the stays'ls took a bight from the galley. Yo, heave ho! What do people expect, and for what does London seek? He had a lot of fun building his sturdy and rollery craft, secured advertising worth more than the boat, and then away, away o'er the bounding main. He is not easily discouraged. The *Snark* doubtless will soon be heard of among the sampans of the Hoang-Ho, and current literature will be made richer by yellow tales of yellow men who sail the yellow sea."[37]

The *Snark,* meanwhile, headed for the Marquesas, a feat thought impossible in a craft like London's, because of erratic equatorial currents and trade winds, which forced ships blown off course to land on the Samoan or Fiji islands, sometimes vanishing forever. Yet sixty-one days later, London reached Taiohea Bay, part of the Marquesas, after nearly dying of thirst. Somewhere beyond the Sandwich Islands, halfway to the Marquesas, either Wada or Nakata left the water tap open during a storm, draining their 1,000-gallon tank, leaving only a precious ten gallons in another container. This forced them to ration water—one quart a day per person. "One has no idea how small an amount a quart is until he is put on such an allowance,"[38] said Martin, who told this curious story about London during the ordeal:

> Almost dead with thirst himself [London] went into his cabin and wrote a sea story about a castaway sailor that died of thirst while drifting in an open boat. And when he had finished it he came out, gaunt and haggard, but with eyes burning with enthusiasm, and told us of the story and said:
> "Boys, that yarn's one of the best I ever did!"
> That night a heavy, soaking tropical rain came on; we spread the awning again and filled our water tanks; and as the big barrel ran over with the gurgling water, Jack said:
> "I'll not kill that sailor; I'll have him saved by a rain like this; that'll make the yarn better than ever!"[39]

The Londons stayed at Nuku-Hiva for several weeks, renting the clubhouse used by Robert Louis Stevenson. They also visited Typee Valley, immortalized in Herman Melville's *Typee,* one of London's favorite childhood books. After sailing around Cape Horn on a whaler in 1841, Melville deserted, becoming a captive of Marquesan cannibals until rescued by another whaler during a bloody battle. But the Marquesas disappointed London, who recalled romantic images of Melville's tales. Most of the natives he called half-breeds, blaming the whites, who brought deadly microorganisms to the South Seas, corrupting islanders.

The islands' canary-sized wasps, giant tropical fruit trees, and poisonous flies impressed London; one attack of flies left him full of itchy welts. He and Charmian, enjoying better days, feasted on taro, poi, and breadfruit, basked in the tropical sunlight, and collected crates of curios: china, exotic carvings, pearls, war clubs, a hula skirt made of human hair from cannibalistic sacrifices, even a century-old artifact from which headhunters had drunk the blood of sailors. (He sent George Sterling a shriveled clitoris from Samoa.) Fred Lockley, editor of *The Pacific Monthly,* later got a shock when he visited the Londons at Glen Ellen. "There was a ghostly semi-twilight in Jack's den, and while I waited for him to turn on the lights I stood in the doorway. He took from an upper shelf a dark, round object about the size of a good-sized coconut and handed it to me. The peculiar touch of it gave me the shivers. When the light was turned on I nearly dropped it, for it was a human head. The hair was coarse and black, the lips were sewed together, and there was an ugly scar on the neck, under the ear."[40]

The *Snark* sailed on December 18 from Nuku Hiva, its deck filled with everything from coconuts to yams and pineapples, Tahiti their new port of call. "Jack wrote as usual, Mrs. London did her typing, and all took their tricks at the wheel," wrote Martin, "but most of the time we just lay around on deck and read or chatted."[41] The mentioned writing was *Martin Eden,* London's portrait of the struggling proletarian author strangled by bourgeois values. The title, derived from Martin's first name and an old acquaintance named Eden, was originally called *Success.* London told Cloudesley Johns he finished this novel before reaching Papeete, Tahiti.

Troublesome news greeted the Londons in Tahiti. An Oakland bank had threatened to attach Flora's house for debts, and eight hundred dollars' worth of checks had bounced in Hilo. London and Charmian, helped with a bank draft from Brett, left Papeete, returning to San Francisco on the *S.S. Mariposa,* finding the states convulsed in depression. Their reserves were sixty-six dollars.

A false sense of well-being and prosperity had hoodwinked Americans, most fast forgetting the frightful nineties, romanticized with mansard roofs, top hats, and gaslight flickering through stained-glass windows. Many things caused "March Panic" or "Silent Panic" in 1907: the Russo-Japanese War, late farm crops, rebuilding San Francisco, railroad overexpansion. All devoured international capital reserves. Who saved the day? "Master of the monopolists" J. Pierpont Morgan, according to John K. Winkler.

> Day after day the captains of finance, both high and low, came trooping into Morgan's plain, severely furnished office, stood before his small, flat desk, and took their orders. Night after night the kings of the Street met in the Morgan Library and reported to the master. During those days of panic Morgan was undisputed monarch. Indeed, in all save name, he was dictator of the United States. The Government itself did his bidding without question. Morgan rose to the emergency magnificently, joyfully. The incense of homage, the feeling of power rejuvenated him. He was a centre of calm in the core of the storm. Eventually he dammed the torrent of panic, turned it aside, and broke it into a thousand little streams to be met and conquered at leisure.[42]

The Londons during these crises? Sailing the South Seas until checks started bouncing. London probably rushed the ending of *Martin Eden* after returning to the *Snark*. (People still buy books during depression years.) Arthur Calder-Marshall says he "just killed Martin for money,"[43] not because of the neurotic writer's manic-depressive nature or for profound philosophical reasons. Such a conclusion seems reasonable, mainly because Martin's suicide lacks motivation. Calder-Marshall believes London actually tried "in his own cabin how to get through the porthole and then, for the drowning scene, drawing on his memory of the Carquinez Straits. With that curious adhesion to actuality, he even used the name *Mariposa* for the ship on which Martin was sailing."[44]

Ninetta Eames and George Sterling, besides Brett, received correction copies of *Martin Eden,* leading to revisions. Although Sterling left intact *The Overland Monthly* sequence in *Martin*

Eden, Ninetta told Brett to remove it, claiming the criticism discredited Roscoe Eames and Edward Payne, both then living in the Bay area. Brett replied:

Dear Mrs. Eames:—

I have just received your letter of July 24th, and I should much like to change 'Martin Eden,' as you suggest. Indeed, I think that there are other changes that might be made in that book to its very decided advantage. In fact, I am a little afraid that the book will not be very successful in its present form, and I look for considerable criticism of the book, when it is published, from Mr. London's most earnest admirers. [This happened.]

I do not think, however, that I could very well take up with Mr. London this matter of its revision, as whenever I have in the past suggested to Mr. London changes in his work, he has not been willing, I think, to consider the matter at all favorably, preferring that his books should go out as he writes them in the first instance.

I am sure that if I write to Mr. London in regard to the matter that you mention, that my letter will be likely, if it has any effect at all, to make Mr. London decide to leave the book as it is rather than to make any changes in it. It might, perhaps, be different if you yourself would put the matter before him clearly, as you have done in your letter to me, as I feel that a friend's criticism and suggestion would be much more likely to receive favorable consideration than a suggestion of a mere business man, even although one of long standing.

In this matter then, I fear that I could only do harm, and not good, by any letter that I should be able to write; and, if the fault in the book to which you direct my attention is to be corrected, it must, I think, be by the efforts of Mr. London's intimate friends and by the efforts of those in whom he has confidence from the standpoint of literary criticism. Mr. London acknowledges, I think, that my business sense is good; but, from our correspondence of the past, I feel quite sure that his attitude toward my suggestions in relation to his work is unfriendly, if not actually hostile.[45]

Brett was right. London refused to make changes in *Martin Eden.*

Ninetta Eames's activities as London's agent during the *Snark* cruise ruptured their relationship. Although she received seven thousand dollars for the serial publication of *Martin Eden* in *The Pacific Monthly* (money London used to buy the Lamotte property, extending his Glen Ellen ranch holdings, instead of clearing bills), she also spent thousands on the ranch without his approval, then asked Brett for another five-hundred-dollar advance. He replied that as of December 1908 London hadn't earned anything over advances! Ninetta also flooded the market with London's stories, rather than waiting for top rates, complaining he ran up bills faster than she could pay them. (He also reduced Bessie's allowance to seventy-five dollars a month, as of January 1909, trying to cut the wrong corners, while maintaining the *Snark* and ranch.) Again Brett wrote Ninetta: "We must not run the risk of publishing anything, I think, which has not yet had serial publication, as to do so would be to deprive Mr. London of a part of his income, and I gather that the serial rights in short stories at present, on account of the immense number of magazines, have become extremely valuable."[46] Ninetta finally refused to send London financial statements, so after returning from the cruise, he replaced her as ranch manager with Eliza.

Critical response to *Martin Eden,* as Brett had predicted, discouraged London, who usually prefaced the publication of a new work with the remark that he'd done nothing like it before, even saying this in the foreword to *Hearts of Three* (1920), one of his hottest potboilers. At the time he called *Martin Eden* his finest work.

Said *The Nation*: "Such of the reading mob as may be attracted to his history are likely to discern a good deal of autobiography therein, and to be stirred piquantly by its daring adumbrations of various well-known proper names. But nothing actionable!"[47] "He writes too eloquently of how he felt and changes too much of what he actually did," added *The Independent*. "A man may shine, autobiographically speaking, as great and good, and yet have a very commonplace life record, which falls far behind his autoidealization. For that reason it seems best to accept this story not as real history, but as an earnest and truthful record of what Mr. London might have been if he had been Martin Eden instead of being limited by himself."[48]

Martin Eden, roughneck sailor and sometime smuggler, saves a fellow from a thrashing and is brought home by him to meet his sister Ruth, fragile figurine whom Martin idolizes at once. Within a few weeks Ruth changes Eden from a clod to near-god. "Love melts his heart and improves his grammar," commented *Current Literature*. "In fact, the blunt sailor, by a marvelous transformation, is changed into a bookworm. He lusts for knowledge with an almost physical passion."[49] The books Martin Eden reads include the works of Herbert Spencer and Friedrich Nietzsche, which *The Dial* called "perverted idealism."[50] Martin finally decides to write, following an apprenticeship of adversity and soul-searching. He becomes a celebrated author, never selling anything new, just works formerly rejected. Ruth, who earlier abandoned him because he refused to write romances, now returns, but Martin scorns her, then commits suicide on the high seas (an inspiration from Swinburne?), after spitting the bitter taste of life from his lips.

Ruth, most likely, is Mabel Applegarth, with a touch of Charmian Kittredge. Arthur Calder-Marshall thinks that "this story, usually taken as his boyhood love's, is also in part a confession of the failure of his second marriage, a confession he could not make openly because he hoped against hope that the birth of a son would redeem it."[51] (Bessie isn't characterized in *Martin Eden*. She planned to remarry during its completion, requesting more money for herself and the girls, something London refused.) Robert Barltrop calls *Martin Eden* "one of the most spiteful books ever written, arraigning people to whom Jack in fact owed something in his development."[52]

London did write several fine stories during the *Snark* voyage, including "The Seed of McCoy" and "The Chinago" set in Papeete, one of his best short studies. The title, a Tahitian name for Chinese coolies, tells about an indentured servant called Ah Cho, executed for a crime because a gendarme confuses his name with the real murderer, Ah Chow. It first appeared in *Harper's Magazine,* then included in *When God Laughs and Other Stories,* London's favorite collection.

He also completed "Samuel" and "The Sea-Farmer" between Australia and Ecuador, both excellent character studies. Margaret Henen in "Samuel," a once beautiful girl, now seems aged and haggard, a mother who has lost four sons called Samuel. The editor of *The American Magazine* rejected "The Sea-Farmer," but admired "Samuel" for which he offered a flat $250, but London did not consider such a small amount. *The Bookman* finally published "Samuel," calling it "an exceptional story. It is not entirely a pleasant tale, it lacks the conventional 'happy ending,' but we don't think any one will question its grim power. When we first read it in manuscript the memory of that lonely, stubborn old mother haunted us for days."[53]

The Bookman also took "The Sea-Farmer," another haunting tale, one of London's best, although it is marred by unconvincing dialect. Captain MacElrath, the lonely seaman of the story, makes readers feel compassion. Unlike the brutal Wests and Larsens, he is small, yet strong and fearless, weary from the sea's toil, longing to buy a farm and settle down. Although married for two years, he has only spent nine days with his wife, each visit forcing their relationship to begin anew. He doesn't even know his baby boy. The South Seas aren't isles of romance to MacElrath, who remembers all the fever in Java, the coal dust in Newcastle, the bitter winter gales between "Voloparaiso" and Sydney.

A collection of mediocre Hawaiian stories called *The House of Pride* completed London's literary output during the *Snark*'s voyage. None of these except "Chun Ah Chun," which traces the rise of a Chinese coolie to wealthy merchant, a favorite London theme, leave impressions. According to James A. Michener,

> Jack London, while writing on the mainland of America, had built for himself a solid reputation as a socialist defender of the underdog, and his works had world-wide acceptance. But when he came to Hawaii and saw at firsthand a population—the Chinese—which had many of the characteristics he had espoused in mainland America, he was completely unable to understand

what he saw. In "Chun Ah Chun," . . . and in other stories he not only failed to comprehend what was happening in the Pacific; he actually denigrated an entire body of people, largely on racist grounds. The story . . . was founded upon events occurring within a real Chinese family, but is, I fear, a pathetic misreading both of the Chinese and of the spirit that activates Hawaii. I have never understood how Jack London could be one man in California, and such a different man in Hawaii. I still cannot understand how he could be a practicing socialist on the one hand and a race supremacist on the other. Yet the story "Chun Ah Chun" does have a sly warmth and much wit and remains one of the focal works in the London repertoire.[54]

Katherine Mansfield, like most women readers, thought less of London's South Seas stories. "For there is not a single story in it which is better than the average magazine supplies. True, his admirers would recognize them as having come from the Jack London shop; but they are machine-made, ready-to-wear tales which depend for their novelty upon the originality of the Hawaiian ornament." She concluded that "his salvation lay in wolves, snow, hardship and toil."[55]

Returning to Papeete, the Londons lingered there for over three months, then embarked again on the ailing *Snark,* this time for Bora Bora, where natives serenaded the crew, wrapped them in garlands, and took the Londons on a stone-fishing expedition with flower-crowned girls. (A French sailor called Ernest joined the crew, but was replaced by a Polynesian named Henry.) The Londons visited with everyone from Queen Vaitupu to the island's governor, staying in his luxurious suite. They left Bora Bora on April 15, 1908.

Each Pacific island offered new exotic adventures, the kind London loved to live, the kind that kept him footloose, his fantasies functioning. A hurricane caught the *Snark* on its way to the Fiji islands. The Londons stayed with hospitable natives on Raitera. The king of Pago Pago honored him. And he visited the tomb of Robert Louis Stevenson in Samoa. Frightful headhunters greeted the crew in Port Mary at Santa Anna Island, the Solomon Islands. Martin wrote in his diary on June 28,

Hundreds of natives ran down the beaches, and, tumbling into canoes, darted after us, all the time screaming at the top of their

voices . . . people who in looks and actions fully justified my
expectations of what South Sea Islanders would be.

They had big heads of bushy hair. Half of them wore nose
rings of tortoise shell and of wild boar tusks. All of them were
adorned with earrings. . . . One had the handle of an old tea cup
in his ear. . . . One of the islanders had tin-ware sardine can-
openers in his ears; but the strangest of all was the one who had
the shell of an alarm clock depending from the cartilage of his
nose. . . .

. . . Their cheeks were tattooed in monstrous designs; little
boys being ornamented just as fantastically as were the elders.
Their teeth were filed to points and were dead black; their lips,
large and negroid, were ruby red. . . .

. . . These natives are all head hunters. This village and the
one across the bay continually at war with each other and each
tribe collects the heads of the other. . . . I'm very much frightened about my right foot. On the shin a large sore, big as a
dollar, has started, and it is eating right into my leg. It seems
that no medicine on board will cure it, and there is no doctor
within thousands of miles that we know of. Jack, I'm afraid, has
one of these eating ulcers, too. If no doctor is on Florida Island,
and if we are no better when we get there, I think we'll sail for
Sydney, Australia, for treatment, and that without delay.[56]

Charmian, London, and Martin Johnson all got malaria. More
ulcerous sores erupted that refused to heal. London's skin
flaked, his hands swelled, he grew a new set of toenails every
twenty-four hours. Nakata got ptomaine poisoning. Martin
noted: "In addition to the ulcers and fever a new trouble has
come into the life of the *Snark* family. Jack's hands have begun
to swell, turn very sore and peel skin. The nails are very hard
and thick and have to be filed. And it is the same with his
feet. . . . The traders and beach-combers could diagnose ulcers
and fever, but not this. Both Jack and Mrs. London are considerably alarmed at this strange manifestation."[57] London's
details about these afflictions repelled George Sterling, who
wrote him: "You rather overworked the Solomon sores in the
Snark book. I suppose they appealed strongly to your imagination, you being a reformer. Why not turn Upton loose on
them?"[58]

Before London sailed for Sydney, Australia, he managed one of the trip's most publicized incidents—an encounter with cannibals. A Captain Jensen, involved in blackbirding, invited Charmian and London aboard the *Minota* to capture slaves along the coast of Malaita. Martin stayed behind, later commenting, "When I think of this practice [slave-trading], I do not really wonder that the natives are so savage against the whites."[59]

Martin and the Londons had survived hurricanes, the disabled *Snark,* inept crewmen, six-inch centipedes, and thousands of cockroaches, yet tropical diseases in the Solomons whipped them. "I was looking forward to getting out of this particular part of the world," said Martin. "It was too wild and raw, too full of sickness and sudden death."[60] London detested the Solomons. On November 15, 1908, they left Wada and two Tahitians with the *Snark* and embarked for Australia on the *Makembo*. Martin went to the Sydney Homeopathic Hospital, the Londons to St. Malo Hospital in North Sydney, where London's diseases baffled doctors.

After recuperating, Martin returned to the Solomons for the *Snark*. (This craft was later sold at auction for three thousand dollars and ended its career transporting slave labor crews in the New Hebrides.) The Londons voyaged home on the *Tymeric,* a tramp collier, sighting land twice—Pitcairn Island of *Mutiny of the Bounty* fame and the isle of Ducie. After reaching Ecuador, they climbed Chimberaze, hunted alligators, and sailed for Panama, where they went horseback riding in the Canal Zone. There they boarded the *Lurrielba,* a United Fruit Company steamer, for New Orleans. They reached Oakland on July 24, 1909.

Chapter 14

One Foot on a Brass Rail

RETURNING FROM HIS two-year South Seas cruise, selling only one in twenty short stories to magazines, London realized he needed another *White Fang* or *The Sea Wolf* to restore the old magic and inspire new challenges. Rising expenses at the Glen Ellen ranch also faced him. But what to write? Then the Klondike called. So he thawed all the literary grub-boxes and sled-lashings. The result was a 1910 romance called *Burning Daylight* in which he even preached old-fashioned ethics to hook readers.

The *New York Herald* bought American serial rights to *Burning Daylight* for $8,000. Needing cash to purchase seven hundred more acres at Glen Ellen, London told Brett that another house had offered a $10,000 advance for hardcover rights. Although willing to advance $5,000, Brett wrote:

> If it is true that a financially responsible publisher is willing to pay $10,000 down on account of royalties on a new novel by you at this time, that is to say, on account of its American sale, I can only reply that I do not understand how it can be done as the sale of not one of the recent books has been sufficiently large to warrant such an advance on account of the book publication of any of the recent volumes. Hence, it seems probable that you will wish at the conclusion of the present contract not to renew it, and I shall be very sorry for this but there seems to be no other outcome as I quite fail to see how so large a sum as $10,000 could be advanced on account of the book publication of either ''Burning Daylight'' or the story ''Adventure'' in this country.[1]

London took Brett's $5,000. The editor, meanwhile, checked this so-called publishing house and learned the truth. "As a matter of fact," he wrote London on June 1, 1910, "the concern in question has no standing whatever, as far as I have been able to find out, and the commercial agencies report their total capital to be about Ten Thousand Dollars, so that they were, apparently, going to pay you the whole of it on account of the publication of one book, which as they have published a number of things from time to time certainly seems strange."[2]

For a while, nevertheless, London severed ties with Macmillan, and let Century publish four books in 1912 and 1913: *Smoke Bellew Tales, The Night-Born, The Abysmal Brute,* and *John Barleycorn.* Perhaps Sinclair Lewis, then a junior editor at Frederick A. Stokes Company, excited London's acquisitiveness by saying that other publishers paid name authors huge royalties. Robert Hichens got a 20-percent royalty for *The Garden of Allah,* instead of fifteen. Richard Harding Davis received $1,000 per short story, Kipling fifty cents a word, Conan Doyle fifty cents a word for Sherlock Holmes, Theodore Roosevelt one dollar a word, and Robert W. Chambers a guaranteed $10,000 for each serial. Century, however, refused London mouth-watering advances. They also asked for two books a year, not three or four, which would have severely reduced his income. When they wouldn't return rights to *John Barleycorn,* London rejoined Macmillan's fold, remaining with them until his death.

The relationship between Brett and London, however, stayed amicable during their temporary separation. Letters continued. Brett even wrote Charmian: "My failure to secure Mr. London's future books for publication came about, I fear, through the impossibility of personally attending to all my correspondence. Some of the matters which arose and which resulted in the parting of the ways I never knew all the particulars or until it was too late to amend the conclusion to which Mr. London felt forced to come."[3]

London named his superhero in *Burning Daylight* Elam Harnish, another Klondike king who can lift nine hundred pounds, travels all day with wet feet at forty-five degrees below zero, and possesses the power and stamina of one man in a million or millions. "He is a monster, not a man," accused Edward Garnett in *Friday Nights*. "The American tendency to exaggeration has in fact annihilated all the finer lines and traits of human personality."[4] The *Dial* said London gloried "in his varied brutalities, which is not surprising when we think of certain of the author's earlier essays in portraiture."[5]

Elam Harnish—also known as Burning Daylight—tires of the icy North and returns to New York City, exchanging one life-lie for another, where con men and tin gods clean his pockets, leading the former titan to retrieve his fortune with a Colt .44, then head west to San Francisco, where he beats the big operators at their own buncos. But civilization turns his muscles to mush, his firm stomach to flab, his tastes to alcohol, reasserting London's thesis that "Five years of simplicity, close to the soil and far from temptation, will make a man of him."[6] A character in "In the Forests of the North" philosophizes about the Indians: "At least they're honest folk and live according to their lights. And then they are amazingly simple. No complexity about them, no thousand and one subtle ramifications to every single emotion they experience. They love, fear, hate, are angered, or made happy, in common, ordinary, and unmistakable terms. It may be a beastly life, but at least it is easy to live."[7] In such simple societies, women play inferior roles. Most of London's Indian women, like Li Wan, "knew no other law than that man was the master of women."[8] Even Freda Moloff tells Floyd Vanderlip, "You are something to cling to,—big muscled, strong, and brave. In short, because you *are* a man."[9]

Dede Mason, Daylight's ladylike secretary, finally redeems his worth, but, like Maud Brewster in *The Sea Wolf*, ruins the novel. (Before meeting Dede, Daylight fears women, calling love a game of destruction for all concerned, an attitude London earlier expressed in *The Kempton-Wace Letters*.) But Dede and Daylight marry, then move to the Valley of the Moon (London's name for the Glen Ellen region), where Daylight buries a fabulous gold mine in adoration of this girl. "When you as 'Burning Daylight' gave up that $50,000,000 fortune (or was it $150,-000,000) you might I think have given a poor publisher a chance to benefit by your generosity,"[10] wrote Brett. *The Independent* also remarked: "We all remember when Mr. London was an ardent advocate in fiction of this very mate, what he called the 'flame woman.' So it would be interesting to know how he came by this later revelation of the nature of his own sex, of the man who, whatever he is or has been, winds up by wanting just the good woman. This is progress for Mr. London."[11]

The *New York Times* made this assessment of *Burning Daylight*:

> The present yarn, with its claptrap title, and its maudlin mixture of false sentiment, tawdry heroics and abysmal ignorance of conventional ways, merely serves to underscore in vari-colored inks the foregone conclusion. In fact, the more Mr. London undertakes to write about men and women the more one longs to have him return to his earlier practice of writing about dogs. The dog at his best is an admirable beast. Man at his beast (so to speak) is unspeakably bad. And either Mr. London writes of man as a beast—or he writes of him as something which never was on land or sea. The moment he steps out of the region where the human animal is pitted against the primal forces of nature in the wilderness, at that moment he loses all grip of the creature and writes of him or her rather more crudely—as to comprehension—than the average schoolboy would.[12]

Apparently pleased with *Burning Daylight*, London starred his last Klondike work, *Smoke Bellew Tales* (1912), with another civilized weakling, Smoke Bellew, who becomes a man's man overnight in the Yukon. (He said that *Cosmopolitan* requested the Klondike setting, although he preferred the South Seas, but acceded to their wishes.) Smoke Bellew gets involved in numerous Klondike adventures. He's accused of murdering a man on the trail, wins a dog race for number three, and loses thousands on a get-rich-quick scheme involving spoiled eggs. London also included several Indian tales in the book. In "The Hanging of Cultus George," a civilized Indian nearly gets strung up before agreeing to become a sled driver, and in "Wonder of Women," Labiskwee, another devoted Indian girl, saves Bellew's life, becoming the most memorable character in this short-story collection disguised as a novel. *The Outlook* wrote that she "practically starves herself to death that he may survive, and dies in his arms—so in a page or two he marries the other girl!"[13] *The Athenaeum* called Bellew a "rather monotonously infallible"[14] hero.

Although the Glen Ellen holdings spread with the receipt of revenues from books like *Burning Daylight* and *Smoke Bellew Tales,* London's life-plan lacked one essential—a male heir to inherit the throne. Bessie had two girls, Joan and Bess, leaving Charmian with the burden of producing an heir. Adela Rogers St. Johns says that he "had been swept by a desire for, a need of, a son as violent as Henry the Eighth's. All he meant to do with his estate, his farm inventions, his aid to the farmer must have a son to carry it on."[15]

When Charmian became pregnant, London's hopes soared for the third time, but she gave birth to an anemic girl called Joy on June 19, 1910. The baby was a girl—and a weakling. (Charmian later lost a second child in Seattle during their 1912 Cape Horn voyage.)

Learning the news about Joy, London fled to San Francisco's tenderloin, planning a good drunk, although the doctor warned that the infant would soon die. London's blast landed him in jail, further damaging his public reputation. It seems he wandered into a dive on the waterfront owned by Tim Muldowney. Although later accounts differed, he entered a ladies' toilet with some papers under his arms, papers Muldowney thought were ads for a venereal disease cure. When Muldowney asked him to leave, London refused, and this led to a brawl. "Muldowney's two bartenders and four entertainers of both sexes witnessed the go without paying $50 for reserved seats," said the *San Francisco Examiner,* whose headline read: "Jack London Fights with a Saloon Man." They added that the "big quarrel at Reno on the Fourth probably will not begin to compare with last night's London-Muldowney scrap in the kitchen at the rear of the Tavern, which is Muldowney's music hall and saloon on Seventh Street between Webster and Franklin."[16]

Unlike fictional fighters such as Wolf Larsen and Burning Daylight, London met his match in Muldowney, who weighed over two hundred pounds. By the time police arrived, London was smeared with blood, his clothes ripped, his eye blackened. Muldowney suffered a kick in the groin. Police hauled both men to the station, where they spent the night behind bars, appearing in court the next day. After reviewing their bruised and bloodied bodies, the judge reset the trial, releasing them on bail. Newspapers, meanwhile, throughout the land reported that London had abandoned his wife and dying daughter, remarks that frenzied him. At the trial he pleaded to Judge George Samuels that "he had been thirsty and had consumed two scotches and soda to cool his parched throat. He stated that he had just started out on a walk, the first in many years, to view again and renew the memories of former years." While the packed courtroom listened with amusement, London denied Muldowney's allegation that he was an "abysmal brute," saying he had "entered the resort and made for a private reception room, not noticing that the door bore the sign 'Ladies.' Muldowney, he said, accosted him, shoved a tray-load of edibles into his chest and ordered him from the place with an oath. When he refused to comply, the saloon man struck him, and he rushed to a clinch." Muldowney contradicted, " 'When I told him to beat it,' he said, 'he hit me two cracks in the eye, just like that,' clapping his hands in rapid succession. 'He struck me first. I don't know what was wrong with him. He didn't act like he was drunk or sober, but he sure did behave like he was crazy.' "[17]

The judge, unable to tell fact from fancy, dismissed the case. But London held grudges. After trying to persuade Joseph Noel to write a follow-up story in the *San Francisco Bulletin,* one abusing Muldowney, London's resentment suddenly switched to Judge Samuels. He placed ads in newspapers, asking for affidavits to discredit the judge, trying to prove that one of the judge's relatives owned the Muldowney property. He finally wrote an open letter to all the area papers, threatening to get the judge.

Judge Samuels replied in the *San Francisco Chronicle*: "It is a foolish letter and does not deserve a reply. I have no controversy with London. I do not understand his motive in sending the letter and so far as browbeating his witness is concerned it is all nonsense. It is a cheap threat when he says he will hold up the actions of my past life, when he admits he knows nothing of my past life. The young man has long been known as an obstreperous youth and at times he gains notoriety of some kind. It is clear that the letter comes from one who has gained little in the way of judgment by experience in the ways of the world which he claims to have had. He is an Oakland boy, and he is still a boy—a foolish boy, at that.''[18]

Local newspapers supported Judge Samuels. "Jack London, in his ridiculous open letter to Police Judge Samuels of Oakland, exhibits himself as a foolish and ill tempered boy. There is a strain of hysteria running through the letter that suggests a towering rage grown somewhat stale by a period of cold storage. The absurd threats with which the document winds itself up to the climax suggest an atmosphere of melodrama of the 'ten, twent', thirt' variety,''[19] wrote the *Call*. The *Chronicle* ridiculed: "From his retreat at Glen Ellen, Jack London, author, traveler in many lands, and plower of the deep sea in cockleshell craft, has written an open letter in which the relater of romances arraigns with a number of vicious punches of his typewriter, the judicial action of Samuels, and cheerfully announces that he is on the trail of the jurist, decked with war feathers and gaudy paint and with a keen tomahawk grasped in his right hand.''[20]

London, who often turned mischief into money, wrote an O. Henry-type short story called "The Benefit of the Doubt," about the incident, which the *Saturday Evening Post* bought for seven hundred fifty dollars. Churchill Williams, the *Post's* editor, feared that Judge Samuels, recognizing his fictional counterpart, would sue, but London said he based 90 percent of his stories on fact. One newspaper caricature showed London on a charging steed, holding a quill lance, while Muldowney called the story "a poor one," but "a great ad.''[21]

Carter Wilson, the leading character in "The Benefit of the Doubt," is another London professor with a social conscience, who has written books about Christ and cave men. Entering a bar where human beasts assault him, Wilson received little sympathy from cops and judge because the saloon-keeper holds a pocketful of votes; the judge, therefore, gives both men the benefit of the doubt, dismissing the case. Later on Wilson finds the judge on his country property, pulverizes him, then pretends the judge attacked him. A village constable again dismisses the case, giving both men the benefit of the doubt.

"I would rather be the heavyweight champion of the world than the King of England or the President of the United States,"[22] London once claimed. The boxing game, like the Klondike and South Seas, provided him with another ideal setting for the "survival of the fittest," an arena where brawn beat brains. (Scientific champ and matinée idol "Gentleman Jim" Corbett, once complained that "the crowd wants blood and the thrill of the kill."[23]) After the Muldowney brawl, eyes bruised and bloated, London went to Reno, Nevada. The *New York Herald* paid him one hundred dollars a day plus expenses to cover the Jack Johnson–James J. Jeffries historic fight. He got lots of blood and lots of thrills.

As early as 1901 London had reported the Jeffries-Ruhlin fight for the *San Francisco Examiner*. After detailing how "the dark man spat blood from his mouth and smiled, and the blood ran down his chin," he philosophized:–"And under this veneer of a thousand years of culture, I, for one, found that the endless savage centuries still lived. I, who had come to note the blood cry of the crowd, came to myself with sickening consciousness to find that my voice too, was issuing forth with lusty joy and thrilling abandon. One does not break lightly from his heritage."[24] (Joseph Noel said London became so involved in fights that his neck veins swelled. This offended Sterling.) He later received one hundred dollars from the *San Francisco Examiner* to cover the Britt-Nelson clash and two hundred seventy-five dollars for the Burns-Johnson bout in Sydney, Australia. Johnson's gold-capped teeth inflamed London. So did everything else about this rags-to-riches black, who liked fast cars, wild women, and the best of times. "Jack London, the late story writer, and Mrs. London were ring-side spectators," Johnson later recalled, "and I think it was at this time that London got the idea of the golden smile with which he often described me later and which was so frequently mentioned in after years."[25] Nat Fleischer, famed boxing sportswriter says in *The Heavyweight Championship* that London "wrote a vivid, not to say, lurid, account of the fight for the *New York Herald,* an account calculated to chill the blood of every member of the master race—that is to say, he appealed to the deep-rooted prejudices of the vast majority of white Americans.''[26]

London hated blacks, not just Jack Johnson. This is a prejudice that surfaces in many stories. David Shelton in *Adventure* calls blacks beasts. David Grief in *A Son of the Sun* compares them to prehistoric monkeys. Dick Forrest in *The Little Lady of the Big House* declares that blacks produced only two important figures: Booker T. Washington and W. E. B. Du Bois, both white-blooded. He even calls the dogs of blacks in *Jerry of the Islands* and *Michael, Brother of Jerry* cowards.

When London entered the press row at Reno on July 4, 1910, he expected James J. Jeffries to whip Jack Johnson—betting four thousand dollars himself on the fight.[27] Since Johnson took Tommy Burns in 1908, Americans had been searching for a "Great White Hope" to wipe the floor with smiling Jack. "Big Jim" Jeffries became their greatest hope—and he failed. Johnson's victory shocked London, the way it shocked millions. Sarcasm seethed in his reports. "This was naive, as well as blatant," says Lester Bromberg in *Boxing's Unforgettable Fights.* "By his description of Johnson's effortless superiority, London had confessed to the pre-eminence of the man, first Negro to become heavyweight champion. Yet, in resentment over Jack's [Johnson's] condescending manner towards an inferior defender, he was appealing to an old hero who had been entirely idle for four years and who hadn't had a testing fight in six years.''[28]

Although London supposedly knew boxing, he still molded shapeless masses from its raw material in fiction. Backwoodsman Pat Glendon in *The Abysmal Brute* (1913), for example, is a cross between Wolf Larsen and Humphrey Van Weyden. He doesn't drink, doesn't smoke, doesn't swear. (A boxer in "The Night-Born" also doesn't drink, doesn't smoke, doesn't swear—and carries his prayer book to the arena.) Pat Glendon reads Browning and Shakespeare's sonnets, attends art museums, and studies color photography—when he isn't hunting, fishing, running forty to fifty miles a day, or innocently pounding opponents in the ring.

Pat Glendon, the abysmal brute, meets Maud Sangster (another Frona Welse) whose father, Jacob, is another Jacob Welse, a captain of industry worth fifty million. She's also a Spencerian individualist, breaking free from Victorian mores by becoming a newspaper reporter and published poet. Maud is also a state tennis champion who walked from San Mateo to Santa Cruz to win a bet; she has played polo with men, dived to the bottom of the Golden Gate, and flown with the bird man. But she's also a feminine female. After she falls for Pat, his life changes, especially when she convinces him that boxing is a rotten game. In a flashing finale, he beats a hairy brute, then makes a ten-page speech about capitalistic corruption.

London's earlier *The Game* (1905), another weak work, is still preferable to *The Abysmal Brute*. Like several of his other novelettes, *The Game* is really a padded short story, which led *The Athenaeum* to remark that he gave "the public rather short measure for its money by sending forth a racy sort of magazine sketch in book form."[29] Reviews were split. The *Atlantic Monthly* called it an "excellent novelette," adding that "if the idyllic side makes a perceptible demand upon your credulity, the result is at least attractive,"[30] and *The Bookman* thought it was "very nearly flawless."[31] *The Independent* commented: "Since Richard Harding Davis wrote 'Gallagher' and George Meredith 'An Amazing Marriage,' prize fighting has become rather common in fiction, but no one has described the brutal scene with more vividness than Jack London. Whether this be a merit or the reverse will depend upon the taste of the reader."[32] *The Critic* panned: "Mr. London must have been under very urgent pressure to produce a book, to consent to acknowledge a story, of this order. It is of the most banal and ordinary stamp, utterly lacking in the dramatic power with which its author has been credited hitherto."[33]

London called Genevieve and Joe, the two main characters of *The Game,* "working-class aristocrats. In an environment made up largely of sordidness and wretchedness they had kept themselves unsullied and wholesome." A shop girl patterned after someone London saw while researching *The People of the Abyss,* Genevieve, a sheltered lass, hates ugliness. She has a "peaches and cream" complexion, stays pristine pure, and re-sembles a piece of Dresden china. "She was all that was pure and good, a holy of holies not lightly to be profaned even by

what might possibly be the too ardent reverence of a devotee."
Joe's a "girl-cheeked, blue-eyed, curly-headed" boyish boxer.
"His skin was fair as a woman's, far more satiny, and no
rudimentary hair-growth marred its white lustre. This [Gene-
vieve] perceived, but all the rest, the perfection of line and
strength and development, gave pleasure without knowing why.
There was a cleanness and grace about it."[34] Maxwell Geismar
says: "The high point of their tedious romance, very much like
the barely disguised strip-tease act that London had used to
redeem the faltering action in *Theft,* was when the peeping girl,
smuggled into a boxing match, saw her young proletarian lover
'naked save for the low canvas shoes and narrow hip-cloth of
white!' "[35]

London pitted Joe against John Ponta, another "beast with
a streak for a forehead, with beady eyes under lowering and
bushy brows, flat-nosed, thick-lipped, sullen-mouthed. . . . He
was coarseness to blackness, and his body was covered with
a hairy growth that matted like a dog's on his chest and shoulders. He was deep-chested, thick-legged, large-muscled, but
unshapely. His muscles were knots, and he was gnarled and
knobby, twisted out of beauty by excess of strength."[36] A real
tough sort. But beauty nearly beats the beast. Joe methodically
tires Ponta with whirlwind blows. While Genevieve, dressed as
a boy, peeks through the peephole, the reader receives a blow-
by-blow account of action. At the last moment, victory within
his grasp, fate trips Joe, causing his death: "In sore travail,
gasping, reeling, panting, with glazing eyes and sobbing breath,
grotesque and heroic, fighting to the last, striving to get at his
antagonist, he surged and was driven about the ring. And in
that moment Joe's foot slipped on the wet canvas. Ponta's
swimming eyes saw and knew the chance. All the fleeing
strength of his body gathered itself together for the lightning
lucky punch. Even as Joe slipped the other smote him, fairly
on the point of the chin. He went over backward. Genevieve
saw his muscles relax while he was yet in the air, and she heard
the thud of his head on the canvas."[37]

One reviewer from the *New York Saturday Times* incensed
London. "Still more one gently doubts in this particular case,
that a blow delivered by Ponta on the point of Fleming's chin
could throw the latter upon the padded canvas floor of the ring

with enough force to smash the whole back of his skull, as Mr. London describes."[38] London replied, calling himself an experienced prizefighter who had been knocked out and knew about such incidents, adding that Jimmy Britt, lightweight champion of the world, liked the book.

London also wrote two short stories about boxing called "A Piece of Steak" and "The Mexican," both superior to *The Game* and *The Abysmal Brute* because of their compression. The former shows his growing awareness that age cripples man's physical prowess. Tom King, a former champ, has passed his prime. Swollen veins, crushed knuckles and worn-out lungs have reduced him to rubble. Hungry for a steak, he recalls when his bull terrier devoured them; now his wife and kids survive on scraps, and he must walk to the arena. Time ravages man. Youth laughs at age—until it catches him on the run. Then glory fades fast. Although King outboxes his opponent, the boy's stamina and endurance turn the tables, and King is knocked cold, forced to return home broken, still famished.

In "The Mexican," youthful fighter Felipe Rivera lives for the Mexican revolution after militarists slaughter his family. Like Tom King, he fights for a burning cause, not acclaim; the odds stacked, he refuses to throw the fight, and wins an all-or-nothing bet. The revolution can continue. How unfortunate London failed to write more such moving stories about sympathetic characters who reach beyond themselves, shaping a better world, somehow coping with the beast within. "Jack London never realized a fraction of his powers," said Russell Blakenship. "Rather he succumbed to the temptation of large checks and often wrote to please the bourgeoisie that he affected to despise so heartily."[39]

Many of those large checks London spent on travel, from trips through the California hills to Bora Bora. In December 1911 he and Charmian went to New York City, planning a return via Cape Horn. London promised to kick the drinking habit and even write a book about it later—*John Barleycorn*—after one last debauch. This became a nightmare for Charmian, left in her hotel room, waiting for the worst, which she reveals in *The Book of Jack London*.[40] In short: London promised to stop drinking, a promise he would fail to keep. And Charmian knew it.

While in New York, London met such celebrities as Victor Herbert, Dr. Charles P. Steinmetz, genius at General Electric, and David Graham Phillips, distinguished American author. Phillips's impeccable dress contrasted sharply with London's flannel shirt and attached collar. They found little in common. "After the meeting I asked London what he thought of Phillips," recalled Isaac P. Marcosson. "His reply was, 'He is too much of a dude. He didn't like me because I wore a flannel shirt.' "[41]

When the Londons finally boarded the *Dirigo* for Baltimore, Charmian breathed relief, although London's shaving his head bothered her. "She aged rapidly under the increasing demands his over-bounding energy made on her," wrote Joseph Noel. "While, to save her marriage, she was the moving spirit in those frequent voyages down to the sea in ships, these trips saved Jack too. Without the excursions to Hawaii and the islands of the South Seas, he would have ended his career long before he did. They took him away from the fever of living."[42]

En route to California on the *Dirigo,* London started his alcoholic memoir, *John Barleycorn,* although resuming the drinking habit. But he rationalized: saloons offered good fellowship, a refuge from the cold and rain, a place to congregate with full-chested manly men. London clung to the illusion that he still preferred taffy and suckers.

The *Saturday Evening Post* serialized *John Barleycorn* in 1913. Century published the hardcover. London struck pay dirt. The Prohibition Party, the Young Christian Temperance Union, and the Women's Christian Temperance Union all pushed it— not knowing London toasted the book's success with a bottle. "That the work of a drinker who had no intention of stopping drinking should become a major propaganda piece in the campaign for Prohibition is surely one of the choice ironies in the history of alcohol,"[43] said Upton Sinclair.

Clergymen, educators, and fundamentalists all waved Barleycorn's banner, providing the same service as American socialists had provided for London's labor tracts. The Prohibition party distributed pamphlets before Century released the book. Groups deluged him with lecture offers. Some reviewers, however, realized the sordid truth. And they resented it.

"It is too excessively frank to convince us that it is wholly a record of thoughts that came into the mind and incidents that happened to the body of its writer,"[44] charged the *Boston Transcript*. *The Independent* added that London's "readers are prone to doubt his sincerity and to attribute the work to mercenary or sensationalistic tendency."[45] The *San Francisco Bulletin* questioned the book's "real logic," suggesting that "perhaps Jack London would see a bigger and truer truth than whiskey can teach him if he could share the attitude toward life of the mother absorbed with her children, the father struggling for his family, and of all the others who are too occupied with sacrifice and service to speculate about the meaning of things."[46] And *The Nation* reasoned: "As a tract against the saloon, and a professed argument for woman suffrage in order that the saloon may be done away with, it will please the prohibitionists and suffragists. [London openly supported women's rights during the book's publication.] As a record of glorious sprees and multifarious good-fellowship, it is capable of exciting thirst in the thirst-minded. As a tract, it suffers from this drawback that the author does not pretend to have 'sworn off,' or even express a wish to swear off."[47] (Cartoonists ridiculed *John Barleycorn*, one caricature showing London hitting a bottle with one of his books.)

London wrung dry the promotion road. His *John Barleycorn* plans even included a film and stage play. He served as vice-president of the National Defense Association that drafted a "No Drunkard Bill," which they hoped the New York Legislature would pass. It allowed each person two yearly drunks. A third drunk lost one's license. "I am absolutely convinced that the no drunkard plan is the finest thing that has yet been presented, considered in the light of all circumstances, for the abolition of drinking,"[48] London commented.

As Carl Sandburg said about London and O. Henry: "Both were jail-birds; no speechmakers at all; speaking best with one foot on a brass rail; a beer-glass in the left hand and the right hand employed for gestures. And both were lights snuffed out . . . no warning . . . no lingering. Who knew the hearts of these booze-fighters."[49]

Chapter 15

The Ranch of Good Intentions

THE FOURTEEN-HUNDRED-ACRE Glen Ellen ranch obsessed Jack London during his last years. It represented a frantic attempt to free himself from the wretched writing game and exert power over man, that "monstrous spectre" and "disease of the agglutinated dust."[1] As Kevin Starr says, "He threw himself into the therapy of ranching, a therapy that in time became an orgy, and finally a dance of death. Through construction of an identity as a great California rancher, London hoped to stave off chaos; instead he invoked a nightmare."[2] Adela Rogers St. Johns recalls:

> Jack built that big ranch up there and so much money was required to run it that he was working harder and doing more than he could do well. He had serials running in every magazine published, and half the time he hadn't finished them when he sold them. And the expenses of the ranch meant he would no longer be able to take off and go to sea whenever he felt like it. I think he got himself into such a tangle that he didn't know how to get out of it.[3]

Located outside the village of Glen Ellen, nearly fifty miles north of San Francisco, this sprawling estate startled American socialists and capitalists alike. Was this the same author who raved about "division of land" in "What Communities Lose by the Competitive System," the essay that won a $200 first prize from *Cosmopolitan*? Was this the same author who traced social losses "to a certain asserted right of the individual to

257

private ownership in land"?⁴ Friends shook their heads. London, however, predicted the ranch would revolutionize scientific farming methods. Although Eliza superintended, he hired the finest stockmen to run it. "When he decided to have a colorful background of Western Bronco busters on his range, he brought out a number of real thoroughbred cowboys from Cheyenne, headed by a genius in that line."⁵ Locals resented the takeover. "Jack London has bought the Glen Ellen blacksmith shop and moved it up to his ranch," said a neighbor. "Good boy, Jack! Take a couple more loads and move the whole town up there!"⁶

The Glen Ellen ranch remained an unfulfilled farm fantasy— not a ranch for ranchers who dug livings from the dirt. "I call this place 'The Ranch of Good Intentions,' " London said in *The Bookman.* "No, it doesn't pay yet [This was several months before London's death, and a decade after he started it] and is, in fact, rather an expensive luxury; but it is bound to bring in good returns in time. I had not much of an idea of farming when I first came here seven years ago. I was tired of cities and city people, and I was looking about for a home in the country when I discovered this hillside place in the Valley of the Moon. I observed that some of the professors at the University of California question that translation of Sonoma, but it is the Valley of the Moon to me."⁷ He told Charmian the ranch would never make money, that he planned to reinvest all profits in more improvements and experiments.

Return to the soil. This became London's threadbare cliche. He, meanwhile, collected checks from New York City for his work. In the wilderness man could live in innocence, remain an individualist, gain freedom and happiness. Civilization lacked guts. He wrote *The Valley of the Moon* to prove the point, Saxon, the laundry girl, marrying Billy Roberts, a professional boxer. Failure litters their cityscape until they decide to farm. In *The Little Lady of the Big House,* Dick Forrest also makes millions off the soil, although Saxon and Billy settle for a rural retreat.

Upton Sinclair remarked that *The Valley of the Moon* was "so poor in quality that you can scarcely believe you are reading"[8] a London work. *The Bookman* added that Saxon and Billy have the "most amazing luck. Everyone they meet, as they travel south through the rich valleys of California, is phenomenally kind and helpful; everything to which they turn their hand becomes gold at their touch. It is all a fairy dream, a new 'Eldorado'; and one closes the book wondering how many adventurous couples, dazzled by the brightness of the picture, are destined to try their fortunes and meet with disillusion."[9] But London was trying to retain the myth of the romantic Old West, along with his own corroded pipe dreams. As Lewis Mumford said, "He was the social platitude of the old West, translated into a literary epigram."[10] Perhaps Sinclair Lewis made the most satirical remarks about *The Valley of the Moon*:

> Indeed, again and again in "The Valley of the Moon" Mr. London recalls the fact that the fathers of his propagandists were forty-niners. But these native Americans have, at the beginning of Mr. London's tale, lost out in the competition against the shrewder Japs, Dalmatians, Greeks and what not, people who have taken up the land carelessly impoverished by the Americans, and made it pay so profusely that they are becoming lords of the land. It is, at first, a melancholy situation.
>
> Here are the children of the gallant forty-niners cramped in Oakland, he a prize-fighter teamster, she a laundry worker, both of them at the mercy of "the bosses" and strike breakers. Yet they are gallant as their forefathers. They leave their accustomed friends and go tramping up the coast, pack on back, looking for "a valley of the moon where they can be free."[11]

Unlike his multimillionaire heroes David Grief, Dick Forrest, and Elam Harnish, London played a losing game with con men and big business in his attempts to become rich. "Like his country, Jack London was corporeally mature, innerly a child," wrote Waldo Frank. "He mastered the outward circumstances of life—and then played with toys. The world was his, by physical and intellectual possession, but he preferred to live in a nursery, and blamed his excess drinking on the fact that no Nurse was there to keep the liquor from his lips."[12]

Because he ignored small print in contracts and stock certificates, swindlers promoting Mexican land deals and a Jack London Grapejuice Company exploited him. Two men calling themselves representatives of the Fidelity Loan and Mortgage Company visited Glen Ellen at one time, offering stocks and a seat on the board of directors for London. He signed a contract of sorts, later claiming that he "became interested from a sociological standpoint."[13] He refused to pay for the stocks, pleading fraud and misrepresentation, leading the men to file a judgment of $4,625[14] against him. The trial packed Santa Rosa's Superior Court. "Verbal hand grenades, shrapnel and 42 centimeter shells fell promiscuously in the court room and from the rate that the case is progressing there seems but little chance to 'get the boys out of the trenches before Christmas,' " joked the *Santa Rosa Republican*.

London, who had offered to settle the stock incident for $250 out of court, was asked why he neglected to complain earlier.

"That was a very baffling conversation," London replied. "You were trying to find out how much I know; you were trying to get my ammunition and I was trying to get yours. I succeeded and you failed."

This didn't end matters. The lawyer tried to prove that London knew about law. Hadn't he been previously involved in other suits?

"This is the second time I have ever been in a civil suit in my life [London answered]. The first time was about a month ago when I was a witness, but was excluded from the court room up to that time, so I am utterly unfamiliar with court conduct."

But hadn't London been involved in a lot of litigations?

"Only in copyright suits. I have had many of them but have always hired the best attorneys possible and have never appeared in court."

"How about breach of contract suits, Mr. London?" was asked.

"Only one, and that was the Balboa Film Company against the Bosworth incorporated, and I simply hired an attorney in the case as usual."

Then the attorney asked London about his familiarity with police courts.

"I have been there when I was on the road. Several times I have been in courts of this character. You know as a boy I bummed about the country considerably and of course got picked up a number of times."

After mentioning the Judge Samuels incident, the attorney commented on London's accurate use of local color.

"Local color is mostly bosh. You haven't time for it. It must be slurred over. Why I get sometimes as high as one hundred letters criticizing me for improper local color after I publish a story."

Even the judge laughed when they asked London if he knew about a corporation director's liability: "No, I don't know exactly, but I do know that it is sometimes darn dangerous."[15]

London lost the case, although he claimed that he had been "flim flammed."[16]

The Millergraph speculation, another financial fiasco, upstaged both the grapejuice company and Fidelity Loan and Mortgage Company affairs. Joseph Noel told London about someone named Miller who invented a lithographic process with three colors. London, again mortgaging Flora's house, sank $4,000 into the shaky scheme. Sterling's uncle added $1,000, Noel $400, and several friends filled the pot. Noel quit his job, moving to New York City as London's watch dog, while Miller looked for bigger backers. According to dates on Sterling's letters to London, this venture continued for several years. "Did you get the Millergraph stock I sent you? I saw Noel several times in N.Y.," Sterling wrote on October 3, 1911. "They'd just started placing the thing and the unions were kicking. It's going to be a fortune-maker, as you thought."[17] Three years later on June 3, 1914, Sterling wrote London that while in Manhattan Noel had taken him "to the Millergraph office and to see Bartlett. B. impresses me as a straightforward man. He spoke encouragingly of the invention."[18] Then on September 30, Sterling followed up: "I don't think *anything* is doing in the 'Millergraph.' Haven't seen Noel since May. He lives in Yonkers, has his family with him, and is sick and probably starving. . . . I'd be starving myself if it wasn't for money that Jimmy lent me."[19]

Entrenched lithographers, of course, controlled this lucrative market, still in its golden age. Miller, needing millions to compete, worked in a basement trying to perfect the process. London feared he would sell out to Wall Street wolves and asked Brett for $25,000 to $50,000 in advances to defray expenses. But Brett didn't bite. London plunged into this the way he often plunged into quick-cash schemes, even writing the company's promotional materials, allowing the use of his name as president on stock certificates. Noel finally recommended Wall Street expertise. This made London bristle, although he finally agreed. Wall Street offered two options: cash in or convert to stocks. He chose the latter. The Millergraph company later went bankrupt. London, who had earlier praised Noel's efforts, grew hostile toward the journalist after this mishap.

London's farm investments also failed as fortune-makers. When a eucalyptus boom swept across California, the United States Forest Service warned that planters had already preempted the market, but London planted 250,000 trees on the 110-acre Lamotte Ranch, then bought the Kohler Ranch, two additions to the original property, endorsing the project in a brochure circulated by the American Corporation of Investors. Publicly he rationalized: "I have been trying hard to get out of the writing game for many years. I never liked to write and only took up the profession as a third and last choice of life. It has been a miserable occupation, but I did it to make money and I made it. I think that my eucalyptus trees will help me make my getaway in the near future and it will be a relief for me to get out of the scorching focus of the public eye."[20]

Then came London's $3,000-pigpen that made area ranchers laugh. Circular in form with running water and electric lights, its pens, radiating from a central feedhouse, were made of concrete. "In twelve years," London defended, "I'll save the price of the thing in saving of labor, by feeding from the center of the ring of pens."[21] The *Santa Rosa Republican* reported:

> Among the latest additions added to the estate by the "Valley of the Moon" author is a fireproof hog pen which will be a model

of sanitation and—yes, comfort—for the family swine. Then there is a crescent-shaped concrete dam, several hundred feet in length, with a width of fourteen feet at the base and four feet at the top. The dam is reinforced with metal pipes from the author's burned home and other fittings from London's grove of redwoods. It is constructed to hold 7,000,000 gallons of water for use in dry seasons. During weather of the other extremes, the dam will prevent overflows.

London has two pedigreed pigs, known as "Doric" and "O.I.C." with which he intends to show other farmers, not only in his own community but over the rest of the world, just how to breed real livestock.[22]

Before entering the palatial pigpen, visitors stepped into a pagoda, where they chemically cleaned their shoes to avoid carrying in cholera germs. One tourist wrote that following this ritual, they "started to drive their Studebaker into the 'Palace Apartments,' but Secretary Byrne called a halt. If feet could carry cholera germs, so could the Goodrich 'Barefoot' tires, with which the car was shod. Before the Studebaker was allowed to proceed further the tires also were washed in disinfectant by an obliging ranch hand."[23] The pigs later died from pneumonia.

Besides the biggest porkers, London bought Jersey cows, thoroughbred shorthorn bulls, white Leghorn fowl, and magnificent horses, including Mountain Lad (who became the supersexed stallion in *The Little Lady of the Big House*) and Neuadd Hillside, his $2,500 shire stallion. Thirty horses devoured barley that ran $40 a ton and hay $20. Luther Burbank, one of London's acquaintances, once talked him into feeding the animals on his spineless cactus.

The Glen Ellen ranch became a showplace of oddities. It was the first farm to use a manure spreader. It had the biggest silo, a mammoth concrete structure, the first in California, forty-three feet high, eleven feet in diameter. "He saw everything from farming through fighting to reading in heroic terms,"[24] says Charles Child Walcutt. Readers of London's stories remember all the monstrous moths, twelve-inch butterflies, birds with ten-foot wingspreads, apple-like barnacles, semi-intelligent flies, even a seventy-pound cat in *Adventure*. Reality, however, cut the heroic down to life-size. The shorthorn bull broke its neck, the Angora herd perished, the Shires' hairy legs couldn't tolerate California's winter mud. Neuadd Hillside died from a rupture. London's workmen loafed and laughed. The ranch's foreman conspired to get a twenty percent kickback from area merchants. Farmers had warned London about the farm when he came to Glen Ellen, but he called them stupid, although admitting he had never handled a plough. The advice of agricultural consultants passed through both ears. "The region was a back-water district," he later said. "The ranchers were poor and hopeless; no one could make any money ranching there, they all told me. They had worked the land out and their only hope was to move on somewhere else and start in to work new land out and destroy its value."[25]

The stillborn Wolf House, London's grandiose "forest castle"[26] built to last a thousand years, became his life's greatest loss. Famed architect Harrison Fisher called it "the most beautiful house in America."[27] This mansion cost $80,000—probably several million on today's market—and took four years to complete.

> In so far as possible the material used in the construction of the house is gathered from the surrounding country. The natural cobblestones, great quantities of which are to be found on the estate, are to be used from the concrete basement to the second story, also for the chimneys, while rough tree trunks will form the architectural lines of the second story and are to be used also for the porte cochere, pergolas, porches, etc. The house will be in the shape of a U with an open court, 45 by 58 feet, the center of which will have a concrete tank, 15 by 40 feet, filled with running water and stocked with black bass and other fish. On all sides of the tank will be a five-foot garden. Balconies made of tree trunks will be built clear around the court.
>
> The main portion of the house will be 86 feet, with two 82-foot wings. All rafters are to be hewn out of rough redwood logs and will be kept in the natural finish. A charming effect is obtained by interlacing the redwood tree trunks in the gables and balconies with fruit tree twigs. The roof is to be of Spanish tile.
>
> The interior is to be carried out along the same lines as the exterior, the rustic effect predominating. London's study or workroom will be on the second floor. It will be a spacious affair,

19 by 40 feet, with the library occupying the same amount of space, and reached by a spiral staircase, just beneath it. These two rooms are quite apart from the rest of the house, and the author is thus assured quiet and seclusion while absorbed in his literary work. A feature of the house is the great living-room, 18 by 45 feet, and extending to a height of two stories, with balconies running entirely around the second floor. An immense stone fireplace will add to the cheerfulness of the room.

The house will contain a hot water heating system, a private electric light plant, a refrigerating plant and laundry, with steam dryer and rotary wringer, a milk and storeroom, root and wine cellar, and a vacuum cleaning plant.[28]

Fire, however, gutted Wolf House on August 27, 1913, shortly before moving-in day. It is said the Londons stayed at the blaze until 6 A.M. Charmian called London's reaction stoical. Others said he wept. Several days before, he had mortgaged Eliza's cottage to complete the Wolf House dream, a total loss except for $10,000 insurance.[29] Although they suspected a discharged laborer, faulty evidence prevented any action. "You poor old Wolf," wrote Sterling. "It's sure Hell, isn't it? Why O why, didn't you have a night-watchman, since you've fired so many Dagoes? But what's the use of questions? I've not seen today's paper, but am hoping that the fire hasn't damaged the canyon much: you can restore houses in a year, but some trees not in a life-time. I suppose those redwoods near the house are gone forever—what a God Damned shame! I wish I had that Dago at the end of a gun!"[30]

Other macabre things had happened at Wolf House. The same year London found a horse shot to death in one pasture. Possum, their pet terrier, also had died strangely in the pool. London never rebuilt Wolf House. Weeds soon claimed the ghost-like structure. Its remains still stand.

After the burning of Wolf House, London's remaining three years became a charnel house of moral and physical dissolution, ending in early death at forty. As Van Wyck Brooks says, "his will to power destroyed his will to live."[31] London caught colds.

His eyelids collected styes. His teeth rotted. Dysentery weakened him. Nephritis (inflammation of the kidneys) and uremia, causing leg cramps and abdominal pains, complicated by rheumatic attacks, turned days and nights into horrors. George Sterling sympathetically wrote: "Too G.D. bad about the rheumatics! I didn't think you'd have them till you were sixty, at least."[32] Joan revealed that he "detest[ed] walking in any of its form, tennis and golf failed to interest him, but he frequently rode horseback when he was on the ranch, until the last months of his life." He also quit swimming. "The lithe, well-knit, graceful body had vanished beneath an unhealthy corpulence,"[33] added Joan. Mary Austin also recalled that he "sagg[ed] a little with the surfeit of success, preferred the lounging drift-wood or the pitch-pine blazing hearth."[34]

Illnesses had bothered London for years. Flora reminded him about liver and kidneys during the road days. London, who despaired that he had inherited death's skull, even called himself a blob in a 1902 letter to Bessie. All these weaknesses and frustrations he transfigured into a success-myth, carefully shaping an image of superior traits, creating a romantic fantasy for the shattered dreams of mass America.

Perhaps Andrew Sinclair's remarks about London's fear that he had syphilis throws additional light on those agonizing last years. (As earlier noted, Bessie mentioned gonorrhea in her divorce suit.) Sinclair, who says London took the drug salvarsan, an early cure for both yaws and syphilis, writes: "In 1911, Jack was turned down for the first time as a bad health risk by an insurance company. No reason was given for his failure to pass. He never took a medical examination for insurance again. And however cheerful he seemed to Charmian about the loss of her child, he brooded over a possible taint in his system that prevented him from having an heir. He believed that his yaws had not been cured properly in Australia. He became a subscriber to *The American Journal of Urology and Sexology,* and collected a small library on venereal diseases. One of the books was heavily underlined, particularly the passages about the transmission of syphilis in the conception of children, the three stages of the disease, and its old cures. Another was a pamphlet called *The Treatment of Syphilis and Salvarsan or 606.*"[35] (This fear may also explain why London and Charmian slept in different bedrooms.)

London's concern about venereal disease probably surfaced long before his discovery of salvarsan. "I was never sick in my life," Wolf Larsen tells Humphrey Van Weyden in *The Sea Wolf*. "Something's gone wrong with my brain. A cancer, a tumor, or something of that nature—a thing that devours and destroys. It's attacking my nerve centers, eating them up, bit by bit, cell by cell—from the pain."[36] In *Martin Eden* Mrs. Morse warns Ruth about unclean sailors, discouraging her from marrying Martin. (Syphilis ran rampant among sailors, many of whom became infected by prostitutes at ports of call.) A character in Frank Norris's *Vandover and the Brute,* the novel London acclaimed, contracts syphilis. Vandover says "To a large extent I really believe it's the women's fault that the men are what they are. If they demanded a higher moral standard the men would come up to it; they encourage a man to go to the devil and then—when he's rotten with disease and ruins his wife and has children—what is it—'*spotted toads*'—*then* there's a great cry raised against the men, and women write books and all, when half the time the woman has only encouraged him to be what he is."[37]

Microorganisms must have intrigued London. He was amazed at how such miniature monsters, millions failing to fill a pinhead, could ravage super brutes like Wolf Larsen, killing them with ease. This neutralized his tenets about the biggest of the big inheriting the earth by devouring smaller creatures. He discussed August Weismann's theories about germ plasm with Cloudesley Johns as early as 1899. He mentioned microorganisms in "The Human Drift" and *The Cruise of the Snark*. In "Stalking the Pestilence," written for *Collier's* during the Mexican revolution, he compared these beasties to colossal armies. And in *The Scarlet Plague* (1915), a science fiction novelette set in 2013, mankind nearly perishes from a modern plague that turns skin scarlet. Germ warfare also destroys the militant Chinese in "The Unparalleled Invasion."

During this period, creditors deluged London with bills, many of which he couldn't pay, although writing three or four books a year. Some sued. Others issued summonses. Chronic neuroses must have depleted his already failing health, because he and Charmian took to water. "I don't see how you can hide very successfully in the tules," wrote George Sterling on October 28, 1913. "I'd guarantee to take a launch and find you in two or three days; and it should be worth a good deal to those pirates to subpoena you. But you never could have hidden hereabouts."[38] The previous February Sterling had written London a mysterious letter, one that implies double-dealings, and the idea of writing under a pen name, although it seems hard to imagine London's producing more work at the time. "The incriminating document has been obliterated (Atlantic Monthly for the letter has been burnt) and the pebble of confession rests forever in the well of discretion (Asiatic for I won't give you away.) It will be a tremendously interesting thing to see if and how you can build up another reputation. It's going to be a hell of a hard thing to do despite your genius. And C.H. isn't likely ever to rise to the popularity of J.L. Your rates too may remain low for much longer than you imagine."[39]

Charmian suffered much from all this turmoil, although she seldom discouraged London's spending sprees. What bothered her most? Probably the phonies and pseudo-philosophers who used London for handouts. This included everyone from hobos to ex-cons. "London usually had satellites about him," wrote Louis J. Stellman. "Sometimes they were the tramp friends of his former days, sometimes long-haired political theorists, artists, impecunious writers or poets. These, in addition to the men famous in various walks of life of which one or two might be found among his visitors almost any day. On the day of my visit, a well known editor sat opposite me—one who spoke familiarly of great names. Another was a friend of his mining days; still another was a socialist poet."[40]

Like Bessie of earlier years, Charmian tired of London's underdogs, refusing to let some of them in the Glen Ellen house. Although Adela Rogers St. Johns remembered that Charmian's "queenly air of ruling Glen Ellen [was] overpowering," she also remembered that stress gradually stifled her spirit. Once when Adela's father and London vanished into the hills for five days, returning stone drunk, she sensed Charmian's frantic desperation:

Peering out hopefully into the dark, Charmian was sharp and bitter. Nothing was ever said between us about drink. A man's

family did not discuss this, nor admit it. Now I knew she *hated*
Glen Ellen. Her longing was to be back on the *Snark,* breathing
the high seas again, seeing strange places, new horizons. I saw
that she was about as domestic as a mountain lioness, of which
she kept reminding me more and more. Of course if her baby
had lived—now as she moved restlessly, never still, I began to
avoid her. This was not the kind of talk I could endure just then.
She had *quit.* It scared me so I felt my insides shake. By nature,
Charmian London wasn't a quitter. Even people who didn't like
her admitted she had more guts than any other female they'd
ever known.[41]

Martin Johnson called Charmian "a brick," someone who
"bears up wonderfully, and is everywhere at once."[42]

Upton Sinclair recalled London's grossness during these last
few years of hopeless despair.

Jack's manners had become those of a nerve-wracked man. He
would take over the conversation and pound the table. If you
disagreed with him he would quarrel. His lively wit had dulled;
his humor was crude horseplay, or crazily complex practical
jokes.

He had purchased some trick drinking glasses, which had tiny
holes around the rim; when a guest tilted the glass to drink, the
liquid would run down his neck. His swimming pool was constructed with a secret passage under the water. Jack would dive
in and swim through that passage and come up in another place,
leaving his guests terrified, sure that he had drowned. A book
bearing the title *A Loud Noise* was left around; when the cover
was opened, a firecracker inside exploded. Rope arrangements
permitted guests' beds to be rocked from another room; hapless
visitors, thus shaken from their beds in the dark of the night,
would dash out of their rooms, shouting "Earthquake! Earthquake!" And Jack would laugh: this was humor, this was fun,
this was wit.

Even after their long, intimate years of friendship, George
Sterling could no longer endure the drunken rituals at the ranch.
His visits to London became ever less frequent.[43]

London's "monumental extravagances and spendthrift madness," as Adela Rogers St. Johns puts it, gradually alienated
friends. "The minute we got out of the wagon that had brought
us up the narrow dusty road, London always had things to show
us. My father would look over the growing acres, the vast barns

and silos, the farm equipment, the houses under construction, and say, 'I approve, this is a fine experiment, but it is feudal. Are you still a member of the Socialist party and what do they say to all this?' Jack London said he was and they too approved, but of course he resigned from the party eventually. My father said the man behind the big stack of blue chips seldom remained a socialist.''[44]

William W. Ellsworth, another friend, also called it quits over London's excesses. "As London grew older and made money from his writings, his wants increased. His place at Glen Ellen was a great money-absorber, and his publishers were asked with growing frequency to make advances from future royalties for one purpose and another. A hundred thousand eucalyptus trees were set out, with a pay-roll of $2,000 a month while the work was going on. They all died. A roof of Spanish tile for his new house cost $3,500, and must be paid for (the house was burned later). A fine stud horse was needed for the farm, price $2,500. Gradually we drew apart; the stud horse was the end.''[45]

This was the same Jack London who had once written in "The Terrible and Tragic in Fiction" that "the pity of it is that the writer-folk are writing for bread first and glory after; and that their standard of living goes up as fast as their capacity for winning bread increases,—so that they never get around to glory,—the ephemeral flourishes, and the great stories remain unwritten.''[46]

London, who wanted seven Saxon sons, ignored Joan and Bess for years, even refusing to finance their college educations, but tried to reconcile differences before his death. "His two daughters were being raised by their mother in Oakland," wrote Joan, who didn't once refer to London as "father" in her severe biography published in 1939. "When they were small he had not missed them especially, and his brief but frequent visits to them had sufficed. . . . When a few years later he asked that Joan and little Bess come to live with him on the ranch for a time so that all might get acquainted with each other, the girls, pawns in a situation neither understood, were unwilling to leave Bess.''[47]

Adela Rogers St. Johns commented on London's tortured conscience—he had offered to build a house for Bessie and the girls at Glen Ellen. When Adela asked him about Charmian, London replied: "Oh—they won't need to see much of each other. . . . It seems to me this would benefit everybody." Such a remark, of course, startled Adela, who thought it was "plain lunacy." When Adela asked, "What does Joan say about it?", " 'She won't answer my letters,' he said in sudden wildness. 'She hasn't answered any of them. Why doesn't she let me talk to her.' His voice held heavy heartbreak and confusion. Disaster signals were on his brow and in the set of his lips.

'I ask her to give me a chance to make her know me. Is that too much?' he cried."

Adela asked London to put himself in the girls' shoes. What would he do under similar circumstances? He thought for awhile, then questioned: "How can a child presume to judge her father? . . . How can a child know what a man feels? What he needs, the measures of his temptations, the obligations to his work—he must venture into the unknown because he is afraid of it, he lives another dimension, he fights wars and sails the seven seas, dares death—"

London, it is apparent, still viewed himself in romantic terms, someone charting the unknown, who sailed turbulent seas, a cross between Daniel Boone and Sinbad the Sailor. He hadn't changed. That night Adela's father told him: " 'A man finds a rut that interests him, it can still be a rut. A rover, a seeker, an adventurer of the body or the spirit, for him it's the same as a grave, only the man is buried alive. Line it with plush, put gold handles on, for the rebel, the revolutionist, it's a coffin!' "

But London wasn't really listening. He shouted back, " 'I am leading a revolution right here!' "[48]

Joan and Bess, however, remembered all the slights, all the insults their mother swallowed, all the money London spent while criticizing Joan for charging schoolbooks. He even wrote her that he didn't want to see the girls or their mother again, that he wouldn't recognize them on the street. Because of his sour experience at Berkeley, London considered college useless for girls. In *The Little Lady of the Big House,* written about this time, he declared that most girls married after graduation and farmed babies. He also felt that education wasn't entirely useful for boys, telling Sophie Treadwell: "It's your education that's to blame for your lack of brass tacks, not you. What a training we give children! If I had a son I would not send him to school until he was ready for the last year in grammar school, and then only that he could get used to our form of democracy. No, I wouldn't give him a free choice of what he wanted to learn any more than I'd give a colt a free choice; or a puppy. I'd train him—freedom—but within limits. No, he would not go to a university; not unless he could run faster than I.''[49]

London's true feelings about the girls surfaced in his will. They received twenty-five dollars a month and insurance—no royalties. He left Bessie five dollars and use of the Oakland house. Charmian, who resented both girls, held the purse strings, which meant they'd have to ask for additional help. Flora got forty-five dollars a month and housing. Even Mammy Jenny received fifteen dollars a month.[50] Everyone benefited—except the girls and Bessie, who contested the will. "The will," said Mrs. London, "was made, I believe, while Jack was in a passion of anger that soon passed off. He was very quick tempered and just as quick to forgive. The will was drawn five years before his death and at a time he learned that he could not have the custody of the children. However, that does not mean that he did not visit them often. I feel certain that if he knew the old will existed and felt his end was so near, he would have provided more generously for his children in a new will.''[51] Due to Bessie's efforts, the court awarded Joan and Bess more money.

Although London treated Joan and Bess badly, avoided Flora during his last years, and abused Bessie, he remained loyal to Eliza, leaving her twenty-five hundred dollars in cash and thirty-five dollars a month in his will. She had staked him in the Klondike, bought his bicycle, paid for false teeth, and gave him loose change when he needed it. He had also defended her during the sensational November 1915 divorce trial that made newspaper headlines. Eliza's husband, James H. Shepard, a former patent attorney, had practiced in Washington and San Francisco. She was "very much younger than her husband. She married him when she was seventeen and he was 'forty-three past.' '' Although they produced a son, Washington Irving Shepard, later executor of the Jack London Estate, and father of

I. Milo Shepard, the present executor of the I. Milo Shepard Estate, the marriage failed. Shepard sued for "cruelty and desertion," while Eliza countersued for "cruelty and for other grounds."[52]

Their marriage, it seems, had failed long before the divorce trial. In May 1913, Shepard caused London's arrest, charging him with "assault and battery" because he and another fellow "attempted to put a stop to a family row in [Shepard's home] and a fight was the result."[53] When Shepard married Eliza, it left London alone, a child without friends. "I was a very poor boy then," said the now famous author, "did not have a cent to my name even to pay for a street-car ride. Then I would meet my sister and she would ask me why I was walking and when I told her I had no money she would open her wallet and give me some money. If she had a dollar or a half-dollar she would divide with me.

"Then, I was born with a cigarette in my mouth, and at times when I did not even have the price of a sack of 'Bull Durham' Mrs. Shepard's monetary gifts assisted in replenishing my smoking supplies. At the time I was struggling along as a poor young fellow endeavoring to do some writing. I made up my mind that if ever I got an opportunity to pay her back I would do so a thousand fold. And I have done so ever since and shall continue to do so. That's why I have given her money, and shall continue to do so."[54]

At one point in the trial, when Shepard accused Eliza of immoral behavior, she jumped up, screaming, "It's a lie." Shepard echoed: "It's an infernal lie. That woman is a perjurer! And I won't hear her lie like that!"[55] The judge removed Shepard from the courtroom. Eliza then testified that he had threatened her with a revolver. It discharged without harming anyone. London, present at the time, had told Shepard to leave the ranch. Jack Byrnes, the cause of Shepard's gun-slinging attack, was a relative whose guest appearance worsened already explosive relations. After weighing the evidence, Judge Mahon granted Shepard a divorce, although he charged:

If he really believed her immoral he would not have ["begged" Eliza to return home]. I do not believe that he believes it now or ever did believe it. I do not think that he has any faith in the allegations he has made against her in this trial.

There is nothing to support his contentions of immorality, nor his charge of cruelty. There is just one point. In view of the circumstances of the trouble on May 3rd the court can arrive at only one decision. The plaintiff knew on that day that Robert [Jack] Byrne was coming to the house. He entered an objection and told his wife not to bring the man there. At the instance of Mr. and Mrs. London she nevertheless invited him to dinner and when they arrived at the Shepard home the plaintiff had a right to object to Byrne's entering the house.

I do not believe that he intended to shoot Byrne or his wife with the pistol, but he did draw the gun. For this gun display he was ordered from the London ranch by Jack London. He went to Oakland and there wrote repeatedly to his wife asking her to come to him. He was willing to forget and forgive, but she would not heed it. This I hold constitutes desertion on the part of the wife. The divorce is therefore granted to the plaintiff and the divorce prayed for by the cross complaint is denied. The property rights are found to lie entirely with the wife. It is not community property and cannot be regarded as such.[56]

This instance of contention sounds similar to an earlier clash in 1875—one between an itinerant astrologer called William H. Chaney and his wife, Flora. A pattern seemed to shadow this family. Another echo was the divorce of London's sister, Ida, reported on December 20, 1905, in the *San Francisco Chronicle*. "They were married in 1888, when the woman was but 17 years of age and the groom [F. H. Miller] 43 years old. Miller deserted his wife absolutely three years ago, but for a long time had not contributed regularly to her support."[57]

Chapter 16

From Vera Cruz to Tinsel-Town

REVOLUTION. MEXICO, 1914. Berserk land of murder and revolt. The Mexican revolution exploded in 1911 when General Francisco I. Madero overthrew Diaz, then was murdered by Victoriano Huerta, a semiliterate Indian with a lust for power. When Huerta's regime, even with support from British oil profiteers, failed to stabilize the country, counterrevolutionaries led by Emiliano Zapata, Carenza, and Pancho Villa drenched the soil with more bloodshed, while Mexican peons played guinea pigs. "In Mexico there was no revolution," reported Richard Harding Davis. "What existed was anarchy. It was a falling out among cattle-thieves. Between Huerta and Villa there was the choice between Lefty Louie and Gyp the Blood. And as to which one was successful in killing the other, so long as he was quick about it, no one cared."[1]

President Wilson, first refusing to recognize Huerta, enforced a policy of "watchful waiting" until Huerta's officers arrested American sailors. He then demanded an apology, including a twenty-one-gun salute—which Huerta ignored. The president sent a force to Mexico under Major General Frederick Funston that took Vera Cruz on April 21, 1914, "killing or wounding 321 Mexicans and suffering 90 casualities of their own."[2] Americans cried: "On to Mexico City!" Enforce the country's honor. Send more troops. Magazines, of course, rushed to the bargaining tables, and correspondents grabbed train schedules for Mexico—including Jack London. Although London had

275

been negotiating with Hearst for several months, he contracted with *Collier's* for eleven hundred dollars a week.

Before embarking for Vera Cruz, London finished *The Star Rover,* one of his last published novels. (He called the first English edition *The Jacket.*) Although admitting its pseudo-scientific and philosophic content, London aimed the work at Christian Scientists, penal reformers, and readers of rousing romances with transcendent values. He based the story on conversations with Ed Morrell, a former San Quentin prisoner. (One character, Jack Oppenheimer, had actually been hanged at Folsom Prison.)

Darrell Standing, *The Star Rover*'s protagonist and a prison inmate, a former professor of agronomics at the University of California's college of agriculture, had killed another academic. Accused of smuggling dynamite from prison, he is laced in a straight jacket by a sadistic warden. Standing survives these ordeals by becoming a star rover, transporting himself back in time through astral projection, reliving race memories. He becomes Jess Fancher, a wagon master's son, who fights Indians provoked by Mormons. Then he's Adam Strang, an Englishman who becomes a mighty Easterner, and finally an ancient Roman centurion during the time of Christ's crucifixion, among other former beings.

The Nation observed: "The truth is, this writer's imagination, with all its affectation of breadth, is singularly narrow and vulgar. . . . Here is an excellent opportunity to paint the horrors of prison life. . . . Here is plenty of chance for the positive propaganda of the gospel of strength. All well enough as a not too fresh flight of fancy—if it were not so hopelessly vulgarized in the handling, did not so patently call for some such title as 'The Immortality of a Bounder.' "[3]

The Bookman added: "The scope of the book is so big, there is such a bewildering mass of material gathered between its covers that it takes true art to leave several striking pictures in the reader's mind as he thinks it over later, and the myriad-figured canvas shrinks to its true proportion. . . . And yet in spite of its differing treatment the true theme of this book shóws that Jack London's evolution is more an outer evolution than an inner one. It is still in his mind the blood superman who is supreme, who is a master of men."[4]

Correspondents debated a new London—the only reporter who brought a wife and valet to Mexico. Bad feelings already existed over "The Good Soldier," an article London supposedly wrote in the *International Socialist Review* about the military. He called American soldiers nonthinking murderers, puppets who obeyed orders.[5] Protests resulted. Some groups urged a congressional investigation. Did London say such things? It seems likely in view of earlier barbs: he had attacked the army to H. R. Lytle during Kelly's forced march, made snide comments about the Japanese soldier in Russo-Japanese war dispatches, and called soldiers "dogs" to Ted Applegarth. Correspondent Edwin Emerson, who read London's reprinted remarks about American soldiers in the *Army and Navy Journal*, said he "believed it to be an expression of Mr. London's true sentiments, for I have repeatedly heard him talk in this very strain."[6]

Philip S. Foner said in *Jack London: American Rebel*: "Whether or not Jack London wrote 'The Good Soldier' will never be known since other articles were published in his name which he did not write. Yet it is difficult to believe that the *International Socialist Review* would have published the article under his name unless they had responsible assurance that it expressed London's sentiments; nor did he protest the publication when it appeared. Again, parts of the article are reminiscent of his descriptions of the guards at the coronation of King Edward in *The People of the Abyss*: 'Myriads of men, splendid men, the pick of the people, whose sole function in life is to blindly obey, and blindly to kill and destroy and stamp out life.' "[7]

Joan London supported Foner, remarking that "from April 1914 until his death he denied it emphatically, yet the rumor persisted. It is significant, moreover, that he did not ask the

International Socialist Review to publish a denial of his authorship. . . . One finds it difficult to believe that a publication such as the *International Socialist Review* would have published the article without assurance from reliable sources that the sentiments it contained were Jack London's. In any case, whether the guess is correct or not, Jack did not trouble to deny his authorship until he discovered that General Funston was withholding his war correspondent's credential because he believed that Jack had written 'The Good Soldier.' "[8]

When General Funston refused London correspondent papers, Richard Harding Davis, London's rescuer in Manchuria ten years before, again intervened. Mrs. Davis later recalled that London "always cherished a high regard"[9] for her husband because of these two incidents.

London endorsed United States intervention in Mexico, calling the peons stupid inferiors, predicting they would praise American conquerors. Our soldiers needed action somewhere. Why not Mexico? When had such order reigned? Weren't the streets clean? Wasn't life safer? He also called Huerta a master among men, but dubbed his followers dummies.[10] (How ironic that London later became a popular American author in Mexico.)[11] Drewey Wayne Gunn concludes in *American and British Writers in Mexico*: "Nowhere does London show any real understanding of the bewilderment that a new system of law had thrust upon the *veracruzanos* or a realization that another system of justice could exist. [James A. Michener made similar remarks about London's insensitivity to Hawaiians.] He simply noticed that the Americans were blond and that the judge was impartially exact. Nothing more than a series of vignettes, 'Law-Givers' was still the only Mexican piece in which he revealed his skill as a writer of fiction."[12]

John Reed, who spent four months in Mexico, opposed American chauvinism in Mexico:

> It is an Anglo-Saxon trait to consider all other races as inferior. A great many of us honestly believe that we will benefit the Mexicans by forcing our institutions upon them. We know nothing about the Latin temperament, and care less. We do not realize that the Latin ideal of liberty is broader than our own. We want to devitalize the Mexican race and turn them into

brown, docile American business men and laborers, as we have the Cubans, as we are turning the Filipinos. . . . And if we can ever withdraw from that distracted country, we will leave things worse than they were before—an exploiting class firmly entrenched in the places of power, the foreign interests stronger, because we supported them, the great estates securely re-established, and the peons taught that wage slavery and not individual freedom is the desirable thing in life.[13]

Lincoln Steffens also sympathized with the Mexicans. "I'd do almost anything for Mexico."[14] He then influenced President Wilson towards the Carranza position, believing that offered the most for Mexico's future. The American government eventually recognized Carranza as Mexico's president. Both Zapata and Villa were later slain.

London's last article for *Collier's,* "Our Adventures in Tampico," showed more interest in warehouses and paraffin plants of the American refineries than Mexican independence.[15] (A character in *Hearts of Three* is a Mexican oil tycoon, and Dick Forrest in *The Little Lady of the Big House* invests in Mexican mining.) Oliver Madox Hueffer recalled London as "a quaint figure in a Palm Beach suit, ducks and a Panama hat. . . . Afterwards he returned and buried himself in the oil-swamps beyond the town in order to get first-hand information of local conditions."[16] London sometimes mixed with Frederick Palmer, Jimmy Hare, and Robert Dunn, completing the weekly *Collier's* assignments to relieve boredom, drank heavily, and played crap, once cleaning out the correspondents, besides several Spanish ambassadors.

I asked Jack London about fiction material, and his hands went up [recalled Dunn]. "Too much. An idea every day." But none was ever written, as far as I know, and he looked peaked, yellow.

"Drink, Bob?" with his wistful mid-morning look. I toasted the White Horse at Fusan, but Jack's mind wasn't on Korea. "In ten seconds I'll feel 'em crawling. The *worms,* Dunn."

"Is that in *John Barleycorn?*" I hadn't read his *Satevepost* temperance tract.

"The white worm, tunneling through our brains!"

"Not mine," I protested. "Jesus, liquor never takes me that way."

We drank on, Jack insisting that booze made his white worms
crawl through any brain, I saying that it hit everyone different,
like love or war, mountains or the sea. We both got pretty tight—
my last clear recollection of Jack. Soon amoebic dysentery nearly
finished him. Once I went up to the room where Jack lay under
a white sheet, against a ratty lattice, like the corpse he would
be in two years or so. But Charmian shooed me out before any
word came from the bed. I wish drink had killed him, instead
of morphine; I hate to accept his suicide. But something about
Jack London was transitory. He was more egoist than either
individualist or socialist. Women counted with him both too
much and not enough. His lack of early schooling was an advantage offset by easy enthusiasms against which he had no
reserves of resistance. He oddly paralleled another of my best
companions, Jack Reed—each a revolutionary to socialists, a
romantic to me. Beginning with humor, both had most of the
weaknesses tagged bourgeois, a word I never heard either use.[17]

Although London praised modern American medicine in
"Stalking the Pestilence,"[18] saying few suffered from amoebic
dysentery in Vera Cruz, he caught it, probably due to weak
resistance, coupled with the mud, malaria, and mosquitoes.
Nakata, faithful since Russo-Japanese War days, nursed him,
while several doctors remained through the crisis, but further
complications with pleurisy nearly killed London, as Robert
Dunn says. Along with Nakata and Charmian, he finally returned to Glen Ellen, his health ravaged.

The impeccable Richard Harding Davis, who brought his own
bathtub and brown bread to Mexico, emerged as America's
hero of the conflict. He once tried to interview cutthroat Huerta,
leading a journalist to say: "That man will go anywhere any
one else will go. He will not quit on the job just because it is
dangerous."[19] Thrown in jail, unable to secure a press report,
Davis nearly faced a firing squad. International figures forced
his release. "Everything they did to us I had written and copy-
righted," he joked. "The serial, dramatic, and 'movie' rights
were all in my name. But, unlike the novelist in Baldpate, I
found acting it much more difficult than writing it."[20] (Davis
performed other brave acts during his long correspondent days.
At the battles of San Juan Hill and El Caney, he not only aided
wounded soldiers under fire, but stayed in rifle pits, agonized

with sciatica, while Jimmy Hare and Stephen Crane begged him to leave.)

London's articles in *Collier's* damaged his reputation as a champion of the underdog, his standing among socialists—if any existed at this time—and his personal integrity. Magazines editorialized. "The extremely readable letters from Mexico in *Collier's* are not written by 'yours for the revolution, Jack London,' but by plain 'Jack London,' " charged *The Nation*. "The flaming challenge of the first signature would not only be inappropriate in a magazine of general circulation, but would be quite out of tune with the context which savors strongly of the individualistic, capitalistic, fiercely competitive spirit of the world that knew not the gospel of Karl Marx."[21] This led George Sterling to write London, "You came down off an awfully high pedestal in John Kenneth Turner's heart in suggesting or approving intervention in Mexico. He thinks you're worse than Whitaker! Gawd! I'm lonesome!"[22]

Joan London called her father's conduct

> a tragic sellout, for he had been subsidized, bought body and soul, by the kind of life he had thought he wanted, and it was destroying him. . . . The several articles he wrote for *Collier's* during his stay in Mexico reveal such a complete *volte face* in his attitude toward the Mexican revolution and America's role in it that one is almost tempted to believe that they were written under his name by an entirely different person. For the second time Jack's reactions to the inhabitants of a foreign country were those of a provincial, middle-class American. All that he had learned from Marx and Engels, his many times reiterated belief in the international revolutionary movement, the solidarity he had expressed so often with the struggle of workers against their oppressors, succumbed to the race prejudice and glorification of the Anglo-Saxon . . . and to the "big-brother" propaganda with which American imperialism masked its self-interest.[23]

The Mexican revolution badly discredited London—impairing both his career and health. Even the socialist party condemned his stand against the peons and his praise of American profiteers. "My boyhood's Socialist hero, Jack London, had died in 1916, no hero any longer in my eyes," wrote Floyd Dell. "A few years earlier, sent to Mexico as a correspondent, he came back singing the tunes that had been taught him by the American oil-men who were engaged in looting Mexico; he preached Nordic supremacy, and the manifest destiny of the American exploiters. He had, apparently, lost faith in the revolution in which he had once believed. His death, as a tired cynic, to whom life no longer was worth living—according to the accounts of his friends,—was a miserable anti-climax."[24]

When World War I roared in Europe, London cursed the barbarian Huns, who used the brute force he preached in books and tracts—survival of the fittest, the strongest of the strong, the futility of human ethics. He declared in *The Overland Monthly* that several million deaths would cleanse mankind of evil, adding this number occurred in peacetime among the world's population.[25]

London's war views lacked logic and vision. He predicted in "The Impossibility of War" (*The Overland Monthly*, March 1900) that

> no longer is it possible to fight men in masses, nor can battles be opened up at close range; and if an attack be insisted upon, the increase in casualties will be frightful. During the time a body of men are attacking a modern battery across a distance of a mile and a half it is estimated that that single battery would fire fourteen hundred and fifty rounds of shell, scattering 275,000 fragments of death among the soldiers of the assaulting party. . . . From the technical standpoint, the improvement in the mechanism of war has made war impossible. Economics, and not force of arms, will decide; not battles, but famine. And behind all, ready and anxious to say the last word, looms the ominous figure of Revolution.[26]

London's tenure in Manchuria, apparently, failed to alter this view. He restated in "The Human Drift" (*The Forum*, January 1911) that economics would prevent future wars. Even stranger, he contradicted a former central tenet, the horrible casualties inflicted by modern weapons, saying more danger confronted workers than soldiers, that shells from an entire fleet killed only one mule.[27] Other soothsayings touched Japan and China. London remarked in "The Unparalleled Invasion" (*McClure's Magazine*, July 1910) that in the early twenties, Japan would pursue art and beauty. China? Starvation and biological warfare would destroy her in 1976.[28]

Collier's offered London an assignment on the Western Front during World War I. He refused. Charmian rationalized after his death—too many commitments prevented it. Besides. Her husband believed failure faced correspondents on all fronts.[29]

Perhaps London's illogical war views, coupled with support of American robber barons in Mexico, helped dilute his popularity among mass readers. (Serious critics avoided him for years.) But he kept stringing stories together in a limp style, repeating words and phrases, overstating issues, shaping shapeless characters—all to keep alive the Glen Ellen dream. In February 1913, before going to Mexico, Brett wrote that Macmillan had "a shocking overstock of 'Adventure,' "[30] a South Seas potboiler. So London took two hundred copies. Macmillan remaindered the rest. They also remaindered *Before Adam* and *The Road*.

This incident is meaningful. Even London's instant novels failed to hold escapist readers. Former fans recalled his Klondike stories. Yet the Yukon gold rush, now a historic event, almost a generation removed from the World War I era, lacked relevancy to American culture. People chatted about Woodrow Wilson, about the Panama Canal, about D. W. Griffith's *The Birth of a Nation*, about Jess Willard's victory over Jack Johnson, about the *Lusitania* disaster. A thousand and one topics—except the white wilderness.

Unable to face facts, London wrote and asked George Brett: Why didn't his books become best sellers? Were other authors better craftsmen? (John Tebbel says London offered *The Saturday Evening Post* free copy to restore his sagging sales.)[31] Had the public lost interest in a former institution? They bought Rex Beach's books. This letter's tone irritated Brett. His January 7, 1915, reply forecasts the collapse of America's golden short-story era, an era when authors like London and Richard Harding Davis made hundreds for single magazine submissions.

I am a little inclined to resent your comments on our exploitation
of your new books, because I believe that your complaint, if it
is a complaint, is made without taking into account the very real
interest and the very considerable exploitation that we do give
to all your books as far as it is possible to do so.

I think that you are also failing to take into account the very
different conditions that obtain today in the trade in relation to
the publication of volumes of short stories and the conditions
that *did* obtain in regard to the publication of such volumes.
Very recently there has been added to the list of magazines
offered to the public dozens, if not hundreds, of new aspirants,
and many of these magazines offer in a single number, for ten
or fifteen cents, as many short stories as are to be found in a
bound volume selling at $1.25 or thereabouts. [*Collier's* sold for
five cents in 1914.] Can we blame the public under these circumstances for no longer buying volumes of short stories in any
considerable number? And does it seem likely that, under these
circumstances, volumes of short stories can be reissued in the
high priced editions any longer, when once the first sale is over,
or nearly so?[32]

Brett's faith in London amazes. For years he continued to
publish shavings from London's book mill, even after he
switched to Century. Brett was a man of infinite patience. He
cared about Macmillan writers and took time personally to read
reviews of the company's many works. He was also a gentleman
publisher. "It is with pleasure," said then-noted novelist Winston Churchill, "that I undertake . . . an appreciation of my
friend and publisher, George P. Brett, the president of The
Macmillan Company. I would repeat the words—friend and
publisher. Mr. Brett has an undoubted genius for publishing,
but he possesses likewise the higher genius for friendship."[33]

One other reason may exist for Brett's loyalty: *The Call of
the Wild*. The American branch of Macmillan Company wasn't
formed until 1896, less than a decade before London's bestseller. Brett became president. The unexpected success of *The
Call of the Wild* strengthened his voice in the book world. It
also strengthened Macmillan's bankroll. Perhaps Brett never
forgot. He was like that. Perhaps he carried London for years
on the basis of past products.

London's reaction to tightening times before World War I? He and Charmian fled, spending more money instead of less, dumping heavier loads of responsibility on Eliza's lap. They sailed for months on the thirty-foot yawl *Roamer* with valet Nakata and cook Yamamoto. They took a four-horse buggy through northern California in 1911. "We have been on the road for several months and to date have covered 900 miles,"[34] he told the *San Francisco Chronicle*. Then they spent five months traveling around Cape Horn on a windjammer in 1912, and basked in the sunlight of Waikiki during the winter of 1915 with four servants and a chauffeur. Again they vacationed in Hawaii between December 1915 and July 1916. "The writer expressed the intention of spending a great portion of his time from now on in the Hawaiian Islands and told of leasing a bungalow in Honolulu," reported the *Santa Rosa Press Democrat* on August 2, 1916. " 'While in the islands,' said London, 'I have spent a great portion of my time in writing stories dealing with the primitive native life, and have visited many of the remote island villages, where the natives still live as in the time of Captain Cook.' " What about Glen Ellen? "London stated that it is still a luxury and that, although he expects to hold it, it will be some time before it becomes a paying proposition."[35] Rumors even spread that he planned to buy a Honolulu hotel.[36]

George Sterling wrote London on December 27, 1914: "Why don't you cruise twelve months instead of six? Then you won't *ever* have to see your 'friends,' " and again the following February 5: "I suppose you're having a great time. I can see the day coming when you and Charmian get a submarine, and escape your friends entirely."[37]

During these last wanderings, London secured some solace in the work of Carl G. Jung, much as he had secured momentary relief from Marx, Spencer, and Nietzsche years before. Richard O'Connor says he was "like a man sliding down the face of a cliff and grabbing at rocks and bushes to stay his fall."[38] Had the myth Jack London palmed on the public for years finally grasped him in a psychic crisis? How fast was his health failing? What about booze and his red-blooded beast craze? What torments hounded London as fate finally sacked his career, his reputation, his lavish income? Perhaps he gained a sense of self-knowledge—which often leaves destruction in its wake.

After reading *Psychology of the Unconscious,* London told Charmian he'd uncovered a new dimension, both terrible and wonderful, something that changed his views.[39] He painstakingly studied Beatrice M. Hinkle's introduction to *Psychology of the Unconscious,* underlining passages such as: "He [Jung] saw in the term libido a concept of unknown nature, comparable to Bergson's élan vital, a hypothetical energy of life, which occupies itself not only in sexuality but in various physiological and psychological manifestations such as growth, development, hunger, and all the human activities and interests. This cosmic energy or urge manifested in the human being he calls libido and compares it with the energy of physics."[40]

Many London Jungian probes appear in *On the Makaloa Mat,* written during this last siege of his long sickness. "The Water Baby," which shows interest in the intrauterine theory—a return to the mother's womb—best expresses such ideas. The leading character, John Lakana, was London's Hawaiian name. The sea-as-a-mother metaphor, with its cradling connotations, wasn't new to London's work. Several critics mentioned Humphrey Van Weyden's water rebirth in *The Sea Wolf.* Martin Eden commits suicide by crawling out a porthole, possibly a symbolic vagina, slipping into the mysterious deep. Charmian also claimed water calmed London's frazzled nerves, offering him a sense of freedom from worldly woes. H. L. Mencken, however, wrote Sterling in 1918: "London's widow I don't know, though I have talked to her by telephone. Her book on their Hawaiian affairs was a silly thing—written like a high-school girl's essay on the unconscious. He and she appear to have carried on love-making in moving-picture terms."[41]

The emphasis on Jung may have obscured other facets of London's Hawaiian stories, namely, his new focus on elitist life-styles, and a disenchantment with gutsy young guys. Characters in *On the Makaloa Mat* belong to the middle and upper classes; most of them are mature and tempered with bittersweet wisdom. (London even started calling himself an old timer, although he hadn't reached forty.) James I. McClintock catches these changing moods: "They dramatize the pathos of aging and disillusioned, even cynical men awaiting death. While violence and death, the triumph of the demoniac, had somehow surprised the earlier protagonists, these last—Jack Lakana, Prince Akuli, and Hardman Pool—are without the capacity for amazement. Carl Jung's system as Jack London found it in *Psychology of the Unconscious,* like the other systems he had found before, had failed . . . to give him a sure faith.''[42]

"On the Makaloa Mat" deals with two elderly sisters, "The Tears of Ah Kim" with a prosperous middle-aged Chinese merchant, "The Bones of Kahekili" with a patriarch–Hawaiian rancher, his life shattered by aging and John Barleycorn. "The Kanaka Surf" sketches a well-muscled couple of the smart set, both super surfers.

"The Kanaka Surf" may also express London's fear of losing Charmian to someone else; he uses the word *charm* to describe the body of Ida, beautiful wife of Lee Barton. A wealthy fellow Lee's age falls for Ida, who doesn't repel his advances. Lee, consumed with jealousy, intentionally intensifies foot cramps during one of the couple's swims in the Kanaka surf, trying to test Ida's devotion, even half-drowning her until he realizes, beyond question, that she loves him. Andrew Sinclair says this story "contains so much autobiographical detail, including the attack of cramp and some of the notes for 'Her Body,' that its description of the surrogate Charmian's flirtation with a wealthy planter can be taken at face value, even if the gossip that reached George Sterling was Jack's self-defensive boast of an affair with a nameless woman. The plot of 'The Kanaka Surf' is confirmed in Charmian's proposed autobiography *Charmette,* which deals with the flirtation as an act of policy.''[43]

George Sterling wrote Margaret Smith Cobb in 1923:

> Jack killed himself because he was in love with two women in two different ways, and couldn't face the pain he'd give one by choosing the other. Of course one was his wife; the other—I can't find out who she was, but Charmian knows, and will have

to tell me some day, when I force her to drop the pretense that he died of uremic poisoning. He died of twelve grains of morphine.

The other one was, I'm almost certain, a white woman living in Honolulu, who has since died of the flu.

When . . . I brought his ashes to the ranch for burial, [a friend] told me that Jack had told him that 'The Little Lady of the Big House' was his (Jack's) own history, but that instead of a woman having to kill herself because she was in love with two men, it was a man who'd have to do so because he was in love with two women. If [I had only known] that at the time Jack said it, I could possibly have averted the tragedy.[44]

Did Jung really influence the form and content of Jack London's work after *On the Makaloa Mat*? Two action-packed dog novels followed with the old Anglo-Saxon racism, the old superheroics, the old frantic flight from reality. In *Hearts of Three* Jung's sun-hero symbolism became a villain Sun Priest, who tries to sacrifice two heroes and a heroine on ancient altars, nearly making them swallow melted gold. As Granville Hicks remarks, "He was curiously juvenile and surprisingly sentimental. He read wisely, but his reading only served to re-enforce his prejudices."[45] Jung's wilderness call also surfaces in "Like Argus of the Ancient Times," a late Klondike tale posthumously published in a 1917 issue of *Hearst's Magazine*. Says James I. McClintock: " 'Like Argus of the Ancient Times' owes little thematically to Carl Jung since, without his aid, London had written many stories in which a hero feels the call of adventure, encounters the hardships of the trail, confronts death and achieves some sense of dignity."[46]

This also regards dreams. Long before reading Jung, London wrote of the "young mining engineer" in "An Odyssey of the North" that "when he did sleep, his brain worked on, and for the nonce he, too wandered through the white unknown, struggling with the dogs on endless trails, and saw men live, and toil, and die like men."[47] The narrator in "The Man with the Gash" says: "Often he dreamed that such was the case, and awoke in the grip of nightmares. A select number of these robbers haunted him through his dreams, and he came to know them quite well, especially the bronzed leader with the gash on his right cheek."[48] Dozens of London characters, both men and dogs, dream dreams, like hundreds of figures in stories by other authors. Even Buck "growled and barked and wrestled with bad dreams."[49] Wolf Larsen mutters, "I often doubt. I often doubt the worthwhileness of reason. Dreams must be more substantial and satisfying." Humphrey Van Weyden adds about the Ghost: "This was the world, the universe itself, its bounds so near one felt impelled to reach out both arms and push them back. It was impossible that the rest could be beyond these walls of gray. The rest was a dream, no more than the memory of a dream."[50] *Before Adam* involves a search for race memories through dreams.

Jungian ideas in London's work shouldn't be taken seriously. He used conceptualists like Jung as pulp-binders, rather than catalysts for character studies as did Stephen Crane, Frank Norris, and Theodore Dreiser. "London, we must remember, was bred on the same basic books that nourished Dreiser— Nietzsche, Darwin, Spencer, Huxley et al.—but the difference between what he and Dreiser did with those ideas, like the difference between his adventuring and that of Crane, is crucially important," write Cleanth Brooks, R. W. B. Lewis, and Robert Penn Warren. "The ideas became, for Dreiser, the fuel for a personal drama. In London they became the fuel for a projected melodrama."[51]

Suppose Jack London had lived through the twenties? His Yukon and South Sea stories might have found a profitable niche in Hollywood—this time through a dream world carried in tin cans instead of between dust jackets. (Woodbridge, London and Tweney list six pages of films based on London's work in *Jack London: A Bibliography*.)[52] *Hearts of Three* (1920), for which Hearst's *Cosmopolitan* paid London $25,000 for serial rights, became a film script written by London, in collaboration with Charles Goddard, producer of "The Perils of Pauline."

What about playwriting? London found stage dialogue and movement difficult. Minnie Maddern Fiske, Bessie's cousin, then America's first lady of the theatre, turned down *The Scorn of Women,* adapted from his short story. "She found it remarkable that anyone could believe that he could justify everything he had ever done," writes biographer Archie Binns. "She laughed at him for his defensive attitude where no one had attacked him. She laughed a little also over his ideal of twentieth-century womanhood—a man's mate who bore his children and endured with him and shared in his dreams and labors—because he had left such a woman for a nineteenth-century coquette who gave him neither help nor children. But she did not laugh much, because she saw it as his tragedy." (London, incidentally, told Brett *The Scorn of Women* charmed Mrs. Fiske.)

Yet London offered Mrs. Fiske another play the next year that "seemed more the result of awkwardness than of design." She returned it with comments. London, always resentful of criticism, replied that his play wasn't unintelligible to certain people, that she didn't understand its intentions, then defended his past behavior as expressions of highest ideals. Mrs. Fiske pencilled on the letter: "Stuff!—Stuffing!"[53]

London once approached Blanche Bates about his melodramas, after attending her road show production of *The Darling of the Gods,* in Oakland. "Mr. London occupied a front seat in the orchestra during the three nights of Miss Bates' engagement," said the *Oakland Tribune.* "He created a great deal of attention at the theater by reason of his peculiar dress for which he has become noted. He is always seen in public places such as the theater, club and social function wearing a negligee shirt and open vest."[54] But Blanche Bates didn't star in *The Scorn of Women* on Broadway, nor anyone else. Macmillan published it in 1906.

Olga Nethersoll expressed interest in *Theft,* another melodrama, but she later turned down this political play that preached love, leaving the faithful Brett and Macmillan to publish it in 1910, again without a staging. (Publishers rarely print plays before they reach Broadway.) Leading character Anthony Starkweather, a capitalist more powerful than a hundred Rothschilds, can't find documents his wife hides behind a Lincoln portrait on the office wall! Corrupt journalists, a teetotaler minister, and Japanese diplomat with a Yale diploma complete the cast, besides an honest congressman, whose father struggled across American prairies behind oxen. *The Bookman* called *Theft* "about as poor a piece of work as a man of talent could be guilty of perpetrating."[55]

London also tried an agricultural play with primitive rhythms called *The Acorn-Planter* for the Bohemian Club's annual high jinks. They refused it. George Sterling wrote: "It's not exactly overloaded with poetry, but seems to me a good, sound, actable play."[56] Macmillan released this in 1916, *The Nation* saying it "curiously demonstrates that a play may be of cyclic duration yet of stationary effect. . . . The dialogue consists, in part, of simple monosyllabic prose, in part of easy, familiar metres moving with a celerity that leaves the question of purely poetic gift in a possibly fortunate abeyance."[57]

According to what London told Sterling, he rushed through the last half of *The Acorn-Planter* in two weeks, one reason for its lack of dramatic force and poor poetic prose. Sterling didn't help matters. Although Sterling wrote "The First Poet," a Bohemian Club play called *Truth,* and titles for a few later Hollywood films, including Douglas Fairbanks's "The Thief of Bagdad," he considered theatre a minor member of the arts, writing Upton Sinclair: "The stage seems to taint, and usually *rots,* about everything that touches it, especially those who are responsible for the stage—partial payment, it may be, for the insincerity of the pseudo-art of acting. But you already know my intolerance for it."[58]

The Sea Wolf intrigued London as a possible film and stage play. After refusing $1,000 from Richard Mansfield, Broadway's Beau Brummel, for rights, Joseph Noel collaborated with London on a dramatized version of the thriller, receiving two-thirds of the profits. Oliver Morosco staged this in San Francisco. He cast Frank Bacon—later the star of *Lightnin'*—as Mugridge, a comic role that stole the show. This angered London. He wanted Wolf Larsen limelighted. So he refused to go backstage and congratulate Bacon, which saddened the old trouper.

London, meanwhile, jockeyed for the sale of Hollywood film rights, neglecting tinsel-town's shadiness. Joseph Noel, who held rights to any dramatic or photoplay productions, thought

The Sea Wolf would benefit from a Broadway staging before cranking the cameras. At first, London agreed to let the Authors' League arbitrate, then changed his mind: "When I said the choice was no longer his, he laughed at the idea of my getting out an injunction to restrain him from making a film of 'The Sea Wolf,' " recalled Noel, "and said he'd fight me through every court in the country. He reminded me that he had the money to do it and that, as I had done, I would be unable to fight back."[59] London then appealed to Noel's sense of comradeship, saying he'd be ruined, and Noel returned film rights of *The Sea Wolf* to London for $5,000. He later rated their worth at $100,000.

Then Hobart Bosworth, Minnie Maddern Fiske's former leading man, visited Glen Ellen with plans to film *The Sea Wolf,* himself cast as Larsen. "[London] became excited and danced around the room, forgetting his appendix bandage, everything in the new possibilities," recalled Bosworth. "Marvelous vitality, marvelous interest in life! In a few days I was back in the North making the sinking ferry boat scenes between Alcatraz and Sausalito, and Jack and Charmian were abroad with us watching all the scenes of the panic among the passengers, and the life boats, like a pair of children."[60]

Bosworth's production of *The Sea Wolf* made film history. "Hollywood meant very little to the feature film until close to the end of 1913," says Kenneth MacGowan, film historian. "Then a West Coast actor sent to New York a seven-reel film that made quite a stir. . . . The actor was Hobart Bosworth and the film was Jack London's *Sea Wolf,* a Pallas Pictures feature, which Bosworth produced and starred in."[61]

Little is known about London's adventure in filmland. It seems fly-by-nighters, who bought film rights to *The Sea Wolf* from Century for marginal costs, swindled him—helped by weak copyright laws. Along with Rex Beach, Booth Tarkington, Ida Tarbell, Ellen Glasgow, Theodore Roosevelt, and other concerned authors, London helped found the Authors' League.

After Congress changed copyright laws, a clear-cut victory for the Authors' League, the organization held a yearly banquet. When President Woodrow Wilson declined to speak in 1913, sending William Jennings Bryan, Secretary of State, Will Irwin recalled:

When Bryan rose to speak, he did not disappoint us. He began: "Young writing men and women of America, do you realize your re-spon-si-bil-ity?" There he paused to let his eloquence sink in, as was his habit, and from a table in the corner of the room came a voice which sounded thin and slight in contrast with Bryan's organ tones, but which carried.

"Bunk!" said the voice. We peeped discreetly. It was Jack London. Evidently he had been indulging the habit which he himself confessed in *John Barleycorn*. Still more evidently he was enjoying himself hugely. Bryan went on to indicate our duty to our country and our Creator, and to deplore tendencies toward impurity and alcoholism in literature. Jack punctuated every pause with an ejaculation—"Oh Hell!" "Hokum!" "Blah!" Then some tactful persons started an ovation whenever the orator paused; this drowned out Jack's criticisms. For diplomatic reasons, the Executive Council of the Authors' League felt it necessary to write to Bryan apologizing for interruptions by "a small minority of the audience"; but as we drew up the letter, we giggled.[62]

Chapter 17

Where Is Time Gone?

DURING 1916, THE LAST year, several pathways of London's life—his feelings about the writing game, his estranged social relations, the downward spiral of his health—reached an inexorable end.

The Macmillan Company published three of London's books during 1916: *The Acorn Planter, The Turtles of Tasman,* a collection of mediocre stories, and *The Little Lady of the Big House,* which Upton Sinclair termed "the most sinister sign in the life of Jack London."[1] This novel London called a masterwork. Both Joan London and George Sterling disagreed, Sterling so vehemently that it damaged their relationship. The public? They bought fewer than 22,000 copies. Because of a continued sales slump, London earned around forty thousand dollars in 1916 from wordsmanship, nearly half of former years, yet expenses at Glen Ellen soared.

Short stories, London's earlier lucrative source, showed a decreasing market with changing times. Walker and Sisson list two between 1914 and 1916 in *The Fiction of Jack London*: "Told in the Drooling Ward," and "The Hussy,"[2] the latter bought from Sterling for one hundred dollars. Miriam Allen deFord comments in *They Were San Franciscans*: "This, however, was not a bare plot but a completed story, and a little gem. It was too slight and too short for London, who was paid by the word, and he expanded and ruined it until it was a prolix manuscript for which he received ten times what he had paid for it. (This episode, incidentally, is given by Irving Stone as an example of London's generosity!) Then he forced Sterling to listen while he read aloud what he had made of the poet's delicate fancy. . . . Perhaps it is no wonder that Sterling had contempt for the magazines and for magazine fiction."[3]

Considering London's longtime hatred of writing, his failing career borders on poetic justice. For sixteen years he reputedly pounded out one thousand words a day, all for fast profits. His style and substance had backslid since *The Call of the Wild* in 1903, and rarely renewed itself in fine-textured stories such as "To Build a Fire," "Samuel," and "The Sea Farmer." He told Emanuel Julius:

> I am nothing more than a fairly good artisan. You may think I am not telling the truth, but I hate my profession. I detest the profession I have chosen. I hate it, I tell you, I hate it!
>
> I assure you that I do not write because I love the game. I loathe it. I cannot find words to express my disgust. The only reason I write is because I am well paid for my labor—that's what I call it—labor. I get lots of money for my books and stories. I tell you I would be glad to dig ditches for twice as many hours as I devote to writing if only I would get as much money. To me, writing is an easy way to make a fine living. Unless I meant it, I wouldn't think of saying a thing like this, for I am speaking for publication. I am sincere when I say that my profession sickens me. Every story I write is for the money that will come to me. I always write what the editors want, not what I'd like to write. I grind out what the capitalist editors want, and the editors buy only what the business and editorial departments permit.[4]

The hero of *The Little Lady of the Big House,* Dick Forrest, seems to be the ultimate literary extension of Jack London's ego, even more so than Martin Eden. He leaves a wealthy home to become a road bum, sails on a windjammer, goes to the Belmont Academy and the University of California where he heads the football team, then journeys to the Klondike, the Philippines, Mexico, and is arrested in Japan. A respected writer on agricultural subjects, he reads all the books London has read, and is painted as a lay philosopher. Forrest becomes a brilliant millionaire farmer, who owns prize-winning Angora goats, bulls, cows, and hogs. While these fecund beasts litter the yard with offspring, and a sex-starved stallion dances in the distant hills, Forrest's wife, Paula, remains barren, possibly because Dick is impotent. (Barrenness and impotency play central roles in many London stories. This might mirror another intense personal neurosis.) The book gushes with sexual symbolism, from flashing knives to super stallions; parts approach pornography, although London swore he wouldn't write anything Joan and Bess couldn't read. Paula, in addition, becomes the playmate of Dick's best friend, leading to her suicide (shades of Martin Eden). This leaves Dick with a pocketful of pedigrees, an eight-hundred-foot house, and 250,000 acres of fertile soil.

At any rate, London hit bottom with *The Little Lady of the Big House*. And critics trounced it.

The Dial. "For interesting it certainly is not, after the first few pages. Perhaps that is because it is not credible that a man who knows so much about running a stock-farm should be satisfied with anything but the stock-farm itself. If he is satisfied with writing about it, we feel that there must be something impracticable about his imagination. If it will not work we do not believe in it, and if we do not believe in it (for the moment) we do not care for it. A sad but real paradox of the artistic life."[5]

The Nation. "In the present yarn he seems to make a desperate attempt at something new. He goes in for a romance of sophisticated life, the motor-car and country-house, diamonds and champagne, money-rolling, intriguing sort of thing. But though he write[s] with the pen of Mr. R. W. Chambers, he remains himself. He does not achieve reality or sincerity in this performance, nor, despite faithful effort, does he attain the enervated voluptuousness of his model. His big man who spends millions, accomplished marvels in agriculture and a dozen other fields and exercises, and tubs himself, and prances about in the role of stallion exulting in his power, and is such a fool that he lets his fabulously lovely wife be philandered with by another."[6]

The Atlantic Monthly, which had published "An Odyssey of the North" in January 1900, wrote a devastating review. "*The Little Lady of the Big House* reproduces merely the fecund— nay, glib—erotomania of three persons who 'fiddle harmonics on the strings of sensualism,' and whose very continence is a mere voluptuous refinement upon desire. In-growing concupiscence, if a subject for the novel at all, ought at least not to masquerade as tragic passion. Is this perverted gusto the half-surrender of one more artist to the baser demands of his market? Or the resort of a thinker too sophisticated for the old naive and cleansing intensities, too undisciplined for the new impersonal meanings of things?"[7]

London's illnesses led to more and more toddies to escape life's lies, while Nakata quietly diluted them with fruit juice. He fell asleep with lit cigarettes dangling from his lips, popped pills, and overdosed with harmful chemicals. The Crowd, which London visited less and less, moved south to Carmel. The few times Bessie and the girls came to Glen Ellen, Charmian treated them badly, forcing Bessie to withdraw, along with the girls. Jimmy Hopper and Upton Sinclair, although both living in the region, failed to visit London. Even George Sterling avoided the ranch, causing London to write him a nasty letter, the last Sterling received from him. Flora, bitter about London's behavior, sold baked goods at home and tried to buy an Oakland newsstand. Both incidents drew adverse printer's ink.

On March 7, 1916, London finally resigned from the socialist party. He accused America's cell of losing its fire. (*The Overland Monthly* published this letter in their May 1917 issue.)[8] The party's response appeared on March 27, 1916, in a *New York Call* article called "How You Can Get Socialism."

> The Socialist Party never spends much time in lamenting over those who occasionally quit its ranks, nor will it do so now. Mr. London's letter, unfortunately, is couched in such vague and general terms that no one can be sure what he means.
>
> London is a fighter. Good. For some reason not stated, he realized his fighting record in the cause is a closed chapter. He has of late found the party too peaceable for his taste. He quits it and goes elsewhere to find a battlefield.
>
> Doubtless this sounds off to us and to most party members. Yet doubtless London is sincere. The reasons may be local or personal, or both. We don't know Glen Ellen, and we do know Jack London. The name of the place does sound rather too idyllic to harmonize with the author of *The Sea Wolf* and *The Call of the Wild*.

We can only assure him that, however tediously peaceable membership in Glen Ellen may be, the workingmen in mine and shop and factory who make up the rank and file of the Socialist Party are fighting—not always the sort of fight that makes good copy for the magazines or good films for the movies—but the steady, unflinching, uncomplaining, unboasting, shoulder to shoulder and inch-by-inch fight that uses the fighters up one by one and sends them to the soon-forgotten graves, but that gains ground for those who fill up the ranks as they fall, that undermines the enemy's defenses and wears him down and keeps on wearing him down until the time comes for breaking his line and making the grand dash that shall end the war.

Live long, Friend London, and keep the pugnacious spirit, that, when the way to victory has been prepared by the unheralded millions, you may be with us once more on that dramatic day. We shall go on doing our best to hasten it for you.[9]

London also decided to build a dam across Graham Creek for cattle and irrigation projects in 1916. This bred more discontent. Local farmers—led by "Mother Mine" Ninetta Eames— charged violation of property rights, fearing he would drain the creek for an artificial lake. London, defending that any water rights flowing through the ranch belonged to him, denied allegations. The case went to court.

"While I have never had my hands on a plow handle in my life, I know more about plowing than any man who has had actual experience for the reason that I have studied from the books and watched experts,"[10] said London at the trial. Did he plan to become a water baron? "I want the water for use on my farms and for no other reason." The prosecuting attorney then quoted a passage from *The Valley of the Moon* in which gentleman-farmer Billy asserts water rights for his farms, and the local boobs be hanged. What did this remark mean? London reaffirmed that *The Valley of the Moon* "was purely fiction and did not represent him at all."[11]

The court denied the injunction, and London won, although he probably considered Ninetta a Judas. He died ten days after inviting plaintiffs to the ranch for a tour and feast. Charmian

said a deadness masked his face during those last days, a terrible
sight unforgettable.[12]

The physicians' bulletin read:

At 6:30 P.M., November 21, 1916, Jack London partook of his
dinner. He was taken during the night with what was supposed
to be an acute attack of indigestion. This, however, proved to
be a gastro-intestinal type of uraemia. He lapsed into coma and
died at 7:45 P.M., November 22.

Dr. W. S. Porter
Dr. A. M. Thompson
Dr. W. B. Hays
Dr. J. W. Shiels.[13]

What really happened during that last night in London's porch
bedroom? Joan London said that "sufficient doubt existed
among the four physicians who attended him to permit the cause
of his death to be stated as 'uremia following renal colic.' "[14]
Charmian, who had taken a walk before retiring, saw London's
light burning. Workers told Sterling they might have heard
footsteps.

At seven o'clock the next morning, Sekine, the Japanese valet
who had replaced Nakata, brought a cup of coffee. He found
London doubled over, unconscious, his face contorted. The
frightened servant got Eliza. She called for Charmian. Finding
London comatose, they called Dr. A. M. Thompson, who di-
agnosed an overdose of narcotics, then asked Dr. W. B. Hayes
of Sonoma for assistance. Although they administered a potas-
sium permanganate solution to London's stomach, massaged
his arms and swollen legs, even instructed workmen to shout
that the dam had collapsed, he refused to revive. His eyes once
flickered and lips moved. Two more physicians arrived, Dr. J.
W. Shiels, and London's surgeon, Dr. W. S. Porter. All efforts,
however, failed to save him.

The big question remains. Did Jack London commit suicide?
A death wish dominated both London's life and letters, evi-

denced in endless passages from stories, both at the start and finish of his career. Joan London called his last years suicidal. Since 1938 when Irving Stone advanced the suicide theory in *Sailor on Horseback,* few have questioned its validity. Stone said Dr. Thompson said that he had found a pad on London's table the day of his death loaded with calculations of amounts of morphine. Although the idea seems reasonable, Stone's statement leaves unanswered questions: Why would a physician conceal this secret for twenty years, then reveal it to a stranger? And why didn't the other three physicians mention the pad? Even Joan London, expressing skepticism over Thompson's belated confession, told Alfred A. Shivers that the family physician, Dr. William S. Porter, disagreed with Irving Stone's suicide theory. Porter, who signed the uremic poisoning death certificate, rejected morphine as the cause of London's death. In 1913 London had his appendix removed. Since that time, Porter had warned him about eating twelve-minute cooked duck, the erosive effects of alcohol, and necessity for daily exercise. London's abuse of his body—not morphine overdoses—caused uremic poisoning and death. So said Porter.[15]

Irving Stone seems to have ignored the toxicological aspects of London's death. Alfred A. Shivers, an ex-pharmacist, offers a penetrating analysis of the situation, surmising that "more than likely, London had injected one or more doses of his drug during a sharp seizure of pain from his kidney stone, and did not give sufficient heed to possible toxicity. Extreme suffering can lead one to risk desperate measures in medication that do not necessarily include self-murder." Shivers, however, also qualifies his conclusions.

Renal colic, an agonizing ailment, causes pain more unbearable than angina pectoris, leading sufferers to double and triple morphine dosages to reduce pain. London had self-administered morphine since early November, even persuading a second doctor to write additional prescriptions. Relief brought gastrointestinal disaster, releasing more and more poisons into the system. Alcohol aggravated the condition, adding to the potency of the morphine. Shivers consulted several experts, none of whom offered a "*mathematically precise figure for what the toxic dose of morphine might be.*" Shivers states that "as an agent for self-destruction, morphine is therefore a most unwise, and unlikely choice for anyone who has better means available, and it should not be hard to find better means."[16] In any case, it would have taken six to twelve hours for the morphine to work, and suicide, incidentally, would have nullified insurance policies. Yet one wonders. Irrational forces ruled London's life; should death be exceptional? Because he had written a letter to Joan inviting her and Bess to lunch doesn't preclude an impulsive act, one perhaps triggered by despair and intense pain.

George Sterling insisted London committed suicide. Jessie B. Rittenhouse wrote in *My House of Life*: "There has been some speculation as to whether London took his own life, but I can only say that Sterling definitely told me that he did, with particulars concerning the cause, when I last saw him in San Francisco, in February of 1924. A friend was present, and also heard the conversation."[17] Robinson Jeffers also remarked that Sterling assured him "that his friend Jack London had died intentionally, of an over dose of morphine, and, not as reported, by process of nature."[18] Mrs. Xavier Martinez attributed London's death to suicide over another woman, something Sterling also suggested; she said he awoke during the night and told Dr. William Porter, "Bill, you cannot do this to me"[18]—meaning, save him.

Unfinished work survived London. He planned an autobiography called *A Sailor on Horseback*, and one on women and alcohol, *Jane Barleycorn*, which would, perhaps, have been an indictment of women. Sections of one study, *Eyes of Asia*, which Charmian said he worked on before dying, appeared in a September 1924 issue of *Cosmopolitan* magazine. This story probably represented a changing world view because it reflects London's growing conviction that Eastern cultures would succeed Anglo-Saxons as the dominant race. One finds a hint of this in *The Mutiny of the Elsinore*, when Asiatic crewmen help Pathurst quell a rebellion of the riffraff (something unthinkable in *The Sea Wolf* a decade earlier). Most men mellow with age. London seems to have followed the pattern, evident especially in "A Northland Miracle" (*The Youth's Companion*, November 4, 1926). This is a late Klondike tale about Bertram Cornell, an evil man who pained his parents as a boy. Redemption comes in the white wilderness when Cornell, who first devours the food of companions, later sacrifices his life to savage Indians, letting the two comrades escape.[20]

In *Eyes of Asia,* furthermore, London preaches universality among men. The protagonist, a fragile and delicate Japanese girl called Cherry, is adopted by affluent Hawaiian aristocrats after being washed ashore on a sampan, both of her parents unknown. Threadbare London clichés clutter the story. The pinches of an amorous suitor thrill Cherry. She carries a Vassar diploma. Her patriarch Polynesian father, who can't eat or sleep, laments about his failing virility and ability to fight.[21]

Charmian completed *Eyes of Asia* for the October 1924 issue of *Cosmopolitan,* her style indistinguishable from London's. Cherry, unable to love an Anglo-Saxon, falls for her Japanese gardener, who became a laborer when his wealthy father died; the blood of Samurai ancestors, however, still fills his veins. Cherry's future dreams include returning to Japan with the gardener in a sampan, then to buy a farm.[22]

A less harsh, less superheroic tone tints these later works of London's, but they fall short of literary excellence. They're poured from plastic molds.

Around seventy persons[23] attended London's funeral, including Eliza and Irving Shepard, Bessie and the girls, and the Reverend Edward B. Payne. Charmian failed to appear. One wonders why. What did George Sterling mean when he wrote Upton Sinclair: "As to Charmian's life of Jack, her chapter inclusive of his death was written carefully to camouflage the fact of his suicide, which was not exactly a compliment to her! And there was the insurance! She fairly *rushed* him to the crematory."[24] Payne delivered the oration and read a mawkish tribute by Sterling:

Oh! was there ever face, of all the dead,
In which, too late, the living could not read
A mute appeal for all the love unsaid—
A mute reproach for careless word and deed?

And now, dear friend of friends, we look on thine,
To whom we could not give a last farewell—
On whom, without a whisper or a sign,
The deep, unfathomable Darkness fell.

Oh! gone beyond us, who shall say how far?—
Gone swiftly to the dim eternity,
Leaving us silence, or the words that are
To sorrow as the foam is to the sea.

Unfearing heart, whose patience was so long!
Unresting mind, so hungry for the truth!
Now hast thou rest, O gentle one and strong.
Dead like a lordly lion in its youth!

Farewell! although thou know not, there alone!
Farewell! although thou hear not in our cry
The love we would have given had we known.
Ah! and a soul like thine—how shall it die?[25]

Sekine made a grand gesture at the cremation. Before flames consumed London's body, he slipped a note into the coffin that read: "Your words are silver. Your silence now is golden."[26] Perhaps Nietzsche put it better: "Woe unto me! Where is time gone? Have I not sunk into deep wells? The world sleeps. Alas! Alas! The dog howls, the moon shines. Sooner would I die, die rather than tell you what my midnight heart thinks now."[27]

Notes

Notes: Chapter 1

1. *San Francisco Chronicle,* January 14, 1876, p. 4.
2. William McDevitt, "Jack London's Father's Autobiography," *Hobbies,* February 1946, p. 121.
3. Fulmer Mood, "An Astrologer from Down East," *New England Quarterly,* 5 (1932), p. 775.
4. Richard O'Connor, *Jack London: A Biography* (Boston: Little, Brown, 1964), p. 15.
5. Fulmer Mood, *New England Quarterly,* pp. 776–77.
6. W. H. Chaney, "Unparalleled Outrages!," *Broughton's Monthly Planet Reader,* 8 (April, May, June 1867), p. 9.
7. W. H. Chaney, "Man Should Be Able to Predict the Future," *Common Sense,* December 19, 1874, pp. 378, 379.
8. W. H. Chaney, *Broughton's Monthly Planet Reader,* p. 11.
9. Luke Broughton, *Elements of Astrology* (New York: L. D. Broughton, 1898), p. 454.
10. W. H. Chaney, *The Astrologer's Vade Mecum* (Baltimore: Eureka Publ. Co., 1902), p. 27.
11. Fulmer Mood, *New England Quarterly,* p. 792.
12. W. H. Perrin, *History of Stark County, Ohio* (Chicago: Baskin & Batty, 1881), pp. 391–92.
13. *Columbus Sunday Dispatch Magazine,* November 14, 1954, p. 23.
14. Joan London, *Jack London and His Times* (Seattle: University of Washington Press, 1968), p. 3.
15. *San Francisco Chronicle,* June 4, 1875, p. 5.
16. Irving Stone, *Sailor on Horseback* (New York: New American Library, 1965), pp. 15–16.
17. John Perry, ed., *Thirteen Tales of Terror by Jack London* (New York: Popular Library, 1978), pp. 11, 23, 25.
18. Jack London, *The Faith of Men* (New York: The Macmillan Company, 1904), p. 203.

19. Jack London, *The God of His Fathers* (New York: McClure, Phillips & Co., 1901), p. 75.
20. W. H. Chaney, "The Great Northwest," *The West Shore,* May 1884, p. 134.
21. W. H. Chaney, "The Great Northwest," *The West Shore,* April 1884, pp. 98, 99.
22. W. H. Chaney, "The Great Northwest," *The West Shore,* May 1884, pp. 134, 135.
23. W. H. Chaney, "The Great Northwest," *The West Shore,* March 1884, p. 72.
24. William H. Chaney, *Chaney's Primer of Astrology and American Urania* (St. Louis: Magic Circle Publ. Co., 1890), pp. 127, 129.
25. Luke Broughton, *Elements of Astrology,* p. 394.
26. William H. Chaney, *Astrological Almanac* (1889), p. 158.
27. William H. Chaney, *The Astrologer's Vade Mecum* (1902), editor's preface.
28. *San Francisco Bulletin,* July 22, 1906, p. 23.
29. Dumas Malone, ed., *Dictionary of American Biography* (New York: Charles Scribner's Sons, 1933), p. 372.
30. Ninetta Eames, "Jack London," *The Overland Monthly,* 35 (May 1900), p. 418.
31. H. M. Tichener, *Life of Jack London* (Girard, Kan.: Haldeman-Julius Co., n.d.), p. 7.
32. Stanley J. Kunitz and Howard Haycraft, eds., *Twentieth Century Authors* (New York: H. W. Wilson Co., 1942), p. 843.
33. Rose Wilder Lane, "Life and Jack London," *Sunset, The Pacific Monthly,* 39 (July–December 1917), pp. 18–19. Reprinted by permission of Lane Publishing Company.
34. Charmian London, *The Book of Jack London* (London: Mills & Boon, 1921), I, p. 36.
35. *Oakland Tribune,* March 16, 1952, Parade Section, p. 7.
36. Joan London, *Jack London and His Times,* p. 22.
37. *San Francisco Chronicle,* December 16, 1894, p. 11.
38. Lewis Mumford, "Jack London," *New Republic,* 30 (March 1–May 24, 1922), p. 145.
39. Kevin Starr, *Americans and the California Dream 1850–1915* (New York: Oxford University Press, 1973), p. 233.
40. Mrs. Jack London, "Bringing Literature to the Screen," *Theatre Magazine,* September 1919, p. 43.
41. Frank Norris, "The Frontier Gone at Last," *The World's Work,* 3 (November 1901–April 1902), p. 1729.
42. Harry Hartwick, *Foreground of American Fiction* (New York: American Book Co., 1934), p. 83.
43. Negley Farson, *A Mirror for Narcissus* (New York: Doubleday & Co., 1956), p. 36.
44. John D. Bergamini, *The Hundredth Year: The United States in 1876* (New York: G. Putnam's Sons, 1976), p. 148.
45. Oscar Lewis, *San Francisco Since 1872: A Pictorial History of Seven Decades* (San Francisco: Ray Oil Burner Co., 1946), p. 17.

46. Lois Rather, *Oakland's Image: A History of Oakland, California* (Oakland: Rather Press, 1972).
47. Karl Baedeker, ed., *The United States with an Excursion into Mexico, A Handbook for Travelers, 1893* (New York: Da Capo Press, 1971), p. 399.
48. Joan London, *Jack London and His Times*, p. 84.
49. Oliver Madox Hueffer, "Jack London, A Personal Sketch," *Living Age*, 292 (January–March 1917), p. 124.
50. Ouida, *Signa* (New York: Peter Fenelon Collier, Publishers, n.d.), pp. 8–9, 44, 71.
51. John Tebbel, *From Rags to Riches* (New York: Macmillan Co., 1963), p. 125.
52. Horatio Alger, Jr., *Ragged Dick and Mark, the Match Boy* (London: Collier Books, 1962), p. 108.
53. Ibid., p. 221.
54. Jack London, *God of His Fathers*, p. 118.
55. Jack London, "Who Believes in Ghosts!," *High School Aegis*, October 21, 1895, p. 2.
56. *Alameda Times-Star*, March 30, 1954, p. 2.
57. "Brother of Famous Author Content Living Alone in his Humble Hut," Scrapbook of Wapsie Farmers Club, The State Historical Society of Iowa.
58. The Macmillan Company, "Jack London by Himself." Reprinted by permission of I. Milo Shepard Estate.
59. George Wharton James, "A Study of Jack London in His Prime," *The Overland Monthly*, 69 (May 1917), p. 368.
60. *Oakland Tribune*, August 5, 1933, p. 13.
61. Jack London, *Children of the Frost* (New York: Macmillan Co., 1902), p. 209.

Notes: Chapter 2

1. Horatio Alger, Jr., *Ragged Dick and Mark, the Match Boy* (New York: Macmillan Co., 1970), p. 39.
2. *San Francisco Chronicle*, December 14, 1949, p. 20.
3. C. T. Peterson, "The Jack London Legend," *American Book Collector*, 7–8 (September 1956–June 1958), p. 16.
4. Charmian London, *The Book of Jack London*, I, p. 102.
5. Harold French, "The Cruise of 'Bay-Pirate Jack,' " *St. Nicholas*, 44 (May–October 1917), p. 850. See also: E. Marshall White, "The Cruise of the Pirate-Ship Moon-Raker," *St. Nicholas*, 12 (November 1884–April 1885), pp. 32–37.
6. Sam S. Baskett, "Jack London on the Oakland Waterfront," *American Literature*, 27 (March–January 1955–1956), pp. 369–70.
7. Jack London, *The Cruise of the Dazzler* (New York: Macmillan Co., 1902), pp. 42, 77, 246.
8. Arthur Calder Marshall, ed., *The Bodley Head Jack London*, 2 (London: Bodley Head, 1964), p. 15.
9. Jack London, *The Cruise of the Dazzler*, pp. 10, 11, 201.
10. Joseph Noel, *Footloose in Arcadia* (New York: Carrick & Evans, 1940), p. 20.

11. Edwin P. Hoyt, *Horatio's Boys* (Radnor, Pa.: Chilton Book Co., 1974), p. 203.
12. Brochure, "Jack London by Himself."
13. Herbert Asbury, *The Barbary Coast: An Informal History of the San Francisco Underworld* (Garden City: Garden City Pub. Co., 1933), p. 198.
14. Jack London, *Tales of the Fish Patrol* (New York: Macmillan Co., 1905), pp. 19–21.
15. Ibid., pp. 33–34.
16. Ibid., pp. 224–25.
17. Shannon Garth, *Jack London: Magnet for Adventure* (New York: Julian Messner, 1944), p. 55.
18. Joan London, *Jack London and His Times*, p. 49.
19. John C. Higgins, "Jack London on the Waterfront," *Westways*, 26 (January, 1934), p. 34.
20. Charles J. Finger, *Seven Horizons* (Garden City: Doubleday, Doran & Co., 1930), p. 446.
21. Frederick P. Schmitt to John Perry, January 12, 1977.
22. Waldo C. M. Johnston to John Perry, December 22, 1976.
23. Ibid.
24. William A. Baker to John Perry, January 6, 1977.
25. George Wharton James, "A Study of Jack London in his Prime," *The Overland Monthly*, 69 (May 1917), p. 370.
26. *New York World*, July 11, 1890, p. 3.
27. Jack London, *The Sea Wolf* (New York: Macmillan Co., 1904), p. 22.
28. Jack London, "One More Unfortunate," *High School Aegis*, December 18, 1895, p. 13.
29. Jack London, *The Sea Wolf*, p. 155.
30. Richard O'Connor, *Jack London: A Biography*, p. 41.
31. Franklin Walker, ed., *The Sea Wolf & Selected Stories* (New York: New American Library, 1964), p. 339.
32. William A. Baker to John Perry.
33. Edward V. Lewis to John Perry, December 30, 1976.
34. Jack London, "Chris Farrington: Able Seaman," *The Youth's Companion*, May 23, 1901, pp. 265, 266.
35. *San Francisco Morning Mail*, November 12, 1893, p. 11.

Notes: Chapter 3

1. Lillian Symes and Travers Clement, *Rebel America* (New York: Harper and Bros., 1934), p. 201.
2. Ibid.
3. Shirley Plumer Austin, "Coxey's Commonweal Army," *Chautauquan*, 19 (1894), p. 333.
4. "Kelly's 'Industrial Army' on Its Way to Washington," *Harper's Weekly*, 38 (1894), p. 416.
5. *San Francisco Chronicle*, December 16, 1894, p. 11.
6. William McDevitt, *Jack London as Poet and as Platform Man* (San Francisco: Recorder-Sunset Press, 1947), p. 13.
7. Charmian London, *Book of Jack London*, I, p. 59.

8. "Tramping with Kelly Through Iowa: A Jack London Diary," *Palimpsest,* 52 (June 1971), pp. 316–46.
9. Andrew Sinclair, *Jack: A Biography of Jack London* (New York: Harper & Row, 1977), p. 22.
10. Robert Barltrop, *Jack London: The Man, The Writer, The Rebel* (London: Pluto Press, 1976), p. 41.
11. Laurence Greene, *America Goes to Press* (New York: Bobbs-Merrill Co., 1936), pp. 296–97.
12. *Boston Evening Transcript,* May 26, 1900, p. 32.
13. Jack London, *War of the Classes* (The Macmillan Company, 1905), pp. 276–77.
14. Joan London, *Jack London and His Times,* p. 84.
15. Jack London, "Rods and Gunnels," *The Bookman,* 15 (1902), pp. 543–44.
16. Josiah Flynt, *Tramping with Tramps* (New York: Century Co., 1899), p. 4.
17. Ibid., p. 54.
18. Jack London, *War of the Classes,* pp. 92–93.
19. George Sterling to Jack London, February 9, 1911. George Sterling letters quoted with permission of The Bancroft Library, University of California, Berkeley, owner of their literary rights.
20. *New York Times,* December 28, 1907, p. 861.
21. "The Road," *Independent,* 64 (January–June 1908), p. 42.
22. Josiah Flynt, *Tramping with Tramps,* p. 65.
23. Jack London to George Brett, March 20, 1903. Macmillan Company Records, Manuscripts and Archives Division, The New York Public Library, Astor, Lenox and Tilden Foundations. All George Brett letters, The New York Public Library.
24. Edward E. Hale, Jr., "The Hobo in Theory and Practice," *The Dial,* 44 (January–June 1908), p. 302.
25. Jack London, "How I Became a Socialist," *Comrade,* March 1903, p. 123.
26. Edwin P. Hoyt, *Horatio's Boys: The Life and Works of Horatio Alger, Jr.* (Radnor, Penn.: Chilton Book Co., 1974), p. 44.
27. Georgia Loring Bamford, *The Mystery of Jack London* (Oakland, Cal.: Georgia Loring Bamford, 1931), pp. 17, 22.
28. Ibid., p. 23.
29. Joan London, *Jack London and His Times,* p. 100.
30. Joseph Noel, *Footloose in Arcadia: A Personal Record of Jack London, George Sterling, and Ambrose Bierce* (New York: Carrick & Evans, 1940), pp. 277–78.
31. *Alameda Daily Argus,* October 21, 1905, p. 6.
32. Application for Admission as Special Student, University of California, Berkeley. Provided by Alda N. Byron, Administrative Assistant, Office of Admissions and Records.
33. Jack London, "First Aid to Rising Authors," *Junior Munsey,* December, 1900, p. 516.
34. Richard O'Connor, *Jack London: A Biography,* p. 76.
35. Transcript of Record, provided by Alda N. Byron, University of California, Berkeley.

36. *Berkeley Daily Gazette*, November 1, 1916, pp. 1, 2.
37. Georgia Loring Bamford, *The Mystery of Jack London*, pp. 28–29, 29.
38. *San Francisco Bulletin*, February 28, 1914, p. 3.
39. *San Francisco Chronicle*, November 24, 1916, p. 3.
40. *Berkeley Daily Gazette*, September 16, 1903, p. 7.
41. Jack London, "Phenomena of Literary Evolution," *The Bookman*, 12 (September–February, 1900–1901), p. 149.
42. Jack London, "Their Alcove," *Women's Home Companion*, September 1900, p. 13.
43. Jack London, "What Life Means to Me," *Cosmopolitan*, March 1906, pp. 529, 527.
44. Ibid., p. 526.

Notes: Chapter 4

1. James S. Easby-Smith, "The Real Klondike," *Cosmopolitan*, 24 (November-April 1897–1898), p. 228.
2. Charmian London, *Book of Jack London*, 1, p. 222.
3. Ibid.
4. Franklin Walker, *Jack London & the Klondike* (San Marino: Huntington Library, 1972), pp. 51–52.
5. Jack London, *A Daughter of the Snows* (Philadelphia: J. B. Lippincott Co., 1902), pp. 7–8.
6. Franklin Walker, *Jack London & the Klondike*, p. 58.
7. A. A. Hill, "The Klondike," *Munsey's Magazine*, 20 (1898–1899), p. 720.
8. Jack London, *The God of His Fathers*, pp. 79–80.
9. Jack London, *The Faith of Men* (New York: Leslie-Judge Co., 1925), pp. 142–43.
10. *The Trail of Ninety-Eight*, Lowell Thomas, Jr., ed. (New York: Duell, Sloan and Pearce, 1962), pp. 25–26, 27, 28. First published in *Home Magazine*, June 1899.
11. Jack London, *The Son of the Wolf* (Boston: Houghton Mifflin, 1900), p. 57.
12. Charmian London, *Book of Jack London*, 1, p. 247.
13. "Jack London by Himself," Macmillan Company brochure. Courtesy of I. Milo Shepard Estate.
14. Franklin Walker, *Jack London & the Klondike*, p. 104.
15. *Buffalo Express* (New York), June 4, 1899, p. 2.
16. Jack London, *The God of His Fathers*, pp. 275, 252, 275.
17. Edward E. P. Morgan, *God's Loaded Dice* (Caldwell, Idaho: Caxton Printers, 1948), p. 127.
18. Jack London, *God of His Fathers*, pp. 157–58.
19. Jack London, "Housekeeping in the Klondike," *Harper's Bazaar* 33 (September 15, 1900), pp. 1227, 1231.
20. Jack London, *Son of the Wolf*, p. 85.
21. Arthur Calder-Marshall, *The Bodley Head Jack London*, 4 (London: Bodley Head, 1964), p. 11.
22. Alva Johnston, *The Legendary Mizners* (New York: Farrar, Straus and Young, 1952), p. 80.

23. Jack London, *A Daughter of the Snows* (Philadelphia: J. B. Lippincott Co., 1902), pp. 245, 247, 252.
24. *Buffalo Express,* June 4, 1899, p. 2.
25. Ibid.
26. Ibid., pp. 2, 3.
27. Ibid.
28. Jack London, *Children of the Frost,* pp. 60, 76.
29. Fred Lewis Pattee, *Side-Lights of American Literature* (New York: Century Co., 1922), pp. 123–24.
30. *Buffalo Express,* June 4, 1899, p. 3.

Notes: Chapter 5

1. Jack London, "The Stampede to Thunder Mountain," *Collier's,* 29 (April–September 1902), p. 10.
2. Jack London, "Getting into Print," *Editor* (March 1903), p. 79.
3. Ibid., p. 78.
4. W. Storrs Lee, *California: A Literary Chronicle* (New York: Funk & Wagnalls, 1968), p. xix.
5. Georgia Loring Bamford, *Mystery of Jack London,* pp. 109, 78.
6. "Men and Women of the Outdoor Life," *Outing,* 44 (1904), p. 486.
7. Joan London, *Jack London and His Times,* p. 263.
8. Charmian London, *The Book of Jack London,* I, pp. 388–89.
9. Ninetta Eames, "Jack London," *The Overland Monthly,* 35 (May 1900), p. 433.
10. Jack London, *Son of the Wolf,* p. 118.
11. James Howard Bridge, *Millionaires and Grub Street* (Freeport: Books for Libraries Press, 1968), pp. 200, 202.
12. Jack London, "Getting into Print," p. 81.
13. Georgia Loring Bamford, *Mystery of Jack London,* p. 97.
14. Jack London, *Son of the Wolf,* p. 204.
15. Richard Vanderbeets, "Nietzsche of the North: Heredity and Race in London's *The Son of the Wolf,*" *Western American Literature,* 2 (1967–1968), p. 233.
16. Grant C. Knight, *The Strenuous Age* (Chapel Hill: University of North Carolina Press, 1954), p. 32.
17. "More Novels," *Nation,* 73 (July–December, 1901), p. 15.
18. "Short Stories," *Athenaeum* (January–June 1902), p. 430.
19. Jack London, *Son of the Wolf,* pp. 103, 5, 60, 60.
20. Ibid., p. 145.
21. Jack London, *God of His Fathers,* pp. 183, 253.
22. Ibid., pp. 176–77.
23. Henry Steele Commager, *The American Mind* (New York: Yale University Press, 1950), p. 110.
24. George B. Waldron, "Five Hundred Years of the Anglo-Saxon," *McClure's,* 12 (1898–1899), p. 188.
25. Jack London, "The Salt of the Earth," *Anglo-American Magazine,* 8 (August 1902), pp. 11, 4, 5, 14, 3, 2, 1, 15, 15, 9.
26. Jack London, *Son of the Wolf,* p. 36.

27. Jack London, *God of His Fathers*, pp. 56, 2, 185.
28. Jack London, *Children of the Frost*, p. 4.
29. Granville Hicks, *The Great Tradition* (New York: Macmillan Co., 1933), p. 195.
30. George Wharton James, "A Study of Jack London in His Prime," *The Overland Monthly*, 69 (May 1917), pp. 364–65.
31. Richard O'Connor, *Jack London: A Biography*, p. 139.
32. Edwin Watts Chubb, *Stories of Authors* (New York: Macmillan Co., 1926), p. 379.
33. Henry Meade Bland, "Jack London," *Overland Monthly*, 63 (May 1904), p. 376.
34. Friedrich Nietzsche, *Thus Spake Zarathustra* (New York: Viking Press, 1966), pp. 115, 126, 114, 37. First published between 1883 and 1892.
35. Mrs. Havelock Ellis, "Nietzsche and Morals," *Forum*, 44 (July–December 1910), p. 425.
36. "Nietzsche in England," *Nation*, 96 (January–June 1913), p. 590.
37. Patrick Bridgewater, *Nietzsche in Anglosaxony* (Leicester: University Press, 1972), p. 165.
38. Charles Child Walcutt, "Naturalism and the Superman in London's Novels," *Papers of the Michigan Academy of Science, Arts and Letters*, 24 (1938), p. 97.
39. Jack London, *Sea Wolf*, p. 1.
40. Jack London, "Rods and Gunnels," *The Bookman*, 15 (1902), p. 544.
41. Joan London, *Jack London and His Times*, p. 209.
42. Friedrich Nietzsche, *Thus Spake Zarathustra*, pp. 12, 31.
43. Friedrich Nietzsche, *The Anti-Christ* (New York: Penguin Classics, 1975), p. 186–87. First published in 1888.
44. Jack London, *Son of the Wolf*, p. 66.
45. Charmian London, *Book of Jack London*, II, p. 363.
46. Jack London, *The People of the Abyss* (New York: The Macmillan Company, 1903), pp. 132, 281–82.
47. Calvin B. Houck, "Jack London's Philosophy of Life," *The Overland Monthly*, 84 (May 1926), p. 136–37, 141.
48. Joan London, *Jack London and His Times*, p. 211.
49. Benjamin Kidd, *Social Evolution* (New York: Macmillan Co., 1895), pp. 142–43.
50. Benjamin Kidd, *Social Evolution*, p. 130.
51. Benjamin Kidd, *Principles of Western Civilisation* (New York: Grosset & Dunlap, 1902), p. 473.
52. Fred Lewis Pattee, *The New American Literature, 1890–1930* (New York: Century Co., 1922), pp. 130, 133.
53. James Gibbons Huneker, *Steeplejack* (New York: Charles Scribner's Sons, 1922), p. 172.
54. Arthur Voss, *The American Short Story* (Norman: University of Oklahoma Press, 1975), p. 168.
55. King Hendricks and Irving Shepard, eds., *Letters from Jack London* (New York: Odyssey Press, 1965), p. 495.
56. Jack London, "Phenomena of Literary Evolution," *The Bookman*, 12 (September–February 1900–1901), p. 150.

57. Jack London, "What Are We to Say?" *Journal of Education,* July 13, 1899, p. 66.
58. John Perry, ed., *Thirteen Tales of Terror by Jack London* (New York: Popular Library, 1978), p. 17–32.
59. Stephen Graham, "Jack London," *English Review,* May 1924, p. 736.
60. G. Jean-Aubry, ed., *Joseph Conrad's Life and Letters* (Garden City: Doubleday, Page & Co., 1927), p. 295. Quotation courtesy of Madame G. Jean-Aubry.
61. David Thorburn, *Conrad's Romanticism* (New Haven: Yale University Press, 1974), p. 10.
62. John Tebbel, *The Media in America* (New York: Thomas Y. Crowell Co., 1974), p. 280.
63. Peter Lyon, *Success Story: The Life and Times of S. S. McClure* (New York: Charles Scribner's Sons, 1963), p. 113.
64. S. S. McClure, *My Autobiography* (New York: Frederick A. Stokes Co., 1914), pp. 247, 234.
65. Dale L. Walker and James E. Sisson, III, *The Fiction of Jack London: A Chronological Bibliography* (El Paso: Texas Western Press, 1972), pp. 1–11.
66. Harlan Hatcher, *Creating the Modern American Novel* (New York: Farrar & Rinehart, 1935), p. 27.
67. "Alaskan Articles That Have Appeared in the Overland," *The Overland Monthly,* 30 (October 1897), p. 382.
68. James I. McClintock, *White Logic* (Cedar Springs, Mich.: Wolf House Books, 1976), pp. 4, 5.
69. William Roscow Thayer, *Theodore Roosevelt: An Intimate Biography* (New York: Grosset & Dunlap, 1919), pp. 120, 252.
70. Trent, William Peterfield et al., *The Cambridge History of American Literature* (New York: G. P. Putnam's Sons, 1918), p. 392.
71. Van Wyck Brooks, *Sketches in Criticism* (London: J. M. Dent & Sons, 1934), p. 249.
72. James R. Giles, "Beneficial Atavism in Frank Norris and Jack London," *Western American Literature,* 3–4 (1968/69–1969/70), p. 26.
73. A. Grove Day, *Jack London in the South Seas* (New York: Four Winds Press, 1971), p. 31.
74. Thomas Williamson, *Far North Country* (New York: Duell, Sloan and Pearce, 1944), pp. 73–74.
75. Jack London, *Son of the Wolf,* pp. 14, 111.
76. Jack London, *God of His Fathers,* pp. 159, 193, 151.
77. Jack London, *Faith of Men,* p. 72.
78. "Jack London by Himself," Macmillan Co. brochure.
79. Martin Severin Peterson, *Joaquin Miller, Literary Frontiersman* (Stanford: Stanford University Press, 1937), p. 110.
80. Hamlin Garland, *The Trail of the Goldseekers* (New York: Macmillan Co., 1906), pp. 237–38.
81. Jack London, "The Terrible and Tragic in Fiction," *The Critic,* 42 (January–June 1903), p. 540.
82. Friedrich Nietzsche, *Thus Spake Zarathustra,* p. 302.
83. Jack London, *Son of the Wolf,* p. 88.

84. "Chronicle and Comment," *The Bookman,* 11 (1900), p. 200.
85. Cornelia Atwood Pratt, "Out of the East and the North," *Critic,* 37 (July–December 1900), p. 162.
86. Jack London, *Son of the Wolf,* p. 7.
87. Jack London, *The Sea Wolf* (New York: Macmillan Co., 1943), pp. 52, 53, 98, 107.

Notes: Chapter 6

1. Jack London, "Getting into Print," p. 81.
2. Jack London, "First Aid to Rising Authors," p. 516.
3. Jack London, "Again the Literary Aspirant," *The Critic,* 41 (July–December 1902), p. 217.
4. Joan London, *Jack London and His Times,* p. 198.
5. "A Reviewer's Notebook," *Freeman,* 4 (1921–1922), p. 407.
6. Louis Kronenberger, "Jack London as Legend," *Nation,* 147–48 (July–December 1938), p. 422.
7. Jack London, "Phenomena of Literary Evolution," *The Bookman,* 12 (September–February, 1900–1901), p. 150.
8. "A Daughter of the Snows," *Athenaeum,* (July–December 1904), p. 140.
9. Jay Gurian, "The Romantic Necessity in Literary Naturalism: Jack London," *American Literature,* 38 (March–January 1966–1967), p. 115.
10. Eleanor Hoyt, "In Lighter Vein," *Book Buyer,* 25 (August 1902–January 1903), p. 522.
11. Jack London, *A Daughter of the Snows* (Philadelphia: J. B. Lippincott Co., 1902), pp. 13, 21.
12. Ibid., pp. 82, 83.
13. Ibid., pp. 55, 60, 58.
14. Jack London, "Stranger Than Fiction," *The Critic,* 43 (July–December 1903), p. 124.
15. Ray Stannard Baker, *American Chronicle* (New York: Charles Scribner's Sons, 1945), p. 138.
16. *San Francisco Bulletin,* May 28, 1902, p. 2.
17. Jack London, "The Proper 'Girlie,' " *Smart Set,* 2 (July–December 1900), p. 117.
18. Jack London to George P. Brett, August 5, 1902.
19. Andrew Sinclair, *Jack: A Biography of Jack London,* pp. 89, 88.
20. Jack London, *The People of the Abyss* (New York: Grosset & Dunlap, 1903), pp. 19, 28.
21. Edward Clark Marsh, "Jack London's 'People of the Abyss,' " *Bookman,* 18 (1903–1904), p. 648.
22. Jack London, *People of the Abyss,* pp. 168, 276, 79, 109.
23. T. D. A. Cockerell, "London on London," *The Dial,* 36 (January 1–June 16, 1904), p. 12.
24. Jack London, *People of the Abyss,* p. 138.
25. Ibid., p. 285.
26. Jack London and Anna Strunsky, *Kempton-Wace Letters* (New York: The Macmillan Company, 1903), pp. 175, 191, 51.
27. Jack London, *People of the Abyss,* p. 36.

28. "Notes," *Nation,* 77 (July–December 1903), p. 384.
29. Grace Isabel Colbron, "Jack London, What he was, and what he Accomplished," *The Bookman,* 44 (September–February 1916–1917), p. 450.
30. Jack London to George P. Brett, August 15, 1903.
31. Edward B. Cassady, "Muckraking in the Gilded Age," *American Literature,* 13 (1941–1942), p. 135.
32. Rebecca Harding Davis, "Life in the Iron-Mills," *Atlantic Monthly,* 7 (January–June 1861), pp. 434, 433.
33. Edward B. Cassady, *American Literature,* p. 137.
34. Benjamin Orange Flower, *Civilization's Inferno* (Boston: Arena Pub. Co., 1893), pp. 13–14.
35. Jacob A. Riis, *The Battle with the Slum* (New York: Macmillan Co., 1902), pp. 14, 36, 37, 69–70.
36. Louise Ware, *Jacob A. Riis* (New York: D. Appleton-Century Co., 1938), pp. 301–9.
37. Herbert Asbury, *The Barbary Coast* (Garden City: Garden City Pub. Co., 1933), pp. 178, 179.
38. Harold W. Pfautz, ed., *Charles Booth on the City: Physical Pattern and Social Structure* (Chicago: The University of Chicago Press, 1967).
39. *San Francisco Chronicle,* December 10, 1906, p. 4.
40. Philip S. Foner, *Jack London: American Rebel* (New York: Citadel Press, 1947), p. 52.

Notes: Chapter 7

1. Hal Waters, "Anna Strunsky and Jack London," *American Book Collector,* 17 (November 1966), p. 30.
2. Jack London and Anna Strunsky, *Kempton-Wace Letters,* pp. 148, 210.
3. Ibid., pp. 87, 143, 176, 67.
4. Ibid., pp. 129, 158.
5. Malcolm Cowley, *The Literary Situation* (New York: Viking Press, 1954), p. 80.
6. Lillian Symes and Travers Clement, *Rebel America* (New York: Harper and Bros., 1934), p. 233.
7. Jack London, *Daughter of the Snows,* p. 87–88.
8. Ray Giner, *The Bending Cross* (New Brunswick: Rutgers University Press, 1949), p. 426.
9. Anna Strunsky Walling, "Memoirs of Jack London," *The Masses,* 9 (July, 1917), pp. 10, 14, 16.
10. Hal Waters, "Anna Strunsky and Jack London," p. 30.
11. Ibid.
12. Joan London, *Jack London and His Times,* p. 217.
13. William English Walling, "The Race War in the North," *Independent,* 65 (July–December 1908), pp. 531, 534.
14. Charmian London, *Book of Jack London,* I, p. 59.
15. *San Francisco Chronicle,* February 16, 1896, p. 20.
16. Alvin A. Teeney, "War of the Classes," *Charities,* 15 (1905), p. 403.
17. Jack London, "The Human Drift," *Forum,* 45 (January–June 1911), p. 5.

18. *San Francisco Chronicle*, February 11, 1897, p. 7.
19. *San Francisco Examiner*, February 11, 1897, p. 14.
20. Jack London, "First Aid to Rising Authors," p. 517.
21. Kenneth S. Lynn, *The Dream of Success* (Boston: Little, Brown and Co., 1955), pp. 84, 85, 86.
22. Jack London, *Daughter of the Snows*, p. 106.
23. Joan London, *Jack London and His Times*, pp. 206, 209.
24. Jack London, *War of the Classes*, pp. 105, 108.
25. Philip S. Foner, *Jack London: American Rebel*, p. 57.
26. Jack London, "What Life Means to Me," *Cosmopolitan*, 40 (1905–1906), p. 528.
27. *San Francisco Bulletin*, February 28, 1914, p. 3.
28. Hobart Bosworth, "My Jack London," *Mark Twain Journal*, 1-5 (1936/37–1942/43), pp. 3–4.
29. Philip S. Foner, *Jack London: American Rebel*, p. 87.
30. H. Addington Bruce, "More Books on Socialism," *Outlook*, 89 (May–August 1908), p. 388.
31. "Current Fiction," *Nation*, 86 (January–June 1908), p. 264.
32. "Socialistic Storm and Sunshine," *Independent*, 64 (January–June 1908), p. 865.
33. "The Iron Heel," *The Arena*, 39 (January–June 1908), pp. 505–6.
34. John Spargo, "Literature and Art," *International Socialist Review*, 8 (1907–1908), p. 629.
35. Joseph Freeman, *An American Testament* (New York: Farrar & Rinehart, 1936), p. 313.
36. Jack London, "The Dignity of Dollars," *The Overland Monthly*, 36 (July–December 1900), p. 53.
37. Jack London, "Again the Literary Aspirant," p. 218.
38. Jack London, *Daughter of the Snows*, p. 184.
39. Jack London, "Revolution," *Contemporary Review*, 93 (January–June 1908), pp. 17–31.
40. Edward Biron Payne, *The Soul of Jack London* (London: Rider & Co., n.d.), p. 55.
41. Jack London, *War of the Classes*, pp. xvi, 96–97.
42. Emma Goldman, *Living My Life* (New York: AMS Press, 1970), flyleaf.
43. Jack London, "Pessimism, Optimism and Patriotism," *High School Aegis*, March 1, 1895, p. 6.
44. *San Francisco Chronicle*, December 21, 1905, p. 2.
45. Marshall Everett, *Complete Life of William McKinley and Story of His Assassination* (Marshall Everett, 1901), pp. 79, 70–71, 72.
46. "Summer-time Fiction," *The Bookman*, 39 (March–August 1914), p. 679.
47. Jack London, *The Contemporary Review*, pp. 17–31.
48. *New York Times*, April 3, 1917, p. 128.
49. L. S. Friedland, "Jack London as Titan," *The Dial*, 62 (January 11–June 14, 1917), 50.
50. Deming Brown, *Soviet Attitudes Toward American Writing* (Princeton: Princeton University Press, 1962), pp. 223, 225, 222, 225.
51. N. K. Krupskaya, *Memories of Lenin* (New York: International Publ., 1930), pp. 208–9.

Notes: Chapter 8

1. Jack London, "The Question of a Name," *The Writer* (December 1900), pp. 177–78.
2. Carl Van Doren, *The American Novel* (New York: Macmillan Co., 1940), p. 238.
3. "Children of the Frost," *Athenaeum,* (January–June 1903), p. 77.
4. "Moon-Face and Other Stories," *Independent,* 61 (July–December 1906), p. 699.
5. "Moon-Face and Other Stories," *Nation,* 83 (October 11, 1906), p. 308.
6. "White Fang," *Athenaeum,* (January–June 1907), p. 161.
7. "A Tireless Romancer," *Current Opinion,* 54 (1913), p. 490.
8. Jack London to George Brett, April 16, 1902.
9. John Berryman, *Stephen Crane* (New York: World Pub. Co., 1950), p. 83.
10. S. S. McClure, *My Autobiography,* p. 172.
11. George Plimpton, "Malcolm Cowley Writing and Talking," *New York Times Book Review,* April 30 1978, p. 7.
12. "Books New and Old," *Atlantic Monthly,* 92 (1903), p. 695.
13. Arthur Bartlett Maurice, "Jack London's 'The Call of the Wild,' " *The Bookman,* 18 (1903–1904), p. 160.
14. "Fiction," *Critic,* 43 (July–December 1903), p. 582.
15. "Literary Table: Glimpses of New Books," *Current Literature,* 35 (July–December 1903), p. 369.
16. "The Call of the Wild," *Athenaeum,* (July–December 1903), p. 279.
17. William Morton Payne, "Recent Fiction," *The Dial,* 35 (1903), p. 261.
18. George Jean Nathan, *The Theatre Book of the Year 1942–1943* (New York: Alfred A. Knopf, 1943), p. 68.
19. Roderick Nash, ed., *The Call of the Wild: 1900–1916* (New York: George Braziller, 1970), p. 2.
20. James I. McClintock, *White Logic,* p. 110.
21. Jack London, *Faith of Men,* pp. 201, 207, 212, 231.
22. Jack London, *The Call of the Wild* (New York: Macmillan Co., 1903), pp. 18–19, 18.
23. Ibid., pp. 15, 25, 32, 33.
24. Ibid., pp. 43, 34–37, 45, 45.
25. Jack London, *Son of the Wolf,* p. 147.
26. Jack London, *Call of the Wild,* pp. 89, 98, 99.
27. Ibid., p. 62.
28. Walter Fuller Taylor, *A History of American Letters* (New York: American Book Company, 1936), p. 317.
29. Philo S. Buck, "The American Barbarian," *Methodist Review,* 94 (1912), p. 718.
30. Jack London, *Call of the Wild,* pp. 144, 145, 157.
31. Ibid., pp. 198–99, 189.
32. Jack London, "Husky—The Wolf-Dog of the North," *Harper's Weekly,* 44 (1900), p. 611.
33. Jack London, *Call of the Wild,* pp. 193, 197, 207, 223.
34. Jack London, *Call of the Wild,* pp. 228–31.

35. Ibid., p. 113.
36. *Berkeley Advance,* March 8, 1906, p. 4.
37. *San Francisco Chronicle,* December 22, 1905, p. 6.
38. "The Dearth of Ideas and Some Recent Novels," *The Bookman,* 38 (September–February 1913–1914), p. 542.
39. Frederick J. Hoffman, *The Modern Novel in America* (Chicago: Regnery, 1951), p. 40.
40. Jack London, *The Sea Wolf,* p. 270.
41. Jack London, *Children of the Frost,* p. 218.
42. Jack London, *People of the Abyss,* p. 279.
43. Jack London, "The Somnambulists," *Independent,* 61 (July–December 1906), pp. 1451–54.
44. Don M. Wolfe, ed., *The Image of Man in America* (New York: Thomas Y. Crowell, 1970), pp. 203–4.
45. Jack London, *Son of the Wolf,* p. 92.
46. Brochure, *Jack London: His Life and Literary Works,* Macmillan Co. Courtesy of the I. Milo Shepard Estate.
47. Theodore Dreiser, *Sister Carrie* (Garden City: International Collectors Library, n.d.), p. 75.
48. Frank Norris, *McTeague* (New York: Doubleday, Page & Co., 1920), pp. 2, 3, 42, 43.
49. Ernest Marchand, *Frank Norris: A Study* (New York: Octagon Books, 1964), pp. 102–3.
50. Robert H. Elias, ed., *Letters of Theodore Dreiser* (Philadelphia: University of Pennsylvania Press, 1959), p. 329. Reprinted by permission.
51. Howard Mumford Jones and Walter B. Rideout, eds., *Letters of Sherwood Anderson* (Boston: Little, Brown and Co., 1953), p. 444. Reprinted by permission.
52. "Animal Stories," *Independent,* 61 (July–December 1906), pp. 1055–56.
53. "Current Fiction," *Nation,* 83 (July–December 1906), pp. 440–41.
54. Grace Isabel Colbron, "Jack London's 'White Fang,' " *The Bookman,* 24 (1906–1907), p. 600.
55. "Nature-Books for the Holidays," *The Dial,* 41 (July 1–December 16, 1906), p. 389.
56. Herbert W. Horwill, "Present-Day Tendencies in Fiction," *Forum,* 38 (July–June 1906–1907), p. 549.
57. Elting E. Morison et al., eds., *The Letters of Theodore Roosevelt* (Cambridge: Harvard University Press, 1952), p. 617. Reprinted by permission.
58. Edward B. Clark, "Roosevelt on the Nature Fakirs," *Everybody's Magazine,* 16 (June 1907), pp. 771–72.
59. Jack London, "The Other Animals," *Collier's,* 41 (March 28–September 19, 1908), pp. 10–11, 25–26.
60. Elting K. Morison, *Letters of Theodore Roosevelt,* VI, (Cambridge: Harvard University Press, 1952), p. 1222. Reprinted by permission.
61. Jack London, *The Call of the Wild,* p. 207.
62. Theodore Roosevelt, "Nature Fakirs," *Everybody's Magazine,* 17 (July–December 1907), p. 428.
63. Barry Lopez, "What Are Wolves? Undoing the Myths," *Travel & Leisure,* 7 (January 1977), p. 7.
64. Barry Lolstun Lopez, *Of Wolves and Men* (New York: Scribners, 1978), p. 218.

65. Jack London, *Faith of Men,* p. 260.
66. Jack London, *Children of the Frost,* pp. 48, 49.
67. L. David Mech, *The Wolf* (Garden City: Natural History Press, 1970), pp. 291, 292, 293.
68. Farley Mowat, *Never Cry Wolf* (Boston: Little, Brown and Co., 1963), pp. 80–81.
69. Bill Mason to John Perry, February 5, 1977.
70. Roger A. Caras to John Perry, September 22, 1976, in *The Custer Wolf* (Boston: Little, Brown and Co., 1966).
71. Roger A. Caras to John Perry, May 14, 1978.
72. Sidney Alexander, "Jack London's Literary Lycanthropy," *Reporter,* 16 (January–June 1957), p. 46.
73. Stephen Graham, *The Death of Yesterday* (London: Ernest Benn, 1930), p. 58.

Notes: Chapter 9

1. Arthur Stringer, "The Canada Fakers," *Canada West,* 4 (October 1908), p. 1140.
2. Ibid., pp. 1140, 1142.
3. Jack London, *Children of the Frost,* p. 189.
4. Ibid., p. 156.
5. Jack London, *The Son of the Wolf,* p. 48.
6. Jack London, *The Call of the Wild,* pp. 71–72, 90, 91.
7. Jack London, "The Terrible and Tragic in Fiction," pp. 542, 540.
8. Sonia Orwell and Ian Angus, *The Collected Essays, Journalism and Letters of George Orwell* (New York: Harcourt, Brace & World, 1968), pp. 26, 25.
9. Alfred S. Shivers, "The Romantic in Jack London," *Alaska Review,* 1 (1963–1964), p. 42.
10. "Lost Face," *Nation,* 90 (January–June 1910), p. 403.
11. Jack London, *God of His Fathers,* p. 29.
12. Jack London, *Children of the Frost,* p. 102.
13. Jack London and Anna Strunsky, *Kempton-Wace Letters,* p. 203.
14. Jack London, *The Game* (New York: Macmillan Co., 1905), p. 69.
15. C. Hartley Grattan, "Jack London," *The Bookman,* 68 (September–February, 1928–1929), p. 669.
16. Jonathan Harold Spinner, "Jack London's *Martin Eden*: The Development of the Existential Hero," *Michigan Academician,* 3 (Summer 1970), p. 43.
17. Earle Labor, *Jack London* (New York; Twayne Publ., 1974), p. 69.
18. T. K. Whipple, "Jack London—Wonder Boy," *Saturday Review of Literature,* 18 (April 30–October 22, 1938), p. 3.
19. Wilfrid Lay, "John Barleycorn Under Psychoanalysis," *The Bookman,* 45 (1917), p. 47.
20. Joan London, *Jack London and His Times,* p. 50.
21. Michael S. Lasky, "James Jones Has Come Home to Whistle," *Writer's Digest,* October 1976, p. 52. Reprinted by permission.
22. John McCole, *Lucifer at Large* (New York: Longmans, Green and Co., 1937), p. 26.

23. Van Wyck Brooks, *Sketches in Criticism* (London: J. M. Dent & Sons, 1934), p. 248.
24. Carl Van Doren, *The American Novel* (New York: Macmillan Co., 1940), p. 238.
25. Alfred Kazin, *On Native Grounds* (New York: Reynal & Hitchcock, 1942), p. 115.
26. James I. McClintock, *White Logic*, p. 85.
27. Anna Strunsky, *The Masses*, p. 14.
28. Maxwell Geismar, *Rebels and Ancestors: The American Novel, 1890–1915* (Boston: Houghton Mifflin, 1953), pp. 144, 215, 195.
29. Jack London, *Son of the Wolf*, p. 89.
30. "Notes on New Novels," *The Dial*, 57 (July 1–December 16, 1914), p. 342.
31. William Morton Payne, "Recent Fiction," *The Dial*, 38 (1905), p. 16.
32. Jack London, *The Sea Wolf*, p. 249.
33. L. Frank Tooker, *The Joys and Tribulatioms of an Editor* (New York: Century Co., 1924), pp. 280, 282–83.
34. Joan London, *Jack London and His Times*, p. 92.
35. Robert Underwood Johnson, *Remembered Yesterdays* (Boston: Little, Brown, and Co., 1923), pp. 121, 127.
36. Porter Garnett, "Jack London—His Relation to Literary Art," *Pacific Monthly*, 17 (January–June 1907), p. 449.
37. "Jack London," *Literary Digest*, 53 (October–December 1916), p. 1538.
38. *Sinclair Lewis: An American Life* by Mark Schorer, Copyright © 1961 by Mark Schorer, McGraw-Hill Book Company, Inc. Reprinted by permission of Brandt & Brandt Literary Agents, Inc., p. 166.
39. Joseph Noel, *Footlose in Arcadia*, p. 194.
40. Georgia Loring Bamford, *Mystery of Jack London*, pp. 137, 136.
41. Ludwig Lewisohn, *The Story of American Literature* (New York: Harper & Bros., 1932), p. 325.
42. Jack London, *The Sea Wolf*, p. 79.
43. Edward Biron Payne, *Soul of Jack London* (London: Rider & Co., n.d.), p. 98. Reprinted by permission.
44. "Recent Fiction," *Nation*, 79 (July–December 1904), p. 507.
45. "A Review of the Season's Books," *Outlook*, 78 (September–December 1904), p. 872.
46. Frederick Taber Cooper, "The Man's Novel and Some Recent Books," *The Bookman*, 20 (1904–1905), p. 219.
47. "New Novels," *Athenaeum*, July–December 1904, p. 801.
48. *San Francisco Chronicle*, September 5, 1914, p. 1.
49. Jack London, *The Sea Wolf*, p. 50.
50. Frank Pease, "Impressions of Jack London," *Seven Arts*, 1 (December 1916–April 1917), p. 523.
51. Jack London, *The Sea Wolf*, pp. 98, 213, 18–19.
52. Ibid., pp. 33, 43, 35, 129, 141.
53. Ibid., p. 115.
54. Ibid., pp. 52, 124, 203–4.
55. Ibid., pp. 79, 108, 109.
56. Ibid., p. 106.
57. Lavon B. Carroll, "Jack London and the American Image," *American Book Collector*, 13 (1962–1963), p. 25.

58. "Jack London," *Nation,* 103 (July–December 1916), p. 502.
59. Robert H. Woodward, "Jack London's Code of Primitivism," *Folio,* 18 (May 1953), p. 43.
60. Jack London, *The Sea Wolf,* pp. 177, 178, 212, 339–40.
61. Bertha Clark Pope, ed., *The Letters of Ambrose Bierce* (San Francisco: Book Club of California, 1922), p. 105. Reprinted by permission.
62. Jack London, *The Sea Wolf,* pp. 354, 362, 366.
63. George Sterling to Jack London, April 1, 1914.
64. George Sterling to Jack London, December 27, 1914.
65. "The New Books," *Outlook,* 108 (September–December 1914), p. 846.
66. Arthur Hobson Quinn, *American Fiction* (New York: D. Appleton-Century Co., 1936), p. 544.
67. "Mere Adventure," *New Republic,* November–January 1914–1915, p. 29.

Notes: Chapter 10

1. *San Francisco Examiner,* August 9, 1959, p. 8.
2. Herbert Croly, *Willard Straight* (New York: Macmillan Co., 1924), pp. 125, 126.
3. Eiji Tsujii, "Jack London Items in the Japanese Press of 1904," *Jack London Newsletter,* 7–8 (1974–1975), p. 56.
4. Lloyd C. Griscom, *Diplomatically Speaking* (New York: Literary Guild of America, 1940), pp. 245–46.
5. Eiji Tsujii, *Jack London Newsletter,* p. 57.
6. Frederick Arthur McKenzie, *From Tokyo to Tiflis* (London: Hurst and Blackett, 1905), p. 65.
7. Ibid., p. 90.
8. Robert Dunn, *World Alive* (New York: Crown Publ., 1956), pp. 117–18.
9. Ibid., pp. 118–19.
10. *San Francisco Chronicle,* February 9, 1920, p. 8.
11. Frederick Arthur McKenzie, *From Tokyo to Tiflis,* pp. 153–54.
12. William Maxwell, *From the Yalu to Port Arthur* (London: Hutchinson & Co., 1906), pp. 95–96.
13. John Fox, Jr., *Following the Sun-Flag* (New York: Charles Scribner's Sons, 1905), pp. 97, 186, 158.
14. *San Francisco Examiner,* September 25, 1904, p. 45.
15. Frederick Palmer, *With My Own Eyes* (Indianapolis: Bobbs-Merrill Co., 1933), p. 242.
16. *San Francisco Examiner,* September 25, 1904, p. 45.
17. Louis Livingston Seaman, *From Tokio through Manchuria with the Japanese* (New York: D. Appleton and Co., 1905), p. 8.
18. Frederick Palmer, *With Kuroki in Manchuria* (New York: Charles Scribner's Sons, 1904), pp. 2–3.
19. Frederick Palmer, *With My Own Eyes,* p. 238.
20. Fairfax Downey, *Richard Harding Davis: His Day* (New York: Charles Scribner's Sons, 1933), p. 2.
21. Richard O'Connor, *Jack London: A Biography,* pp. 220–21.
22. Frederick Palmer, *With My Own Eyes,* p. 242.
23. *San Francisco Chronicle,* June 29, 1904, p. 16.

24. *San Francisco Chronicle,* July 1, 1904, p. 16.
25. Carrie Rand Sterling to Gertrude Partington, April 27, 1905. Partington Collection, Bancroft Library, University of California at Berkeley.
26. Joseph Noel, *Footloose in Arcadia,* p. 150.
27. Jack London, *Children of the Frost,* p. 25.
28. Jack London, *Daughter of the Snows,* p. 111.
29. Jack London, *Sea Wolf,* p. 225.
30. *San Francisco Chronicle,* June 30, 1904, p. 9.
31. *San Francisco Chronicle,* August 7, 1904, p. 25.
32. Joan London, "The London Divorce," *American Book Collector,* 17 (November 1966), p. 31.
33. Jack London, *Sea Wolf,* p. 68.
34. Reprinted from *My Lifetime in Letters* by Upton Sinclair by permission of the University of Missouri Press. Copyright 1960 by the Curators of the University of Missouri, p. 31.

Notes: Chapter 11

1. Letters of George Sterling to Jack London.
2. Michael Paul Orth, "A Biography of George Sterling," (M.A. thesis, San Francisco State College, 1963). A fine study of Sterling's life, with a valuable bibliography.
3. Ambrose Bierce, *The Collected Works of Ambrose Bierce,* 10 (New York: Neale Publ. Co., 1909–1912), p. 181. Reprinted by permission.
4. Upton Sinclair, "My Friend George Sterling," *The Bookman,* 66 (September–February 1927–1928), p. 30.
5. Ambrose Bierce, "An Insurrection of the Peasantry," *Cosmopolitan,* 44 (1907–1908), p. 224.
6. Ann N. Ridgeway, ed., *The Selected Letters of Robinson Jeffers* (Baltimore: Johns Hopkins Press, 1968), pp. 54, 35, 29, 38. Reprinted by permission.
7. Guy J. Forgue, ed., *Letters of H. L. Mencken* (New York: Alfred A. Knopf, 1961), p. 229. Reprinted by permission.
8. Gertrude Atherton, *My San Francisco* (Indianapolis: Bobbs-Merrill Company, 1946), p. 100.
9. Walter Neale, *Life of Ambrose Bierce* (New York: AMS Press, 1969), p. 333.
10. M. E. Grenadier, *Ambrose Bierce* (New York: Twayne Publ., 1971), p. 70.
11. Michael Paul Orth, *Biography of George Sterling,* pp. 118, 120.
12. Bertha Clark Pope, ed., *Letters of Ambrose Bierce,* pp. 113, 150.
13. George Sterling, "The Shadow Maker," *American Mercury,* 6 (September–December 1925), pp. 13–14.
14. Ibid., p. 10.
15. M. E. Grenadier, *Ambrose Bierce,* p. 71.
16. Joan London, *Jack London and His Times,* p. 259.
17. George Sterling to Jack London: August 7, 1906; July 9, 1913; October 26, 1912.
18. Jack London and Anna Strunsky, *Kempton-Wace Letters,* pp. 19–20.
19. Guy J. Forgue, ed., *Letters of H. L. Mencken,* p. 332.

20. Michael Paul Orth, *Biography of George Sterling,* p. 211.
21. Walter Neale, *Life of Ambrose Bierce,* pp. 305–6.
22. W. A. Swanburg, *Dreiser* (New York: Charles Scribner's Sons, 1965), p. 261.
23. Arnold Genthe, *As I Remember* (New York: Reynal & Hitchcock, 1936), p. 75.
24. Miriam Allen deFord, *They Were San Franciscans* (Caldwell, Idaho: Caxton Printers, 1947), p. 309.
25. Richard O'Connor, *Jack London: A Biography,* pp. 375–76.
26. Theodore Dreiser, *Sister Carrie,* p. 4.
27. William Inglis, *Champions Off Guard* (New York: Vanguard Press, 1932), p. 110.
28. John Perry, *James A. Herne: The American Ibsen* (Chicago: Nelson-Hall, 1978), pp. 159, 158.
29. William McDevitt, *Jack London's First* (San Francisco: Recorder-Sunset Press, 1946), p. 13.
30. Jack London, "The King of Mazy May," *Youth's Companion,* 73 (1899), p. 629.
31. Jack London, "A Lesson in Heraldry," *National Magazine,* 11–12 (1899–1900), p. 636.
32. Kevin Starr, *Americans and the California Dream,* p. 230.
33. Jack London, *The Sea Wolf,* pp. 259–60.
34. Robert Barltrop, *Jack London: The Man, the Writer, the Rebel,* p. 68.
35. Joan London, *Jack London and His Times,* p. 260.
36. Robert Forrey, "Male & Female in London's *The Sea Wolf,*" *Literature and Psychology,* 22–24 (1972–1974), pp. 137–38.
37. George Sterling to Jack London, December 14, 1911.
38. Mary Austin, "George Sterling at Carmel," *American Mercury,* 11 (May–August 1927), p. 68.
39. Arnold Genthe, *As I Remember,* p. 74.
40. Upton Sinclair, *The Cup of Fury* (Great Neck, New York: Channel Press, 1956), p. 71.
41. George Sterling to Jack London, November 18, 1910.
42. George Sterling to Jack London, February 1, 1913.
43. Franklin Walker, "Jack London's Use of Sinclair Lewis Plots, Together with a Printing of Three of the Plots," *Huntington Library Quarterly,* 17 (November 1953–August 1954), p. 64.
44. Jack London, "The Dignity of Dollars," *The Overland Monthly,* 36 (July–December 1900), pp. 53–56; ibid., 50 (July–December 1907), pp. 592–95.
45. Richard O'Connor, *Jack London: A Biography,* p. 328.
46. Mark Schorer, *Sinclair Lewis,* p. 169.
47. Ibid., p. 187.
48. Ibid., p. 186.
49. Harry E. Maule and Melville H. Cane, eds., *The Man from Main Street* (New York: Random House, 1953), p. 124. Reprinted by permission.
50. "Recent Fiction and the Critics," *Current Literature,* 42 (January–June 1907), p. 111.
51. L. A. M. Bosworth, "Is Jack London a Plagiarist?" *Independent,* 62 (January–June 1907), pp. 373–75.
52. *San Francisco Call,* October 19, 1906, p. 15.

53. "Chronicle and Comment," *The Bookman,* 25 (1907), p. 115.
54. George Sterling to Jack London: July 7, 1906; October 16, 1906; September 28, 1906; October 22, 1906.
55. Bertha Clark Pope, ed., *Letters of Ambrose Bierce,* p. 153.
56. "The Old Story," *The Bookman,* 23 (1906), p. 369.
57. Clipping, *New York Telegraph,* November 27, 1906, Theatre Collection, Library of Performing Arts at Lincoln Center, New York.
58. Frank Norris, *Vandover and the Brute* (Garden City: Doubleday, Doran & Co., 1928), p. 242.
59. Franklin Walker, "Frank Norris and Jack London," *Mills College Magazine,* 56 (Spring 1966), p. 16.
60. Frank Harris, "Mr. Jack London: Knave or Fool, or Knave and Fool?", *Vanity Fair,* 83 (July–December 1909), p. 103.
61. Frank Harris, "How Mr. Jack London Writes a Novel," *Vanity Fair,* 82 (1909), p. 454.
62. Frank Harris, "Mr. Jack London Again," *Vanity Fair,* 83 (July–December 1909), p. 519.
63. Philippa Pullar, *Frank Harris* (London: Hamish Hamilton, 1975), p. 332.
64. Franklin Walker, "A New Jack London Bibliography," *CEA Critic,* 34 (1971–1972), p. 29.
65. *Oakland Tribune,* November 28, 1932, p. B3.
66. Jack London, "Getting into Print," p. 82.

Notes: Chapter 12

1. *San Francisco Examiner,* August 27, 1905, p. 47.
2. P. S. Williams, "Jack London, Lecturer," *The Overland Monthly,* 48 (1906), p. 249.
3. *San Francisco Examiner,* March 16, 1911, p. 1.
4. Philip S. Foner, *Jack London: American Rebel,* p. 70.
5. Joan London, *Jack London and His Times,* p. 297.
6. William Trufant Foster, "Random Notes on Public Speaking," *Quarterly Journal of Speech,* 33 (1947), p. 139.
7. Jack London, "Revolution," *Contemporary Review.*
8. *Los Angeles Examiner,* January 9, 1905, p. 7.
9. *Common Sense,* January 14, 1905, p. 1.
10. *Daily Californian,* January 23, 1905, p. 1.
11. Ibid.
12. *California Writers Club Quarterly Bulletin,* 4 (December 1916), p. 9.
13. *San Francisco Call,* August 31, 1911, p. 1
14. *San Francisco Examiner,* February 25, 1902, p. 9.
15. *San José Mercury,* January 29, 1908, p. 1.
16. John Ellis, "Tribute to Mother Jones," *Miners Magazine,* January 25, 1906, p. 13.
17. William Whalen to John Perry, July 16, 1976, Harvard University Library.
18. *Harvard Advocate,* January 19, 1906, p. 1.
19. *San Francisco Chronicle,* December 19, 1904, p. 14.
20. "Jack London and Silk-Stocking Society," *Miners Magazine,* April 13, 1905, p. 12.
21. *San Francisco Chronicle,* December 21, 1905, p. 2.

22. *Santa Rosa Democrat,* December 21, 1905, p. 1.
23. *Boston Post,* December 27, 1905, p. 8.
24. "Jack London at Harvard and Faneuil Hall," *Arena,* 35 (1906), p. 187.
25. *Boston Herald,* December 27, 1905, p. 2.
26. Ibid.
27. Michael Paul Orth, "A Biography of George Sterling," p. 144.
28. Philip S. Foner, *Jack London: American Rebel,* p. 71.
29. *San Francisco Call,* November 21, 1905, p. 4.
30. *Boston Transcript,* December 27, 1905, p. 2.
31. *New York Times,* January 20, 1906, p. 1.
32. Ibid.
33. Jack London and Anna Strunsky, *Kempton-Wace Letters,* p. 70.
34. *New York Times,* January 20, 1906, p. 1.
35. Ibid.
36. P. S. Williams, *The Overland Monthly,* p. 250.
37. Upton Sinclair, *Cup of Fury,* p. 51.
38. Upton Sinclair, "About Jack London," *The Masses,* 10 (November–December 1917), p. 17.
39. Upton Sinclair, *The Autobiography of Upton Sinclair* (New York: Harcourt, Brace & World, 1962), p. 248.
40. Guy J. Forgue, editor, *Letters of H. L. Mencken,* p. 97.
41. Upton Sinclair, "About Jack London," p. 17.
42. Jack London, "Jack London and 'The Jungle,' " *Wilshire's Magazine,* 6–10 (October 1904–December 1906), p. 13.
43. Leon Harris, *Upton Sinclair: American Rebel* (New York: Thomas Y. Crowell Co., 1975), p. 81.
44. Philip S. Foner, *Jack London: American Rebel,* pp. 72–73.
45. *San Francisco Chronicle,* April 16, 1905, p. 34.
46. *San Francisco Chronicle,* October 2, 1939, p. 11.
47. Alexander Irvine, *From the Bottom Up* (New York: Doubleday, Page & Co., 1910), pp. 251, 253.
48. Ibid., p. 255.
49. "Jack London to Yale Men," *Yale Alumni Weekly,* January 31, 1906, pp. 343–44.
50. Philip S. Foner, *Jack London: American Rebel,* p. 75.
51. Mark Shorer, *Sinclair Lewis* (New York: McGraw-Hill Book Co., 1961), p. 104.
52. "Jack London to Yale Men," p. 343.
53. Joan London, *Jack London and His Times,* p. 301.
54. Jack London, "Things Alive," *Yale Monthly Magazine,* March 1906, pp. 77, 79.
55. Ira Kipnis, *The American Socialist Movement 1897–1912* (New York: Greenwood Press, 1968), p. 299.
56. David A. Shannor., *The Socialist Party of America* (New York: Macmillan Co., 1955), pp. 56–57.
57. *New York Times,* February 1, 1906, p. 8.
58. *New York Times,* February 5, 1906, p. 8.
59. "Derby Neck Under Jack London's Yoke," *Wilshire's Magazine,* 6–10 (October 1904–December 1906), p. 6.
60. *New York Times,* February 10, 1906, p. 8.

61. Will Irwin, *The Making of a Reporter* (New York: G. P. Putnam's Sons, 1942), p. 84.
62. Joan London, *Jack London and His Times*, p. 136.
63. William McDevitt, *Jack London as Poet and as Platform Man* (San Francisco: Recorder-Sunset Press, 1947), pp. 20, 16.
64. *Minneapolis Tribune*, February 3, 1906, p. 3.

Notes: Chapter 13

1. Joshua Slocum, *Sailing Alone Around the World* (London: Rupert Hart-Davis, 1955), pp. 33, 32.
2. George Sterling to Jack London, May 25, 1906.
3. R. S. London, *The Hunting of the Snark: An Agony in Eight Fits* (New York: Clarkson N. Potter, 1975), p. 6.
4. Ibid., p. 19.
5. "Jack London at Sea," *The Bookman*, 28 (1908–1909), p. 5.
6. George Sterling to Jack London, July 1, 1906.
7. Osa Johnson, *I Married Adventure* (Philadelphia: J. B. Lippincott, 1950). Reprinted by permission of Harper & Row, Publishers, Inc., p. 44.
8. Ibid., p. 45.
9. Martin Johnson, *Through the South Seas with Jack London* (New York: Dodd, Mead & Co., 1913), pp. 40, 38.
10. George Sterling to Jack London, April 18, 1906.
11. Walter Lord, *The Good Years: From 1900 to the First World War* (New York: Harper & Bros., 1960), p. 138.
12. Jack London, "The Story of an Eye-Witness," *Collier's*, 37 (March 31–September 22, 1906), p. 22.
13. *San Francisco Call*, April 21, 1907, p. 35.
14. *San Francisco Chronicle*, April 23, 1907, p. 13.
15. Martin Johnson, *Through the South Seas with Jack London*, p. 51.
16. David Klein and Mary Louise Johnson, *They Took to the Sea* (New Brunswick: Rutgers University Press, 1948), pp. 21–22.
17. Ibid., pp. 336, 338.
18. Osa Johnson, *I Married Adventure*, p. 51.
19. Ibid.
20. Joshua Slocum, *Sailing Alone Around the World*, p. 144.
21. Edwin Emerson, "As to Jack London," *United States Army & Navy Journal*, 51 (1913–1914), p. 556.
22. Martin Johnson, *Through the South Seas with Jack London*, p. 67.
23. Ibid., p. 72.
24. *San Francisco Chronicle*, May 29, 1907, p. 12.
25. Jack London, "To Build a Fire," *Youth's Companion*, May 29, 1902, p. 275.
26. Jack London, *Son of the Wolf*, p. 35.
27. Andrew Farrell, ed., *Writings of Lorrin A. Thurston* (Honolulu: Advertiser Pub. Co., 1936), pp. 105–6.
28. Ibid., pp. 108–9.
29. *San Francisco Chronicle*, August 18, 1907, p. 46.
30. Martin Johnson, *Through the South Seas with Jack London*, pp. 117, 119, 128–29, 130.

31. Charmian London, *Our Hawaii,* pp. 125–26, 130.
32. *Honolulu Sunday Advertiser,* January 23, 1910, p. 8.
33. Andrew Farrell, ed., *Writings of Lorrin A. Thurston,* pp. 121–22, 124.
34. George Sterling to Jack London, February 23, 1915.
35. *San Francisco Evening Globe,* May 10, 1909, p. 1
36. Martin Johnson, *Through the South Seas with Jack London,* p. 102.
37. "London at Sea," *Sunset Magazine,* 19 (1907), p. 400.
38. Martin Johnson, *Through the South Seas with Jack London,* p. 150.
39. Ibid., pp. 151–52.
40. Fred Lockley, "Impressions of and Observations of the Journal Man," *Oregon Journal,* January 5, 1923, Section I, p. 8.
41. Martin Johnson, *Through the South Seas with Jack London,* p. 150.
42. John K. Winkler, *Morgan the Magnificent* (New York: Vanguard Press, 1930), pp. 218, 258–59.
43. Arthur Calder-Marshall, ed., *The Bodley Head Jack London,* 3 (London: Bodley Head, 1964), p. 16.
44. Ibid.
45. George Brett to Ninetta Eames, July 29, 1908. Letters from George Brett are in Macmillan Company Records, Manuscripts and Archives Division, The New York Public Library, Astor, Lenox and Tilden Foundations.
46. George Brett to Ninetta Eames, May 24, 1909.
47. "Current Fiction," *Nation,* 89 (1909), p. 406.
48. "Martin Eden," *Independent,* 67 (July–December 1909), p. 980.
49. "Recent Fiction and the Critics," *Current Fiction,* 47 (July–December 1909), p. 695.
50. "Recent Fiction," *Dial,* 47 (July–December 1909), p. 386.
51. Arthur Calder-Marshall, *The Bodley Head Jack London,* 3, p. 10.
52. Robert Barltrop, *Jack London: The Man, the Writer, the Rebel,* p. 133.
53. Jack London, "Samuel," *The Bookman,* 37 (March–August 1913), p. 285.
54. James A. Michener, *A Hawaiian Reader* (New York: Appleton-Century-Crofts, 1959), pp. xiv–xv.
55. Katherine Mansfield, *Novels and Novelists* (New York: Alfred A. Knopf, 1930), p. 257.
56. Osa Johnson, *I Married Adventure,* pp. 57–58.
57. Ibid., pp. 58–59.
58. George Sterling to Jack London, October 29, 1911.
59. Martin Johnson, *Through the South Seas with Jack London,* p. 283.
60. Ibid., p. 313.

Notes: Chapter 14

1. George Brett to Jack London, May 19, 1910. Letters from George Brett are in Macmillan Company Records, Manuscripts and Archives Division, the New York Public Library, Astor, Lenox and Tilden foundations.
2. George Brett to Jack London, June 1, 1910.
3. George Brett to Charmian London, August 1, 1912.
4. Edward Barnett, *Friday Nights* (New York: Alfred A. Knopf, 1922), p. 259.
5. William Morton Payne, "Recent Fiction," *The Dial,* 49 (1910), p. 384.
6. Jack London, *Faith of Men,* p. 244.

7. Jack London, *Children of the Frost*, p. 10.
8. Ibid., p. 206.
9. Jack London, *God of His Fathers*, p. 293.
10. George Brett to Jack London, January 9, 1911.
11. "Some Notable Books of the Year," *Independent*, 69 (1910), p. 1092.
12. *New York Times*, November 5, 1910, p. 622.
13. "The New Books," *Outlook*, 102 (September–December 1912), p. 320.
14. *Athenaeum*, 4472 (July–December 1913), p. 37.
15. Excerpts from *Final Verdict* by Adela Rogers St. Johns. Copyright (c) by Adela Rogers St. Johns. Reprinted by permission of Doubleday & Company, Inc., p. 354.
16. *San Francisco Examiner*, June 22, 1910, p. 1.
17. *San Francisco Chronicle*, July 9, 1910, p. 4.
18. *San Francisco Chronicle*, August 2, 1910, p. 4.
19. *San Francisco Call*, August 3, 1910, p. 4.
20. *San Francisco Chronicle*, August 2, 1910, p. 4.
21. *Oakland Enquirer*, April 1, 1910, p. 20.
22. *San Francisco Examiner*, Sporting Section, February 21, 1909, p. 35.
23. James J. Corbett, *The Roar of the Crowd* (New York: Garden City Pub. Co., 1926), p. 300.
24. *San Francisco Examiner*, November 16, 1901, p. 2.
25. Jack Johnson, *In the Ring and Out* (London: Proteus, 1977), p. 131.
26. Nat Fleischer, *The Heavyweight Championship* (New York: G. P. Putnam's Sons, 1961), p. 141.
27. *Oakland Enquirer*, July 21, 1910, p. 12.
28. Lester Bromberg, *Boxing's Unforgettable Fights* (New York: Ronald Press, 1962), p. 63.
29. "New Novels," *Athenaeum*, (July–December 1905), p. 138.
30. "Notes on New Novels," *Atlantic Monthly*, 97 (1906), p. 49.
31. Frederick Taber Cooper, "The Individual Note and Some Recent Books," *The Bookman*, 22 (September 1905–February 1906), p. 35.
32. "Literature," *Independent*, 58 (January–June 1905), p. 1480.
33. "The Book-Buyer's Guide," *Critic*, 47 (1905), p. 285.
34. Jack London, *The Game*, pp. 45, 66, 112, 113–14.
35. Maxwell Geismar, *Rebels and Ancestors*, p. 179.
36. Jack London, *The Game*, pp. 117–18.
37. Ibid., pp. 169–70.
38. Richard O'Connor, *Jack London: A Biography*, p. 239.
39. Russell Blakenship, *American Literature* (New York: Holt, Rinehart and Winston, 1949), pp. 567–68.
40. Charmian London, *The Book of Jack London*, II, pp. 241, 255.
41. Isaac F. Marcosson, *Before I Forget* (New York: Dodd, Mead & Co., 1959), p. 516.
42. Joseph Noel, *Footloose in Arcadia*, p. 231.
43. Upton Sinclair, *Cup of Fury*, p. 165.
44. *Boston Transcript*, August 20, 1913, p. 18.
45. "The New Books," *Independent*, 76 (October–December 1913), p. 36.
46. *San Francisco Bulletin*, September 17, 1913, p. 8.
47. "Notes," *Nation*, 97 (July–December 1913), p. 190.
48. *New York Times*, November 3, 1915, p. 1.

49. Stephen Graham, *The Death of Yesterday* (London: E. Benn, 1930), p. 60.

Notes: Chapter 15

1. Jack London, *A Daughter of the Snows*, p. 219.
2. Kevin Starr, *Americans and the California Dream 1850–1915*, p. 210.
3. Chris Boyle, "Adela Rogers St. Johns, Reliving the Good Life," *Writer's Digest*, April 1980, p. 31. Also courtesy of Adela Rogers St. Johns.
4. Jack London, "What Communities Lose by the Competitive System," *Cosmopolitan*, 30 (1900–1901), p. 59.
5. Bailey Millard, "Jack London, Farmer," *The Bookman*, 44 (September–February 1916–1917), p. 152.
6. L. Rudio Marshall, "Mrs. Jack London's New Viewpoint," *The Overland Monthly*, 69 (May 1917), p. 401.
7. Bailey Millard, "Jack London, Farmer," p. 152.
8. Upton Sinclair, *Cup of Fury*, p. 164.
9. "The Valley of the Moon," *The Bookman*, 38 (1913–1914), p. 542.
10. Lewis Mumford, *The Golden Day* (New York: Horace Liveright, 1932), p. 247.
11. *Sinclair Lewis on the Valley of the Moon*, pamphlet distributed by Harvard University Press through Harvey Taylor, Rare Book Room, Cornell University.
12. Waldo Frank, *Our America* (New York: Boni and Liveright, 1919), p. 37.
13. *Santa Rosa Republican*, December 14, 1915, p. 8.
14. *Santa Rosa Republican*, May 24, 1915, p. 4.
15. *Santa Rosa Republican*, December 15, 1915, p. 1.
16. *Santa Rosa Republican*, January 28, 1916, p. 3.
17. George Sterling to Jack London, June 3, 1914.
18. George Sterling to Jack London, September 30, 1914.
19. George Sterling to Jack London, October 3, 1911.
20. *San Francisco Chronicle*, January 8, 1911, p. 78.
21. *Santa Rosa Press Democrat*, October 27, 1915, p. 6.
22. *Santa Rosa Republican*, February 20, 1915, p. 8.
23. *San Francisco Chronicle*, December 31, 1916, p. 38.
24. Charles Child Walcutt, *American Literary Naturalism* (Minneapolis: University of Minnesota Press, 1956), p. 89.
25. "Jack London, Farmer," *Literary Digest*, 46 (January–June 1913), p. 1195.
26. *Oakland Tribune*, August 23, 1913, p. 1.
27. Ed Dieckmann, Jr., "The House That Jack Built," *National Parks Magazine*, 35 (November 1961), p. 5.
28. "Jack London's Unique Country Home," *Architect and Engineer*, 25 (July 1911), pp. 49, 51.
29. *Santa Rosa Press Democrat*, September 11, 1913, p. 5.
30. George Sterling to Jack London, August 24, 1913.
31. Van Wyck Brooks, *The Confident Years: 1885–1915* (New York: E. P. Dutton & Co., 1952), p. 235.
32. George Sterling to Jack London, September 21, 1916.

33. Joan London, *Jack London and His Times,* p. 371.
34. Mary Austin, "George Sterling at Carmel," *The American Mercury,* 11 (1927), p. 69.
35. Andrew Sinclair, *Jack: A Biography of Jack London,* p. 170.
36. Jack London, *Sea Wolf,* p. 343.
37. Frank Norris, *Vandover and the Brute* (New York: Doubleday, Doran & Co., 1928), p. 85.
38. George Sterling to Jack London, October 28, 1913.
39. George Sterling to Jack London, February 12, 1912.
40. Louis J. Stellmann, "Jack London—The Man," *The Overland Monthly,* 70 (October 1917), p. 386.
41. Adela Rogers St. Johns, *Final Verdict,* p. 358.
42. Martin Johnson, *Through the South Seas with Jack London,* p. 63.
43. Upton Sinclair, *Cup of Fury,* pp. 165–66.
44. Adela Rogers St. Johns, *Final Verdict,* p. 353.
45. William W. Ellsworth, *A Golden Age of Authors* (Boston: Houghton Mifflin Co., 1919), p. 102.
46. Jack London, "The Terrible and Tragic in Fiction," *Critic,* 42 (January–June 1903), p. 543.
47. Joan London, *Jack London and His Times,* p. 324.
48. Adela Rogers St. Johns, *Final Verdict,* pp. 354, 355, 356, 357.
49. *San Francisco Bulletin,* February 28, 1914, p. 3.
50. *San Francisco Chronicle,* December 2, 1916, p. 1.
51. *San Francisco Chronicle,* June 29, 1917, p. 2.
52. *Santa Rosa Press Democrat,* November 24, 1915, p. 5.
53. *San Francisco Chronicle,* May 6, 1913, p. 2.
54. *Santa Rosa Press Democrat,* November 25, 1915, p. 5.
55. *Santa Rosa Press Democrat,* November 24, 1915, p. 5.
56. *Santa Rosa Republican,* November 24, 1915, p. 1.
57. *San Francisco Chronicle,* December 20, 1905, p. 13.

Notes: Chapter 16

1. Richard Harding Davis, "When a War Is Not a War," *Scribner's Magazine,* 56 (July–December 1914), p. 43.
2. John W. Caughey and Ernest R. May, *A History of the United States* (Chicago: Rand McNally, 1965), p. 436.
3. "Current Fiction," *Nation,* 101 (July–December 1915), p. 548.
4. Rupert Scott, "Some Novels of the Month," *The Bookman,* 42 (September–February, 1915–1916), p. 720.
5. Jack London, "The 'Good' Soldier," *International Socialist Review,* 14 (1913–1914), p. 199.
6. "Edwin Emerson's Opinion of Jack London," *United States Army and Navy Journal,* 51 (1913–1914), p. 1436.
7. Philip Foner, *Jack London: American Rebel,* pp. 115–16.
8. Joan London, *Jack London and His Times,* p. 349.
9. Gerald Langford, *The Richard Harding Davis Years* (New York: Holt, Rinehart and Winston, 1961), p. 240.
10. Jack London, "The Red Game of War," *Collier's,* May 16, 1914; "With Funston's Men," May 23, 1914; "Mexico's Army and Ours," May 30,

1914; "The Trouble Makers of Mexico," June 13, 1914; "Lawgivers," June 20, 1914.

11. Arnold Chapman, *Spanish American Reception of U.S. Fiction* (Berkeley: University of California Press, 1966), p. 42–56.
12. Drewey Wayne Gunn, *American and British Writers in Mexico* (Austin: University of Texas Press, 1969), p. 69.
13. *New York Times,* April 27, 1914, p. 4.
14. Justin Kaplan, *Lincoln Steffens* (New York: Simon and Schuster, 1974), p. 212.
15. Jack London, "Our Adventures in Tampico," *Collier's,* June 27, 1914.
16. Oliver Madox Hueffer, "Jack London, A Personal Sketch," *New Statesman,* 8 (1916–1917), p. 206.
17. Robert Dunn, *World Alive: A Personal Story* (New York: Crown Publishers, 1956), p. 202.
18. Jack London, "Stalking the Pestilence," *Collier's,* 53 (March–September 1914), pp. 11–12, 28–29.
19. Fairfax Downey, *Richard Harding Davis: His Day,* p. 243.
20. Richard Harding Davis, "When a War Is Not a War," p. 50.
21. "Socialists and Rebels," *Nation,* 99 (July–December 1914), p. 7.
22. George Sterling to Jack London, June 27, 1914.
23. Joan London, *Jack London and His Times,* pp. 353, 350.
24. Floyd Dell, *Homecoming* (New York: Farrar Rinehart, 1933), p. 283.
25. Jack London, "Jack London on the Great War," *The Overland Monthly,* 69 (May 1917), p. 434.
26. Jack London, "The Impossibility of War," *The Overland Monthly,* 35 (March 1900), pp. 279, 282.
27. Jack London, "The Human Drift," *Forum,* 45 (January–June 1911), pp. 1–14.
28. Jack London, "The Unparalleled Invasion," *McClure's,* 35 (May–October 1910), pp. 308–14.
29. Charmian London, *Our Hawaii,* p. 318.
30. George Brett to Jack London, February 6, 1913.
31. John Tebbel, *George Horace Lorimer and The Saturday Evening Post* (Garden City: Doubleday & Co., 1948), p. 66.
32. George Brett to Jack London, January 7, 1915.
33. Donald Sheehan, *This Was Publishing* (Bloomington: Indiana University Press, 1952), p. 56.
34. *San Francisco Chronicle,* August 8, 1911, p. 3.
35. *Santa Rosa Press Democrat,* August 2, 1916, p. 5.
36. *Santa Rosa Republican,* August 18, 1916, p. 4.
37. George Sterling to Jack London: December 27, 1914; February 5, 1915.
38. Richard O'Connor, *Jack London: A Biography,* p. 391.
39. Charmian London, *Book of Jack London,* II, (New York, 1915), pp. 322–23.
40. Beatrice M. Hinkle, "Introduction" to *Psychology of the Unconscious,* p. xxvi.
41. Guy J. Forgue, *Letters of H. L. Mencken,* p. 132.
42. James I. McClintock, "Jack London's Use of Carl Jung's Psychology of the Unconscious," *American Literature,* 42 (March–January, 1970–1971), p. 347.
43. Andrew Sinclair, *Jack: A Biography of Jack London,* pp. 227, 228.

44. George Sterling to Margaret Smith Cobb, September 5, 1923.
45. Granville Hicks, *The Great Tradition* (New York: Macmillan Co., 1933), p. 194.
46. James I. McClintock, *White Logic,* p. 157.
47. Jack London, *Son of the Wolf,* p. 199.
48. Jack London, *God of His Fathers,* p. 117.
49. Jack London, *Call of the Wild,* p. 51.
50. Jack London, *Sea Wolf,* pp. 155, 166.
51. Cleanth Brooks, R. W. B. Lewis and Robert Penn Warren, *American Literature: The Makers and the Making,* 2 (New York: St. Martin's Press, 1973), p. 1633.
52. Hensley C. Woodbridge, John London, and George H. Tweney, *Jack London: A Bibliography* (Georgetown, Cal.: Talisman Press, 1966), pp. 282–88.
53. Archie Binns, *Mrs. Fiske and the American Theatre* (New York: Crown Pub., 1955), pp. 117, 145–46.
54. *Oakland Tribune,* January 27, 1905, p. 1.
55. "Mr. London's 'Theft,' " *The Bookman,* 32 (1910–1911), p. 450.
56. George Sterling to Jack London, February 23, 1915.
57. O. W. Firkins, *Nation,* 103 (July–December 1916), p. 151.
58. George Sterling to Upton Sinclair, July 2, 1909.
59. Joseph Noel, *Footloose in Arcadia,* pp. 238–39.
60. Hobart Bosworth, *Mark Twain Journal,* p. 5.
61. Kenneth MacGowan, *Behind the Screen* (New York: Delacorte Press, 1965), p. 163.
62. Will Irwin, *The Making of a Reporter* (New York: G. P. Putnam's Sons, 1942), p. 84.

Notes: Chapter 17

1. Upton Sinclair, *Mammonart* (Pasadena, California: the Author, 1925), p. 369.
2. Dale L. Walker and James E. Sisson, III, *The Fiction of Jack London: A Chronological Bibliography,* pp. 28–29.
3. Miriam Allen deFord, *They Were San Franciscans* (Caldwell, Idaho: Caxton Printers, 1947), p. 319.
4. Emanuel Julius, "The Pessimism of Jack London," *Western Comrade,* June 1913, p. 91.
5. "Recent Fiction," *The Dial,* 60 (January 6–June 8, 1916), p. 473.
6. "Current Fiction," *Nation,* 102 (January–June 1916), p. 647.
7. Wilson Follett, "Sentimentalist, Satirist and Realist: Notes on Some Recent Fiction," *Atlantic Monthly,* 118 (July–December 1916), p. 495.
8. "Jack London's Resignation from the Socialist Party," *The Overland Monthly,* 69 (May 1917), p. 446.
9. *New York Call,* March 27, 1916, p. 6.
10. *Santa Rosa Republican,* November 10, 1916, p. 8.
11. *Santa Rosa Democrat,* November 11, 1916, p. 6.
12. Charmian London, *Book of Jack London,* II, p. 378.
13. *San Francisco Chronicle,* November 23, 1916, p. 1.
14. Joan London, *Jack London and His Times,* p. 375.

15. Ibid., pp. 47–48, 48, 51.

16. Alfred S. Shivers, "Jack London: Not a Suicide," *Dalhousie Review*, 49 (1969–70), p. 52.

17. Jessie B. Rittenhouse, *My House of Life* (Boston: Houghton Mifflin Co., 1934), p. 220.

18. Ann N. Ridgeway, ed., *Selected Letters of Robinson Jeffers*, p. 93.

19. Michael Paul Orth, *A Biography of George Sterling*, p. 206.

20. Jack London, "A Northland Miracle," *Youth's Companion*, 100 (November 4, 1926), pp. 813–14.

21. Jack London, "Eyes of Asia," *Cosmopolitan Magazine*, 77 (July–December 1924), pp. 24–31, 148, 150–56.

22. Charmian London, "How Jack London Would Have Ended Eyes of Asia," *Cosmopolitan*, 77 (July–December 1924), pp. 78–79, 124, 126, 128, 130–31.

23. *San Francisco Chronicle*, November 25, 1916, p. 8.

24. George Sterling to Upton Sinclair, August 8, 1924.

25. *San Francisco Examiner*, November 25, 1916, p. 5.

26. *San Francisco Chronicle*, November 25, 1916, p. 8.

27. Friedrich Nietzsche, *Thus Spake Zarathustra*, p. 320.

Jack London
Bibliography

The Son of the Wolf, Tales of the Far North (1900): Houghton Mifflin.
The God of His Fathers and Other Stories (1901): McClure, Phillips.
A Daughter of the Snows (1902): J. B. Lippincott.
The Cruise of the Dazzler (1902): Century.
Children of the Frost (1902): Macmillan.
The People of the Abyss (1903): Macmillan.
The Call of the Wild (1903): Macmillan.
The Kempton-Wace Letters (with Anna Strunsky, 1903): Macmillan.
The Faith of Men and Other Stories (1904): Macmillan.
The Sea-Wolf (1904): Macmillan.
War of the Classes (1905): Macmillan.
The Game (1905): Macmillan.
Tales of the Fish Patrol (1905): Macmillan.
Scorn of Women (play, 1906): Macmillan.
Moon-Face and Other Stories (1906): Macmillan.
White Fang (1906): Macmillan.
Before Adam (1907): Macmillan.
Love of Life and Other Stories (1907): Macmillan.
The Road (1907): Macmillan.
The Iron Heel (1908): Macmillan.
Martin Eden (1909): Macmillan.
Lost Face (1910): Macmillan.
Theft: A Play in Four Acts (1910): Macmillan.
Burning Daylight (1910): Macmillan.
Revolution and Other Essays (1910): Macmillan.
When God Laughs and Other Stories (1911): Macmillan.
Adventure (1911): Macmillan.

The Cruise of the Snark (1911): Macmillan.
South Sea Tales (1911): Macmillan.
The House of Pride and Other Tales of Hawaii (1912): Macmillan.
Smoke Bellew (1912): Century.
A Son of the Sun (1912): Doubleday, Page.
The Night-Born (1913): Century.
The Abysmal Brute (1913): Century.
John Barleycorn (1913): Century.
The Valley of the Moon (1913): Macmillan.
The Strength of the Strong (1914): Macmillan.
The Mutiny of the Elsinore (1914): Macmillan.
The Scarlet Plague (1915): Macmillan.
The Star Rover (1915): Macmillan.
The Little Lady of the Big House (1916): Macmillan.
The Acorn-Planter: A California Forest Play (1916): Macmillan.
The Turtles of Tasman (1916): Macmillan.
Jerry of the Islands (1917): Macmillan.
The Human Drift (1917): Macmillan.
Michael, Brother of Jerry (1917): Macmillan.
The Red One (1918): Macmillan.
On the Makaloa Mat (1919): Macmillan.
Hearts of Three (1918 London: Mills and Boon) (1920): Macmillan.
Dutch Courage and Other Stories (1922): Macmillan.
The Assassination Bureau, Ltd. (finished by Robert L. Fish, 1963): McGraw-Hill.
Letters from Jack London (edited by King Hendricks and Irving Shephard, 1965): Odyssey Press.
Jack London Reports (edited by King Hendricks and Irving Shephard, 1970): Doubleday.
Daughters of the Rich (edited by James E. Sisson, 1971): Holmes Book Company.
Gold (three-act play written with Herbert Heron; edited by James E. Sisson, 1972): Holmes Book Company.

INDEX

337